MONASTERIES AND MONASTIC ORDERS

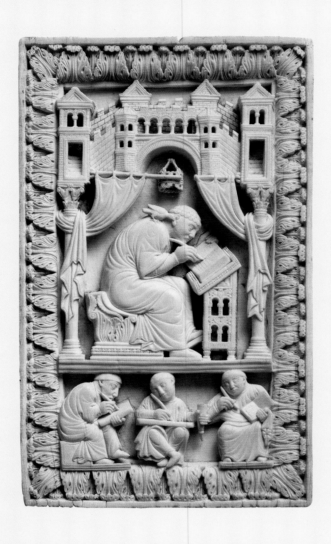

3 1705 00409 3834

Kristina Krüger

MONASTERIES
AND
MONASTIC ORDERS

2000 Years of Christian Art and Culture

Edited by Rolf Toman
With a contribution from Rainer Warland
Photographs by Achim Bednorz
Production by Thomas Paffen

SEO Library Center
State Library of Ohio
40780 Marietta Road, Caldwell, OH 43724

WITHDRAWN

h.f.ullmann

Rome, early Christian catacombs on the Via Latina

Fulda, former monastic church of St. Michael, crypt

Pomposa, former Benedictine abbey, porch

Serrabone, former priory church, singers' platform

Fontenay, former Cistercian abbey, chapter house

Crusader Bible, New York, Pierpont Morgan Library

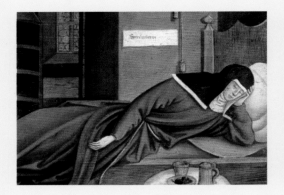

Recumbent Franciscan nun, Germanisches
Nationalmuseum

City scene, fresco, A. Lorenzetti, Siena, Town Hall

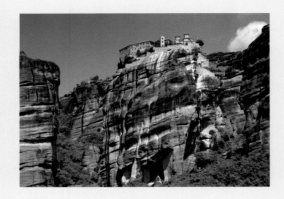

Varlaam monastery, Meteora, Greece

Grieving monks on the tomb of Philip the Bold, Dijon, Musée des Beaux-Arts

Ulm-Wiblingen, library of the former Benedictine abbey

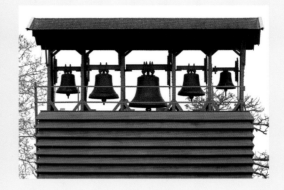

Taizé, the bells of the ecumenical community

◀ **Mönchengladbach, the Franciscan parish church of St. Barbara.** Up until a few years ago many Franciscans congregated in the monks' choir behind the altar. Today the monastery has shrunk down to a few friars. Their work of spiritual guidance requires strength and "angelic" patience.

▶ **St. Gallen, library.** Monastic culture is primarily associated with medieval monks' tireless work as scribes, as well as the monastic theology of the orders' great scholars. As magnificent as these efforts were, it is just as important to remember monastic prayer, which, well into the modern age, has been ascribed even more significance.

Editor's Foreword

In the Middle Ages the monastic lifestyle of the Christian orders was seen as an alternative to a life "in the world." It did not, however, mean a life apart, but rather a life that in many respects had a decisive influence on "this world." Some abbeys, especially the large monasteries, were powerful and influential, not only within the realm of the Church but also as lords of land and property. One of the greatest intellectual authorities on ecclesiastical policy in the 12th century was the Cistercian abbot Bernard of Clairvaux: an important theologian and mystic, Bernard was passionate in his religious zeal, the preacher of the Second Crusade, took asceticism to the limits of physical endurance, and was torn between his worldly work and the tranquility of his monastery.

One does not necessarily have to look to such great individuals as St. Bernard, the most popular saints of the Middle Ages, and the founder of the Franciscan order, St. Francis of Assisi, to highlight the work of the monasteries in the world. We have a multitude of unknown monks in the monastic scriptoria to thank for many handwritten books: not only a large proportion of Christian literature, but also for the preservation of classical philosophical, historic, and natural history texts, very few of which would have survived at all had it not been for their assiduous copying.

The cultural achievements of the monasteries encompass much more, however. Ancient artistic techniques such as illumination, ivory carving, and the work of the goldsmith were fostered and further developed; musical developments included the Gregorian chants; magnificent monasteries and masterpieces of church architecture from the High and Late Middle Ages in particular have been preserved, some of them with abundant sculptures and splendid murals. Monastery schools and monks as university teachers exemplify the educational tradition of the cloister. Monastic institutions are also reminiscent of charitable works: soup kitchens, the accommodation of pilgrims, the nursing of the sick in hospitals, and much more. All of these are examples of the tasks performed in the monasteries—or outside them—both the work of monks in the world.

There is another kind of monastic "work" that is overlooked today because few people continue to be really willing to recognize the significance of prayer. Monastic life was subject to two demands: prayer and work—*Ora et labora*—and prayer or liturgical celebration with song and prayer for a long time took priority. The tripartite teaching of the High Middle Ages, with its division of labor between prayers, crusaders and laborers, is far removed from our present day reality. Monastic prayer as a paid service for departed souls, enabling these to be released

from purgatory more quickly, as was common practice in the Middle Ages, is more likely to be met with incomprehension today: prayer is widely seen as a personal matter. In order to be able to understand Christian monasticism, however, one needs to keep this metaphysical aspect of monastic "work" in mind, otherwise a decisive component of this enduring institution remains hidden.

This book provides a history of Christian monasticism from its origins in the 3rd century to the present. The main focus is on Western Latin monasticism and, in addition to the diverse cultural aspects mentioned above, the book also covers the numerous monastic orders, the circumstances surrounding their emergence and expansion, as well as their rules and customs. The largest part of this portrayal is dedicated to the Middle Ages, the era in which Christian monasticism reached its height and enjoyed its greatest significance as an institution. As impressive as the baroque monastic residences may appear to visitors today, the monks' lifestyle had very little to do with these images of courtly splendor. Early monastic communities were mostly based on the claim or ideal of providing the world with a role model for a truly Christian life. It is not that this ideal has completely vanished from view in the modern age, nor has there been a lack of new orders endeavoring to redefine Christian life in communities—but the former self-image of monasticism as a meaningful institution and its external esteem disappeared with

the Enlightenment, and more especially in the political aftermath of the French Revolution, which led in many parts of Europe to the abolition of monasteries and the persecution of monks and nuns.

A separate chapter is dedicated to Byzantine monasticism, highlighting its structural features in contrast to those of Western Latin monasticism. The course of its historical development and its geographic spread, on the other hand, play only a background role here. A special feature of the book is the closing chapter on hermits. Some of the hermits named by German-Belgian writer and journalist Freddy Derwahl are known to him personally and, understandably, his approach to his subject is without the distance characterizing the other chapters. Derwahl has a great respect for the "voices crying out in the wilderness," one that, as editor, I share with him. Having come into contact with monks and monasteries as a teenager, as a boarding school pupil, and as a monastery visitor on a temporary basis, I am firmly of the opinion that the institution of monasticism is in no way obsolete, even if it appears "old-fashioned" to the majority of people in this day and age. To my mind it is more time-honored than antiquated.

I

Early Monasticism

Chi-Rho—the Greek letters XR forming a monogram of Christ—on the façade of the Kisan Gate in Damascus, Syria.

Judaism, the Bible, and the Promise of the Messiah

Judaism is the oldest of the three monotheistic religions. It is based on the covenant that God made with the Israelites on Mount Sinai, after he had led them out of slavery in Egypt. This covenant's laws—including the Ten Commandments—are recorded in the Torah (Hebrew for doctrine, i.e. the Five Books of Moses in the Old Testament). Together with the books of history and the prophets, the psalms and the remaining scriptures, they make up the Hebrew Bible, which tells the story of Israel from the days of the patriarch Abraham to the centuries before the Common Era.

The canon of books comprising the Hebrew Bible was adopted by the Christians with few deviations. It was termed the Old Testament, which essentially means "testimony of the ancient covenant." As testimony of the new covenant mediated by Jesus this was supplemented with the New Testament, which comprised the Gospels, the history of the Apostles, the Letters from the Apostles, and the Book of Revelation. The psalms and the prophets had initially predicted a Messiah who would resurrect the Kingdom of Israel, and with whose coming a New Age would begin. At first this belief referred explicitly to kingship whose consecration ritual was anointing with oil (Messiah from the Hebrew *maschiach*, the Anointed), but changed over the course of time to take on the notion of a spiritual leader. The side issue of liberation from political oppression remained alive, however, especially under Roman occupation. Consequently, in addition to Jesus of Nazareth, Simon Bar Kokhba, leader of the Jewish insurrection of 132–135/36, was also sometimes seen as the Messiah.

The Significance of Monasticism in the Christian Religion

Monasticism and the ascetic way of life have always played a special role in Christianity, more so than in other religions. The example of individuals or whole groups of believers living a life detached from the world and consecrated to God has always been an important element in the shaping and transmission of Christian religiosity. The history of the Christian Church has been influenced to a considerable extent by monks, monasteries, and monastic orders. The significance of such movements, defined by pious withdrawal from the world, in some epochs such the Middle Ages remains plainly visible today—in the churches and monasteries that still characterize our cities and landscapes. However, in the years following the Reformation, which led to the dissolution of many monasteries, Catholic revival movements continually aroused new interest in the monastic way of life, reformed existing monasteries, and founded new ones. Even today, a monastery might sometimes be accorded special significance in the communication of Christian beliefs in a largely secular world—for example the ecumenical community of Taizé in Burgundy.

The prominent position of monasticism itself and of individual monasteries in particular is a feature distinguishing Christianity from the other two great monotheistic religions. Neither ascetic movements, monasteries, nor monastic orders have ever played a similar role in either Judaism or Islam. Neither did the ancient world of the Romans and the Greeks know such monastic lifestyles. So where does the close link between Christianity and movements of ascetic withdrawal from the world come from? Before examining the historical development of monasticism, we should once again take a look back at the beginnings of the Christian religion in the context of this fundamental question.

The Beginnings of Christianity

In Jerusalem, the capital of the Roman protectorate of Palestine, the time around AD 30 saw the execution of the Jewish religious teacher, Jesus of Nazareth, which led to the emergence of a new Jewish sect. Its followers saw Jesus as the Messiah promised by the prophets (Greek *Christos*, the anointed, i.e. the messenger of God) and testified to his resurrection from the dead. They very soon began to propagate this conviction, not only among their Jewish co-religionists but also among the Greek-speaking, non-Jewish population of Palestine and the neighboring Mediterranean region, as far as Rome. The gentile followers of Jesus were absolved from adherence to the laws of the Jewish faith, such as those relating to diet and to circumcision. This saw the sect develop into an independent religious community.

As early as the 2nd century there were Christians in many, sometimes remote, areas of the Roman Empire. The State treated the Christians with suspicion—not because they were followers of a man sentenced by Rome to a dishonorable death by crucifixion as an insurrectionist guilty of high treason, but because, in the name of their God, they rejected the Roman imperial cult and the deification of the Emperor.

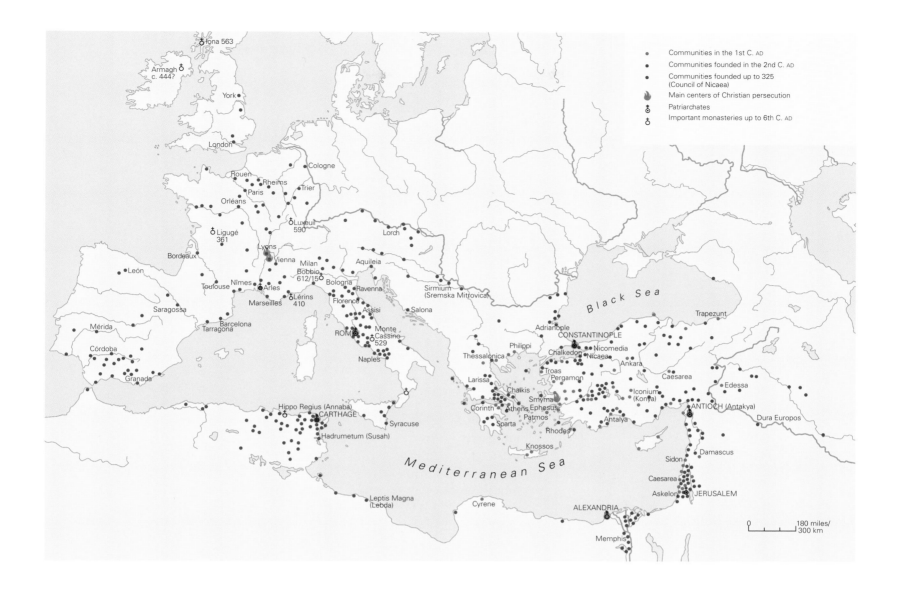

Communities in the 1st C. AD
Communities founded in the 2nd C. AD
Communities founded up to 325 (Council of Nicaea)
Main centers of Christian persecution
Patriarchates
Important monasteries up to 6th C. AD

Despite repeated persecution during the first three centuries of its existence, Christianity gained in influence within the Roman Empire and, with the Edict of Milan (which brought toleration) in 313, finally became a publicly recognized religion with the express support of Emperor Constantine I. This rise from an insignificant sect to the imperial religion and, from 391, to the sole state religion of the global empire appears surprising at first and has always prompted questions about the reasons for this "astonishing" success. If one takes a closer look at the situation, however, it appears to be considerably less spectacular.

In around 313, Christians made up no more than 5–10 percent of the population of the Roman Empire. Extrapolated over the 280 years of Christian missionary work since Jesus' crucifixion, this gives an annual conversion rate of below 0.04 percent of the population, which is hardly extraordinarily high. Other cults and religions that were widespread in the Roman Empire, such as the Mithras cult for example, sometimes achieved very similar growth rates. Christianity differed from other religious communities, not in the speed with which it spread, but in the steadiness and duration of its expansion, which continued unabated despite persecution.

Contrary to what is often assumed, it was not primarily the public preaching that played a decisive role in the expansion of Christianity; instead, personal persuasion and the living example of Christian believers constituted a significantly more effective route to conversion. The points of contact for Christian missionaries outside Palestine were always the Jewish communities that had formed in the towns around the Mediterranean. However, the proclamation of Jesus as the promised Messiah met with only limited success among the Jews; gentiles soon made up the majority of Christians. During the 1st and 2nd centuries, many members of the urban elite in the Greek towns around the Eastern Mediterranean were won over to the new faith. Due to the integration of the former independent city-states into the Roman Empire with its central administration, they had lost their traditional political and administrative spheres of influence and Christianity offered them a way

The Spread of Christianity up to the Mid-5th C.
The most important points of contact for Christian missionaries were the Jewish communities in the towns of the Hellenic world. The initial Christian expansion therefore took place primarily in the Eastern Mediterranean area, extending as far as Rome. It was only in the second phase that Greek immigrants, in particular, also brought Christianity into the towns of the Western Mediterranean, from where it spread to the whole of the western Roman world.

Rome, Catacombs of Domitilla, apse area in the room of the *pistores* (bakers) with extensive murals, 4th C. In addition to secular scenes from the lives of those buried here, the catacombs also contain numerous paintings with Christian content.

Early Monasticism   13

Damascus, Chapel of St. Paul, constructed in 1939 in the so-called Kisan Gate (Bab Kisan), from the Mamluk era (14th C.). The chapel is said to mark the place where, according to legend, the newly converted Christian Paul was lowered down the city wall in a basket in order to be able to leave the city unnoticed by the angry Jewish community.

The Temptation of St. Anthony, the right inner wing of the Isenheim Altar, c. 1512, by Mathis Gothart Nithart, known as Grünewald, (Colmar, Museum Unterlinden). In the second half of the 3rd century, St. Anthony, known as the Father of all Monks, went into the desert as a young man in order to meet with God. There he was afflicted by the demonic powers of his own imagination and put to the test. Bishop Athanasius of Alexandria, who visited Anthony several times, wrote a description of the life of the great hermit shortly after his death (356).

out of the existential crisis into which they had plunged. From now on, instead of issues of the earthly *polis* (Greek for city), they concerned themselves with matters of the "Kingdom of Heaven."

In Rome and in the towns in the west of the Roman Empire, the new doctrine at first spread primarily within the Greek-speaking, oriental immigrant milieu and, to a lesser extent, among the educated upper class who were able to speak Greek. This was because the Gospels and the Letters from the Apostles were written in Greek and a Greek translation of the Hebrew Bible, the Old Testament, had already long been in existence. Latin translations of individual scriptures from the Old and New Testaments were first mentioned only in the late 2nd century, however, and there was no complete Latin Bible translation prior to the middle of the 3rd century.

Members of the landed classes who made their wealth available to the religious community were particularly important for the early Christians. During the first few centuries, religious services took place solely in private homes or in so-called house churches, for which the wealthy had made their houses available. Prominent Roman women, in particular, showed an early interest in Christianity and not infrequently their involvement included their property. Jewish Christians also took up an important position among the early communities. By virtue of their origins, they were familiar with the religious scriptures that formed the basis of Jesus' teachings. They were therefore well versed in theology and had practical cult experience, which the gentile Christians lacked, coming from the very different religious culture of the Greeks and Romans with their multitude of gods.

Asceticism and Abstinence

Irrespective of whether they lived in the rural areas of Palestine or Syria, in one of the Hellenic coastal towns and metropolises of the Eastern Mediterranean, or else in a town in the West of the Roman Empire with a Greek or Jewish settlement, all 1st-century Christians had one thing in common: they believed in the imminent return of Jesus and the impending end of the world that would ensue. The return of the Messiah was a long time coming, however, and the end of the world did not occur. Reactions to this failure were extremely varied, though some form of renunciation of the "contemporary age" was almost always at the forefront.

The most radical reaction to this situation derived from the notion that it was possible to advance the coming of the Kingdom of Heaven through an exemplary Christian life of absolute chastity. Complete sexual abstinence, combined with strict fasting and a withdrawal from the activities of normal life, was intended to transform the body and lead to the threshold of a new world. This was to coerce heaven down to earth, so to speak, and enable Christ's victory over death to be shared. By estranging the human body from the laws of biology and thereby disrupting society's reproductive system, one would in this way, according to the theory, induce or at least accelerate the end of the world.

This position represented a complete break with the principles and ideals of the classical world. It meant a renunciation of the discipline of the Greco-Roman state, which encouraged reproduction for the preservation of society. And it also meant a repudiation of the ancient attitude to the body and its impulses, which aimed for the control of appetites but not their complete suppression, and which was directed towards sensible use of the body but not its ruination.

In a subversive but, at the same time, a very active manner, radical Christians readied themselves for the fight against the state and society, which represented the generally accepted maxims of social life, using their abstemious bodies and, when necessary, their lives given in martyrdom, so that the world would collapse "like a sandcastle" due to a lack of offspring and make way for the Heavenly Kingdom. Between the 2nd and 4th centuries retreats populated by ascetics arose everywhere on the perimeters of Christian communities. In Palestine where, since the time of Jesus, wandering preachers, like the Apostles, had roamed the streets and proclaimed the Gospel, individuals and entire groups of hermits entered the solitude of the Judean Mountains, consecrated themselves to celibacy, abstained from enjoying meat, and fasted.

Hermits lived in the arid steppe hinterland of the Syrian coastal towns, while in Egypt ascetics attempted survival in the desert beyond the fertile land. In the towns, virgins in Christian households consecrated themselves to chastity and married couples lived together in celibacy. Although, in relation to Christians in their entirety, it was always only a minority who undertook the withdrawal into the inner or external "desert" and lived a life of abstinence and asceticism, the emergent Christian churches were strongly characterized by the moral intransigence of these radicals and the discussion surrounding their lifestyle. In many circles, celibacy was seen as a sign proclaiming the imminence of a "new Creation."

The stance taken by important theologians towards the issues of marriage and sexuality, beginning with the Apostle Paul, made an essential contribution to this view. Paul, a Jew who had been converted to Christianity by a vision of Jesus, and who had dedicated himself to missionary work among heathens, was influenced by Jewish ideas about the body that one might consider as the roots of Christian deliberations on abstinence. In Jesus' time, there had indeed been communities of pious men within Judaism who wanted to overcome, through a life of celibacy, the "obduracy of the heart" standing in the way of observance of the law of God. These groups belonged to sects such as the Essenes or the Qumran community. However, there were also married members in these sects, in addition to the reclusive, abstinent adherents, and the groups of celibate men had not broken off contact with society. Their goal with their pious, abstemious life was to bring about the emergence of a "new Israel." In contrast, though, to the later Christian ascetics, who wanted to bring about the collapse of society through a rejection of reproduction, they had no intention whatsoever of turning against marriage and the family. Their notion of a "new Israel" was one of a proliferating people.

Qumran, caves in the cliffs. During the period 1949–56, on the western shores of the Dead Sea, archaeologists unearthed a monastery-like complex that had possibly been inhabited by adherents of the Essene community. In 1947 Bedouins had discovered the first of the famous "Dead Sea Scrolls" in nearby caves, which contained the oldest known Bible manuscripts. Eleven caves with more or less complete texts were found in total.

Paul's negative position on sexuality was clearly based on concepts deriving from a comparable mindset. He made the human body, the "flesh," the source of the "evil drive" that was directed against the will of God, though as a general rule he expressly declined to promote his personal stance that a life of abstinence is better than one of marriage. Yet the arguments that he developed in order to justify marriage were characterized by such a fundamental distrust of the dark powers residing in the "flesh" that, ultimately, they achieved the opposite of their declared intention: Paul's views provided the theological rationale for a two-level Christianity, with the abstinent version emerging as clearly more demanding and therefore the one to be aspired to. With his view of the "flesh" as the gateway to sin, Paul had a persistent influence on the Christian image of man, underpinning the esteem of the lifestyle that declared war on this very "flesh" and its needs: a life of sexual abstinence, consecrated to God.

Thebaid, idealized landscape with hermits, by Gherardo Starnina (Florence, Uffizi). The area of Upper Egypt around Thebes, a cradle of hermitism, is portrayed here as an undulating fantasy landscape. Instead of hermitic solitude there is brisk activity taking place between the figures, most of whom are in groups of two. Only a few of the figures are alone, at prayer, or lost in meditation. The life of the hermits is set against a peaceful natural background that allows one to forget all the hardships of the desert. Starnina's *Thebaid* reflects the historical reality only in that the early Christian hermits did not in fact go unobserved, nor did they remain alone. Their example was a role model and the first hermit colonies soon came into being.

St. Pachomius, Bulgarian icon. Pachomius, contemporary of St. Anthony, is seen as the founder of cenobiticism. Each of the monasteries he founded had the character of a settlement, with numerous houses for 20 to 50 monks.

At the beginning of the 5th century Jerome, a Father of the Latin Church, lived as a recluse near Bethlehem in Palestine, working on an improved Latin translation of the Bible. All around him, on the perimeters of Christianity's holy sites, was a multitude of people—both men and women—who had turned their backs on the world in a life of asceticism and abstinence and, as individuals or in small groups, lived solely in praise of God or studied the Holy Scriptures. They were not a new phenomenon in this landscape. Their lifestyles were part of a manifestation of the Christian faith that had been familiar in Palestine and Syria for centuries. Yet we know little about these hermit colonies, called "lauras." Presumably, the lives of these hermits did not require any written regulation. The origins of monasticism, as we know it—a community living according to fixed rules within a walled off area—lie not in Palestine, but in Egypt. From his retreat near Bethlehem Jerome, through his writings, undertook to make known to the Western world the first monastic rules and the life of the Egyptian desert fathers.

Egypt: Pachomius, Anthony, and the Hermits of Kellia

Hermit colonies had also been formed in Egypt as early as the 4th century. Pupils and followers gathered around these exemplary ascetics. Following his conversion to Christianity at the age of about 20, Pachomius (c. 292–346), a young man from the area around Thebes, joined a hermit living on the edge of the desert. His notion of a life detached from the world was different to that of his hermit companions, however. In 323, together with a group of like-minded individuals, he founded a monastery in the remote village of Tabennisi, where they lived together according to binding principles applicable to all and under Pachomius' spiritual leadership. The followers of Pachomius grew rapidly in number. At the end of his life he was the head of nine monasteries (for men). Two establishments for women were led by his sister Mary. Life in these populous communities, which are thought to have comprised several

thousand members, needed a detailed system, which Pachomius set down in writing. This Coptic language monastic rule, which was then translated into Greek and, around 404 into Latin by Jerome, provides us with information on the internal organization of Pachomius' monasteries.

These had more in common with rural settlements than did the later Western monasteries that we know. Groups of monks lived in houses within the walled monastery complex, each monk having his own cell in the house. The kitchen and refectory, the care of the sick, and a hostel for monastery visitors were housed in separate buildings. Everyone gathered together in the morning for the daily religious service (with readings, prayer, and the singing of psalms) in the church, which was described not as an *ekklesia* but simply as a *synaxis* (Greek for assembly room). Meals were also taken together. The monks worked in their cells for the rest of the day. While praying and singing psalms they made craft products by hand, the sale of which provided the monastery's livelihood. The evening service was held in the individual houses. On Saturday evening and Sunday morning, Mass was celebrated by an external priest; there were no clergy in the monastery itself. Monks who wanted to join the community first had to live in the visitors' house outside the monastery gates, learn prayers and psalms, and become familiar with the rule. Upon entering the monastery, they made a vow. There was no private property; the monks all wore the same clothing, and nobody was allowed to leave without permission. Infringements of the rule were punished. Twice a year all the monks from the monasteries headed by Pachomius attended large gatherings in the leading monastery, Pbow.

The monks' cenobitic, i.e. communal, life differed from that of the solitary hermits primarily in the discipline required of each individual and the binding unity of the living arrangements. The daily handicraft work carried out in meditation or prayer, however, was also common among the hermits, who earned their livelihood by means of a craft or by working in the fields.

Anthony (251/52–356) is considered the model hermit and the first of the Desert Fathers. He came from a wealthy Christian family from the Arsinoë (today Fayum) area. As a young man he sold his possessions, gave away his

Monastic Terminology

The word monk derives from the Greek *monos*, alone. Ascetics living by themselves were originally called *monachoi*, recluses, who were also referred to as hermits (from the Greek *eremos*, meaning alone, abandoned) or anchorites, from the Greek *anachorein*, to withdraw. Hermits who lived close by one another could form a colony or laura. Monks who lived together and gathered regularly for prayer and meals, however, were called cenobites, from the Greek *koinos bios*, living together. The hermits often set up in their cells, separate from the bedroom, a prayer room called an oratorium, from the Latin *orare*, meaning to pray. Hermit colonies often had their own church for communal Sunday celebration of Mass, while monasteries located near Christian settlements with a church often forewent the construction of their own church initially and contented themselves with an oratorium.

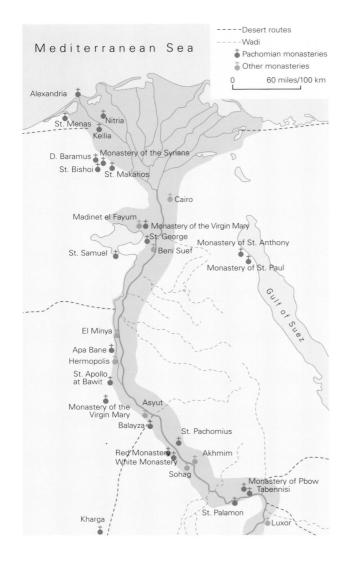

Map of Coptic monasticism.
- - - - Desert routes
- - - Wadi
Pachomian monasteries
Other monasteries
0   60 miles/100 km

Mediterranean Sea

Alexandria
St. Menas   Nitria
Kellia
D. Baramus   Monastery of the Syrians
St. Bishoi   St. Makarios
Cairo
Madinet el Fayum
Monastery of the Virgin Mary
St. George
St. Samuel   Beni Suef   Monastery of St. Anthony
Monastery of St. Paul
Gulf of Suez
El Minya
Apa Bane
Hermopolis
St. Apollo
at Bawit
Asyut
Monastery of the
Virgin Mary
Balayza
St. Pachomius
Red Monastery   Akhmim
White Monastery
Sohag
Monastery of Pbow
Tabennisi
Kharga   St. Palamon
Luxor

Map of Coptic monasticism. Egypt was largely Christian at the time of the Arab conquest (639–42). Between the 4th and 7th centuries, the Egyptian Christians, known as Copts, though burdened by taxes and levies with the country under Byzantine rule, developed a cultural life of their own, which included the erection of churches and monasteries. In the 8th century, the situation deteriorated for the Copts as a result of the Islamization of the country.

The Kellia hermitage complex, 4th C., remains of one of the earliest anchorite-monastic settlements southwest of Alexandria. The majority of the hermits and monks of Coptic Christianity came from the lower social classes. Their tuition was based on the example and rules of older monks.

money, retreated into the desert beyond his village, and tried to leave all of his ties behind. In an indefatigable battle against the powers of his own imagination which, despite all of his isolation, taunted him with tempting images, he wrestled with the physical impulses of sexuality and hunger until his body was again as pure "as Adam's." His break with his social surroundings, however, did not mean giving up his connection with the world. He remained in contact with those of similar ideas while retreating from the Libyan desert into ever more remote areas east of the Nile and ultimately to the Red Sea region. In later years he gathered pupils around him, traveled to Alexandria twice and corresponded with important theologians and church figures such as Athanasius, bishop of Alexandria. Anthony was famous even during his lifetime, and the description of his life written shortly after his death by Athanasius became a model for the Christian's successful inner battle against the temptations of sin. Anthony's biography, translated into Latin by Euagrios of Antioch as early as 388, became one of the most widespread and influential of the saints' biographies within Christianity.

Ascetics had also begun to settle south of Alexandria in the infertile land west of the Nile Delta, even prior to the middle of the 4th century. They chose a way of life that lay in between Anthony's absolute solitude and Pachomius' ordered monastery. The rapidly growing hermit colonies of Nitria, Kellia (Greek for cells), and Sketis (today Wadi Natrun) extended along a series of locations where groundwater was to be found directly underneath the desert sand. The individual cells in a settlement were clustered around the church at their center, but were far enough away from each other that the occupants were not within hearing. Each kellion (the singular of kellia) was enclosed by a wall and inhabited by two monks—an older, experienced monk and his pupil. In addition to two separate bedrooms there was a kitchen and a larder as well as an oratorium with an alcove in the east wall where the daily morning and evening officium (service) was held. On Saturdays and Sundays all of the monks in the settlement gathered for a communal service in the church.

The hermits and monks of the 4th century were no longer radical subversionists who wanted to bring about the end of the world using all the means at their disposal. This no longer seemed to be a priority once Christianity had been promoted, in 313, to the primary religion in the Roman Empire. What remained, however, was the anxiety about the true Christian life and the right path to God. With the increasing number of Christians, who now led a peaceful life safe from state persecution, the ascetic movements now experienced a new appreciation. The direct route to God through abstinence and withdrawal from the world was widely seen as exemplary and was highly regarded morally. The prayers of the monks were accorded special powers. For their part, the recluses had established themselves in their way of life. Their asceticism now followed proven rules, which they passed on to their pupils and advice-seeking visitors. These "desert tourists" who sought out the hermit fathers in their Egyptian solitude in the decades around the year 400 also included travelers from the West such as Jerome and John Cassian. These recorded the lives and teachings of the Desert Fathers and, through their writings, publicized these Eastern experiences in the countries north of the Mediterranean.

The Beginnings of Monasticism in the West

In addition to religious fervor, the increasingly unstable political situation at the end of the 4th century was another reason for the spread of ascetic tendencies in the West of the Roman Empire. Attacks by Germanic and Gothic tribes, internal political disputes, and the ensuing public instability cast a dark shadow over the material world and encouraged withdrawal into the spiritual domain. Monastic life had already developed in different locations in the western Roman Empire by the second half of the 4th century. Small groups of Christians, primarily from educated circles, joined together on a personal basis to lead an informal ascetic life, which was more strongly characterized by individual piety than by striving to adhere to binding rules. Such, often short-lived, monastic communities are reported by Jerome in Trier and Rome—both perhaps not coincidental locations, where Bishop Athanasius of Alexandria had spent several years in exile. In Rome Christian house communities, which included women belonging to the Roman senator class in particular, initially lived in urban dwellings before some of the members retreated to a more strictly monastic life in country villas. Others, like Jerome, went to Palestine. Similar forms of the personal withdrawal of smaller communities to their own properties are reported in the writings of Bishop Victricius in Rouen and Sulpicius Severus (c. 400) in southern France (Prémillac) and can also be inferred for many other places: excavations of numerous late antiquity villas throughout the western Romanized region have revealed church and chapel buildings, some of which date to the 4th century and were often still in use into the 7th century. Some of them later became the starting point for the foundation of important monasteries, such as St. Maximin in Trier or S. Vincenzo al Volturno in Abruzzo.

Rome, anonymous catacombs on the Via Latina, 2nd half of the 4th C. (?), wall paintings portraying Jesus and his followers at the Raising of Lazarus.

Pfalzel near Trier, a nunnery founded c. 700 by an aristocratic woman in a Roman country palace of the 4th century. The rooms in the east wing of the symmetrical four-winged complex were set up as the church. The courtyard gallery, which, according to the excavation findings, dates from the 4th-century construction period, could be used by the nuns as a kind of cloister.

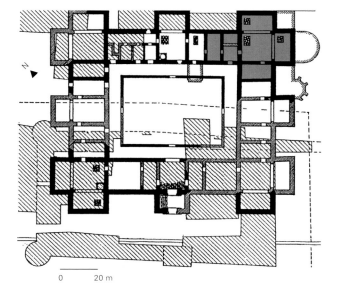

0   20 m

Diptych of Boethius, (Brescia, Musei Civici d'Arte e di Storia). This early Christian panel shows St. Augustine between St. Jerome and St. Gregory.

Layman—Cleric—Priest—Monk

In contrast to the simple believers, who were referred to as *laymen*, *clerics* are members of the religious body who are ordained. The prerequisite for religious office is the corresponding ordination. Those offices associated with a lower ordinations (including *lectorship* and *acolyte*) quickly lost their significance and since the Middle Ages have served only as transitory steps en route to higher ordination, such as *subdeacon*, *deacon* and *presbyter*. Subdeacons and deacons carry out readings and assist at the altar; the *priest* celebrates Mass. The highest level of the presbytery is the office of bishop. A *monk* does not have to be ordained provided he does not hold any office of the church. He is distinguished from a layman through his *profession*, the monk's vow, which he makes upon entering the monastery.

▶ **Marseilles, Saint-Victor,** views of the crypt and its decorative sculpture, which includes reused Roman sarcophagi. The spacious crypt contains the oldest remains of the monastery founded in the early 5th century by the hermit John Cassian. As a location he chose the resting place of St. Victor, a Roman officer who converted to Christianity and is said to have been martyred under Maximian.

Augustine

The clerical community that had built up around Bishop Eusebius of Vercelli (died c. 371) and the Church Father and Bishop Ambrose of Milan (c. 340–97) represented an ascetic lifestyle that was closely linked with the structures of the Church. It was here that Augustine (354–430), the great Doctor of the Church in the Latin West who was baptized in 387 by Ambrosius in Milan, also found inspiration for his own ideas of the appropriate lifestyle for Christian office-holders and clergy. After returning to his North African homeland he founded a monastery in Thagaste in 388. Following his appointment as bishop of Hippo Regius in 395 he committed his clergy to a monastic life based on the example of the original Christian community as described in the histories of the Apostles, and recorded their principles in his own rule. This was concerned not with the organization of daily routine nor with specific issues, but focused on mutual love, harmony, and lack of ownership as the basis of communal life and prescribed the humility and chastity of the individual as its prerequisites. Although Augustine's founding of the monastery and his episcopal example made little impression during his lifetime, the Rule of St. Augustine experienced an unexpected renaissance during the reform efforts of the High Middle Ages.

Martin of Tours

Martin of Tours (316–97) introduced another link between the office of bishop and monastic life. Following his appointment as bishop of Tours in 371, Martin, who had already founded a monastery in Ligugé near Poitiers in 361, was not willing to completely forego periods of ascetic withdrawal from the world. He therefore erected a new monastery on the other side of the Loire opposite his episcopal city. Easily accessible but at the same time effectively separated by the river from his official residence, the "Magnum Monasterium" (Latin for large monastery; from which the French name Marmoutier is derived) served him as a retreat detached from the world, beyond the reaches of his official duties. In fact, Martin's monastery resembled a hermit colony with a chapel more than it did a monastic establishment. A written rule never existed but it is known from the biography of Martin by Sulpicius Severus that the monks, who were referred to as pupils, lived in wooden buildings or caves in the cliffs along the river and did not undertake any handiwork, solely pursuing their studies and the copying of texts; the monastery presumably provided their training as clergy. Martin's monastery did not survive beyond his death and there are no archaeological traces of his wooden buildings.

In the first half of the 5th century, Bishop Germanus of Auxerre followed Martin's example and built himself a monastic retreat on the river bank opposite Auxerre. This monastery model, however, remained as a bishop's semiprivate retreat and was not imitated. Instead, the decisive development for Western monasticism stemmed from Provence.

The Provence Monasteries, the Rhône Valley, and the Rule of the Master

During the first decades of the 5th century there settled in Provence two Egyptian travelers influenced by their encounters with the Desert Fathers. John Cassian (c. 360–430/35), who had spent a long period with the Kellia monks, founded the Saint-Victor monastery near Marseilles between 410 and 415. There he wrote two works in which he recounted his Egyptian experiences, the *Collationes patrum* (Conferences with the Fathers) and *De institutis coenobitorum* (Monks' Practices).

Honoratus (died 429/30), who in addition to Egypt had also traveled to Palestine, initially withdrew into the solitude of the Massif de l'Estérel. In around 405, together with a group of companions who shared his beliefs, he founded the monastery of Lerinum (Lérins) on a Mediterranean island off the coast of Cannes, which he accorded a fixed rule. The monastery of Lérins subsequently became a kind of school for southern Gallic clergy. Beginning

Provencal coastal landscape near the monastery island of Lérins. In the Middle Ages the small island off the coast was repeatedly attacked by pirates and plundered.

Islands of Lérins and Saint-Honorat with fortress and new monastery. In the early 5th century, Honoratus, who had become familiar with Egyptian and Syrian monasticism, founded a monastery on the island named after him, in which he wanted to combine both the hermitic and cenobitic ideals.

with Honoratus himself, who was appointed bishop of Arles in 426, the monastery produced, into the 6th century, numerous bishops who spread monastic ideas through their own writings, such as Bishop Caesarius of Arles (470/71–542). A series of monasteries founded in the hinterland of episcopal cities, primarily in the Rhône Valley, can be attributed to former monks from Lérins. The so-called Jura Fathers were also influenced by Lérins; this was a group of three named hermits and their pupils who, in the middle of the 5th century, retreated to the remote valleys of the Jura, north of Lake Geneva, where they founded the monasteries of Romainmôtier and Condat (Saint-Claude), amongst others.

The first monastic rule in Latin, the anonymous *Regula magistri* (Rule of the Master), which contains detailed information about the internal organization of a monastery, originates from either Italy or the Lérins area. It is also the longest of all the rules. Its 95 chapters describe the daily routine of a model monastery with twelve monks and one abbot. Aside from the individual specifications regarding the religious service and asceticism, the Rule of the Master goes into detail about the basic conditions of monastic life, such as obedience, silence, and the twelve steps of humility. These are intended to enable the monks to overcome sin and to lead a life in the perfect love of God, the reward for which, one day, will be heavenly salvation. The prominent position and special responsibility of the abbot, who is bound to the rule himself, are emphasized. In addition to the church, there is also a communal dormitory in the monastery, with the abbot's bed in the middle, and a communal dining room, where the abbot's chair is also in a prominent position. It is not known which individual monasteries followed the "*Regula magistri*." In addition to southern France, it was certainly also widespread in central and southern Italy, where copies of its text have been preserved.

Benedict of Nursia

Among those familiar with the Rule of the Master, as well as the teachings of the Egyptian monks, was a young man who had withdrawn into the mountains of Subiaco, east of Rome, in the year 500. His life's work was to become the main basis for the later development of Western monasticism.

Benedict (c. 480–547) came from Nursia (today Norcia) in Umbria and had gone to Rome to study, but soon fled into rural solitude, where he began a hermit's existence. The fame of his pious life attracted pupils and sympathizers. Although his interim leadership of a religious house in Vicovaro was a failure, he later moved to Montecassino, where he founded his own monastery in 529, over which he presided as abbot. For this monastic settlement, situated on the top of the mountain, visible from afar, he wrote a rule that he wanted to be understood as a fundamental instruction, extending beyond Montecassino, for the "service of God."

The Rule of St. Benedict has 73 chapters, in which all of the essential issues of monastery life are addressed. These include the monastery constitution with the abbot at the head, the spiritual basis of monastic life, religious services, offices and duties, lapses and punishments, regulations governing eating, work, and clothing, the admission of new monks, and the election of the abbot and his deputy. Benedict thus provided not only general spiritual guidelines, but also concrete regulations for issues significant to the practical implementation of communal life in the monastery. This is likely to have been the reason for the later widespread dissemination of his rule.

In the first seven chapters, which contain the basic parameters and details of the spiritual attitude and goals of monastic life, Benedict made close reference in parts to the *Regula magistri*. The subsequent detailed regulations for the religious service, however, provided a new focus: the monks' daily *officium*, comprising the nightly vigil and the day's seven offices, at each of which the monks gathered for communal prayer, was the central element of monastery life for Benedict. This *Opus Dei* (service to God) had to take priority over everything else. This is also reflected in the mitigation of the ascetic conditions: the monks' fasting should not be at the expense of the ability to pray. Benedict required that the regulations of his rule be adapted to the respective circumstances and, for example, that allowances be made for climatic conditions and the different abilities of the individual monks, especially in the case of illness or age-related problems. So as not to leave such decisions solely up to the discretion of the abbot, a council of experienced monks was consulted.

The religious service, which for Benedict stood at the centre of monastery life, was a Liturgy of the Word without Eucharist. It took place in the monastery's oratorium, a prayer room not necessarily with an altar. For Mass, which was celebrated only on Sundays and feast days, the monks either went to a church outside the monastery or they invited an external priest to

Sainte-Trinité (◄) and **Saint-Caprais** (▲) chapels on Saint-Honorat. Seven chapels strewn over the island are relics of the former hermits'. Among the best preserved is the early 11th-century Sainte-Trinité Chapel.

St. Benedict of Nursia, Subiaco, S. Benedetto/Sacro Speco, fresco in the upper church.

▼ ▶ **Subiaco, S. Benedetto.** The monastery erected above what was once Benedict's cave, also known as Sacro Speco, is constructed over several levels. The upper and lower churches, as well as the chapel and the stair panels, have been covered time and again with frescoes from the 8th to the 16th centuries.

Officium—Mass—Liturgy of the Hours

The term officium (Latin for service) refers to service to God, i.e. the religious service, the main components of which are prayer, readings, and psalm recitations. If the officium is combined with the Eucharist, i.e. with the consecration of bread and wine in remembrance of Christ's Last Supper, then it is Mass. Mass has a set composition, with some of the components fixed and others following the liturgical calendar. The readings from the Gospels are spread through the year according to a fixed pattern. While the Egyptian monks only had a morning and an evening officium, Basil (c. 330–79), the founder of Eastern monasticism, had already divided the religious service into six Offices of the Day and a nocturnal office. The eight prayer times daily prescribed in the Rule of St. Benedict became canonical for the Latin Church. This division of the religious service into individual offices, which each take place at a fixed time, is known as the Liturgy of the Hours.

the celebration. Priests who lived as monks in the monastery shared the same status as the other monks, holding no preferential position.

In addition to prayers and psalms, the daily officium, for which everyone gathered in the oratorium, also comprised readings from the Bible and the writings of the Church Fathers. In order to be able to take active part, the monks therefore had to be able to read. The acquisition of education, the study of the Scriptures, and the transcription of the texts required for the readings thus became essential elements of monastery life.

Only 30 years after Benedict's death in 577, Montecassino was abandoned by the monks in their flight from the Lombards. Lombard rule meant the end of Late Antique society and the establishment of a new order that no longer functioned according to the laws of the Roman state. Benedict's knowledge and his monastery rule would have been lost in the commotion and upheaval if Pope Gregory the Great (590–604), who was himself a monk or a proponent of monasticism, had not dedicated the second book of his famous *Dialoge* to the founder of Montecassino, thus preserving his influence for posterity.

Specific key features of a monastery as we know it were already evident in the Rule of Pachomius. This basic model was completed by Benedict's monastery rule and given an orientation through the primacy of the religious service, one that remained consistent throughout the Middle Ages up until today—albeit not as the only possible direction for monastic life. It restrained the ascetic impetus of the early monks in favor of the religious service and the praise of God, in order to make way for measured abstinence from food and a disciplined lifestyle devoid of all forms of superficiality. The renunciation of any form of sexuality, however, remained an absolute commandment. As the source of the cravings "of the flesh," the monk's body was under constant observation and was seen as the gateway to sin, in the sense of St. Paul. However, the victory over the impulses of sexuality ennobled the monk and made his prayers a precious commodity. Seen as exemplary, monastic life also contributed to the legitimation of the Christian Church over the new, still heathen, rulers and the new, Germanic upper class. In the only partly and often only superficially Christianized society of the Early Middle Ages the monks became *the* Christians par excellence and monasteries places of superlative Christian life.

Scenes from the life of St. Benedict, Subiaco, Sacro Speco, frescoes in the upper and lower church.

▲ Benedict receives the monk's habit from Romanus and withdraws to a grotto in Subiaco. Master Conxulus, 13th C., lower church.

▼ Benedict's conversation with his sister Scholastria, School of Umbria and the Marches, 15th C., upper church. According to Gregory the Great, the siblings met annually for a spiritual discussion.

▲ Benedict sees his sister's soul—in the form of a dove carried by angels—ascend to heaven. School of Umbria and the Marches, 15th C., upper church.

▼ Benedict observes one of his monks allowing himself to be tempted by the devil. The monk is punished with a beating by his abbot (following scene, not shown here). School of Umbria and the Marches, 15th C., upper church.

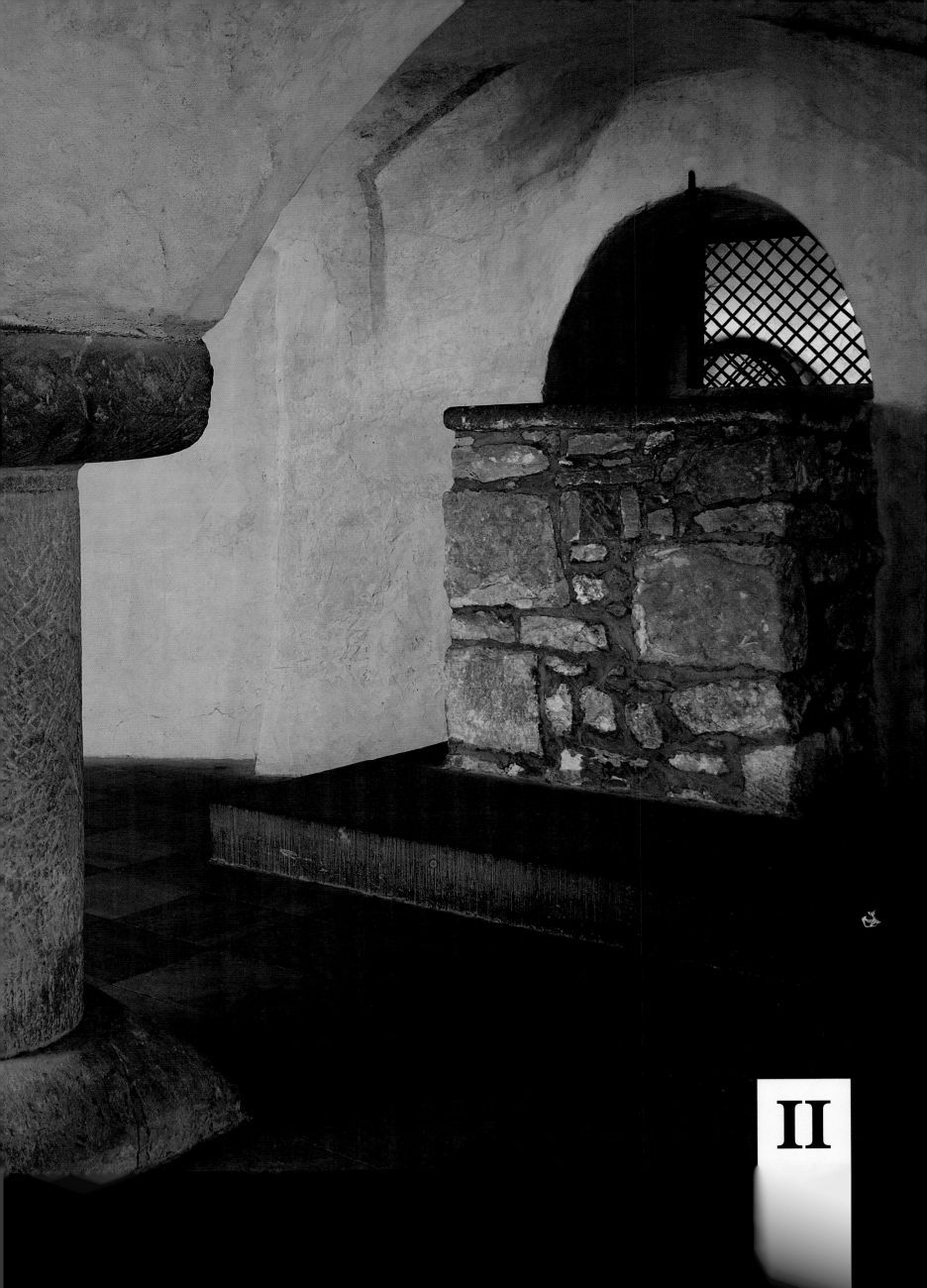

II

Monasticism in the Early Middle Ages

The End of the Roman Empire

The deposition of the last Western Roman Emperor in 476 spelt the end of the global Roman Empire and saw the division of Western Europe into kingdoms ruled by immigrant Germanic tribal and military leaders of differing origins. The Visigoths took power in southern Gaul and on the Iberian Peninsula, the Franks established themselves in north eastern Gaul and in the regions on the western banks of the River Rhine, while, after a brief interlude, Italy fell to the Ostrogoths under Theodoric. In the Greek-speaking East, however, with the capital at Constantinople, Roman rule continued and was to outlive the whole of the Middle Ages as the Byzantine Empire. Consequently, the division of the Roman Empire into East and West, which had already been in existence at an administrative and governmental level since the 4th century, was confirmed under new auspices. Although the new Germanic kings formally recognized the sovereignty of the Eastern Roman Emperor and continued to bear honorary Roman titles, the West went its own way from here on. Even the Byzantine Empire, which was becoming increasingly restricted to Greece and Asia Minor due to ongoing territorial losses, was in fact no more than a medieval successor state of ancient Rome.

However, the break-up of the Roman Empire was barely perceived as a hiatus by its contemporaries. A profound change had in fact taken hold in the ancient world long before 476. As early as the first centuries following the birth of Christ and even more so from the middle of the 3rd century, Germanic groups and their followers had been crossing the Limes (the northern border) and the Danube border into the Roman Empire. Since attempted military reprisals against them had not met with long term success, the intruders were allocated imperial land and allowed to settle as confederates who were required to perform military service and to defend the imperial borders against encroachments by further *barbari* (Latin for foreigners). Germanic auxiliaries and mercenaries made up an increasing proportion of the Roman army, and Germanic tribal rulers from both sides of the Limes were able to climb the career ladder as military leaders within the Roman services. Contact with Roman civilization led to the acculturation of the Germanic ruling class well beyond the imperial borders. In this way, not only did Latin, Mediterranean consumer and luxury goods, and Roman fashion reach Germanic circles on both side of the Limes, but so did knowledge of Christianity. At the beginning of the 5th century the equilibrium, which had been established so painstakingly through barbarians fighting barbarians, collapsed. At the time of the Germanic seizure of power following incursions for plundering and conquest throughout the empire, many members of the ruling class had already converted to Arian Christianity.

Ravenna, Theodoric's Mausoleum. The powerful Ostrogoth king Theodoric (451–526) had this tomb, resembling the Late Antique portrayals of the Holy Sepulchre, built during his lifetime: both are typical of late Roman tomb construction.

Anglo-Saxons
Angles
Suebi
Saxons
Slavs
Tournai
Cologne
REALM OF THE
THURINGIANS
Cambrai
Soissons
Mainz
Rheims
Trier
REALM
Regensburg
Bulgars
Orléans
Alamanni
Lombards
OF THE
Bavarians
Dijon
REALM
FRANKS
REALM OF THE
Raetia
Noricum
Pannonia
OF THE
BURGUNDIANS
Geneva
GEPIDIANS
Milan
Verona
Pavia
Aquileia
Lugo
REALM OF
Cantabrians
Toulouse
Arles
Genoa
REALM
Dalmatia
THE SUEBI
Marseilles
OF THE
EASTERN ROMAN
Braga
Basques
OSTROGOTHS
EMPIRE
Constantinople
Adrianople
REALM OF THE
Corsica
Rome
Monte
Nicomedia
Lisbon
Toledo
Barcelona
Cassino
Thessalonica
VISIGOTHS
Naples
Epirus
Larissa
Mérida
Sardinia
Nicopolis
Symrna
Córdoba
Athens
Ephesus
Balearics
Corinth
Seville
Palermo
Cartagena
REALM OF THE VANDALS
Lilybaeum
Messina
Caesarea
Carthage
Syracuse
Hippo Regius
Hadrumetum
Crete
Mediterranean Sea

Realm of the Franks c. 486 AD
Conquests up to 551 BC

The downfall of the Roman state also saw the demise of the structures that had supported it. Although most of the new rulers did attempt to adopt and utilize these structures, the change of power usually meant a new start at a lower level. Tax revenues sank, administration and infrastructure functioned on a local basis only, and communication and national trade were heavily restricted. Roads, bridges, and water supplies were seldom repaired, public facilities such as administrative buildings, military complexes, baths, and theaters were used for other purposes or else fell into ruin, schools were closed. Roman law was replaced by a new, largely Germanic system. Education and training took place only within the family environment or else at court, and cultural, medical, and technical expertise became forgotten. The consequences were a decline in life expectancy and a marked drop in the quality of life for all, with the exception of the small, very wealthy Germanic and provincial Roman upper classes.

The Christian Church emerged from the upheaval strengthened as the only surviving institution. An increasing number of high-ranking Romans had converted to Christianity since the Edict of Milan proclaimed religious toleration in 313 and Constantine I lent support to the Christians. Many had entered into the service of the Church as office-holders in later life. At the time of the Germanic acquisition of power, the Church was therefore the domain of the well-educated, provincial Roman upper class with their experience of administration. In some towns the bishop's miter was firmly in the grasp of a few families. At the same time, from the 4th century, the systematic elaboration and expansion of the church organization, its dioceses closely resembling the divisions of the Roman Empire, represented the only remaining structure still functioning on a national basis. Despite the new rulers' Arian beliefs, recourse to the wealth of administrative, political, and cultural competence concentrated within the Catholic Church was inevitable and the involvement of the bishops in the administration of the new kingdoms was merely a question of time. The complete conversion of the Germanic population to Catholicism in the late 6th or 7th centuries opened the way for successful, enduring cooperation and, in the long term, led to the amalgamation of the Roman with the new Germanic ruling classes.

Europe in the first third of the 6th C. The Germanic migrations in the 4th and 5th centuries had led to the global decline of the Roman Empire and, with the deposition of the last Western Roman Emperor Romulus (Augustulus) in 476, to the collapse of the Western Roman Empire. The western territories had fallen under Germanic rule well before that. From 493 Italy was ruled by the Ostrogoth Theodoric, who acted as a mediator between the Romans and the Goths.

Arians and Catholics

In contrast to the Catholics, the Arians believed that Jesus, although created by the Holy Ghost, was "dissimilar" to man and therefore to God. This concept was rejected by the bishops gathered at the Council of Nicaea in 325 in favor of the teaching that Jesus was fully human and simultaneously fully divine and consubstantial with God the Father. This doctrine was subsequently considered *orthodox* (Greek for faithful). Although Arianism was thus officially declared a *heresy* (Greek for false doctrine), in opposition to the *Catholic* (Greek for complete, universal, correct) Church, it still attracted numerous followers well into the 5th century, especially among the Germanic population. As long as the Visigoths in Spain and the Ostrogoths, as well as later the Lombards, in Italy were confessed Arians, there were Arian "national churches" in these countries, whose bishops were appointed by the king. Evidence of this is still visible today with the 5th and 6th-century duplication of church buildings in Ravenna, where the corresponding Arian versions stand next to the "orthodox" cathedrals and baptisteries.

The New Role of the Monasteries

It was not only the bishops who played a decisive function in the societies that developed under Germanic rule; a new role also fell to the monasteries. While, in Late Antiquity, these had been primarily a place of personal retreat for Christians who, for ascetic reasons, wanted to withdraw from the world either for a while or on a lasting basis, they were now entrusted with social responsibilities by both the Church and the secular leadership. They found themselves at the centre of society instead of on its fringes. From places of austerity monasteries became places of service to God and the Christian community. The monasteries' new tasks lay primarily in the areas of education and study, relief for the poor, intercessory prayer, land development, and missionary work.

The social changes had turned what had previously been obvious or marginal activities on the part of the monks into sought-after skills: the reading and writing (or copying) of texts, study, and the transmission of ancient works, including those in Greek, as well as the passing on of this knowledge to the younger generation. Together with the cathedral schools set up by the bishops, many monasteries became educational centers where the scholarship transmitted from antiquity was compiled in the form of manuscripts, studied, and annotated in an attempt to preserve it through teaching and copying. With their contemplative lifestyle devoid of a focus on external activities and the apprenticeship laid down for novitiates at the outset, the monasteries were without doubt predestined for a role as places of study. This applied even more so in a society where the lives of upper class men were characterized by military activity, with no allowance for tuition in reading and writing. The knowledge conveyed in the monastery schools was not restricted to theology but also included the secular, in particular the disciplines outlined in the Late Antique canon *Septem Artes liberales* (Latin, Seven Liberal Arts), namely grammar, rhetoric, dialectic, arithmetic, geometry, music, and astronomy. In the Early Middle Ages the canon was often not taught in its entirety. Instead, the main focus was on grammar and rhetoric, with the teaching of the other disciplines dependent on the teacher's skills and the manuscripts available in the library.

Glendalough, former monastery settlement, tower (▲), west façade of the "cathedral" (▼) and St. Kevin's Church (▶), 9–11th C.

Glendalough developed from a 6th-C. hermitage founded by St. Kevin (died 618), which, under his pupils and successors, became one of the largest monastery settlements in Ireland and an important pilgrimage destination. In addition to the buildings, restored in the 19th and 20th centuries, some of the early Christian gravestones have also been preserved.

Study requirements were compatible with ascetic preoccupations only to a limited extent. In contrast, the regular training of pupils was only initially possible with the assured basic provision of all of the necessities of life. Donations and the endowment of the monasteries with grants of land therefore served as a guarantee for this basic provision even during times of hardship. Extensive protection from material need was in fact one of the main advantages of monastic life in the Early Middle Ages.

Although the amount of land necessary to safeguard the monks' livelihood constituted a considerable obstacle to the foundation of a monastery, many large property owners did not hesitate to take this step; after all, the transfer of their property to a monastery was repaid by the monks living there in a multitude of ways. The founding of a monastery was not an altruistic act but rather a trade-off, with the monks undertaking both spiritual and secular tasks in return for their livelihood. These tasks varied according to the social and political position of the benefactor and their personal motivation.

It was in this way that bishops, who were traditionally responsible for the relief of the poor in their communities, also founded aristocratic lay monasteries that they entrusted with charitable or social services. One example is the founding of a monastery known as a *xenodochium* (Greek/Latin for hostelry) by Bishop Syagrius of Autun shortly before 600, which performed the task of accommodating pilgrims and paupers coming to the town. In this way, facilities dating from Late Antiquity were resurrected on the initiative of individual office-holders using their own personal means, or with donations from further benefactors. It was not uncommon for rulers to be involved with such social endowments in cooperation with the local bishop. Hence Syagrius was also able to secure the support of the Burgundian Queen Brunichild for his establishment of the "monastery hostelry."

Like the bishops, kings too were interested in monasteries as elitist centers of learning and not just with regard to spiritual duties. They, like other aristocrats, also endorsed the greater utilization of their lands through monastic husbandry with the founding of monasteries on their properties. This was accompanied, as a rule, by the development of a new infrastructure that included transport connections as well as the settlement of farmers, manual workers, and merchants. And last, but not least, with these foundations beholden to royal or aristocratic benefactors, the establishment of monasteries also served the safeguarding of power.

Missionaries setting up monasteries as bases for their work in heathen regions followed similar paths. The monasteries functioned as Christian propaganda centers and were intended to provide the local population with a demonstration of Christian life, while at the same time forming a nucleus of ecclesiastic organization in newly Christianized areas. The missionary activities were usually closely coordinated with rulers hoping to establish their political influence or expand their territories through Christianization. Irrespective of the concrete social function assigned to the monasteries they founded, all benefactors were entitled to intercessory prayer by the monks in the institutions they had set up. This was an important extension of the concept of monastic life, which had originally been directed solely to the unremitting praise of God.

From now on, the monks' praise of God no longer constituted a life's purpose detached from worldly concerns and independent of third party interests, as a witness to the faith solely in service of the spiritual perfection of the individual. Instead, the monks now acted as the link between the benefactor and God, as mediators performing intercessory prayers to the Heavenly Father on behalf of their earthly patron. As a result of the monasteries' obligation to perform such intercessory prayers, an obligation that persisted after the death of the donor and, ideally, was to continue until doomsday, the monks' prayer lost its worldly indifference and became a specific commitment for a benefactor. They were thus able to score points in heaven without practicing asceticism themselves or dedicating their life to spiritual perfection.

Gregory the Great, reworked consular diptych (ivory, early 6th C.) as binder for a 9th-century gradual. A gradual contained the songs and music of the Mass; the name derives from the chanting after the reading, which was usually sung mounting the steps (Latin *gradus*) to the ambo, a raised reading platform. (Monza, Museo del Tesoro del Duomo).

The building, also known as the Tempietto Longobardo (Lombard Temple), was probably built as a royal commission. It was either a palace chapel or served as an oratorium for the adjacent nunnery, which was first mentioned in 830. According to sources dating back to the 13th century, the oratorium and monastery were founded by the Lombard queen Piltrudis. Of the six female stucco figures, which were originally painted in color, the two inner figures are dressed as spiritual women and their hands are raised in a gesture of prayer. The four outer figures, on the other hand, are aristocratic ladies with martyr's crowns.

Figural capital with Biblical motifs: Daniel in the Lions' Den. The original status of the church of S. Pedro de la Nave near Zamora, built in the second half of the 7th century, is unknown. The external architectural compactness of the building corresponds to the figural capital decoration in the interior, which is based on a coherent theological agenda. As with the portrayals of the Apostles, the scenes from the stories of Daniel and of Isaac are also focused on salvation.

S. Frutuoso de Montélios, near Braga. The ground plan of the church, built c. 660, has the shape of a Greek cross with straight, closed cross arms. St. Fructuosus, who built the church and to whom it is now consecrated, was archbishop of Braga and founded several monasteries in Galicia, Portugal, and Andalusia, for which he compiled a *Regula monachorum* (Monks' Rule), a characteristic example of Hispanic monasticism in the Early Middle Ages.

Development of the Successor States of the Roman Empire

Following the acquisition of power by the Germanic leaders, Arian or heathen, the situation of churches and monasteries initially looked very different in the individual successor states of the Roman Empire.

Italy

Stability and a considerable degree of governmental continuity prevailed in Italy under the Ostrogoth Theodoric I (493–526). His Arian faith took a back seat in the face of practical political needs: the administration was renewed with the involvement of the Catholic bishops and the capital city of Ravenna was expanded. It was only with the 535–53 war between Theodoric's successors and the generals of Justinian I, the Eastern Roman Emperor, over control of Italy, and the Lombard conquest from 568, that the break came with late Roman connections. Almost all of the monasteries were destroyed during the raiding and plundering by the Lombards, which continued for decades, including the Montecassino monastery founded by Benedict of Nursia. The repeated sieges of Rome, which lay in Byzantine territory, led to ongoing political antagonism between the Popes, who saw their autonomy under threat, and the Lombard rulers.

Hispania

On the Iberian Peninsula the relationship between the Arian Visigoths and the Roman population was tense for other reasons. Visigoth legislation, which was based on clan membership and religious faith, led to social discrimination against all non-Arians, especially Catholics and Jews. Only once the rule of the Visigoths had been reinforced militarily through the subjugation of the realm of the Suebi in the northwest of the peninsula and the Byzantine-occupied south extensively recaptured, did King Reccared implement the conversion to the Catholic faith at the Council of Toledo in 589. This abolished the political and religious discrepancies between the Visigoths and the Catholic majority and paved the way for close cooperation with the Church. The dignitaries of the Church, who came from the former provincial Roman upper class (as they did everywhere else), were thus incorporated into the new power structures.

Luke the Evangelist, from a Spanish Bible, 920 (León, Archivo de la Catedral, Cod. 6). The monastic scriptoria, which were founded in the 10th century by immigrant Mozarabic monks from Andalusia, are seen as the cradle of early Spanish illumination. The famous *Facundus Beatus* codex (today in the National Library in Madrid) originated in St. Isidore's scriptorium in León. Spain's oldest illuminated Bible, this was created in the Albares monastery (perhaps Abellar near León?).

Baptism of the king of the Franks Clovis I, Christmas 498, miniature, c. 1250. Clovis's (466–511) aggressive politics of domination fuelled his rise from a minor Frankish king to the most powerful ruler of Gaul. Given his position, his conversion to Catholic Christianity was a decisive step in the Christianization of Europe.

A number of churches dating from the time of the Visigoths' conversion to Catholicism have been preserved, such as the church of S. Juan de Baños de Cerrato (province of Palencia), built according to a large inscription by King Recceswinth (649–72). The original status of most of these churches (monastery or community church?) is frequently unclear due to a lack of detail regarding their construction periods and systematic archeological research. This also applies to the churches and chapels discovered in some Late Antiquity country villas. We do not know whether these were community churches for the local population or villas converted into monasteries, as is evidenced by sources relating to southern France and the Rome area. Early buildings from the monasteries founded in the Visigoth era, such as S. Isidro de Dueñas (province of León) or St. Cugat del Vallès in Catalonia (both 7th century) have not survived.

What we do have, however, are two monastery rules from around 600. These are, firstly, the *Regula monachorum* (Monks' Rule) from the important Doctor of the Church and archbishop Isidore of Seville (600–36), but it does not contain much new material as compared to older rules. The other is a nuns' rule compiled by Isidore's older brother and predecessor as archbishop, Leander of Seville (578–99), for the Florentina Sisters who lived as nuns (*De institutione virginum et contemptu mundi*). Isidore's works document the close contact with Pope Gregory the Great and the active communication that were maintained despite wars and the political divisions within the Church.

Visigoth rule came to an end with the Arab conquest of the Iberian Peninsula in 711. Only a small area in the northwest of Spain remained under Christian rule, becoming the nucleus of the Asturian kingdom and the later *Reconquista* (Spanish for reconquest), which originated from there. The Christian dioceses and monasteries, however, remained in existence in Islamic Andalusia because Christians and Jews enjoyed protection as "Peoples of the Book." Even though the number of Christians decreased steadily from the 9th century due to conversions to Islam, there was therefore a certain degree of Christian continuity until the recapture of large areas of Andalusia in the 13th century. This uninterrupted tradition found expression in the maintenance of Visigothic Hispanic rites, which were still followed in some Andalusian churches until the 15th century.

Clovis's Frankish Kingdom

The Visigoths and Ostrogoths made up barely 5 percent of the overall population in Hispania and Italy. In contrast, earlier immigrant movements, as well as the confederate settlements in northwest Gaul and the areas on the left bank of the River Rhine, had led to a significantly larger proportion of non-Romans within the population. Apart from Germanic peoples, and more especially Franks, this included Alans, Sarmats, and Huns, amongst others, all of whom were non-Christian. Christians who, as former Romans, were mainly resident in the towns, again became a minority in these regions, while the flat country where the immigrants settled was largely heathen.

The Frankish Merovingians, who gained power in northern Gaul in the second half of the 5th century, came from a family of military leaders in the service of the Romans. In contrast to many others of Germanic origin, they had not converted to Aryanism but had remained faithful to the old Roman gods. They realized earlier than the Goths, who persisted with their own brand of religion, what opportunities cooperation with the Gallo-Roman upper class would open up. This is precisely what King Clovis I had in mind when he was baptized in Rheims by Bishop Remigius at Christmas 498 and converted to the Catholic faith: the religious and social discrepancies were to disappear and Franks and Gallo-Romans amalgamated into a new union, in order to consolidate

Frankish rule. With the baptism in Rheims the Frankish kingdom became the *fille aînée de l'église*, the eldest daughter of the Catholic Church. However, despite this successful political maneuver, the conversion of the nobility took place at a slow pace, even taking into account the report by Gregory of Tours that 3000 men from the Frankish army were also required to be baptized following the example of their king. The areas settled by the Franks continued to be predominantly heathen for a long while. The impetus for the renewed Christianization of these areas came not from the south this time, but from the north.

Ireland, Land of Missionaries

Away from the conquests and upheavals of the migration era on the Continent, Christianized 5th-century Ireland had undergone peaceful and sustained development. Christianity was firmly anchored in society. From the start of the 6th century numerous monasteries were founded, which were places of strict asceticism but also played a very active role in church politics. It was not the bishops but the abbots of important monasteries who controlled the church dioceses, which were based on clan structures and kingdoms (or parts of them). In addition to church administration, prayer, and asceticism the monks also dedicated themselves to study. The instruction at the monastery schools was based on the Late Antiquity teaching canon of the *Artes liberales*, but with the emphasis on grammar for the purposes of learning Latin. Irish monks copied liturgical texts, the Bible, and the works of the Church Fathers, and also had contacts with Rome and with the East as far as Syria. Their ideal of an ascetic, peripatetic life (Latin *peregrinatio in eremo*, pilgrimage in the desert; in the sense of "in foreign lands") ultimately resulted in missionary activities on the Continent and in neighboring England. The stepping stone to England was the island monastery of Iona, which is situated off

▲ ▼ **Skellig Michael, former monastery with monks' cells.** The storm-battered island of Skellig Michael lies 7 miles (12 km) south of the Iveragh Peninsula. A number of small, dry-stone houses that served as monks' cells in the Early Middle Ages are preserved here. They are also known as the "Gallarus type oratoria," after the best preserved examples and date back to between 600 and 800. They are found only along the west coast of Ireland.

▼ ▶ **Kells, St. Columba's House and the Cross of Sts. Patrick and Columba,** east side, 9th C. The monastery at Kells was first mentioned in 807 in the Annals of Ulster. It served as a place of refuge for monks from the Scottish island monastery of Iona, which was attacked by the Vikings. Saints' relics were most probably stored on the upper floor of St. Columba's house.

▼ **Idealized illustration of an Irish monastery,** after A. Hamlin. The monastery complexes, usually with circular enclosures, housed several huts and churches and/or oratoria, almost all of which were built of wood until the 12th century. As, in addition to monks and priests, these settlements also accommodated artists, craftsmen, and pupils, doubts were sometimes cast upon their "monastic" character.

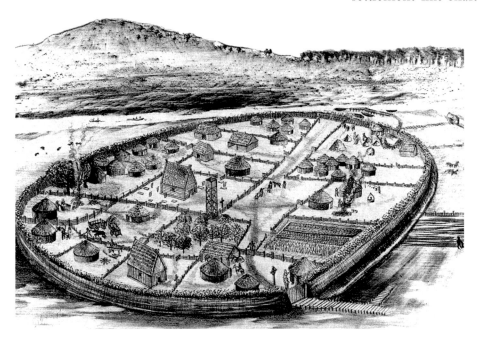

the west coast of Scotland, and which was founded by Columba the Elder in 563.

Since Irish monastery buildings were made almost exclusively from wood until the 12th century, our knowledge of early monasteries such as Clonard, Clonmacnoise, Kildare, Glendalough, Durrow, Bangor, or Iona is largely derived from written sources. The enclosed monastery complexes included churches, mostly simple rectangular buildings, and must have had a settlement-like character. Descriptions tell us that the interiors of the wooden churches were decorated with paintings and tapestries, as well as extensive metal and gold work. Only on the west coast, where dry-stone buildings were constructed without mortar using stones piled on top of one another, have monks' cells (simple round constructions) been preserved, at the island monastery at Skellig Michael, and a small church with parabolic external walls in Gallarus; these possibly date to the 8th century. The oldest walled stone churches date back to the period after 800, such as St. Columba's House in Kells (post-807) and St. Ciaran in Clonmacnoise (pre-880). Many of the early handwritten texts from Irish monasteries that have been preserved contain exquisite illuminations, such as the *Book of Durrow* (mid-7th century, presumed to be from Durrow) and the famous *Book of Kells* (c. 800, presumed to be from Iona).

Britannia

Britannia, abandoned by the Romans at the start of the 5th century, was taken over by the Angles, Saxons, and Jutes. Augustine, sent from Rome by Pope Gregory the Great, began his missionary activities in 597 at Canterbury in southern England. The monastery diocese of Lindisfarne in Northumberland, founded in 635 by Irish monks from Iona, was the starting point for his mission in the North. Numerous monasteries and dioceses were established through to the end of the 7th century and the Christianization of England was completed. Anglo-Saxon monks had since joined their Irish colleagues on journeys to the Continent to bring their faith to the remaining heathen areas, or to those districts that had relapsed into heathenism.

The new establishments in the North included the twin monasteries of Wearmouth (674) and Jarrow (683), whose library was developed into one of the best in contemporary northern Europe by the founding abbot, Benedict Biscop, with manuscripts that he had acquired on his journeys to Rome. This library became the workplace for the most important church writer of the Early Middle Ages, the Venerable Bede (673/74–735). Bede's assertion that the abbot had employed construction workers and glassblowers from Gaul to construct the monastery buildings in the "manner of Roman stone structures" has been confirmed by excavations in Wearmouth and Jarrow: both monasteries have stone churches and other buildings, and the remains of colored window glass and glassblowers' workshops have been found at both sites. The artistic book culture of northern England was also well developed during this era, as is evidenced by the *Book of Lindisfarne*, a gospel book created on the island of Lindisfarne at the end of the 7th century and containing outstanding illuminations.

Iona, interior view of the monastery church, 13th C. (none of the building dating from the Early Middle Ages has survived). Iona, founded by St. Columba in 563 on the island of the same name off the west coast of Scotland, was the leading Hiberno-Scottish monastery of its day. Despite its remote location, it played a significant role in the Christianization of Northumbria and is considered to be the place of origin of the famous ancient Irish codex, the *Book of Kells* (see p. 38).

Book of Lindisfarne, **the initials IN of the Gospel of St. Mark (◄) and John the Evangelist (▼),** late 7th C. (London, British Library, Cotton MS. Nero D. IV, folio 94 recto and folio 209 verso).

under the influence of the important monastery at Clonmacnoise. One of the most famous crosses here is the "Cross of the Scriptures" (illustration below right). Both of the crosses shown here date to the first quarter of the 10th century.

With its artistically skilled decoration, the *Book of Kells*, presumed to have originated on the island of Iona around 800, outshines all other European works of this period. The page of the Chi-Rho (the monogram of Christ), at the start of the Gospel of Matthew, pictured opposite, is the most impressive example of Hiberno-Scottish art's obsession with detail. In the midst of the confusing multitude of illuminations, symbolic indications of the Eucharistic body of Christ are combined with elaborate, naturalistic animal imagery.

◀ ▼ **Clonmacnoise,** high crosses in the former monastery complex; below, the famous "Cross of the Scriptures."

▶ *Book of Kells,* Chi-Rho page, c. 800, 330 x 241 mm (Dublin, Trinity College Library, Ms. A. 1.6 (58), folio 34 recto).

Early Medieval Art in Ireland

Most of the preserved evidence of early medieval art in Ireland, the greatest examples of which include highly decorative stone high crosses as well as book illumination, originated in monasteries or in monastic circles. The high crosses were erected on road sides, in cemeteries, and in other holy places. Many Irish high crosses are characterized by their decoration, comprising biblical scenes and ornamental motifs, as well as their ring or circle, which encircles the intersection between the shaft and the arms, stabilizing the latter. The hollowing out of the ring, together with the fact that the center of the cross almost always displays an image of the crucifixion, encourages the interpretation of the ring as a cosmic symbol with Christ at its center. The best known and preserved crosses include the two large examples from the former Monasterboice monastery: the "West Cross," measuring almost 23 ft (7 m), is the highest in Ireland, and the smaller "South Cross" or "Muiredach Cross" (illustration right), so named after an inscription on its west side. Most of the crosses still surviving today are to be found in central Ireland, where they were erected

Monasterboice, "South Cross," also called the "Muiredach Cross."

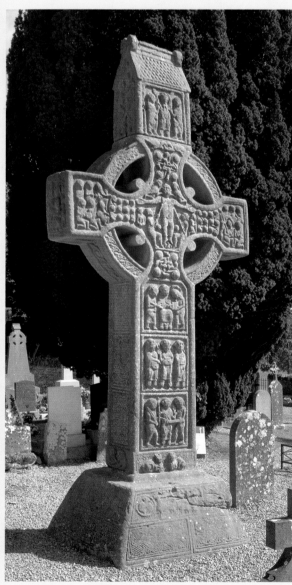

b;eunamo

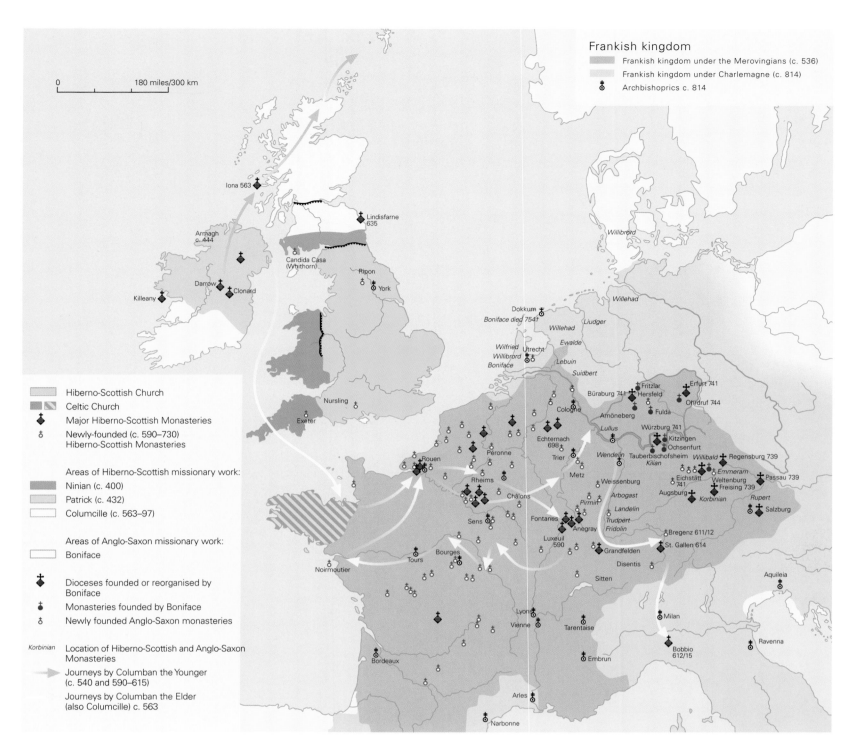

Frankish kingdom

Frankish kingdom under the Merovingians (c. 536)
Frankish kingdom under Charlemagne (c. 814)
Archbishoprics c. 814

0   180 miles/300 km

Iona 563
Lindisfarne 635
Armagh c. 444
Candida Casa (Whithorn)
Ripon
York
Darrow
Clonard
Killeany
Willibrord
Dokkum
Boniface died 754†
Willehad
Liudger
Willehad
Wilfried Utrecht
Willibrord
Boniface
Lebuin
Suidbert
Ewalde
Fritzlar
Hersfeld
Erfurt 741
Büraburg 741
Ohrdruf 744
Cologne
Amöneberg
Fulda
Nursling
Lullus
Würzburg 741
Exeter
Echternach 698
Wendelin
Kitzingen
Ochsenfurt
Tauberbischofsheim
Kilian
Willibald
Regensburg 739
Péronne
Rouen
Trier
Eichstätt 741
Emmeram
Weltenburg
Freising 739
Passau 739
Rheims
Metz
Weissenburg
Arbogast
Augsburg
Korbinian
Rupert
Châlons
Pirmin
Landelin
Salzburg
Sens
Fontaines
Trudpert
Fridolin
Anegray
Bregenz 611/12
Luxeuil 590
Grandfelden
St. Gallen 614
Bourges
Disentis
Aquileia
Tours
Sitten
Noirmoutier
Lyon
Milan
Vienne
Tarentaise
Ravenna
Bordeaux
Bobbio 612/15
Embrun
Arles
Narbonne

Hiberno-Scottish Church
Celtic Church
Major Hiberno-Scottish Monasteries
Newly-founded (c. 590–730) Hiberno-Scottish Monasteries

Areas of Hiberno-Scottish missionary work:
Ninian (c. 400)
Patrick (c. 432)
Columcille (c. 563–97)

Areas of Anglo-Saxon missionary work:
Boniface

Dioceses founded or reorganised by Boniface
Monasteries founded by Boniface
Newly founded Anglo-Saxon monasteries

Korbinian Location of Hiberno-Scottish and Anglo-Saxon Monasteries
Journeys by Columban the Younger (c. 540 and 590–615)
Journeys by Columban the Elder (also Columcille) c. 563

The Hiberno-Scottish missionary movement. While the Irish were focusing their missionary work on central France, the Anglo-Saxons were active on her northern and eastern peripheries, i.e. outside the territory of the former Roman Empire. While the Irish had tried to free their monasteries from episcopal control, the Anglo-Saxons wanted to integrate their missionary areas into the organization of the church.

Columban and Hiberno-Frankish Monasticism

The monk Columban (Columban the Younger) landed on the Breton coast in around 591, together with twelve companions. From there he headed for the Vosges Mountains, where he made contact with the Merovingian-Burgundian royal court and founded a first monastery in Annegray. Following initial difficulties, the increasing success of his mission and the permission of King Childebert II of Austrasia and Burgundy enabled Columban to found two further monasteries in quick succession: Luxeuil and Fontaines. Both settlements enjoyed a brisk influx of young Frankish aristocrats. Columban compiled rules and two Handbooks of Penance for the three communities, which are said to have numbered over 200 monks.

The ten chapters of the *Regula monachorum*, dating from 595, contain basic principles of ascetic monastic life and regulations for spiritual obligations, as well as for the organization of the day, with the Liturgy of the Hours and meal times. Special emphasis is placed on the control of lust, to which an entire chapter is devoted. The *Regula coenobalis* (also called the *Regula partum*) is a collection of punishments for lapses in the monastery, which was expanded upon by Columban's successors. Two Handbooks of Penance comprise additional, voluntary acts of penance for the monks. In contrast to the Rule of St. Benedict, the monastic life propagated by Columban places a clear emphasis on asceticism and penitence. The severity of Irish monasticism he expressed was moderated by successive abbots of Luxeuil (Eustasius,

610–29; Walbert, 629–70), however. A "mixed rule," comprising parts of the Rule of St. Columban and of the Rule of St. Benedict was introduced in place of the Rule of St. Columban alone.

Luxeuil, which played a leading role among the three Vosges monasteries, attracted monks from all corners of the Frankish kingdom. Monks from Luxeuil, on the other hand, found their way to Frankish bishop's thrones or exported Hiberno-Frankish monasticism by emigrating to other monasteries or founding new settlements. The first abbot of the double monastery at Remiremont, founded in the Vosges Mountains in 620 as a settlement where monks and nuns lived at the same location, albeit strictly separate from one another, came from Luxeuil. Monks from Luxeuil were summoned to the double monastery at Faremoutiers, founded in 620, while the derelict monastery at Romainmôtier, once revived by the Jura Fathers, was resettled by monks from Luxeuil in c. 640.

Beyond the direct influence of Luxeuil, however, it was Columban's concept of missionary work through the founding of monasteries that was to prove most successful: based on the example of the "model monastery" at Luxeuil, the Frankish aristocracy and the Merovingian kings realized that the settlement of monks who lived according to their strict spiritual discipline was an effective means not just of Christianization, but also of developing underutilized areas. This realization paved the way for a series of significant monastery developments both on the part of the royal court and also by individual aristocratic families. In 635, Audoin, educated at the royal court, and his brother founded the monasteries of Jouarre and Rebais east of Paris. As bishop of Rouen Audoin initiated and/or supported the founding of St. Wandrille (c. 650) and Jumièges (654) on the lower stretches of the River Seine. The property in the Ardennes on which St. Remaclus founded the monasteries Stablo and Malmédy was left to him by King Sigibert III. In 657–61, together with her son Chlothar III, Queen Balthild established the Corbie monastery near Amiens and assigned it to monks from Luxeuil, before she founded the Chelles nunnery near Paris in 658–59, to which she herself retreated in 665. In 650 the Pippinid family, of which the Carolingians were members, founded the double monastery of Nivelles on their property, as well as the St. Trond monastery after 654. Due to the support of the propertied nobility, the Hiberno-Frankish monks' sense of purpose provided the impetus

Jouarre, Crypt of St. Paul, 7–8th C., relief of Christ enthroned with the Evangelists' symbols from the head of the sarcophagus (▲) of Bishop Agilbert of Paris (died 673/90), and the sarcophagi of the first abbesses (▼). With the entry of female family members, the monastery, founded c. 635 by one of the brothers of St. Ouen (Audoin), archbishop of Rouen, developed into a nunnery with an adjacent clerical convent.
The crypt is part of the former St. Paul burial church, which, together with the monastery church of Notre-Dame (today a 19th-century reconstruction) and the clerical church of St. Pierre (later a parish church), comprise the monastery's family of churches. It was probably redesigned as a hall crypt in the 11-12th centuries, reusing the ornate early medieval columns and marble capitals.

Miniature with scenes from the life of St. Boniface
(672/75–754), baptism of a Friesian on completion of
successful missionary work (above): the violent death of
Boniface, the famous monastery founder and missionary
bishop (below). *Fulda Sacramentary*, c. 1000 (Bamberg,
Staatsbibliothek, Cod. lit. 1, fol. 126 verso).

Müstair, St. John's Monastery, southern apse of the
monastery church with statue of Charlemagne. The church
and the murals in the nave are Carolingian, while those in the
eastern apses date to the second half of the 12th century, as
probably does the stucco imperial figure underneath a Late
Gothic dais.

for an acculturation movement that served to consolidate royal and aristocratic power at the same time.

Despite the success of the monastery he founded, Columban himself had
to leave Luxeuil in 610 as he had fallen out with King Theuderic II of Burgundy over the latter's lifestyle. Following a brief sojourn at the court of
Chlothar II of Neustria he went to Metz, where the Bregenz area was allocated to him as a missionary target by Theudebert II of Austrasia. Columban
preached Christianity to the Alamans at both Lake Constance and Lake
Zurich with varying degrees of success before he had to retreat to Italy following Theudebert's loss of power in 612. He was awarded protection and an
open ear by the Lombard king Agilulf, despite the latter's Arian faith. In St.
Peter's Church, assigned to him by Agilulf, Columban founded his last
monastery: in Bobbio on the banks of the Trebbia River, south of Piacenza, in
613–14, where he subsequently died in 615. Bobbio became the starting
point for new monastic life in northern Italy and, as of the late 7th century,
housed one of the most important Scriptoria (writing rooms) of the Lombard
kingdom. The monastery acquired wealthy possessions and remained closely
linked to the royal court, particularly following the Lombards' conversion
to Catholicism.

One of Columban's pupils, Gallus, settled in the area surrounding Lake
Zurich. The St. Gallen Monastery was later erected on the site of the hermitage where he spent his life. Other representatives of Hiberno-Frankish
monasticism entered southern German territory in the 7th and 8th centuries,
such as the Irishman Kilian in the Würzburg area and Pirmin from Meaux on
the Upper Rhine, where in 724 he founded a monastery on the island of
Reichenau in Lake Constance.

The Anglo-Saxon Mission

A new phase of missionary monasticism began in 690 under the influence of
the Anglo-Saxon Willibrord, one that differed from what had gone before in
a number of respects. While the Irish carried out their missionary work
inland, the Anglo-Saxons were active on the northern and eastern peripheries
of the Frankish kingdom, outside the territories of the former Roman
Empire. They sought not only the support of the rulers, but also close cooperation with Rome. While the Irish had always tried to maintain their monasteries outside episcopal influence, the Anglo-Saxons, on the other hand,
aimed to incorporate their missionary areas into the church organization.
Settlements and missionary bases were intended to pave the way for the
founding of dioceses, which had not previously existed east of the Limes.
Finally, and this was the most significant point for the development of monasticism, they did not compile their own monastery rules; instead, they brought
into their monasteries the *Regula Benedicti* (Rule of St. Benedict), which
Augustine of Canterbury and his pupils had introduced in England.

Willibrord's main activities extended westwards into southwestern Friesland, which is today part of the Netherlands. He founded a diocese based in
Utrecht and erected a monastery in Echternach (now in Luxembourg) in
697–98 on a property assigned to him for this purpose, in order to be able to
organize and consolidate his missionary work there. Echternach experienced
the first of its golden periods under Willibrord, as is evidenced by the important manuscripts compiled in the monastery scriptorium.

Boniface began his missionary work among the Friesians in 719 at Willibrord's side, before he moved on to Hesse and Thüringia two years later. He
traveled to Rome three times during the course of his work, which covered
nearly three decades. The monasteries he founded included those in Fritzlar,
Ochsenfurt, Hersfeld, and lastly in Fulda; he reorganized the already existing
Bavarian dioceses of Regensburg, Passau, Salzburg, and Freising; and founded
the dioceses of Würzburg, Büraburg and Erfurt, as well as the monastery diocese of Eichstätt. Although the Pope appointed him archbishop of Mainz, at
the end of his life he returned to Friesland, where he met his death as a missionary in 754. Boniface initiated the Christianization of central Germany
with his establishment of monasteries and dioceses and set an important
course for the organization of the Church and future urban development.
Boniface and Willibrord had acquired not only new territories but also the

Frankish nation for the Church with their missionary work. In doing so, they worked more closely with the ambitious Carolingians, whose own lands lay in the northeast of the Frankish kingdom than they did with the Merovingian kings. The acquisition of power by the Carolingians brought with it a new era of national unity and enduring prosperity for Christian Europe.

Monasteries in the Carolingian Empire: Between Imperial Service and Monastic Reform

Charles Martel (718–41), officially "*Maior Domus*" (Latin for "mayor of the palace") in the service of the Merovingians, but de facto autocrat, had extended Frankish territory in the north and east through crusades against the Friesians, Thüringians, Alamans, and Bavarians, and consolidated Frankish rule in southern Gaul in battles against the Arabs. His son Pepin the Younger (741–68), elected Frankish king in 751 and anointed in 754 by Pope Stephen II in St. Denis near Paris, conquered the former Byzantine areas of central Italy under threat from the Lombards, following a plea for help from the Pope. Instead of returning them to Byzantium, he gave them to the Roman Church, thus founding the Papal States. His son Charlemagne (768–814) completed the conquest of the Lombard kingdom in 774 and in 795 regained the "Spanish Mark," present day Catalonia, from the Arabs. In 800 he had himself crowned emperor by the Pope in Rome, reminiscent of the tradition of the *Imperium Romanum*.

Under Charlemagne's rule and that of his son, Louis the Pious (814–40), all the European countries that had belonged to the Western Roman Empire, with the exception of England and Islamic Spain, were reunited under one jurisdiction. The organization of land control into counties, in which the counts officiated as the emperor's deputies, served to create a unified administrative structure. Royal decrees and edicts were intended to standardize legal practice. The construction of roads, and messenger systems, enabled commu-

Müstair, St. Johann's Monastery, view of the complex from the northeast. The monastery, located in Switzerland near the border with South Tyrol's Vintschgau, was founded at the end of the 8th century by Bishop Constantius or Bishop Remedius of Chur. Originally a Benedictine abbey for monks, it was converted into a nunnery (also Benedictine) in the first half of the 12th century and has remained as such today. A relic of the Holy Blood kept in the monastery made Müstair a pilgrimage destination. The Carolingian church's building design, a hall with three apses, is typical for the Rhetian alpine region. In the interior of the church is the most extensive surviving cycle of early medieval wall paintings in the whole of Europe (dating to c. 800). Müstair is a UNESCO World Heritage Site.

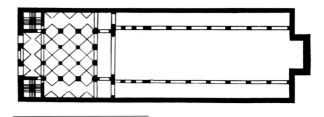

▲ ▶ **Lorsch: ground plan of Lorsch II and "gatehouse",** consecration of the monastery church 774, gatehouse c. 860–70. The gatehouse stands alone in an elongated atrium, adjacent to the west building and the Late Romanesque narthex of the former St. Nazarius monastery church. The reconstruction shows a pier basilica with a nave and two side aisles, a rectangular altar space but no transept.

Imperial Monasteries: Immunity and Royal Protection

The Carolingians accorded special rights to important monasteries and abbeys. In particular, this included the "immunity" ("freedom from rule") and royal protection, which always appear together in Louis the Pious' documents. In order to be able to enjoy these privileges, the monastery voluntarily placed itself under the authority of the emperor or king. In return the latter promised to provide special protection for the monastery, confirmed and guaranteed its possessions, and exempted it from specific taxes. The monastery in turn accorded the monarch and his entourage the right to hospitality, i.e. accommodation and meals. Since the royal entourage was extensive and taking care of it costly, the imperial monasteries had to have sufficient lands available in order to be able to entertain the royal court, so donating to them was in the ruler's own interests. In addition to buildings for housing the monarch and his family, some imperial monasteries also had their own royal chapel. The monasteries at Reichenau, Lorsch, and Farfa, amongst others, provide examples of such private royal oratories.

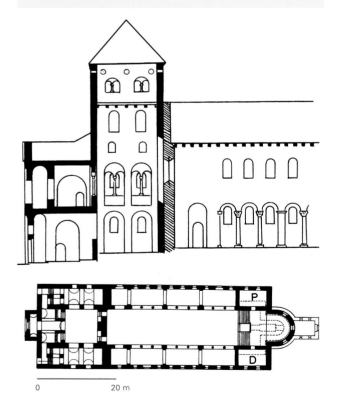

Essen-Werden, priory church of St. Salvator, post-799 (church, ring crypt added c. 835) and 943 (west building). Sectional view through the west building (reconstruction) and ground plan.

▶ **Corvey, former abbey church,** west façade. The Benedictine abbey, founded in 822 by monks from Corbie, was named with reference to the mother house. The Carolingian west building (see p. 50) was converted to a twin tower façade c. 1150; the surviving original building below the windowed extension (873–85) in all probability had a central tower.

nications to function between the various parts of the empire. Peace and legal security in large areas of the empire allowed a resurrection of trade and traffic. The concentration of the most important scholars at the royal court, the gathering of knowledge from antiquity, and the support of monasteries and monastic schools led to a cultural blossoming.

Numerous important monasteries were founded in the decades around 800. Others received donations and immunity privileges that freed them from local dependencies and made them directly subject to the empire. In return they had to accommodate the imperial court on its travels through the empire, providing the ruler and his attendants with accommodation and meals. At the same time, abbots and the scholars of the monastery schools were accorded political offices, entrusted with concrete political duties for the Church or were summoned as advisors to the imperial court. Due to this direct integration into the practical implementation of governmental business, the founding and development of monasteries became an internal political measure of high priority, and, in the same manner, the furtherance of monastery schools served not exclusively cultural but in addition national political interests.

Liudger, the first Bishop of Münster, came from a noble West Friesian family. He was brought up in the monastery founded by Willibrord in Utrecht and educated in Anglo-Saxon York by Alcuin, later head of Charlemagne's court school. In 799 he founded the Werden monastery on his own property in his Westphalian missionary area, where he was later buried. Members of his family continued to lead the dioceses of Münster and Halberstadt for several generations and also presided as abbots over the Werden monastery and daughter monastery at Helmstedt in the Halberstadt diocese. Around 845 Altfrid, advisor to the king and bishop of Hildesheim, erected a nunnery in neighboring Essen, also on his own property. In 822, Adalhard, a cousin of Charlemagne, former administrator and abbot of the important Corbie monastery near Amiens, founded Corvey on the Weser (*Corbeia nova*), an important Christian outpost on what was at the time newly subordinated Saxon territory. Two further monasteries in the west of the Frankish kingdom developed into important centers under the leadership of members of the royal court school: Centula (Saint-Riquier) Abbey in northern France received a large, elaborate new building under Abbot Angilbert (790–814) and is said to have numbered 300 monks; under the Anglo-Saxon scholar Alcuin (abbot 796–804) Saint-Martin's Abbey at the saint's tomb in Tours became one of the largest production centers for biblical manuscripts in the Frankish kingdom. At the abbey of Saint-Germain in Auxerre, erected at the tomb of Bishop Germanus, was one of the most important monastery schools of the 9th century. The monasteries founded by Boniface at Fulda, that of Pirmin on Reichenau, and that of St. Gallen also developed around 800 into

large abbeys with significant schools and libraries.

In Italy, particularly the monasteries founded in the late Lombard era with royal or ducal support underwent a further revival under Carolingian rule. These included the double monastery SS. Salvatore e Giulia in Brescia, erected in the middle of the 8th century, Monte Amiata Abbey founded in the same year, the monastery at Montecassino, which was resettled in 729, and the S. Vincenzo al Volturno monastery in the Abruzzi Mountains, founded shortly after 700, as well as Farfa Monastery founded a few years previously in the Sabina Mountains. Farfa was the first Italian abbey to be promoted to an imperial monastery.

The Carolingians aimed at unification both in affairs of state and those of the Church. With a reform of the liturgical books, which contained the essential texts and rituals for the religious offices, they harmonized services throughout the Frankish kingdom based on the Roman liturgy. Charlemagne commissioned scholars such as Alcuin to work on a revision and improvement of the Latin Bible text. In accordance with their self-image as protectors and champions of Christianity, the Carolingian monarchs did not shy away from intervening in the internal business of monasteries and churches in order to impose a unified rule on the monks, namely the Rule of St. Benedict. These "Carolingian monastery reforms" culminated in the Councils of Aachen in 816–19 convened by Louis the Pious.

Benedict of Aniane

The initiator and imperial representative of the reform movement via the implementation of the Rule of St. Benedict was a Visigoth aristocrat. Following the death of his brother during the Frankish campaigns against the Lombards, Witiza, son of the Count of Maguelonne, had withdrawn from secular life and entered Saint-Seine Abbey in Burgundy. Dissatisfied by the lack of stringency of the life there, he founded his own monastery in 779 on a property in Aniane, west of Montpellier. After experimenting with anchorite and other ascetic lifestyles he ultimately decided in favor of the adoption of the Rule of St. Benedict, which he subsequently advocated as the only authoritative monks' rule. As an expression of this conviction, he himself adopted the name Benedict and dispatched monks from Aniane, which soon numbered more than 300, to other monasteries in the southwest of the Frankish kingdom, to teach the Rule of St. Benedict. After taking office in 814, Louis the Pious summoned him to the court in Aachen and commissioned him to supplement the often only generally worded specifications of the Rule of St. Benedict with concrete regulations on implementation. This was intended to remove the discrepancies existing between individual monasteries in the practical application of the rule in favor of a uniform way of life. The adop-

▲ ▲ **Auxerre, former abbey church of Saint-Germain, crypt,** c. 840–63. The crypt, perplexingly multipartite on the ground plan, is an outer crypt with an apex rotunda. At the center is the *Confessio* with the tomb of St. Germanus, a small room with a nave and two side aisles, the three parallel barrels of which are supported by oak architraves each on two columns. In 1927 murals dating from the era of construction were discovered in the northern arm of the tower gallery. Floral patterns are visible in the intrados beyond the decorated columns and on the vault supports, while scenes from the life of the martyr Stephen are visible under the arches.

Flavigny-sur-Ozerain, former monastery church of Saint-Pierre, inner apse of the crypt, 2nd half of the 9th C. The only slightly later complex at Flavigny is similar in many respects to that at Auxerre.

◄ **Christ panel, cover of the *Lorsch Gospels* with ivory panels,** early 9th C. (London, Victoria and Albert Museum). In the Middle Ages gospel books in particular had very valuable covers. This gospel book from Aachen, dating to c. 810, originated from Charlemagne's royal workshop. Lorsch Abbey, where this famous codex was housed from 830 (when it was first mentioned in the abbey's library catalogue) until the 15th century, was one of the most important of the Carolingian royal monasteries.

The Regulations of Benedict of Aniane

The so-called *Regula sancti Benedicti abbatis Anianensis* is not a self-contained monastery rule but merely contains the supplementary regulations for the implementation of the Rule of St. Benedict. These are arranged as individual regulations in 77 chapters and, in addition to issues regarding the religious service, the calendar of religious festivals, and the rites and practices to be observed, it relates primarily to practical monastery life (eating, drinking, and fasting, personal hygiene and clothing), the official hierarchy (abbot and provost, ranked according to age at entry), and the monastery organization (handicraft in the monastery, travel and inspection of monastery lands, tributes to the poor; dormitory next to the church), as well as the admission of novices and contacts with laymen (accommodation of guests, visits by family members). This was an Anian "rule" based on the earliest form of the *Consuetudines* or monastic customs. Sometimes simply called "practices," these practical habits differed in nature from monastery to monastery, depending on the differences in climate and geography, natural resources and vegetation, as well as on building practices and specific spiritual traditions. The actual extent to which the regulations of Benedict of Aniane were actually implemented is a matter for dispute due to the lack of written evidence. Nevertheless, many of the Anian regulations relate to issues that were taken up repeatedly in subsequent *Consuetudines*. There is no doubt, however, that the Councils of Aachen and the influence of Benedict of Aniane played a decisive role in the binding implementation of the monastery rule of St. Benedict of Nursia throughout the Frankish kingdom.

Romainmôtier, monastery complex buildings in the 8–11th C., showing the two churches.

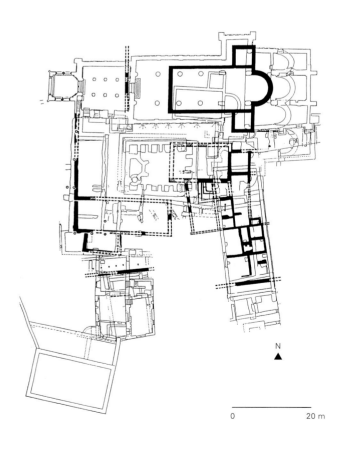

N ▲

0   20 m

tion of the new, unified rule and its implementation throughout the empire was agreed upon at the Aachen Councils of 816 and 817, attended by the abbots of all of the monasteries in the Carolingian domains. During the same period Emperor Louis founded Inden Monastery close to Aachen in order to make it a model religious house under Benedict's leadership and an example for the whole of the empire.

The Council of Aachen in 816 also led, for the first time, to the drawing of a firm distinction between monks and canons. Clerics who performed communal religious services in churches but who did not subjugate themselves to the monks' strict life devoid of possessions were known as canons or capitulars. A binding classification within the one or other way of life, based on precisely defined features, was now introduced in the place of what had previously been seamless transitions. Canons and their female counterparts, canonesses or female capitulars, were also obligated to follow their own set of rules, the *Institutiones Aquisgranenses*. Due to their lesser degree of asceticism, canons and canonesses, who were not required to surrender their private property upon entering a community, were seen as spiritually inferior to monks and nuns.

The Monasteries and their Inhabitants

Pachomius' Egyptian monasteries had been similar to village settlements, while Anthony and his pupils, as well as the hermits of Kellia, lived in simple cells comprising one or two rooms. The private monasteries in Late Antiquity villas and the early monks in Lérins and Montecassino had used buildings that have not survived and the specific details of which are therefore unknown, but all of them must have been very different. Furthermore, most of the older monasteries had disappeared and their usually wooden buildings destroyed. Once monasteries were again built in larger numbers in the 7th and 8th centuries there was no building tradition stipulating how they were to look. Neither did the monastery rules contain any concrete specifications. Only the regulation that meals were to be taken together and the requirement for a communal dormitory for all monks provide indications of the layout. The construction of the early monasteries was therefore oriented towards two key aspects: the need for a church building and the requirement of rooms for communal meals and sleeping.

Since the utilitarian monastery buildings were modified, rebuilt, and torn down far more frequently than the churches, our knowledge of early monastic structures is based primarily on archaeological excavations. The Jura monastery of Romainmôtier is one of the few early medieval monasteries about which we know a fair amount, relatively speaking.

The oldest building remains in the area of the former monastery, south of the still existing Early Romanesque monastery church of the 11th century, are post-holes from wooden structures that presumably date back to the monastery's founding phase in the 5th century. The first church was a simple hall with a semi-circular apse and transept-like annexes underneath the present-day church. The stone monastery buildings were later erected to the south of the church, under the east wing of the later cloister, which undoubtedly housed the monks' dining room and dormitory.

The monastery complex was soon modified, however: the buildings under the east wing were altered and the northern part was torn down in order to make way for a second church. This was also a hall with a rectangular choir. The two church buildings stood next to one another from then on. The north church was later replaced by a larger new construction of the same shape, and the south church was fully renovated at least once using the same foundations. The monks' buildings were adjacent to the south side. Further monastic structures were erected on the site of the later west wing of the cloister. Assuming that the monks' facilities did comprise a dining room, dormitory, living room, and pantry, the existence of two churches next to each other in what was a relatively small monastery is surprising. Even though the lack of precisely dated findings means that we do not know exactly when the individual churches were erected, the excavations have shown that there were two monastery churches well into the 10th century, that is, for the entire duration of the Early Middle Ages.

Groups of Churches

These findings are not unique to Romainmôtier. Groups of churches comprising two or three buildings were in fact a common feature of early medieval monastery complexes. The double monastery of Nivelles, founded c. 650, has three churches: one to the north for the male clerical community, a large one in the center for the nunnery, and a cemetery church further south, to which the tomb of the first abbess, Gertrude, was attached. Following her canonization the cemetery church was replaced by a new, larger building as of the 9th century, which was dedicated to St. Gertrude and ultimately became the monastery's main church. Contemporary sources from Centula/Saint-Riquier tell of three churches that were connected to one another via walkways. A representation of Centula in the 11th-century monastery chronicle of the monk Hariulf, which has survived as a later engraving, shows churches connected to one another by means of galleries in the form of a kind of cloister with an irregular rectangular shape. There is also frequent evidence, including excavations, from the early English monasteries, of several churches built within some of these.

The reason for the construction of such groups of churches, which are also found at cathedrals, is unknown. The conjecture that, originally, one church had served the Arian and the other the Catholic cult is contradicted by the occurrence of groups of churches in the solely Catholic Frankish kingdom. It is possible that the individual buildings in a family of churches were originally intended for specific purposes. The example of Nivelles, with male, female, and cemetery churches, would seem to confirm such a division of purpose. Such functional allocations are not, however, evident in every case. It is also conceivable that an early church had only one altar and could serve only one saint's cult. The construction of a second altar, because of the acquisition of relics from an additional saint, for example, then required the building of a new church. This explanation is no longer applied to the Carolingian era, however. Written sources from Centula and the famous St. Gallen monastery plan, as well as surviving buildings like St. Johann in Müstair with its three apses, tell us that there were numerous different altars in Carolingian monastic churches. In this case the retention of groups of churches in the monasteries of the period c. 800 is best explained as the adherence to a tradition, which had already been firmly anchored in monastic life due to liturgical practices such as processions between the different churches.

Double Choir Churches

In addition to the widespread existence of groups of churches, the Carolingian monastery complexes following the period around 800 also exhibited a second, almost contradictory, tendency: the combination of two cult centers in the same building. The large abbey church at Centula, consecrated in 799, is such an example. While, on the one hand, it was part of the abbey's triple church group, its walls also accommodated two different cult centers, with contemporary sources making a clear distinction between them: to the east was the *ecclesia sancti Ricarii* with the tomb of St. Richarius and to the west the *ecclesia sancti Salvatoris*. Both parts of the building, the "Richarius church" and the "church of the Saviour," were connected to each other via a *vestibulum*

Centula (today Saint-Riquier, Picardy). This illustration of the abbey complex based on a hand drawing of the 11th C. (engraving of 1612) shows three churches connected with one another via walkways.

Müstair, monastery church, detail of the east end with three apses.

Corvey, former abbey church, interior view of the west building and ground plan. On the upper floor, above the vaulted ground floor hall, is a west choir enclosed on three sides by galleries, the walls of which were originally decorated with life-sized stucco figures between the arches. Written sources provide no evidence at all of the frequent assumption that this was an "imperial church." Instead the large gallery opening on the west side (▶)—accessible only via the stairs, which were secured by lockable doors was possibly used to house and display precious relics.

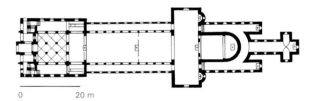

0   20 m

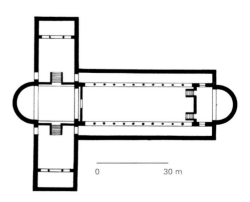

0   30 m

Fulda, abbey church, c. 790–819, ground plan. The column basilica with a nave and two side aisles, as well as west and east crypt, faces west. The width of the open ("Roman") transept, based on the example of St. Peter in Rome, is especially conspicuous.

(Latin for atrium) and were situated on a higher level, reached via a staircase. In architectural terms this means that the abbey church at Centula was a so-called double choir church with east and west choirs, which were connected to each other by a nave. Both choirs were higher than the nave because the east choir was located over the crypt with the tomb of St. Richarius and the west choir over the entrance to the abbey church. It is unclear, however, whether the east and west choirs were already crowned with towers by c. 800, as can be seen in the 11th-century illustration (see top of p. 49), as the Carolingian abbey church has not survived.

A surviving construction in the west building at Corvey is possibly comparable to the west choir at Centula. There the abbey church dating from 844 was initially extended to the east with a choir and outer crypt, before the west building, consecrated in 885, was erected. Above the low, vaulted entrance to the church was the Choir of St. Johann, a high, square room, which was once enclosed on three sides by galleries. To the east an open arcade provided the connection to the nave. Remains of the elaborate decoration with wall paintings and stucco figures have survived. The exterior of the building, with its twin tower façade erected in the 12th century, no longer, however, corresponds to its original form.

The abbey church at Fulda acquired a special form of west choir. Between 802 and 817, a wide west transept and a west apse were added to the church, which had been begun in 790, with a nave and two side aisles, and an east apse. The open transept and the crypt under the west apse are a clear indication that the Fulda church was based on St. Peter's in Rome, which was copied as precisely as possible. As with the tomb of St. Peter in Rome, Fulda housed the tomb of St. Boniface in the west crypt. As a crypt had also been built under the east apse, the east and west choirs were higher than the nave, as was also the case in Centula und Corvey.

The St. Gallen monastery plan also shows a church with an east and a west choir, both ending in apses as at Fulda. The excavated monastery church of St. Gallen, however, is a rectangular construction closed to the east. The somewhat smaller church to the west was erected at a later stage on the same axis but facing west. The two churches were connected to each other by an atrium situated between them. Despite the differences in construction, the bipolar alignment of both buildings does provide a structural harmony between the excavated church and the plan church. In the excavated monastery church this is still emphasized by the fact that they are two separate buildings that are back to back. What is also striking is that the term *vestibulum* used at Centula for the nave became a reality at St. Gallen: an atrium did indeed connect the two churches, with St. Michael's Chapel on the upper floor.

Processional Liturgy

The liturgical practices at Centula under Abbot Angilbert (790–814) are described in the *Institutio Angilberti*. From this we know that the abbey's various churches and altars were used for celebrating the feast days of the saints venerated there with religious services. All of the feast days relating to Christ, such us Christmas (birth), Easter (resurrection) and Ascension Day were celebrated in the Salvator choir, all of the Mary and Apostle feast days in the church consecrated to the Mother of God and the Twelve Apostles, and so on. In addition to the celebration of these saints, the Richarius choir was also used for the daily religious service, for which there was no consecrated altar in the monastery. Even on an everyday basis, however, part of the Liturgy of the Hours was sometimes held in another church. What the *Institutio Angilberti* describes, therefore, is an abbey in a constant state of flux. The monks were not bound to one place for the fulfillment of their spiritual obligations. Instead, they moved from one church to another according to a fixed pattern, from one choir to another, and from altar to altar. With their processional movements, which followed the liturgical times of the day and the festivals of the church year, the prescribed sacral topography determined by the family of churches and the altar arrangements constituted a detailed image of the monastery as a heavenly settlement populated by a multitude of saints.

Tassilo Chalice from Kremsmünster Abbey, Austria, c. 780, copper, gold-plated, with soldered silver leaf. The donor inscription for this precious communion chalice cites Tassilo and his wife Liutpirc. The Bavarian Duke Tassilo III was a benefactor of the abbey, upon which he bestowed great riches. In 788 Tassilo was deposed by his cousin Charlemagne and despatched a monastery.

Teuderic Reliquary from Saint-Maurice d'Agaune, Switzerland, 8th C., with imitation Roman cameo, gold cloisonné, and garnets. Liturgical objects and reliquaries are outstanding pieces in the church's treasury. The abbey, founded in 515 by the Burgundian King Sigismund at the supposed site of the graves of the martyrs of the Theban legion, is one of the oldest monasteries in Europe. Its rich church treasury includes several priceless examples of medieval gold work.

The St. Gallen Monastery Plan—the Ideal Monastery

The St. Gallen monastery plan, already mentioned several times, provides us with the most comprehensive outline of what an early medieval monastery complex was to comprise and what the ideal layout of the buildings was to be.

It is a large parchment plan detailing the ground plan for a monastery complex, which is housed in the monastery library at St. Gallen. A dedication text is addressed to Abbot Gozbert of St. Gallen (816–37), but does not give the name of the initiator, although it is assumed that the plan originated on the island of Reichenau around 830. The representation of the buildings by means of simple lines, all of the same consistent thickness,

dynamic diagram for the construction of a monastery and enables comparisons with excavation findings.

The double choir church noted previously formed the center of the monastery complex. To the south was the core area of the monastery with the monks' living quarters. These are arranged around a courtyard directly adjacent to the church, lined with arcades on all four sides—a cloister, which appears here in its "classic form" for the first time. The east side of the cloister includes a two-story building, the ground floor of which houses a room with underfloor heating, serving as the monks' workplace and living room, and the upper floor the monks' dormitory, called the dormitorium. Two smaller buildings to the south, the bathroom and the latrine, are reached via corridors. The

beer cellar. Between this building and the church is a narrow room with benches at the sides, constituting the entrance to the cloister area and which also serves as a conversation room or parlatorium (also locutorium), where the monks receive visitors from outside the monastery.

With the distribution of the most important monastery buildings around a cloister in the shape of a quadrangle, the St. Gallen plan provides the authoritative outline for the layout of religious houses in the High and Late Middle Ages. The St. Gallen plan's only major deviation from later conventions is the lack of a chapter house for the monks' morning meetings. This almost always encompassed the part of the east wing close to the church. The St. Gallen plan, however, provides for the monks' gatherings in the cloister wing

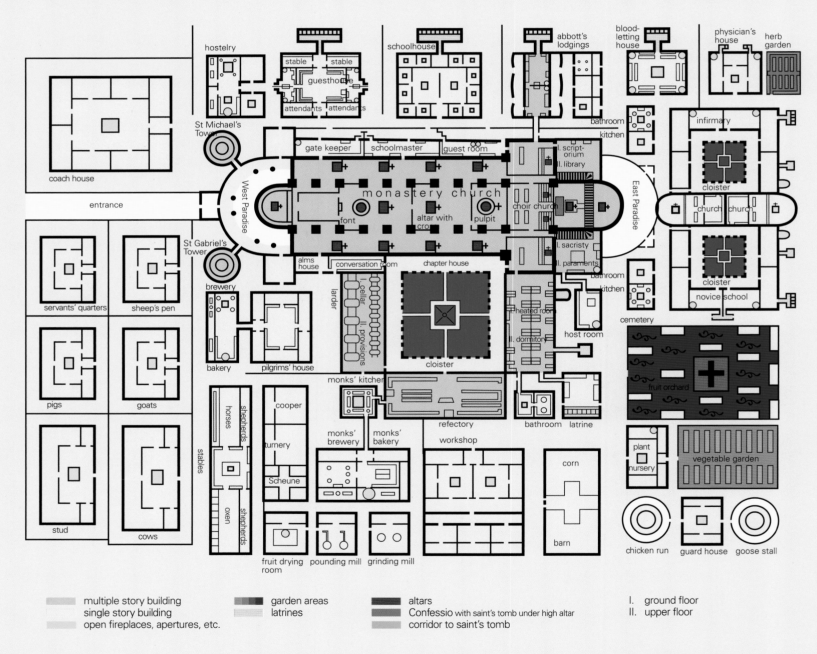

multiple story building
single story building
open fireplaces, apertures, etc.

garden areas
latrines

altars
Confessio with saint's tomb under high altar
corridor to saint's tomb

I. ground floor
II. upper floor

does not correspond to present-day conventions and makes the reading of the plan more difficult. The identification of the buildings, however, is made easier due to the labeling. The plan also shows interiors and furnishing, as well as giving diagrammatical indications of vertical masonry and of underfloor installations. This wealth of information provides a

whole of the south wing of the cloister incorporates the monks' dining room, the refectorium, with a cloakroom above it. The monastery kitchen is in the southwest corner and has a direct connection to the refectorium, as well as access to the bakery and the monks' breweries. The west wing is a large storage building, the basement of which serves as a wine and

adjacent to the church, which is equipped with benches for this purpose.

The Conclave

The conclave is a separate area within the monastery complex reserved solely for the monks. Visitors are prohibited from entering the conclave (passive conclave) and the monks are not allowed to leave

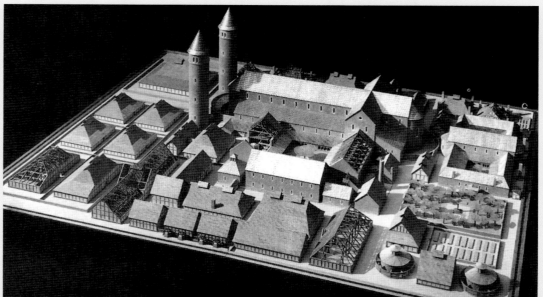

Model of the St. Gallen monastery complex
according to the plan of c. 830.

the conclave without permission (active conclave). The conclave encompasses the monks' living quarters, the dormitory, living room, and dining room grouped around the cloister, as well as the adjacent gardens and parks, the novice house and the infirmarium (infirmary). The part of the monastery church in which the monks perform their daily Liturgy of the Hours, namely the monks' choir, is also part of the conclave. This is a separate area with seats for the monks (choir benches or choir stools), situated in front of the sanctuarium (sanctuary) at the high altar. It is separated from the nave by a rood screen, which delineates the conclave area from the part of the church accessible to all believers. If it is a larger church with a transept then the monks' choir, as is the case in the St. Gallen monastery plan, is located in the crossing, i.e. in the east part of the church's central aisle between the transept arms.

The entrance to the conclave is marked by the monastery gate, which is usually in the west wing of the cloister quadrangle and where older, more experienced monks serve as portarii or gate keepers. Directly behind that is the conversation room, where visitors may be received. There is a series of other facilities in the monastery in addition to the church and the monks' living quarters. These include the library and scriptorium as well as the sacristy and armarium, where liturgical books, equipment, and vestments, as well as precious relics, are kept and are always to be found in direct proximity to the altar space. However, separate library and scriptoria buildings have not been identified to date in monasteries of the Early and High Middle Ages. Instead, it is assumed that a heated room was used for writing work, as is shown in the monastery plan in the east wing of the cloister, in which other activities also took place. Separate schoolhouses, like that north of the church on the St Gallen plan, have also not yet been identified. Fixed components of a monastery complex, on

the other hand, included a novitiate for accommodating and training novices and an infirmarium for the care of sick and ailing monks. On the monastery plan they are located opposite each other around two courtyards east of the church. The intentional symmetry here is a clear indication of the ideal nature of the diagram. The accompanying kitchens and bathrooms, as well as the physicians' house and the blood-letting house are unlikely to have existed in reality. Just as improbable is a separate church for novices. On the other hand, there was often a church in the proximity of the infirmary, available not only to the sick but was also frequented regularly by the monastery's members. A monks' cemetery as well as the vegetable and herb gardens were part of the basic features of the monastery complex.

A further important monastic duty was the accommodation of guests. For this purpose, more important monasteries had

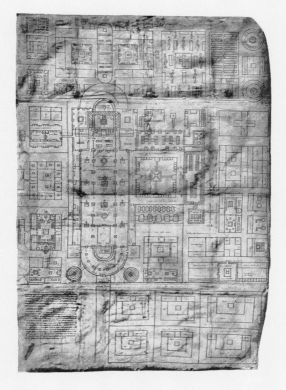

St. Gallen monastery plan, c. 830, St. Gallen monastery library.

not just a simple guest house, but three different facilities, which are also indicated on the St. Gallen plan. Outside the monastery gate southwest of the church was a house for pilgrims and paupers, the provision of board and lodging for whom had been one of the monasteries' earliest tasks. A specific monk, the eleemosynary (from the medieval Latin *eleemosyna*, meaning alms), took care of such groups of people. More esteemed travelers, on the other hand, were accommodated in another building, which the St. Gallen plan places to the northwest of the church. Special guests had the honor of eating with the monastery's abbot. In order to be able to receive and accommodate such guests in the appropriate manner the abbot had his own prestigious house either outside or on the edge of the conclave.

The Monastery and its Surroundings

Stables to the west and workshops and mills in the south complete the layout of the complex portrayed in the St. Gallen monastery plan. The monks were not in a position to carry out themselves all of the work necessary for daily monastery life. Therefore, they employed manual workers and servants who worked for a wage to do the milling of grain, baking of bread, making wine and beer, tailoring and shoemaking, as well as the repair of buildings and the like, but also for heavy labor in the monastery such as chopping wood, preparing fires, heating water, and the feeding of guests. The monasteries also needed special materials such as fine fabrics for altar cloths and liturgical vestments, ink and colors for writing and painting, and large quantities of animal hide for producing parchment. They therefore attracted traders and merchants, and in times of large building projects, also stonemasons, masons, carpenters, joiners, glaziers, and painters, as well as sculptors and goldsmiths. Monastery servants, handworkers, and traders settled with their families close to the monastery. The settlements that then developed often became the origins of towns such as Fulda, Essen, and St. Gall itself.

S. Vincenzo al Volturno. View of the abbey complex with broken columns from the large basilica of Abbot Joshua (792–817).

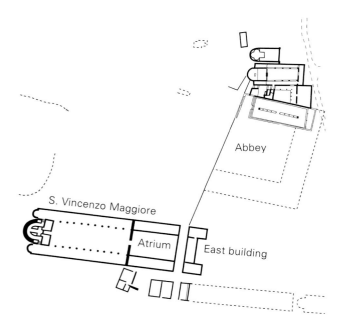

S. Vincenzo al Volturno.
▲ Ground plan of the abbey with the two older churches (above) and Abbot Joshua's large basilica (below).
▶ Chapel forecourt north of the old abbey church with 9th-century tombs.

Prosperity and Ruin

At the start of the 8th century, three Lombard aristocrats, with the support of the Duke of Benevento, founded an abbey on the plateau fed by the Volturno river at the foot of the Abruzzo Mountains, about 30 miles (50 km) northeast of Montecassino. The three men had become acquainted with monastic life in Farfa and took turns at presiding over their monastery as abbots during the initial years. They established their abbey in the ruins of a Roman villa, which had existed as a rural settlement into late antiquity. They erected the abbey church, consecrated to St. Vincent, on the foundations of this location's two churches and adjacent chapel, both simple column buildings with a west apse. The western parts of both churches were rebuilt in the second half of the 8th century, whereby the abbey church acquired a tower gallery constructed externally around the apse. The rise of S. Vincenzo only really began under Frankish rule, however. The abbey developed into an important community during the last decades of the 8th century, attracting the attention of both the king and the Pope, while the monastery possessions grew through donations and acquisitions. At the beginning of the 9th century the Frankish abbot Joshua (792–817) undertook the rebuilding of the entire complex, the key feature of which was the construction of a large, new abbey church on undeveloped land south of the old monastery. Excavations over the last 20 years have revealed a long column basilica with a nave and two side aisles, consummating in the west in three apses, the middle one of which had a galleried ring crypt. In addition to its size, the elaborate decoration of this building, with its marble columns, reused antique capitals, a floor made from colored stone slabs cut into geometric shapes and arranged in patterns (*opus sectile*), wall paintings, and glass windows overshadowed all other churches in the region, including those erected shortly beforehand in Montecassino under Abbot Gisulf. At the same time, new buildings were erected close to the two original abbey churches, including a long refectory divided into two aisles by a central row of columns and an adjacent meeting room. Both rooms were painted with imitation marble and images of the saints. The older abbey church was converted into a residence for esteemed guests. A three-aisled hall with an *opus sectile* floor and wall paintings was constructed in place of the nave, the lower part of which was adorned with imitation marble and the upper part figures. This residence included a garden with adjacent dining room that was bordered by a partly built and a partly painted portico as a kind of antique peristyle courtyard. Under Abbot Epiphanius (824–42) the chapel acquired a crypt with outstanding wall paintings. All of these buildings had stained glass windows. The workshops in which these magnificent decorations were made lay to the south of the new abbey church, where a separate refectory was built for the craftsmen. Excavations have revealed kilns for roof and floor tiles, for bronze and copper work, a pit for bell founding, a carving workshop making combs and figurines of the saints, a goldsmith's and an enamel workshop, as well as an extensive glaziers' workshop—the oldest identified in early medieval Europe—where a variety of goods including

bowls, plates, goblets, numerous lamps, and window glass were produced or fabricated.

On October 10, 881 S. Vincenzo was attacked by Saracens—Arab pirates who had settled in southern Italy—set on fire and destroyed. Archaeologists have found the attackers' spearheads among the remains of the burnt out buildings. Since the Arabs plundered not only in their own interests but also on behalf of the Bishop and Duke of Naples, effective protection was hardly possible. Two years later the same fate befell Montecassino; Farfa was razed to the ground in 898. The surviving monks gave up their monasteries and sought refuge in the towns, where they remained for decades. Even after their return, some of the parts of the S. Vincenzo abbey complex were not rebuilt.

The Normans had been beleaguering England and Ireland from the end of the 8th century. They made more frequent appearances along the north and west coasts of the Frankish kingdom from 840. During their raids they managed to reach far into the interior on the rivers with their small, versatile ships, plundering and sacking monasteries and towns. Shortly after 860 the Hungarians began carrying out raids into the east of the Frankish kingdom. At times these extended far into southern Germany and beyond, into the western part of the empire. The Carolingians had lacked centralized power since the division of the imperial territory amongst Louis the Pious' sons. The rulers of the three Frankish part-kingdoms were hostile to one another and unable to provide effective resistance to the attacks. Internal power struggles and coalitions with the attackers worsened the situation further. The result was enduring insecurity, destruction, and the flight of more population groups into the towns or the interior.

Hence, in the second half of the 9th century the European revival that had been ongoing since the Merovingian era came to an abrupt end. The political conflicts following the decline of the central Frankish power and the attacks by Arabs, Normans, and Hungarians all contributed towards bringing about the end of a period of national stability, economic development, intellectual exchange, and cultural prosperity. The countries of Europe then relapsed into a profound provincialism which lasted for more than 100 years.

S. Vincenzo al Volturno. Chapel north of the old abbey church with west-facing apse and rectangular entrance to the crypt; on the left is the entrance to the crypt staircase.

S. Vincenzo al Volturno. Chapel north of the old abbey church. View of the north arm of the shamrock-shaped crypt with its wall paintings, built under Abbot Epiphanius (824–42); an altar dating back to the construction period is in front of an alcove in the east wall.

Brescia, SS. Salvatore e Giulia, Italy

The last Lombard king Desiderius and his wife Ansa founded the S. Salvatore nunnery in Brescia in 753 and it received relics of St. Giulia shortly thereafter. Donations and privileges made the convent one of the wealthiest in northern and central Italy. Following secularization it was used as a barracks and is today a museum.

The S. Giulia and S. Maria churches in Solario belong to the nunnery, as does the early medieval convent church S. Salvatore, where part of the decoration has survived. It is a flat-roofed basilica with wide arcades on Roman spolia columns with capitals that are partly antique, partly specially made. The lintels of the arcades and their undersides bore elaborate stucco decoration with interlacing, tendrils, and palmette friezes, the walls were covered with a superlative cycle of saints' images and Bible scenes, only the remains of which survive, and the rood screen and ambo were adorned with exceptionally finely worked reliefs. As with the Tempietto Longobardo in Cividale, which is comparable in some of the details, the dating of the wall paintings and stucco to between the mid-8th and the 9th century is a matter of dispute.

View through the upper floor arcades of the southern nunnery courtyard towards the campanile (13–14th C.), on the left the adjacent nuns' choir and its deep blind arcades (post-1466) and the S. Giulia church (16th C.), and on the right the S. Salvatore church (8/9th C.). The churches are inter-connected via the sub-structure, similar to an atrium, of the nuns' gallery.

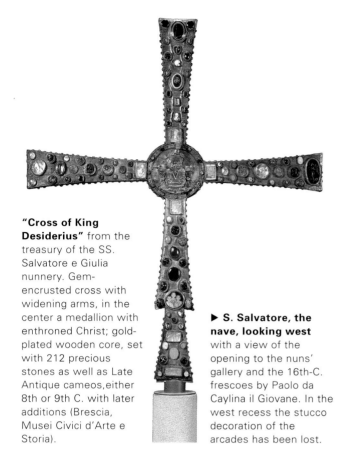

"Cross of King Desiderius" from the treasury of the SS. Salvatore e Giulia nunnery. Gem-encrusted cross with widening arms, in the center a medallion with enthroned Christ; gold-plated wooden core, set with 212 precious stones as well as Late Antique cameos, either 8th or 9th C. with later additions (Brescia, Musei Civici d'Arte e Storia).

▶ **S. Salvatore, the nave, looking west** with a view of the opening to the nuns' gallery and the 16th-C. frescoes by Paolo da Caylina il Giovane. In the west recess the stucco decoration of the arcades has been lost.

Milan, S. Ambrogio, Italy

The church of the S. Ambrogio monastery, founded in 784, is one of the most important Romanesque buildings in Italy. It rises above a Late Antique martyr basilica, which the great Father of the Church and Bishop of Milan, Ambrose (c. 340–87) had constructed and where he is buried. In contrast to the majority of north Italian churches of this era, the building, work on which began c. 1100, with a wide central aisle and galleries over the side aisles is vaulted throughout. A forecourt in the style of an early Christian Roman atrium, lined with high arcades, extends in front of the façade, which is flanked by two towers. The façade is a two-story atrium with tiered, triumphal arch-like arcades in the gable. The high altar with the tomb of St. Ambrose and Sts. Gervase and Protase has a complete altar cloth made from precious metal dating to 840, with scenes from the life of Christ and of Ambrose, and it is crowned by a 10th-century dais, the gable walls of which are decorated with stucco reliefs.

An octagonal cupola spans the altar recess. The small, Late Antiquity church of S. Vittore in Ciel, with mosaics from the 5th century, is located in the conclave area south of S. Ambrogio.

Golden frontal of the high altar with Christ Enthroned, surrounded by scenes from his life—the only surviving complete altar cloth from the Early Middle Ages. The founding bishop, Angilbert (in office 824–59), and the artist Volvinus are portrayed on the back.

▲ **S. Vittore in Ciel d'Oro,** view of the dome lined with Late Antiquity gold mosaic.

▶ **View of the elegantly tiered arcades of the atrium façade** through the 12th-century atrium, which is framed by two uneven towers, the one on the right originating from the 9th C.

▶ **View of the pulpit.** It was rebuilt following the collapse of a vault in 1196 and rises as arcades supported by columns over an early Christian sarcophagus with illustrations from the New Testament.

▶▶ **Interior looking east** towards the high altar dais. The generous width and the high ribbed vaulting make S. Ambrogio one of the most magnificent vaulted Romanesque buildings in Italy.

Pomposa, Italy

The origins of the abbey belonging to the towering and imposing campanile are obscure. Although it was first mentioned in only 874, it is assumed to have originated in the 8th or early 9th century. Pomposa prospered in the 11th century: Abbot Guido extended the church and renovated the abbey buildings, Abbot Mainard began the construction of the campanile in 1063, and Abbot Girolamo developed the library. The abbey was subject alternately to the Bishop of Comacchio and the empire and was a mediator of amicable relations between the Emperor and the Pope. Assigned in 1339, it was reformed in 1492 through affiliation to the congregation of S. Giustina, but this was repealed in 1653. The library, which possessed many works by classical Roman writers, was highly valued by the humanists in the 14th and 15th centuries. Today, the surviving abbey buildings, the former east wing of the cloister, house a museum.

The largely 9th-century abbey church was probably renovated prior to the addition of the 11th-century atrium with its stone reliefs and stained glass inlays. It is a basilica with a nave and two side aisles, with wide arcades on reused antique columns and capitals, and a broad apse with a raised floor level over a crypt. Although the present day wall paintings are by 14th-century artists, the interior of the church, with its complete wall paintings and magnificent *opus sectile* floor, provides a good idea of the appearance of churches in the Early and High Middle Ages.

▲ **Campanile.** Next to the low atrium with its three large arcade openings, the free-standing campanile rises high into the sky, the number of windows increasing from floor to floor.

▶ **The Miracle of S. Guido.** Detail of wall painting in the refectory, 1316–28.

▶▶ **View of the interior.** The interior of the basilica, supported by elegant arcades on slim, antique columns, is characterized by the pale, reflective *opus sectile* floor and the subdued colors of the wall paintings.

Saint-Benoît-sur-Loire, France

The transfer of the relics of St. Benedict of Nursia from the ruined Monte-cassino to Floriacum (Fleury) Abbey, founded around 650, made this into one of the most prominent monasteries in the Latin West. After the success of monastery schools and scriptoria under the Carolingians and their destruction by the Normans, in the decades c. 1100 the abbey again rose in prestige under Abbots Abbo and Gauzlin and maintained far-reaching contacts in England, Italy, Germany, and

◄◄ **View through the nave to the choir.**

◄ **Choir gallery,** through the arcades of the circular choir, separated from the elevated choir end by the altar of St. Benedict.

▲ **Early Romanesque capital from the atrium tower.**

Catalonia: hence the recording of the monastery practices from Fleury for St. Michael in Hildesheim. Fleury retained its importance as a role model for monastic life and its extensive library, where the history was kept of this abbey continuing over several generations, until well into the 12th century. Following its demise in the Hundred Years' War, the abbey enjoyed a last phase of prosperity through its affiliation to the congregation of Saint-Maur in 1627. Abolished during the Revolution, the abbey was resettled in 1944 by monks from La Pierre-qui-Vire Abbey.

Following the transfer of Benedict's relics, the church of Sainte-Marie, one of the original tripartite group of churches, became the abbey church of Saint-Benoît. Today it comprises the atrium in the west with its famous sculpted capitals, begun by Abbot Gauzlin, the 12th-century nave and the east section with the transept and choir, consecrated in 1107. The difference in elevation between the long choir with its exceptional *opus sectile* floor and the elevated circular choir with St. Benedict's altar, raised above a crypt, and the adjacent choir gallery reflect a typical early medieval layout. Small openings (*fenestellae*) in the crypt walls enable a view of the relics.

◄ **Atrium tower** (French. *tour-porche*) with a chapel above the open ground floor arcades.

◄◄ **Crypt.** View from east to west of the repository of St. Benedict's relics, which is encircled by robust round pillars.

Jumièges, France

Together with Audoin (French, Ouen), later Archbishop of Rouen, and Wandrille, founder of the nearby Fontenelle monastery, Philibert, the founder of Jumièges, was in his younger years a member of the Merovingian royal court. Queen Balthild endowed his abbey, erected in 654 on a bow in the Seine, with extensive lands. Philibert had to leave Jumièges after he fell out of favor and then founded a further monastery on the Atlantic island of Noirmoutier, where he died c. 685. His body was taken to Tournus in Burgundy during flight from the Normans. In 841 Jumièges was also ransacked by the Normans and resettled only in 942. In the 11th century, energetic abbots ensured the rebuilding of the abbey church, the Gothic choir being renewed in the 13th century. The abbey suffered plundering and losses in the Hundred Years' War and the monks fled as a result of religious wars. Affiliation to the congregation

▶ **West front of the abbey church of Notre-Dame** with protruding center flanked by two towers.

▲ ▲ **West walls** of the transept and crossing tower; behind, the 11th-century nave. Views from the southeast and east.

of Saint-Maur in 1617 brought renewed prosperity. Following the sale of the abbey during the Revolution the choir was demolished in 1802 and used as a stone quarry until 1824. The new owners retained and maintained the ruins until the abbey was bought by the state in 1947.

As in all Merovingian monasteries, Jumièges had three churches, of which the abbey church of Notre-Dame and the church of Saint-Pierre to the south have survived in part. Next to them the picturesque remains of the ruined abbey buildings include the chapter house, storehouse, gatehouse, and abbot's palace. The impressive west front, framed by high towers, of the abbey church, consecrated in 1067, indicate that it previously served as a west choir. While only the foundations of the Gothic east choir have survived, the Romanesque nave has been largely preserved. The west section of Saint-Pierre is assumed to originate from the Carolingian era.

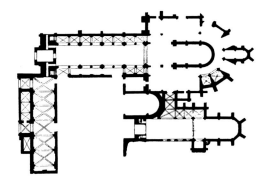

◀ **The church from the south** with remains of the abbey buildings, the west towers, and the only surviving high west wall of the crossing tower.

Reichenau, Germany

The abbey founded on the island in Lake Constance in 724 enjoyed the first of its golden periods under the Carolingians. The abbots had close ties to the court and often held the office of bishop at the same time. The monastery had a large library and produced scholars such as Walahfrid Strabo. The famous St. Gallen monastery plan was produced at Reichenau. Renewed prosperity in the 10th and 11th centuries led to the flourishing of the art of book illumination, with the decorated manuscripts from Reichenau the epitome of Ottonian illumination. From the 12th century the monastery played only a marginal role, which benefited the survival of the early and high medieval buildings. In addition to the abbey church in Mittelzell, these include the churches in Nieder- and Oberzell, both of which are renowned for their wall paintings. Reichenau was declared a UNESCO World Heritage Site in 2000.

The remains of one of the oldest known cloisters, from the early 9th century, were discovered north of the abbey church—a double choir basilica of 1008–48 with a west transept and a west choir crowned with towers, a renovated Romanesque nave, a Carolingian east transept, and a Late Gothic choir. The church of Sts. Peter und Paul in Niederzell, consecrated in 799 and renovated in 1100, has Romanesque wall paintings in the apse, while the St. Georg church in Oberzell, erected at the end of the 9th century, has the most complete cycle of 10th-century wall paintings north of the Alps.

The abbey church in Mittelzell from the northeast. The high Late Gothic east choir parallels the Early Romanesque west choir on the other side of the double choir building.

◄ **St. Georg in Oberzell from the southeast** with straight choir end and short, solid choir tower above the altar recess.

▲ **St. Georg in Oberzell.** Wall paintings with the miracles of Jesus: the Storm at Sea.

▼ **The nave of St. Georg's Church** with the 10th-century wall paintings. The individual registers and scenes are separated from one another by decorative strips with geometric motifs.

Monastic Book Illumination in the Middle Ages

From the Early Middle Ages through to the 12th century, the reproduction of texts largely took place in monasteries. It was a collective endeavor, although it can be assumed that, among the monks, some were especially talented at writing while others proved to be more skilled at painting decorative letters and pages, and others still tended towards the more technical tasks of book production. Little is known about these aspects of the division of labor in the monasteries, even though we have ample details of the individual work processes involved in the production of books, as is shown by the illustrations below.

The early handwritten records can hardly be referred to as "books," in fact. The rotulus commonly used in antiquity, an approximately 30-33 ft (9-10 m) long book roll, which was still used only sporadically in the Middle Ages, was first replaced as of the 4th century by the *codex* (Latin *cauda*, meaning tree trunk). It refers to the bound leaf book with which we are familiar; its prevalence

Three initials with illustrations of the process of book production in a manuscript text from Hamburg dating from 1255: buying parchment (above), scraping the writing block (below left), ruling lines (below right) (Copenhagen, Kongelige Bibliothek, Ms. 4, 2°).

was related to the change in writing material from papyrus to parchment. The great boom in Christian book culture came—literally—on the backs of animals, i.e. it was based on processed animal hide as a writing material. The production of a large book cost numerous calves their lives: "the hides of 250 calves were required for the Winchester Bible, and for a full monumental Bible some 500 animals are required." This alone explains the extraordinary value of medieval books. Then there was also the work of the scribes and bookbinders, as well as the cost of the valuable binding itself. Paper, invented in China in the 2nd century, came to be used in the West only much later. Even after printing was invented by Gutenberg in the middle of the 15th century, parchment was often still used for high quality books.

From the 13th century, when the number of literate individuals grew, the demand for books became greater, and the circle of people commissioning books expanded, book production was increasingly transferred from the monasteries to more and more specialized "workshops" in the towns. The medieval universities made a significant contribution to the growing demand for books, their requirements of course focusing more on scholarly books than on artistic masterpieces. Greater numbers of luxury products for bibliophiles, on the other hand, were ordered in court circles and made by privileged court artists. Book illustrations, the art of miniatures, was a well-paid business in the Late Middle Ages. The occupation of "miniator" derives from the Latin *minium*, the name of the vermilion pigment that was initially used for pen drawings or for the contours of initials. In the Late Middle Ages, the term "miniature" was expanded and reinterpreted to become associated with painting in reduced formats, namely that within the handwriting itself. In the Early and High Middle Ages writing in particular was seen as a pious

The monk Eadwine writing, from the Eadwine Psalter, c. 1170 (Cambridge, Trinity College Library, Ms. R.17.1, folio 283 verso).

service to God and numerous texts and images testify to its esteem. It was believed that the scribe would be absolved of as many sins in purgatory as there were letters and lines in a book. Of course, the promise of reward in the afterlife no longer applied to the later professional writers; they received payment for their work during their lifetime.

The Contents of the Books

The majority of the books produced in the monasteries were of religious content. These included liturgical books, which were used in the religious service, and devotional books, which served the purposes of personal piety. Elaborately decorated devotional and prayer books for laymen, so-called Books of Hours, were a specialty of the Late Middle Ages, and their production was no longer the task of the monasteries. The Bible took a special place among religious books in so far as it served as the basis for both the liturgical works and the devotional books. The liturgical books included the psalter, the gospels, and the evangelistary, which are based on specific excerpts from the Bible (the Psalms of the Old Testaments, gospels), as well as the sacramentary, missal, and temporal, which contain the readings and prayers used in the Mass, and finally the breviary and the gradual, with the anthems for the religious service and the Liturgy of the Hours.

The most important secular books deriving from the monastery scriptoria include antique works on natural history as well as richly illustrated encyclopedic works, including the *Hortus Deliciarum* by Abbess Herrad von Landsberg (died 1196). The manuscript text, which provided comprehensive teaching on issues of faith, the church, and nature, was destroyed by fire in Strasbourg in 1870.

Important Monastery Scriptoria
Following the great age of scriptoria in the British Isles (Iona, Durrow), which we have to thank for such richly illuminated gospels as the *Book of Durrow*, the *Book of Lindisfarne*, and the *Book of Kells*, Carolingian book illumination (780–860) constituted another apogee for this art form. Characterized by imperial ambitions and the highest of demands, this illumination referred back to both antique and also Byzantine traditions. Important manuscripts, such as the *Godescalc Evangelistary* and the *Coronation Gospels*, originated in the court scriptorium in Aachen and later, following Charlemagne's death, primarily to the west of the empire. Special emphasis is deserved by the monastic scriptoria at Corbie, Rheims, Tours, Fulda, Lorsch, St. Gall, and Trier.

Of the scriptoria involved in Ottonian book illumination, which flourished 960–1020, the abbey of Reichenau on Lake Constance was by far the most significant. It was from here that such famous works as the *Gospels of Otto III*, the *Bamberg Apocalypse* and the *Pericope Book of Henry II* originated. Created largely in the imperial abbeys, the book illustrations fostered by the Ottonian emperors also had personalized features, as is evidenced by the significant representations of rulers in the individual texts. They also highlighted "ecstatic-expressive sign language" and "intensity of the color's own light" as specialties and marks of quality. In addition to the scriptorium at Reichenau, those at St. Gall, Trier, Regensburg, Salzburg, Fulda, Corvey, and Hildesheim are also worthy of mention. The only school of painting that did not work for the Ottonians was based in Cologne under Archbishop Heribert (999–1021). In addition,

the early Spanish *Beatus Apocalypse* was created in around the same era as Ottonian book illumination.

The last great period in which the monastic scriptoria were able to maintain their significance in face of other writing workshops was the Romanesque era, from the middle of the 11th to the 13th century. The emphases changed during this period, however, as is evidenced by the fact that the illustration of scholarly works became more widespread. The new 11th and 12th-century monastic orders, whose newly founded monasteries had to

Gospels of Otto III, ornamental decorated page with the introductory words *Quoniam quidem* from the Gospel of St. Luke, Reichenau, end of the 10th C.(Munich, Bayerische Staatsbibliothek, Clm 4453, folio 104 recto).

be equipped with books, again constituted a counterbalance. The resultant demand for books, however, could no longer be met by monks alone. Laymen also worked in the monastic scriptoria as of the 12th century. The internationalism of the Romanesque movement also led to a Europe-wide expansion in the book illumination field. Only the English "giant Bibles" are seen as Romanesque specialties within this wealth of production.

Three Vatican codices with decorative bindings. Bindings decorated with figures such as that of the codex on the right—Christ in the mandorla as an ivory relief, the four Evangelists' symbols on enamel plates—were later increasingly replaced by purely ornamental binding.

III

Benedictine Monasticism in the High Middle Ages

The State of the Monasteries and the Monastic Reforms of the 10th Century

The events of the 9th century had a long term, devastating effect on the monasteries. Attacks, the ensuing flight of the monks, raids and destruction damaged the material basis of the monastic life that had developed in Europe since Benedict and Columban. The orderly use of landed property for agriculture was considerably hampered under these conditions, and the bartering and sale of products at markets disrupted. Goods traffic and travel, communication and cultural contact over larger distances were possible only to a limited extent due to the lack of security, such that material deprivation was accompanied by intellectual impoverishment as well.

Then there was also the fact that the monasteries were especially at risk because, as prosperous institutions and guardians of the saints and their treasures, they belonged to the small class of gold and precious metal owners. Liturgical objects like chalices and patens, the golden crucifixes and gem-encrusted reliquaries that embellished altars, embossed and gilded book covers, and other valuable items became sought-after objects of plunder and made the monasteries prime targets. Due to their usually unprotected locations on open land or outside city gates, the raiding parties found them practically presented on a platter. In such cases flight was often the only way to escape the ongoing threat. Yet retreating behind the protective walls of the towns, which were often far away from the monastery and its lands, was usually the prelude to alienation of the monastic property, which had to be regained later through protracted legal disputes.

Under these circumstances, where all attention was initially focused on ensuring the survival of the monastery's members and thereafter on preserving the community itself and maintaining its livelihood, the monks' spiritual tasks naturally fell somewhat by the wayside. Over the years, the persistent insecurity and the adverse external conditions accorded the exceptional circumstances of monastic life a kind of habitual status, with the monasteries' own tradition to some extent lapsing into obscurity. When the Norman

The Golden Gospels of Echternach
(*Codex Aureus Epternacensis*), c. 1030, Nuremberg (Germanisches Nationalmuseum, Hs. 156142, fol. 78 recto).
The entire text of this richly decorated book, originating c. 1030 in the Benedictine abbey of Echternach, is written in gold. It contains 16 full page miniatures, each comprising three scenes. The page shown here tells the story of the rich man and the poor Lazarus. In the top picture the rich man is dining with his guests, while the

beggar Lazarus knocks on the door outside—in vain. Lazarus dies alone on the bare ground, obtaining just compensation only after his death. While his soul is taken directly up to heaven by the angels (central picture), the rich man's soul is received by the devil and given over to the fires of hell (bottom picture). Such graphic warnings were directed at all those whose lifestyles deviated from the path of the righteous, and also at monks who neglected their vows.

attacks came to an end in the first half of the 10th century, individuals or sympathetic groups in various places set about renewing the neglected spiritual routines and leading the monks back to the way of life propagated in the Rule of St. Benedict. This movement for the return to a regulated life was referred to as monastic reform. The efforts and conflicts surrounding the renewal of monastic spirituality were not restricted to internal monastery and church debates. The issue of a regulated monastic life became a decisive factor in the external perception of the monasteries.

The objective of the reform endeavors of the 10th century was always the reinstatement of the Rule of St. Benedict, whereby the practical embodiment of monastic life was usually oriented towards the Aachen regulations of Benedict of Aniane. The observance of the reforms therefore differed less   in terms of content and more in the legal and political parameters within which they developed. Two principal orientations took shape within the reform of monasticism.

Monastery reforms and reform movements were initially self-corrections and reversions to stricter adherence to the (predominant) Rule of St. Benedict. The Cluniac reforms constituted the most powerful monastic revival movement of the Middle Ages. The emergence of new orders in the 11th and 12th centuries can also be seen in the context of this reforming spirit. They did, however, also seek to incorporate the older ideals of anchorite and hermitic life.

The Lotharingian Reforms

One of the reform's focal points was in Lotharingia. The "Middle Kingdom," which had passed to Louis the Pious' son Lothair upon the division of the empire, had belonged to the East Frankish kingdom since 925, where, in contrast to the western part of the empire, the new dynasty re-established consolidated royal power in the 10th century. The hallmark of the Lotharingian reforms was that the spiritual renewal endeavors were largely driven by the bishops. In recognition of their duty of supervision towards the monasteries they installed reform abbots in order to ensure adherence to the Rule of St. Benedict, and attended to the restitution of alienated lands, in order to

Frauenchiemsee, gatehouse of the Benedictine nunnery of Frauenwörth, view from the south, late 10th C. Duke Tassilo III founded a Benedictine convent on the Frauenchiemsee in 780, over which Irmingard, one of Louis the German's daughters, presided in the middle of the 9th century. The two-story gatehouse, the oldest surviving structure in the nunnery, is located to the north of the present day complex. On the ground floor it comprises an open hall with three barrel vaults running perpendicular to the longitudinal axis.

provide the material basis for regulated monastic life. A group of clerics and hermits from the Dioceses of Toul, Metz, and Verdun who wanted to realize the monastic ideal of life according to the Rule of Benedict of Nursia gathered together shortly after 930. The regulations of Benedict of Aniane formed the model for the discipline and religious austerity to which they aspired. The search for a suitable location was met by the offer from Bishop Adalbero of Metz in 934 to take over the abbey at Gorze. Situated close to Metz, Gorze had been founded in 757 by Bishop Chrodegang of Metz, who had prescribed the as yet uncommon adherence to the Rule of St. Benedict for his monks as well as confirmation of the elected abbot by the bishop of Metz. In the 9th century this meant that the bishops often took up the office of abbot of Gorze themselves or that the monastery and its lands were assigned to laymen. The unavoidable consequences were property misappropriation and a decline in monastic discipline.

Under the new leadership of the group of reformers the abbey soon underwent a significant revival. In order to ensure its livelihood with the rising number of monks, the bishop had to effect the return of the monastery lands, some of which had been given to relatives. Within a few years the reforms had been adopted at other Lotharingian monasteries, including Saint-Martin near Metz, Saint-Hubert-en-Ardenne, Stablo, as well as Saint-Arnoul and Saint-Félix in Metz. A fresh start also took place in other monasteries at the same time as the new phase in Gorze. Independent reform centers developed in Saint-Èvre in Toul and St. Maximin in Trier, which also exported strict observance of the Rule of St. Benedict to further monasteries.

In addition to the spiritual charisma of the reform monasteries and the need that stood behind such a revival of Benedictine ideals, the political influence and personal relationships of the bishops also played a significant role in the success and propagation of the reforms. The bishops turned to the King in order to be able to confirm the restitution of property to their reform monasteries and to mediate in disputes. In 937 Otto the Great, who supported the reforms, sent for monks from St. Maximin in Trier for his newly founded abbey, St. Mauritius in Madgeburg. It was from here, too, that the first abbot of the St. Pantaleon monastery founded by Otto's brother, Archbishop Bruno of Cologne, came in 964. Bruno had had a spiritual upbringing and had established contact early on with the leading personalities involved in the reforms. For his embassy to the court of the caliph in Córdoba in 953 Otto relied upon monk Jean de Vandières, a leading member of the Gorze reform group and later abbot of Gorze. The active support of the bishops, incorporation into the church hierarchy, and royal protection, as well as certain ties to the ruling dynasty, were factors that constituted the social parameters of the Lotharingian reforms.

Cologne, St. Pantaleon, west end of the former abbey church, consecrated in 980. Archbishop Bruno (953–65), brother of Emperor Otto I, founded the monastery outside the then city walls of Cologne and commissioned the building of a new church, which housed the relics of St. Pantaleon. The interior of the middle tower of the west end, largely reconstructed and renovated in the 19th century, has high arcades opening onto the side rooms and the gallery level.

Cluny

Odo, a former canon from Saint-Martin in Tours, entered Baume Abbey in the French Jura c. 908. Disappointed by the secularization of spiritual life at the start of the 10th century, he had, according to his biographer, initially set out with a companion in search of a place where the monastic way of life was still strictly adhered to, but ultimately returned to Tours discouraged. There he received a message from his companion that he had found what they were looking for: the monastery at Baume under its Abbot Berno, who had founded nearby Gigny and who, on the grounds of his reputation as a reformer, had been entrusted with the leadership of a further religious house. Odo, an educated man who came from a scholarly family and had studied in Paris, came to Baume with 100 manuscripts in his luggage; there he was immediately assigned to the training of the monks.

The small monastery network experienced further growth shortly thereafter. On September 11, 909 or 910, Duke William of Aquitaine founded the abbey of Cluny and placed it under Abbot Berno. The property with which he endowed his monastery, the *villa Cluniacum* in the Grosne valley west of Mâcon and the churches belonging to it, had been bequeathed to him by his sister Ava. As at Gigny and Baume, the Rule of St. Benedict was to be followed in the new house. After Berno's death the monks were to elect an abbot from within their own ranks. William forbade any secular involvement in the business of the monastery and forwent all of his own rights relating to its founding. Neither he, family members, nor third parties were to have powers of disposal over Cluny in any form. In order to safeguard his foundation in its southern Burgundy location remote from the king's influence, William assigned the monastery and all of its property to St. Peter himself and placed it under the protection of the latter's representative on earth, namely the Pope.

The regulations laid down in the founding charter—strict adherence to the rules, independence from secular power, assignment to St. Peter, and papal instead of the usual royal protection—were to shape the long term future of Cluny. They were unusual but in no way unique. Benefactors had often tried, in vain, to safeguard foundations from family claims. The fact that this independence was in fact achieved in the case of Cluny is due not least to William having been childless and the early death of relatives entitled to inherit. Abbeys such as Vézelay or Aurillac had already been placed under the protection of the Pope, and William's retainer Ebbo adopted the wording of Cluny's founding charter word for word when establishing his own monastery in Déols in 917. The assignment of Cluny to St. Peter was also predetermined by the dedication to him of the church, which belonged to the *villa Cluniacum*. In addition, Gigny, which was managed together with Cluny, was dedicated to St. Peter and enjoyed papal protection privileges. What is unusual about Cluny's founding charter, however, is the special wording, which served to emphasize and exaggerate the positions of St. Peter and the Pope, and to ensure awareness of the corresponding church and legal conditions. The documents drawn up in Bourges are signed by a certain *Oddo Levita*, a "cleric Odo," as scribe. It is

Cologne, St. Pantaleon, interior view from the southern side aisle of the west building. The core structure from the 10th C. was a large hall church; the addition of the nave and two side aisles followed in 1160–70.

▼ ▼ **Cluny, model of the abbey church (Cluny III); from western viewing point towards the former church,** begun in 1088. Abbot Hugo (1049–1109) worked on the planning of the new church for years before building started, as it needed to accommodate the large number of monks at Cluny. The final consecration took place in 1130. The extent of the once 600 ft (187 m) long building is best appreciated from the point where the church's main portal was once located. The surviving south arm of the great transept appears like a church in itself. Behind it stretched the complex east section of the church, which culminated in an ambulatory with five radiating chapels.

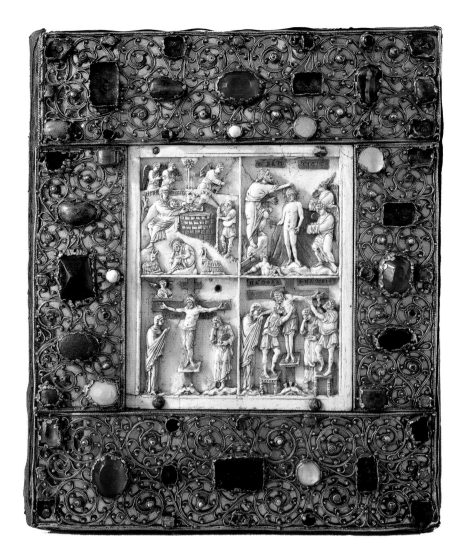

Book cover, ivory relief with four scenes from the life of Christ, Constantinople, 2nd half of the 10th C.; gold work, Quedlinburg, c. 1225. *Otto-Adelheid Gospels*, from the Quedlinburg Treasure, c. 1000. (Quedlinburg, St. Servatius Stiftskirche-Domgemeinde).

Monasticism according to Odo of Cluny

Odo is one of the few 10th-century personalities known to us through their writings. His ideas about the monks' way of life and their worldly duties are clearly expressed. The original Jerusalem community as described by Luke the Evangelist in the Acts of the Apostles was Odo's role model for monastic life: as led by the Apostles and the followers of Jesus in absolute community of property and without personal possessions, made possible by unity of faith, altruism, and the overcoming of egoism. While, in the Acts of the Apostles, the miracle of Pentecost, the descent of the Holy Ghost, is the prerequisite for this type of life, Odo also saw the reverse as being true: a communal life in faith and mutual love, the renunciation of personal possessions, and abstinence enabling the "receiving" of the Holy Ghost and the incorporation of the example of the early Church. The intention was to hold up a Christian alternative to contemporaries in a world torn apart by greed and selfishness. Ultimately, the monks' duty was to contribute to an overall revival of Christianity and to facilitate the spread of peace on earth through their apostle-like lives. The external signs of this mission were the monk's habit—the simple, even rough, clothing that was the same for everyone and made from coarse, colorless cloth—and generosity towards the needy.

presumed to have been none other than the new monk Odo from Tours. The fact that Cluny became an outstanding monastery and influential reform center is due primarily to the vision, abilities, and sense of purpose of its abbots. When Odo became abbot in 927, Cluny was a small monastery of just twelve monks, modest possessions, and a still incomplete monastery complex. In defiance of the regulation regarding the free election of the abbot, Berno had designated his successor himself, but had obtained the monks' approval beforehand—a course of action that was to set the tone at Cluny. While Berno installed his nephew Wido as abbot of the monastery group centered on Gigny and Baume, which were linked to his family possessions, the abbeys of Cluny, Déols, and Massay, which had been assigned to him personally, went to Odo. On the one hand, this partition of Berno's monastery network, and the lack of descendants on the part of the benefactor William of Aquitaine, gave Cluny freedom from secular rule but, on the other, left it without effective protection. Odo immediately set about turning this uncertain situation into a positive one. In 927 he obtained confirmations of possession for Cluny from the Pope and the West Frankish king. He traveled to Rome a few years later and effected a confirmation and endorsement of the papal protection set down in the founding charter. Odo was in Rome four times during the fifteen years he was in office and obtained seven papal deeds.

Odo's concept of monasticism as the continuation of the early Church and of monks as the apostles of a Christian revival, but doubtlessly also his consistent lifestyle and his proven "love of poverty, " must have impressed his contemporaries. Within a few years he had advanced to become head of a monastery network that was not only more extensive but also disproportionately more important than that of Berno. Cluny was thus endowed with other monasteries (Romainmôtier, Charlieu), in order that they be run according to the same principles and in unity with the abbey on the River Grosne; there were also property endowments which required that daughter houses be founded there by Cluny (Sauxillanges, Souvigny). Primarily, however, Odo was entrusted with the reformation of a series of renowned abbeys, including Aurillac, Saint-Julien in Tours, and Saint-Benoît-sur-Loire, as well as S. Paolo fuori le Mura in Rome, Farfa, and other Italian monasteries. While, for reform purposes, the assignments were conferred on Odo in person, monastery endowments were made to "the Abbot and the monks of the monastery of Cluny." Independent of the abbot's person they became the property of the monastery and belonged henceforth to the Burgundian abbey. This planted the seed of a new type of monastery network, in that the individual monasteries were legally affiliated to a reform center on an ongoing basis. Odo had the privilege not only of being able to admit monks from outside, but also of being able to take over other abbeys for reform purposes, as confirmed in a papal deed in 931. Although Odo also acquired a papal protection deed for other monasteries that he managed, such as Déols and Saint-Benoît-sur-Loire, the reform privilege remained unique to Cluny. It legitimized Cluny's status as a permanent center of reform.

In contrast to the far reaching contacts and the cosmopolitism of its abbot, under Odo the material basis of monastic life at Cluny remained limited. This changed only under his successor, Aymard (in office 942–54/65), when Cluny gained in profile and prestige in its surrounding region and generous, continuous endowments by the local nobility to the abbey became established. Majolus (954/965–94), initially appointed *coadiutor* (Latin for assistant, deputy) by Aymard, who went blind at an early age, and then designated as abbot, continued Odo's travel and reform activities and maintained close contacts with the leading personalities of his era, in particular the Burgundian royal family and the German emperor Otto I, his wife Adelheid and Otto II. While the monastery network continued to grow as a result of new transfers, Maiolus, like Odo, was active as a reforming abbot in important old abbeys, which remained independent of Cluny, as was the case with Marmoutier near Tours, Saint-Germain in Auxerre, and the island monastery Lérins.

England's Monastic Reform: the *Regularis Concordia*

While the monastic reform on the Continent exhibited very different characteristics from one monastery to another, in England the attempt was made to unify monastic life, in the second half of the 10th century. As with the Carolingian reform, the initiative here came from the ruler. The Council of Winchester, convened by King Edgar together with the leaders of the reform movement, Bishop Æthelwold of Winchester and Archbishop Dunstan of Canterbury, met between 970 and 973. In the spirit of the Councils of Aachen, 816–19, the attempt was made to establish the practices and observances that were to apply equally in all English monasteries. The reasons for the intended regularization included the inadequate implementation of the Rule of St. Benedict in English religious houses and the spread of mixed clerical observances, as well as political interest in the control of the monasteries and in intercessory prayer for the king. The *Regularis Concordia* (Latin for "harmony according to the rule"), adopted as the outcome of the Council of Winchester, clearly showed the influence of Continental reform monasteries such as St. Peter in Ghent and Saint-Benoît-sur-Loire, with which Dunstan and Æthelwold maintained close contact.

As with the Aachen resolutions, for how long and how effectively the *Regularis Concordia* held sway over English monastic life is unclear. A phase of new, formative influences had begun by the time of the Norman Conquest of 1066. Also, almost nothing survives of the churches and especially the monasteries of the 10th century. Nevertheless, the installation of communities of monks instead of clerics in various episcopal seats, as a result of the reform, had far reaching consequences and led to the particular English institution of the "cathedral monastery."

Monastic Reform as Ongoing Process

The reforms of the first half of the 10th century had brought about a revival on Benedictine monastic life. The desire for spiritual renewal, often to a large extent driven by both secular and spiritual monastery leaders, led in some respects to rapid expansion of the reforms. Spiritual discipline could disappear again just as quickly, however, and the exhilaration of a new beginning could easily evaporate. The monks' social environment was becoming increasingly sensitive to issues of rule observance, such that "reform" came to be seen

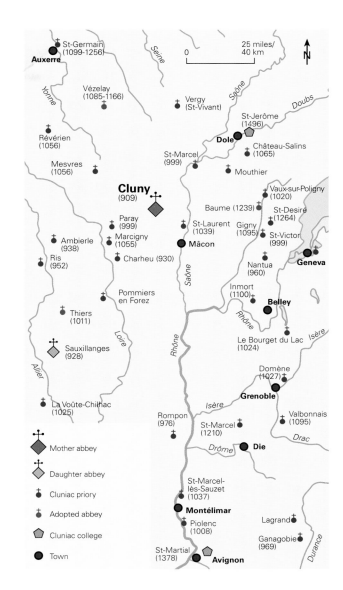

Spread of Clunian reforms in the region (after Patrice-Cousin). In 1109 the order numbered 1,184 houses with a Cluniac orientation (daughter abbeys, priories, adopted abbeys) in Europe, 883 of which were in France.

Benedictional of St. Æthelwold, bishop of Winchester, 970–80 (London, British Library, Add. Ms. 49598, fol. 99 v.). The miniature shows St. Benedict as a high dignitary. Bishop Æthelwold, who probably commissioned the work, was one of the authoritative minds behind the English monastery reform in the last third of the 10th C.

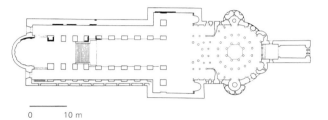

▲ ▼ **Dijon, former abbey church of Saint-Bénigne** (a cathedral since 1805), rotunda, rotunda capital and ground plan. The crypt of Saint-Bénigne is the only surviving part of a previously extensive complex, which was built by William of Volpiano, abbot of the monastery from 990. The building had an expansive crypt extending under half of the nave. In the east it adjoined a rotunda, which had columned galleries on three stories around a central opening extending from the crypt to the roof. The rotunda capitals are among the oldest sculptures decorated with figures in Burgundy.

0   10 m

increasingly as the requirement for permanent spiritual (self) renewal on the part of the monasteries, as well as being an effective instrument of political control. The further course of the 10th and the whole of the 11th century therefore constitute a series of continuing reforms. Up until the middle of the 11th century this was mostly intervention by renowned reforming personalities who had been appointed as heads of the relevant abbeys. It was not unusual for such reform abbots, as houses were successively assigned to them, to accumulate entire monastery networks, which then fell apart again after their deaths.

A prominent example of such a reforming career is that of William of Volpiano (962–1031). Coming from a noble family with close connections to the Italian royal and German imperial courts, he was brought up in Locadio Abbey (diocese of Vercelli). It was from here that Abbot Maiolus summoned the stringently observant monk to Cluny, where William took a second vow, underwent a probation period as prior of a Cluniac monastery and was then appointed to Saint-Bénigne in Dijon as reform abbot, with twelve monks from Cluny. William introduced Cluniac practices in his abbey, extended its possessions, and turned it into a famous reform monastery that attracted numerous monks, especially from Italy. He crowned his work with the rebuilding of the abbey church, consecrated in 1016. Shortly after his arrival at Saint-Bénigne, the bishop of Langres assigned to him further Burgundian monasteries for reform (Saint-Pierre de Bèze, Moûtiers-St.-Jean, amongst others). Between 996 and 1026 the bishops of Metz and Toul subjected to reform almost all of the monasteries that had previously undergone the Lotharingian reformation, including Gorze, Saint-Arnoul in Metz, and Saint-Èvre in Toul. From 1001 the Duke of Normandy commissioned William with the reform of La Trinité de Fécamp, Saint- Ouen in Rouen, Jumièges, Mont-Saint-Michel and with the administration of the newly founded Bernay. In 1026 Robert the Pious of France summoned William to the royal abbey of Saint-Germain-des-Prés in Paris. Since the simultaneous management of so many monasteries was simply not possible, William appointed his pupils as the

abbots of most of them, following a short, personal period in office himself. In particular, Fruttuaria Abbey (today S. Benigno Canavese near Turin), founded by him on family property, remained important as a reform center even after his death.

A comparable reform network, albeit with a focus on the Lotharingian reforms, was also built up by Richard of Saint-Vanne (c. 970–1046). Following his training and career as a cleric in Rheims he decided to become a monk. He sought the advice of Abbot Odilo of Cluny, who recommended entering the abbey of Saint-Vanne in Verdun, where Richard was elected abbot in 1004 with the support of the bishop of Verdun. The radical reformation of Saint-Vanne, which was accompanied by property acquisitions and the rebuilding of the abbey, was followed by the assignment and reform of over 20 further monasteries in the area between Verdun, Rheims, and Liège. Prior to a long pilgrimage to Jerusalem in 1026 Richard asked Odilo of Cluny to inspect his primary monastery at Saint-Vanne and revise the monks' practices. Like William of Volpiano, Richard frequently handed the running of the reformed monasteries to his pupils, but retained supervision of the abbeys assigned to him.

Poppo (978–1048), a pupil of Richard's entrusted with administrative duties within the monastery network, had himself made pilgrimages to Rome and Jerusalem before he had become a monk. In 1020 Poppo was "lured away" by Emperor Henry II and was swiftly appointed Abbot of Stablo and Malmédy.

Parallel to his work at Stablo (spiritual renewal, restitution of alienated lands, reorganization of monastery property, rebuilding of the abbey church, art donations), Poppo undertook the reformation of a series of important abbeys within imperial territory, including St. Maximin in Trier, Limburg an der Haardt, Echternach, Hersfeld, and St. Trond. During the course of these activities Poppo became one of the imperial church's leading representatives, also serving the emperor in diplomatic missions.

The reforms of William, Richard, and Poppo left a legacy of large, new church buildings and valuable works of art, but their monastery networks disintegrated with the deaths of their abbots, unless they left behind deep bonds between the abbeys or the consciousness of common monastic practices. Of the 10th-century reform centers, only Cluny enjoyed long term success and appeal; the Cluniac monastery network was the only one to outlive the coming and going of its abbots and in the 11th century it was only among the religious houses linked to Cluny that a sense of togetherness began to develop. This continuation of the Cluniac achievement was the work of Abbot Odilo of Cluny.

Limburg an der Haardt, ruins of the former Benedictine abbey church, 1025–45, view of the north transept arm. The former Benedictine abbey in Limburg an der Haardt was one of those on imperial territory that were reformed by Poppo in the first half of the 11th century. The structure of the exterior with pilaster strips and blind arches, as well as a twin tower façade, identify the abbey church as a typical example of Early Romanesque architecture under the Salian emperors, whose most famous construction is the first Speyer Cathedral (Speyer I).

Odilo's Cluny: the Angel-like Monks as the Saviors of Souls

Odilo, designated by Maiolus and elected by the monastery as abbot in 994, proved himself as heir and adept pupil of his predecessor Odo. Like Odo three quarters of a century before, Odilo set to work defining the function of the monks within society in the late 10th and early 11th century. Odo had developed his ideas of monastic life based on the example of the early Church and regarded his "apostle-like" monks as messengers of a Christian revival in a Europe torn by heathen attacks and internal power struggles. In Christian society c. 1000, which was no longer under such acute threat from outside and was at least in part peaceful, Odilo saw the monks' first duty as ensuring the salvation of the faithful: Christendom was to be saved from eternal damnation through the monks' prayers and their intercession for the deceased. The performance of intercessory prayers was therefore the primary spiritual task, and who but the monks were in a better position to fulfill this duty? Their abstinence, ideally also their virginity, and their lives detached from the world gave them a status high above that of the secular clergy, accorded them a purity not dissimilar to that of the angels, and lent their prayers more weight in the face of God. The monks' intercessory prayers were therefore disproportionately more effective than those of all other believers. They therefore stood at the apex of Christian society, which in Cluny, based on the works of the Carolingian monastery school of Saint-Germain in

Angels carry the soul of Saint Bertin to heaven, detail of an altarpiece, c. 1480. The monks of Cluny also saw themselves as the angel-like saviors of souls, whose prayers for the deceased freed the latter's souls from hell.

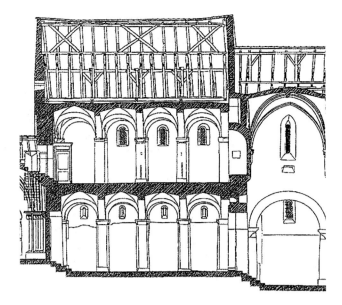

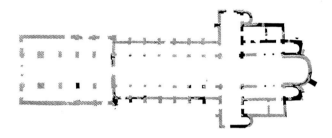

▲▲ **Romainmôtier,** cross-section through the narthex of the Cluniac priory.

▲ **Ground plan of Cluny II,** consecrated 981, with the narthex erected under Abbot Odilo.
To avoid disturbing the celebration of the Liturgy of the Hours and to create a set location for performing the many Requiem Masses, Abbot Odilo had a new building erected west of the abbey church, an idea also adopted by other, larger Cluniac houses. This west building comprised a passageway, often with several recesses, to the church, and a chapel above it, the east apse of which, in the church's interior, extended from the wall as a semicircular overhang. As with the narthex's exterior, usually crowned with façade towers, this architectural accentuation of the upper story chapel served to display the narthex as the site of intercessory prayer.

Consecration of the high altar at Cluny III by Pope Urban II in 1095, miniature from a 12th-century manuscript (Paris, Bibliothèque Nationale, Ms. Lat. 17716, fol. 91 recto).

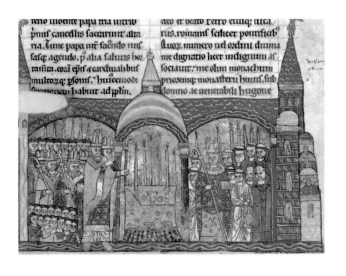

Auxerre, was seen as a horizontal tripartite pyramid: below were the peasants, in the middle the weapon-bearing nobility, and above them the clergy. At the top of this third level were the monks, at least those who lived in abstinence and pursued their spiritual duties as conscientiously and fervently as the monks at Cluny and the monasteries belonging to it. Abbot Odilo's concern was to strengthen and consolidate the proximity of the "angel-like" monks of Cluny to heaven in this world.

In order to do justice to their claim on the supreme position, the Cluniacs had to do more for the salvation of the faithful than did others. During Odilo's term in office (994–1048), therefore, prayers of remembrance and intercessory prayers for the deceased systematically acquired a previously unknown degree of intensity at Cluny. Although benefactors and those in power had previously sought to secure the intercessory prayers of the monks, the monks' prayers of remembrance had been for their deceased brothers and brotherhoods of prayer with other monasteries had been established; the powers of the holy sacrifice of the Mass, performed for the deceased, to erase sin had also been a firm conviction dating back to Pope Gregory the Great (595–604). However, none of these means of influencing the afterlife to ensure the salvation of the deceased had been applied as consistently as they were in Cluny under Abbot Odilo.

Of course, the particular efforts on the part of the Cluniacs in this regard did not go unnoticed by their contemporaries, nor was that the intention— on the contrary: by means of specially circulated descriptions of miracles, Cluny successfully spread the news of the extraordinary effectiveness of Cluniac intercession. This propaganda was also reflected in the related accounts recorded by the historian Radulfus Glaber, a monk from Saint-Bénigne in Dijon, and by Odilo's biographer, Iotsald. These tell of hermits living on the periphery of the inhabited world, in topographic proximity to "realms of the damned," who regale passing pilgrims with stories of the many souls saved from hell by Cluniac prayer. The pilgrims are tasked with taking this news to Cluny and asking the Cluniac monks not to relent in their effective efforts for the souls of poor sinners.

The Cluniac Monastery Network

The Cluniac model of intercessory prayer for the deceased, as developed by Odilo, was an overwhelming success. For more than a century it brought Cluny a continuous stream of donations, the assignment of numerous other monasteries to be reformed, interments in the abbey cemetery, and a growing number of new monastic vocations. The representatives of secular and spiritual power in the 11th century—German emperors, Castilian kings, Popes and church reformers—all sought to have prayers of remembrance said for them at Cluny. The Burgundian abbey became the epitome of impeccable monastic life and pious, committed spirituality. The Cluniac monastery network gained members throughout Southern and Western Europe. Cluniac monasteries were no longer to be found only in Burgundy, the Auvergne, and in the Jura region, but everywhere: from Portugal via Spain, through southern France, and Italy as far as Lotharingia, northern France, and England.

Odilo's measures and the new orientation that he propagated had encouraged the coherence within the monastery network and led to the development of a comprehensive Cluniac self-image. Reformed monasteries no longer remained independent but were incorporated into the network. Since there were too many adopted monasteries for them to be run by one individual from Cluny, the abbot appointed priors in the individual houses, who undertook their management on site. The monasteries, which had formerly been of equal rank, thus became dependent priories, but talented monks from such houses now enjoyed career opportunities at Cluny or other Cluniac priories. At the same time, there were obvious advantages to belonging to the monastery network, especially with regard to the significantly higher propensity for making donations to the Cluniacs, but also in terms of the exoneration of their houses from supervision by the diocesan bishops. Odilo had adopted and successfully pursued this aspect of Odo's policies. Cluny's ranking immediately under Rome, initially little more than the grandiose wording of a legally articulate monk, gained in substance through

the many papal privileges and the abbots' close contacts with the papacy. Step by step, Odilo had turned the wording and its vague content into reality by enforcing Cluny's independence within church law with the help of further papal deeds. Hence, first the abbey itself and then all of the monasteries belonging to it were exempted from episcopal control and placed under the sole supervision of the Pope. The communal prayers of remembrance for all Cluniac brothers, the unifying of the network, and their independence gave the Cluniac monks an awareness that they were something special and that they constituted an independent elite within the Roman Church—the *Cluniacensis ecclesia*.

While the Cluniac model was being imitated in other monasteries, and the Cluniacs' monastic practices (*Consuetudines*) adopted, or at least used as an orientation, in the first half of the 12th century the ongoing success of intercessory prayer for the deceased led to a crisis for the Burgundian abbey itself. Increasing numbers of monks, especially under Odilo's successor, Hugo of Semur (1049–1109), and numerous new vocations, in part by geriatric laymen, swelled the entries in the necrology, increased the monks' liturgical duties, and made the feeding of the poor for the sake of the deceased into a supply problem for the living. Abbot Peter the Venerable (1122–56) saw himself forced to counter the shortages and grievances—caused in part by the many lay brothers who did not know Latin and who were therefore unable to perform the liturgy—with specific measures. He limited the feeding of the poor to a maximum of 50 per day, irrespective of the number of names in the necrology. He also introduced drastic restrictions on the admission of illiterate adults into the monastery and expedited the training of monks as priests. As the Mass-related duties, especially in small priories, were barely manageable, the abbot introduced a common day of remembrance for all deceased Cluniac monks. However, surviving necrology manuscripts with entries extending into the 15th century, show that, among the *Cluniacensis ecclesia*, individual intercessory prayer for the deceased was still adhered to in the Late Middle Ages, despite all of the difficulties.

Berzé-la-Ville, Château de Moines, chapel frescoes, 1st quarter of the 12th C. Apsidal dome with *Maiestas Domini* (Christ in Majesty). The wall paintings at Berzé-la-Ville, near Cluny, are among the most impressive Romanesque frescoes in France.

Intercessory Prayer in Cluny in the 11th century

After *vespers* and *matins* the monastery congregation celebrated the intercessory prayer service for the deceased. In the High Mass invocations were said for benefactors and friends, and the monks remembered recently deceased affiliates of the monastery; the morning Mass was solely dedicated to intercessory prayer. In accordance with Odilo's regulations, a day of remembrance for all deceased believers was held in all Cluniac houses on November 2, with every priest conducting a Requiem Mass and all the other monks

singing psalms and saying the Lord's Prayer. This is the origin of All Souls' Day, which is still observed today. The most intensive ministration, however, was reserved for the deceased brothers. After his death, each Clunian monk was entitled to seven morning Masses celebrated by the congregation, the citing of his name in all intercessory prayers during the first weeks after his death and in all psalms or Lord's Prayers said for him. In particular, he received a *tricenarium* comprising 30 Requiem Masses. During this time his daily food ration was given to a poor person, for whom the community was also obliged to perform intercessory prayer. His name was entered into a book of remembrance (the "necrology," and a Requiem Mass was said for him every year on the anniversary of his death, and food donated to a pauper.

Cluniac Monastery Complexes

The great abbey church at Cluny erected in 1088–1131 (Cluny III) was largely destroyed after the French Revolution, but we do have details of its structure obtained through excavations and from plans and diagrams from the era prior to the demolition. Also, two parts of the complex, the greater and smaller south transept, have survived and provide us with a good impression of the architecture of this once large medieval church. The building style of Cluny III, with its antique architectural elements such as channeled pilasters and Corinthian capitals, was emulated only to a limited extent within the monastery network. Nor had there ever been a specific Cluniac style. Instead, the Cluniac churches spread throughout Europe were the products of regional architectural traditions, which differed greatly from one another in design, technical aspects, and materials.

Due to recent excavations there are now increased indications of common features in Cluniac monastery complexes as of Odilo's time in office, but these relate to neither design nor stylistic characteristics, rather to the layout of the church and monastic buildings. These common attributes, which were based on liturgical practices, followed the example of the older abbey church at Cluny, consecrated in 981 (Cluny II), and the newly built cloister erected under Odilo, with its surrounding buildings. Although neither Cluny II nor the medieval abbey buildings have survived, the essential aspects of their layout are outlined in a description of the monastery in a rite text from the Odilo era, as well as in older plans and limited excavations. These structures include the double-story narthex to the west as the site of intercessory prayer, which was common to all Cluniac churches, and the link between the narthex and the cloister, erected for processions, and for which the cloister's west wing over the nave façade had to be moved out to the west. This characteristic location of the west wing with its portal through to the narthex is evident not just at Cluny (as testified to in the rite text) but also in Romainmôtier, Payerne (narthex) and Charlieu. Furthermore, in addition to the abbey church, there was also a second, smaller sacral building between the eastern cloister wing and the infirmary; this was used by the abbey congregation twice a day and was usually dedicated to Mary and/or All Saints (Cluny, Romainmôtier, Charlieu, Souvigny, La Charité-sur-Loire, Saint-Martin-des-Champs in Paris, amongst others). Ultimately, the excavated east part of Cluny II, with its sweeping transept and sanctuary accompanied by side choirs, stood as a model for simplified versions of this type of choir in the priory churches newly erected under Odilo at Payerne and Paray-le-Monial (excavated), as well as Romainmôtier (surviving).

Cluny, the great south transept of the former abbey church of Saint-Pierre-et-Saint–Paul, 1088–pre-1115, which is crowned with an octagonal tower with two open arcade stories.

▶▶ **Cluny, museum in the former abbey granary,** 2nd half of the 13th C. A grain mill once stood in the two-aisled, rib-vaulted hall of the ground floor. The surviving sculptures from the abbey church have been on display here since 1949: a Romanesque altar table and the eight capitals of the ambulatory columns. Each capital measures 31 in (80 cm); the column shafts were 29 ft (8.85 m) high.

Cluny, ground plan of the entire complex, reconstruction of the situation c. 1150 (after K.J. Conant)

1 Cluny III church
2 Narthex of Peter the Venerable
3 Sacristy
4 Abbot's chapel
5 East part of Cluny II church
6 Atrium
7 Cloister
8 Well/wash room
9 Refectory
10 Chapter house
11 Parlatorium (conversation room)
12 Calefactorium (heated room)
13 Chamber
14 Novitiate
15 Novices' cloister
16 Latrines
17 Storerooms
18 Kitchens
19 Bread room
20 Bakery
21 Small cloister
22 Abbot Peter the Venerable's great infirmary
23 Infirmary courtyard
24 Sainte-Marie Church
25 Monks' cemetery
26 Notre-Dame cemetery chapel
27 Stables
28 Coach house
29 Abbot Peter the Venerable's hospice
30 Abbot Hugo's hospice
31 Gates
32 Forecourt
33 Great courtyard

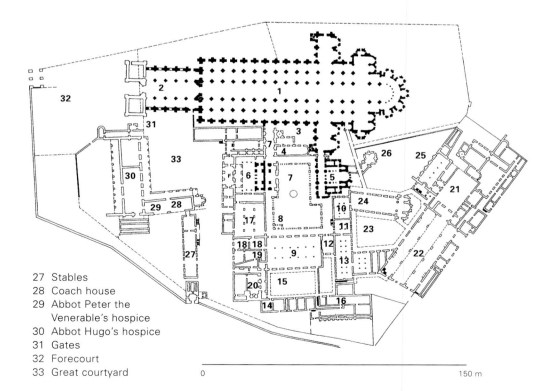

Cluny's Spiritual and Secular Roles: the Myth and the Reality

Cluny was not the only important reform monastery of the 10th and 11th centuries, but it was without doubt the most authoritative. This was due less to its abbots' good contacts with secular rulers and far more to the unusually long period of its influence as a reform center. This longstanding impact, on the other hand, was due to the intellectual capacities of its abbots, their prominent personalities, and their long terms in office. Maiolus, Odilo, and Hugo of Semur each ran the monastery for 40 to 60 years and were therefore able to ensure a continuity that was lacking elsewhere. Furthermore, Cluny's independence proved to be an important factor in its uninterrupted progress: no bishops or secular authorities were able to meddle in the abbey's affairs and its patrons—emperor, king and Pope—were far removed and had no political power base in Burgundy.

The Burgundian abbey's exceptional position has time and again, however, led to an overestimation of Cluny's power and influence in issues of (church) politics. The development of the huge monastery network had nothing to do with a quest for a "Cluniac" empire. The enforced subjugation of abbeys such as Saint-Martial in Limoges or Saint-Sernin in Toulouse was the result not of Clunian intrigue, but of local power struggles. Old, traditional monasteries that were assigned to Cluny to be reformed usually retained their status as abbey and a certain degree of liturgical autonomy, especially with regard to local saint cults. Many of them later regained their independence. The Cluniac influence on the "Gregorian Reform," the most extensive church reform in the second half of the 11th century, which was intended to combat simony, nepotism, and the misappropriation of church property, was also considerably less than is often assumed. The endeavors of the Gregorian reformers, particularly in the early phase, did comply with Cluniac concepts and they also received active support from Abbot Hugo of Semur during this time. However, the political ambitions of Gregory VII were naturally viewed with circumspection in Cluny: too strong a papacy would have impaired the abbey's own independence. Also, in the political conflicts surrounding the investiture dispute, those at Cluny were not prepared to place loyalty to abstract principles above personal ties. Hugo of Semur was godfather to Henry IV, and that is why the emperor—contrary to church regulations—was still included in the prayers of the Cluniacs even during the period of his excommunication. The first priority was the saving of threatened souls; everything else was secondary.

High Medieval Monasticism in Conflict with Cluny

A series of 11–13th century rite texts have survived that allow us to follow, using the liturgical regulations, the concrete influences and relationships between the individual monasteries and reform centers. Where church and monastery buildings from this era still survive today, it is also possible to check the testimony of the texts against the buildings themselves.

Imperial Territory

A proven means for familiarizing oneself with the practices of a reform monastery, without becoming dependent upon it, was to acquire a copy of the *Consuetudines* practiced there. Interestingly enough, Cluniac influence, without incorporation into the monastery network, can be seen in the 11th and early 12th centuries, particularly in communities that had already been reformed at an earlier point in time by Cluny or by abbots affiliated to Cluny. The only complete manuscript of Cluniac rites at the time of Odilo comes in fact from the Italian abbey at Farfa, which had been assigned to Odo for reformation. Barely a century later, the abbot of Farfa undertook a second Cluniac reform under his own direction. Several copies of the Cluniac rites from the end of the 11th century, recorded by the monk Bernard on behalf of Abbot Hugo of Semur, come from monasteries in northern France and present day Belgium. Forming part of the "permanent reform area" of Lorraine,

Abbot's portrait, fresco detail from Berzé-la-Ville, 1st quarter of the 12th C. Cluny's development and success benefited from the unusually long terms in office of its abbots. In the two and a half centuries from the foundation to the middle of the 12th century, hardly more than half a dozen abbots were in charge of the abbey:
Berno (910–27)
Odo (927–42)
Aymard (942–65)
Maiolus (965–94)
Odilo (994–1049)
Hugo of Semur (1049–1109)
Peter the Venerable (1124–56)

Farfa, view of the abbey complex. The Benedictine abbey in Farfa near Rome was founded c. 700 by the traveling Frankish monk Thomas (its foundation in the 6th century by Bishop Laurentius of Spoleto is less assured). For many centuries, Farfa was one of the wealthiest and most powerful abbeys in Italy. Its golden age began at the start of the 11th century with the outstanding Abbot Hugo (998–1038), who sought cooperation with Cluny without giving up the independence of his abbey in the process. For its part, Farfa influenced other monasteries in Italy, including Subiaco.

some of these abbeys—including St. Trond as well as Saint-Jacques and Saint-Laurent in Liège—had already been reformed in the first half of the 11th century by Richard of St. Vanne or his pupil Poppo of Stablo. Following Cluny's indirect influence communicated via Richard, reference was then made back to the original c. 1100 and led to the implementation of the Cluniac rites themselves. In Saint-Bénigne in Dijon, too, an abbey reformed by Maiolus' pupil William of Volpiano, efforts were made at the end of the 11th century to bring about a "refreshing" of their own observance by means of the current *Consuetudines* from Cluny in monk Bernard's version. A further, freer adaptation of Bernard's text to the conditions at Saint-Bénigne derives from the 13th century. Fruttuaria Abbey near Turin, founded by William, was itself a renowned reform monastery in the second half of the 11th century, which exported its *Consuetudines* to other monasteries, including Siegburg near Cologne and St. Blasien in the Black Forest. At St. Blasien a version of the *Consuetudines* was compiled on the basis of a rite text from Fruttuaria, but the latter indicates the influence of the *Consuetudines* of Bernard of Cluny, which were obviously incorporated therein. However, both versions adopted only those parts that were in line with their own ideas. Hence, the version of the *Consuetudines* from St. Blasien makes no mention of a west building (as at Cluny), even though Bernard frequently refers to the narthex, and excavations in Fruttuaria have also proven the existence of a narthex there. Excavations and written evidence clearly contradict one another here.

The ruins of the abbey at Hirsau, on the other hand, provide the best confirmation of the text version. Abbot William of Hirsau (1071–91) wanted to introduce the Cluny rites in his abbey and therefore asked his friend Ulrich of Zell, a Cluniac, to write down the Cluniac practices for him. Ulrich's records were not detailed enough for William, however. He therefore sent monks to Cluny three times to clarify questions and to have further texts copied, including the *Consuetudines* of Bernard. On this basis he then compiled his own rite text for Hirsau, the *Constitutiones Hirsaugienses*, in which he adopted extensive excerpts of the Cluniac *Consuetudines* word for word. Yet this was still not enough for William. In order to align the external conditions at Hirsau as closely as possible with those at Cluny, he built a new abbey complex in open countryside. All of the essential elements of the Cluny II monastery are reproduced at Hirsau—the narthex, the layout of the choir, the three altars for morning Mass on the east wall of the sanctuary, the characteristic bend in the cloister at the transept, and the St. Mary's church. The length of the Hirsau church exceeded that of the 100 years older church at Cluny so distinctly, however, that the cloister could not extend to the narthex, so the connection was made via a passage in the extension of the north wing at the side of the church.

▲ ▼ **Hirsau, former Benedictine abbey,** sculptural decoration on the "Owl Tower"; remains of the cloister. The early history of this Benedictine abbey dates back to the first half of the 9th C. It was only under Abbot William (1071–91) that the previously insignificant Black Forest monastery achieved its status as an important reform center. William introduced the Cluniac *Consuetudines* in 1079, and in 1083 he began construction of the large Sts. Peter und Paul Basilica. The Hirsau Reform associated with his work extended to more than 120 monasteries in the imperial territory.

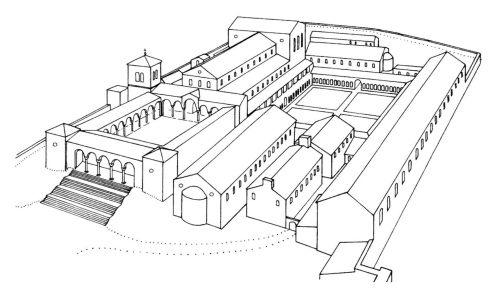

▶ **Montecassino, abbey complex, c. 1080,** reconstruction by Conant. Montecassino also experienced a new flowering in the second half of the 11th century.

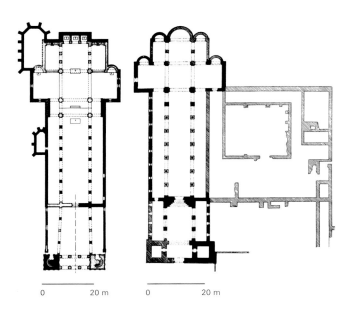

0   20 m   0   20 m

▲ **Ground plans of Hirsau (left) and Paulinzella (right).**
The church buildings of the monasteries reformed from Hirsau exhibit analogies that permit one to speak of the "Hirsau school of building." These are related to the liturgical requirements of the reform monasteries and to the layout at Cluny. Important features are: three cell choir, and a narthex to the west with towers.

Schaffhausen, cloister of the former Benedictine abbey of All Saints, which was once one of the monasteries reformed from Hirsau. The complex, which largely survives and has been restored, is today a museum.

Since the incorporation of all monasteries in the empire into the Imperial Church under the emperor was not reconcilable with the Cluniac ideal of freedom, the abbots at Cluny were always very reserved when it came to the founding or adoption of religious houses on imperial territory. Only in the former kingdom of Upper Burgundy (present day western Switzerland) was there quite a large number of Cluniac monasteries; east of the Rhine, however, there were hardly any. Cluniac practices permeated the German-speaking realm regions after they were first spread by Hirsau, which had developed its own, widespread reform activities. In addition to the southwest (St. Georgen, Schaffhausen, Petershausen near Constance), the Hirsau Reform spread to the east in particular (Paulinzella, Petersberg in Erfurt, Michaelsberg in Bamberg, the Berge abbey near Magdeburg) and the southeast (Prüfening in Regensburg, Admont, Melk). The reformed monasteries remained independent abbeys, bound only by their common practices, which also enabled old, traditional monasteries such as Corvey on the Weser and Gengenbach in Baden to adopt the Hirsau *Consuetudines*. Together with St. Blasien and Siegburg, which was settled by monks from Fruttuaria and was especially influential in the Cologne area, the Hirsau Reform became the most important reform observance in the German-speaking territories.

In addition to Fruttuaria and Farfa, the old Benedictine abbey at Montecassino also experienced a new golden age in the second half of the 11th century. Under Abbot Desiderius (1058–87) Montecassino played a mediating role between the Pope, the emperor and the Normans, who had recently come to power in lower Italy, where Byzantine enclaves enabled the abbey to maintain cultural contacts with the Greek East. The abbey had an important scriptorium and was a focal point for scholars. The magnificently decorated abbey church at Montecassino, newly built during Desiderius' term in office, with its open transept and three directly adjoining apses, served as a model for church architecture throughout lower Italy until well into the modern age.

France

In France, too, there were other reform centers apart from Cluny. These included Marmoutier and Saint-Benoît-sur-Loire, both of which stood at the apex of a monastery network. While in Marmoutier, reformed by Maiolus, it was known in the 11th century that the practices followed there, and passed on to other monasteries, were "Cluniac" ones, the two reformations of Saint-Benoît by abbots from Cluny appeared to have left no traces there. Neither the *Consuetudines* from the 1000 era nor those of the early 13th century contain any indication of the work of Odo of Cluny from c. 930 or of the introduction of the Clunian rites by Abbot Macarius (1145–61). Instead, the liturgical practices described in the texts, including an Easter play at St. Benedict's tomb, differed greatly from those common in Cluny.

◀ **Glastonbury, ruins of the Benedictine abbey church**
◀ **St. Mary's Chapel,** exterior view from the south; and interior view to the east, 1184–86. Glastonbury was one of the oldest and wealthiest abbeys in England. Its freestanding St. Mary's Chapel, the *Vetusta ecclesia*, was both the core and pride of the abbey. The small rectangular building is full of vaulted arches, both inside and outside, and there are zigzags, rosettes, and numerous other Late Romanesque motifs everywhere.

▲ **Castle Acre, former Cluniac priory church,** west façade, mid-12th C. The priory was founded in 1089 by William de Warenne II. Construction of the church was begun shortly thereafter; six of the nave recesses and the façade with its typically English row of blind arches are still standing.

▼ **Bury St. Edmunds, former Benedictine abbey,** gate tower, begun post-1081. The golden age of the abbey, founded in the 7th century began in the 2nd half of the 11th century, when the fortified complex including its huge church was erected, the layout of which is still recognizable today. One of the most famous scriptoria of the age was established here in 1121 by Abbot Anselm.

England

Under the Italian prior Lanfranc (1045–63), the Le Bec Hellouin abbey in Normandy gained in importance through its monastic school and the *Constitutiones* compiled by Lanfranc. In 1063 Duke William of Normandy appointed him as abbot of his newly founded abbey of Saint-Étienne in Caen. Following the conquest of England Lanfranc became archbishop of Canterbury in 1070. While appointing Norman clergy to run the English church, he dedicated himself to the restoration of monastic life at his cathedral monastery. His influential *Constitutiones*, which had an impact well beyond Canterbury, were a compilation of practices from a variety of monasteries and sources and do not show any specific Cluniac influence. However, the Cluniac priory at Lewes founded in 1077, which was followed over time by over 30 further adopted communities, was the beginning of an English branch of Cluniac monasticism.

There are numerous church buildings from the first phase after the Norman invasion whose dimensions constitute a conscious break with the more modest measurements of Anglo-Saxon constructions. These include both the churches of older abbeys, such as St. Augustine's in Canterbury or St. Albans, as well as those of cathedral monasteries such as Canterbury, Winchester, or Ely. What they all have in common is a markedly long nave, a protruding transept with an east chapel, and an elaborate choir, in the form either of a tiered choir or an ambulatory with radiating chapels. Both the widespread occurrence of ambulatories and the use of rib vaults in the rebuilding of the Durham Cathedral c. 1100 constituted trend-setting, innovative aspects of Anglo-Norman architecture.

Southern France and Spain

While Norman monasteries had regular contact with England after 1066, a number of southern French abbeys maintained close ties to religious houses on the other side of the Pyrenees, especially in Catalonia. In contrast to the rest of Spain, after the reconquest of Catalonia from the Arabs by the Carolingians in the 9th century, the Hispanic liturgy had already been given up there and the Roman rites adopted. Many Catalans had also been making journeys to Rome or Jerusalem since the second half of the 10th century, during a peaceful phase of brisk exchange with Islamic Andalusia. At that time the newly founded S. Pere de Rodes monastery was placed under the Pope and received Roman privileges. The monk Garin, from Lézat Abbey in the Toulouse region, was appointed head of the most important Catalan abbey of the 10th century, Saint-Michel-de-Cuxa. Gerbert d'Aurillac, later Pope Sylvester II, came to the S. Maria de Ripoll abbey for study purposes. The attraction of Catalonia continued to increase in the 11th century due to the wealth acquired in Andalusia, which was initially based on mercenary services, and later on tribute payments from the neighboring Muslim city states. During this time the reform abbey of Saint-Victor in Marseilles began an active policy of acquisition in Catalonia. At the end of the 11th century a series of important Catalan monasteries had become affiliated to the Marseilles abbey, including Ripoll.

S. Pere de Rodes, side aisle of the former monastery church, consecrated in 1022. High side aisles with their half-barrel vaults support the nave barrel vaults. Particularly noticeable are the columns standing on high bases between the nave and the side aisles (for further information on S. Pere de Rodes, see p. 98).

▼ ► **Ripoll, S. Maria abbey church,** reconsecrated in 1032, east building with seven apses; detail of the porch area, mid-12th C. The former S. Maria Benedictine abbey, founded in 879 in Catalonia, experienced its first flowering under Abbot Oliba (in office 1007–46), who was also abbot of the Saint-Michel-de-Cuxa monastery. The Ripoll scriptorium was famous: during Oliba's time the stock of manuscripts increased from 121 to 246, including important tracts on astronomy and geometry. With its complex iconographic display, the porch, built after 1150, is one of the most important Romanesque works in Spain.

Benedictines in the High Middle Ages

In the 9th and early 10th centuries, a highly developed architecture existed in the west of Spain, in the Kingdom of Asturias. Several complete, vaulted churches, which were plastered and their interiors decorated with murals, still survive today, at least in part. Unfortunately, in many cases we do not know whether these buildings were monastery or parish churches. No other types of monastery building have survived. Nevertheless, an inscription does identify the church of S. Miguel de Escalada, in the province of León, consecrated in 913, as a building belonging to a monastery (re)founded by emigrants from Córdoba. In contrast to the Asturian buildings, the designs and techniques from Escalada and other 10th-century churches in León show the influence of the Islamic architecture in Andalusia, with their horseshoe arches; with the exception of cupolas over the apses, they have no vaulting. The monasteries settled by Andalusian emigrants produced illuminated manuscripts with the apocalypse commentary of a monk named Beatus of Liébana. The sometimes full page, multicolored illustrations are strongly influenced by the Arab-Islamic culture from which the monks came. As in all other Spanish religious houses, with the exception of Catalonia, the liturgy of these monasteries followed the old Hispanic rites of the Visigothic era. Nor did this change in the 11th century when the rulers made their first contacts with the reform monasticism north of the Pyrenees. In 928 King Sancho III of Navarra had the Cluniac *Consuetudines* introduced to the monastery of S. Juan de la Peña, and Fernando I of Castille-León, towards the end of his reign, paid an annual sum to Cluny in order to be included in their intercessory prayers. His son, King Alfons VI, assigned the first of the Spanish monasteries to Cluny in the 1070s, which in time led to the development of a prestigious Spanish branch of the monastery network, and he later resumed

S. Miguel de Escalada, former monastery church, consecrated in 913. The ashlar construction of the towers originates from 1155, after Alfonso VII had given the monastery to the canons of Saint-Ruf in Avignon. The Mozarabic portico comprising 12 horseshoe arches over narrow columns provides an elegant counterpart to the bulk of the compact tower.

◀ ▲ **S. Juan de la Peña, abbot's chapel and cloister.** The monastery, built in the 9th century under an imposing, overhanging cliff, developed from an 8th-century hermitage. The Benedictine community adopted the Cluniac reforms in the 11th century and a new church was built during this era. Of the old monastery buildings, all that survive are the church, the Gothic abbot's chapel, and the remains of the cloister from the second half of the 12th C.

his father's payments. It was only in 1085, however, that the Hispanic rites were renounced in favor of the Roman, upon the express intervention of the Pope. This officially brought Spain back into line with the general practice of Roman Catholic Church. Nevertheless, the actual abandonment of local traditions in favor of the Roman liturgy did in fact take considerably longer and in many places was undertaken only slowly and reluctantly. In contrast, the narthexes, erected at the end of the 11th century, of the Cluniac priory and royal monastery at Sahagúnare testimony that the practice of Cluniac intercessory prayer, in which the kings had already invested large sums of money, was implemented without circumstance and without delay.

St.-Michel-de-Cuxa, France

Like the keep of a fortress, the imposing bell tower dominates the monastery complex, one that enjoyed great esteem in the Middle Ages. As the most significant abbey in the Roussillon region, Cuxa was a key source of impetus for all of the monasteries in this area. Cuxa had the scholarly and widely traveled Abbot Garin, who ran the monastic community from 964 to thank for its importance. He had the present day abbey church of Saint-Michel consecrated in 974, which, together with the church of Saint-Germain dating from 953 (which no longer survives), made up the abbey's family of churches. In 978 the Venetian doge Pietro Orseleo sought a retreat in this Pyrenean monastery, in order to renounce secular life. He was accompanied by the hermit Marinus and his pupil Romuald, the later founder of the Camaldulian order. The renowned scholar Gerbert of Aurillac (940/50–1003), later Pope Sylvester II, stayed at Cuxa.

The abbey experienced its golden age when Bishop Oliba of Vich (c. 971–1046), offspring of the most prominent Catalan noble family, took up the office of abbot in Cuxa in 1008, in addition to Ripoll. In the following decades the church acquired a square ambulatory, the transept towers and, to the west, a double-story centrally oriented building of which only the basement with the "Crypt of the Virgin of the Crib" survives. The Romanesque cloister with its significant sculpted capitals is from the 12th century.

Much of Saint-Michel has today been reconstructed and the sculptures, after undergoing a genuine odyssey, have been regrouped. The French Revolution had left the abbey to fall into rack and ruin. Following the collapse of the church roof in 1835 and further damage as a result of the north tower falling down, a veritable

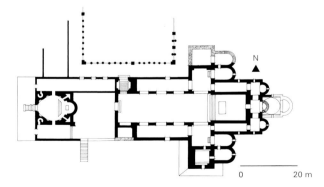

St.-Michel-de-Cuxa, completed c. 1040, view of the abbey church and bell tower from the southeast. Until the 19th century the church was flanked by a similar tower on the northern side, which was decorated with pilaster strips and arched friezes.

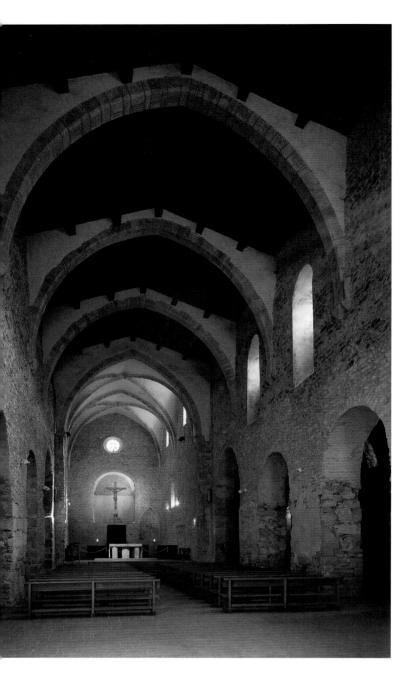

▲ **Cloister.** The original pieces reassembled in Cuxa have made possible the partial reconstruction of the cloister. The former square at least is evident.

clearance sale of the monastic art treasures, and even parts of the buildings, took place in the 19th and 20th centuries. Many pieces are today in the Metropolitan Museum in New York, where the Romanesque columns and capitals from Cuxa compose the cloister wing forming the center of the "Cloisters" complex opened in 1938. Cuxa was resettled in 1919 by monks from the Cistercian abbey Fontfroide, who began reconstruction work. Monks from the Spanish monastery at Montserrat took up residence in 1965, with their church and cloister open to visitors today.

◀ ▶▶ **Church, looking east; and southern side aisle.** The basilica, with a nave and two side aisles, is largely pre-Romanesque. The massive supporting pillars are the wall sections between horseshoe-shaped "cut-out" arcades.

▼ **Crypt of the Virgin of the Crib.** Of the chapel to the west only the basement survives. The building, square on the outside, is circular on the inside. The annular vaults are supported by a single, massive column.

In 1007 Count Guifred of Cerdagne and his wife founded an abbey at a church of Saint-Martin in the Pyrenees, situated at an altitude of over 3250 ft (1000 m) in the Canigou Massif. Two consecration dates exist for the church, namely 1009 and 1014 (or 1026). Despite its modest dimensions, it is an unusual building—double-story with a nave and two side aisles on each floor, ending in apses, and vaulted throughout. On the upper floor, short, monolithic columns support the three parallel barrel vaults; on the lower floor the columns also used in the east recesses already had to be cladded with masonry piers during the construction phase; in the west recesses the vaults are supported by solid cross-piers. North of the choir rises a wide, square bell tower with two open, windowed floors, in which is St. Michael's Chapel, consecrated in 1009. The remains of the two-story cloister originate from the 12th century. The abbey, dissolved in 1783, served as a quarry in the 19th century, was reconstructed in a changed form in 1902 and, since 1988, has again housed a religious community, which stages multimedia tours.

◄ **Monastery complex,** southern elevation with abbey buildings, partly restored in modern times: the cloister in the center, the southern flank supported by the buttressed walls, the church and tower to the rear, right.

▲ **Interior view of the upper church looking east.** The short columns supporting wide arcades and the narrow nave give the space very compact proportions.

▼ **The south wing of the cloister**—a visionary creation from the 20th C. with capitals from the second half of the 12th C.—provides a view of the landscape today.

S. Pere de Rodes, Spain

Towards the middle of the 9th century the nobleman Tassi effected the promotion of a small monastic settlement on the Peralada Peninsula to an independent abbey, which was placed under the protection of the Pope. Tassi's son Hildesind became the first abbot (947–91). The monastery was subsequently supported by the Counts of Ampurias–Roussillon. The existing church was consecrated in 1022. Rodes was an important pilgrims' destination in the Early and High Middle Ages: a visit to Rodes was a substitute for the pilgrimage to the tomb of St. Peter in Rome—this was a privilege that was otherwise enjoyed only by the famous abbey of Cluny.

Excavations have shown that the inaccessible location has been settled since Late Antiquity. The church is a hall with a nave and two side aisles, and a lower transept and ambulatory above a crypt; it incorporates the remains of a previous structure. All parts of the building have been vaulted from the beginning. In the nave the annular vault is supported by two columns on top of one another: quarter circle barrel vaults in the side aisles divert the thrust towards the exterior walls. This elaborate system of vaults was imitated in other churches in the region. The columns standing on top of one

another are derived from antique buildings and are directly based on the Great Mosque of Córdoba. The delicate chamfer ornamentation on the exquisite capitals could also have been inspired by caliphate art. The monastery complex was abandoned in 1798 and has been a ruin since then. Extensive restoration work has taken place in recent years.

▲ Northwest elevation of the monastery complex in the mountains above the Catalan coastal town of Port de la Selva.

▶ View through the church's high nave with the double columns in the choir.

▼ Relief from the former west portal, "Master of Cabestany," late 12th C. The Calling of the Apostles Peter and Andrew (Barcelona, Museu Marès).

Cloister courtyard with fountain.

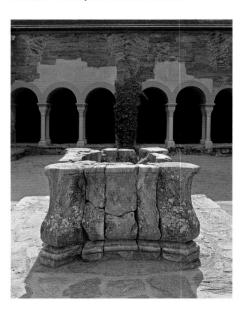

▲ View of the monastery from the southeast.

◄ Capital from the c. 1100 construction period: mythical creatures entwined in tendrils, their heads turned towards each other.

▼ View into the cloister, through the arcades of the north wing to the south and west galleries.

►► Reliefs from the period c. 1100: the resurrected Jesus encounters two disciples on the road to Emmaus (above); Doubting Thomas (below). The fine craftsmanship and clear outline of the figures is in harmony with the subtlety of the composition: the disciples standing behind one another in rows with their heads slightly bowed to the left emphasize the stance of the resurrected Christ, who, with raised arm, presents Thomas with his wounded side. He is portrayed much larger than the other figures.

S. Domingo de Silos, Spain

The monastery's origins lie in the 7th century. Refounded following the *Reconquista* (recapture) of the region by the Counts of Castile and granted comprehensive privileges, it enjoyed a spiritual and material flowering under Abbot Domingo (1040–73), its namesake, turning the provincial monastery into a focus of Castilian religious life. The church was subsequently enlarged and construction of the cloister was started. There was a large library and an important scriptorium. After a period of decline the monastery became affiliated to the congregation of Valladolid in 1512 and centuries of well-ordered monastic life followed. The buildings were renovated and extended in the 17th and 18th centuries and the church was rebuilt in neoclassical style. Dissolved in 1835, Silos was resettled in 1880 by monks from the French monastery at Solesme, who turned it into a center for historical research.

The famous cloister with its magnificent sculptures was begun at the end of the 11th century. The east and north wings, with their finely carved capitals portraying mythical creatures, in particular originate from this period, as do most of the corner pillar reliefs. The south and west wings were built in the second half of the 12th century, with the remaining reliefs and scenic capitals in a fluid drapery style; evidence tells us that the building work took place between 1158 and 1175. The cloister was extended into a second floor at the beginning of the 13th century.

Moissac, France

Founded in the 7th century, the abbey of Moissac experienced its most successful period after being affiliated to the abbey of Cluny in 1048. Under Abbot Durandus (1048–72), also Bishop of Toulouse from 1059, Moissac played a key role in southwestern France in the spread of both church and Cluniac monastic reforms. Donations increased the abbey's possessions and made extensive building projects possible. Moissac's spiritual and artistic impact lasted until the middle of the 12th century. Thereafter the abbey underwent only sporadic revivals under individual, committed abbots. The Hundred Years' War and the plague

The south porch of the west building at Moissac, one of the most important Romanesque sculpted porches. The tympanum shows Christ returning for the Last Judgement, surrounded by Evangelist symbols, two angels, and the 24 Elders. The door pillar features pairs of lions, on top of each other. The left side of the porch archway portrays the Apostle Peter; opposite him on the left side of the door pillar is Paul. On the right side of the porch archway is the Prophet Josiah; on the left side of the door pillar the Prophet Jeremiah.

▶ **Detail of the south porch.** Jeremiah from the left side of the door pillar. Behind the figure, which is aligned to the narrow pillar, is the indication of a column, the capital of which overhangs the prophet's head.

blighted the property base and the number of monks. The affiliation to Cluny was dissolved in 1461 and 1618 saw the conversion to a secular foundation, which was in 1790. After the partial collapse of the abbey buildings in the 18th century, the cloister only narrowly escaped destruction with the construction of the Bordeaux–Sète railway line in the mid-19th century.

The abbey church rebuilt under Abbot Durandus and consecrated in 1063 was replaced by a new Gothic structure in the 15th century. The west building with its large, sculpted porch on the south side originates from Abbot Roger's era (1115–c. 1135).

The celebrated cloister, which is dated by an inscription to the year 1100, was erected under Abbot Ansquitil (1085–1115). Abbot Bertrand de Montaigut (1260–95), who undertook a comprehensive renovation of the abbey buildings, had the arcades rebuilt in the 13th-century Gothic style. The cloister forms a proper square, enclosed by brick built arcades of pointed arches. The arcades rest on wide, protruding capitals that are supported alternately by single and double pillars. The square corner pillars feature high embedded marble slabs with reliefs of standing apostles under blind arches. The square center pillar opposite the entrance to the chapter house bears an image of Abbot Durandus. The capitals and their slabs feature elaborate sculptures. Each capital displays the corner volutes adopted from Corinthian-style capitals and a central accentuation reminiscent of abacus ornament. Figural motifs portraying scenes from the Old and New Testaments and from the lives of the saints predominate, however, over purely foliage and tendril decoration.

▲▲ **Two cloister capitals.** Left, intertwined tendrils; right, a figural motif.

▲ **View into the cloister.**

◄ ▶ **Reliefs from the left atrium wall:** Under arcades, the parable of the pauper Lazarus and the rich man (above), Avaritia and Luxuria (personifications of avarice and extravagance), tormented by the devil (below). Detail of the upper panel (▶): the death of the rich Man, whose soul is sacrificed to the devil.

The Cloister—Center of the Monastery

The cloister, for us a self-evident, in fact central, element of the monastery complex, around which the most important monastic buildings are grouped, did not yet exist in the early monasteries and the origins of its development are unclear. There is no evidence that it was derived from the peristyle courtyards of Roman villas or from the atria of early Christian basilicas, even though the surrounding porticoes of both have close similarities with the cloister.

The cloister in fact developed independently of a concrete architectural model and out of the need to provide a link, via covered passageways, between buildings with a close functional relationship. Its genesis lay in the grouping of the monastery buildings around an interior courtyard. Provided this was more or less properly shaped as a square, the second step could then be to enclose it by means of galleries, which facilitated communication between the individual buildings.

Early Cloisters

Romainmôtier Abbey provides an example of the gradual conversion of an older monastery complex into one with a closed layout. Prior to the 10th century an additional structure had already been incorporated on the south side, between the western and eastern buildings. Hence the formation of a built-up courtyard, enclosed on three sides, to the west and south of the two abbey churches, which was only closed completely, however, in the late 10th century. In other religious houses there were already significantly more regulated layouts in existence in the 8th and 9th centuries—newly founded

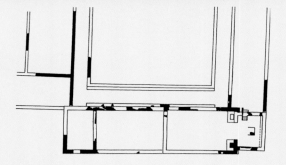

▲ **Reichenau-Mittelzell,** mid-8th C. (after Reisser/Zettler). The cloister wing on the church side (square of the cloister indicated only) was equipped with benches.

monasteries in missionary territory—that did not have to take older structures into consideration and perhaps aimed at a completely enclosed square for reasons of protection. Excavations have shown that even the first wooden monastic buildings in Reichenau-Mittelzell formed a square north of the abbey church. They were replaced by stone structures during the

▲ **S. Domingo de Silos,** cloister, c. 1100.

course of the 8th century. The east building adjacent to the choir was connected to the church via doors. To the west were the abbey gate and a hostelry. There were benches for sitting on both sides of the long room on the north side of the church, a feature also found on the St. Gallen monastery plan. Since the plan lacked a chapter house, it is to be assumed that the monks in St. Gallen, like those in Reichenau, gathered in the cloister wing on the church side, where the benches were situated.

As in Reichenau-Mittelzell, the first Lorsch-Altenmünster abbey complex, erected after 760, was also grouped in a square around a courtyard north of the church. In the imperial model monastery at

Inden, consecrated in 817, on the other hand, the buildings appear to have been located to the west, where the church was situated in a large courtyard. At Müstair the monastic buildings were also to the west, albeit extending to the south along the church axis. At Corvey and Lorsch, the elongated courtyards surrounded by porticoes, reminiscent of the Roman basilica atria, to the west of the church, are to be distinguished from cloisters, however. Both have freestanding buildings in the center, at right angles to the courtyard's longitudinal axis, of which construction only the gatehouse at Lorsch survives.

Propagation and Regulation

In contrary to what is sometimes assumed, the Councils of Aachen did not aim to impose the Carolingian "model monastery," with the St. Gallen plan as its prototype. Yet, indirectly, they did facilitate the spread of the cloister due to the implementation of the *Vita communis* for canons, which necessitated the construction of monastic buildings at cathedrals and priories.

The function of the buildings around the cloister varied in earlier times. At Reichenau underfloor heating was installed in the west wing in the 9th century and the east wing was then no longer heated. This indication of the domestic quarters and monks' living room being transferred from the east to the west wing contradicts later practices, according to which the granary and storerooms were always in the west wing.

In individual cases, the layout of the monastic buildings in a regular square around the cloister provided the opportunity for a multitude of variations room

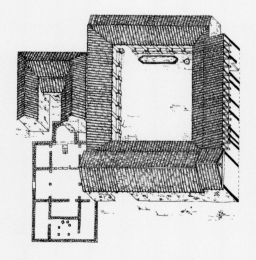

▲ **Villa Fortunatus** reconstruction of its layout in the 6th C. Integration of a church (ground plan) into a 3rd-century villa with a peristyle courtyard. The baptistery at the end of the church, opposite the apse, is more indicative of a community than a monastery church.

▶ **Noirlac,** east wing of the cloister with 14th century tracery filling the arches.

layouts and distribution. The external closure also facilitated the separation and control of the monks' conclave. For this reason proper cloister complexes became more widespread from the 9th century, onward becoming a standard element of monastery architecture in the 12th century, frequently with the incorporation of individual features.

The Cistercians' filial structure, which facilitated the passing on of construction concepts from mother to daughter house, played a significant role in this standardization. By the 11th century, however, new buildings in the many Cluniac priories had already contributed to the spread of monastery complexes with cloisters at the side of the church and an increasingly established room sequence based on the requirements of the *Consuetudines* as well as the example of the mother house.

Room Distribution in a Standard High Medieval Monastery Complex

East wing: adjoining the church transept, often the sacristy, sometimes also an armarium (book chamber); always the chapter house (distinguished always by open arcades on the portico sides), *auditorium/parlatorium* (room where discussions could take place), passageway to the infirmarium, stairs to the dormitorium and monks' living room (camera: brothers' room); on the upper floor a dormitorium and access to the latrines.

South wing/north wing: calefactorium (heated room), refectorium (opposite the entrance the fountain house for hand washing prior to eating) and the kitchen(s); on the upper floor, utility rooms, if available, such as the cloakroom,

▲ **The Cistercian abbey at Hauterive,** benches for monks in the cloister.

and also further heated rooms, etc.

West wing: granary and storerooms, beer and wine cellar, almonry; monastery gate and conversation room for receiving visitors; passageway to the cloister.

Cistercian lay brothers' wing: the storage cellar; on the ground floor the refectory (close to the kitchen) and the lay brothers' living room, as well as the abbey gate with passageway to the cloister; on the upper floor the lay brothers' dormitorium.

Functions

The cloister had a multitude of functions. It was here that the daily gathering of the monks took place, initially in the wing on the church side with the benches, then later in the chapter house, the open arcades of which enabled listening in and therefore ensured the "public" nature of the gathering. Following the chapter meeting and nones the monks were allowed to talk to one another in the cloister. In summer it was a place of individual morning reading, and communal evening reading (the collation), before compline. The monks' daily ablutions took place in the cloister fountain house, where hands were washed before meals and feet following barefoot penitential processions. The monks also gathered in the cloister for shaving and hair cutting. In many monasteries the congregation crossed the east wing twice a day on the way to the chapel behind the chapter room. On Sundays and feast days the monks passed through the cloister in a celebratory procession with singing before returning to the church. Burials could also take place in the cloister. The privileged graves were located in the east wing in front of the entrance to the chapter house or the church, while the graves of ordinary monks were in the courtyard. Apart from anything else, the cloister was a place of calm, reflection, relaxation, and silent prayer.

Design

From early times great emphasis was placed on the design of the cloister. In the first half of the 11th century, Abbot Odilo expended a great deal of effort to have marble columns brought to Cluny for the new cloister. Italian cloisters of the 12th century often exhibit a multitude of different column types, including spiral and encrusted.

▲ **Serrabone,** twin capital decorated with mythical creatures. Bernard of Clairvaux considered such capitals to be completely inappropriate in a monastery.

The capital sculptures in High Romanesque cloisters in southern France and in Spain are especially celebrated. Bernard of Clairvaux, who viewed all kinds of three-dimensional images with suspicion, campaigned against the figural portrayals of multiple mythical creatures commonly found on the capitals. Figural depictions were subsequently abandoned in Gothic cloisters, which were nevertheless more ambitious and resourceful in their architectural design: the multitude of Gothic pillars and other features, as well as the elaborate window tracery of the High and Late Gothic eras, let the capital fade from central element into the background.

Saint-Savin-sur-Gartempe, France

In the second half of the 11th century this Benedictine abbey, founded in the 9th century, acquired a new building that houses the most extensive and significant cycle of Romanesque wall paintings in France. The abbey's archive was burnt by the Huguenots in 1562 and so only a little is known about its medieval history. The hall church, with a nave and two side aisles, has a transept with east chapels and an ambulatory with five radiating chapels. There is a crypt underneath the slightly elevated sanctuary. A high atrium tower rises to the west, topped by a spire.

The wall paintings from the period c. 1100 originally covered the whole of the interior but in the transept and choir they have been lost. In the nave, colossal tall, round pillars and piers composed of semicircular responds support an open round vault, only the west recess of which has supports, and which serves as the surface for a painting cycle running in four registers from west to east and from east to west. It portrays scenes from the Old Testament Books of Genesis and Exodus: the Creation, Paradise Lost, Cane and Abel, Noah, the stories of Abraham and Joseph, Moses and the Exodus from Egypt. The paintings in the crypt illustrate the stories of Saints Savinus and Cyprianus, while those in the ground floor

atrium show the Apocalypse and in the chapel above it the Passion and Resurrection of Christ.

▼ **Exterior view of the abbey complex,** with graduated eastern sections dominated by the spire of the west tower; and exterior of the cloister's east wing.

▲ **Noah's Ark,** detail of the wall painting on the nave's barrel vault.

▶ **View of the nave looking east.** The high, elongated space culminates in the continuously painted barrel vault. The painting includes architectural elements (marbling of the pillars, painting of grooves) and capitals.

Saint-Guilhem-le-Désert, France

The significance of this once much-visited monastery and its saint—as its name indicates, it is situated in a remote location at the foot of the Cevennes Mountains—is today more familiar to the expert in medieval poetry. More famous than the historical Count William (Guilhem in Occitan) of Toulouse is his heroic fictional double, the much lauded Guilhem d'Orange of the *chansons de geste*. William, son of the Count of Autun, was a cousin of Charlemagne, and rose from military leader to Duke of Aquitaine. Under the influence of his friend Benedict of Aniane in 804 he founded a *cella* in Gellone, the later Saint-Guilhem, to which he retreated as a monk in 806 and where he died in 812, having earned the reputation of a saint. The transfer of his remains to the *confessio* (niche for relics) under the choir at the end of a church erected in the 10th century marked the beginning of the pilgrimages to his tomb. This *confessio* was integrated as a crypt into a new building begun

▶ **The monastery church from the south** with the remains of the monastic buildings and the lower cloister.

◀ **View of the nave looking east.**

▼ **The church and monastery from the east** against the scenic backdrop of the mountain landscape. Left of the choir in the East wing, renovated in the 17th century by the Maurinians, behind which is the west tower of the 12th-century church.

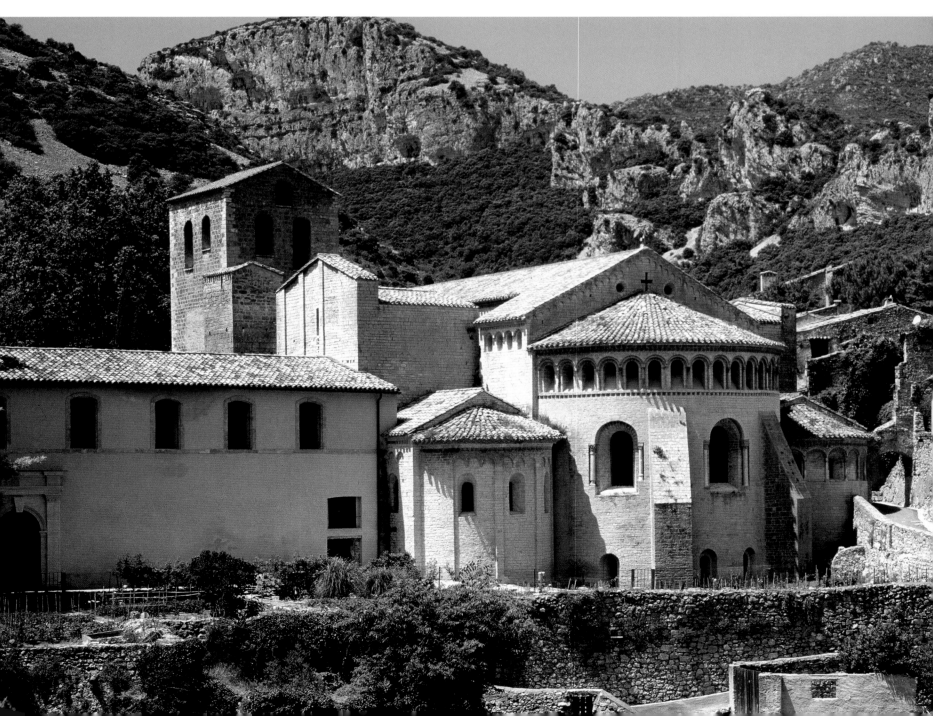

after 1050, of which the present day nave and apse recesses in the extended side aisles form part. Only c. 1100 was it decided to replace the narrow, rectangular choir of the 10th century with a wide, three apse construction, the main apse of which was built last, on the outside around the old choir, before this was then torn down.

During the monastery's golden age in the 12th and 13th centuries, Saint-Guilhem was an important staging post on the Road to Santiago de Compostela and was also frequented by crusaders embarking for the Holy Land. In the 12th century, as with other churches in the region, a gallery for the monks' choir was built in the two western nave recesses. Whether this was a measure undertaken to counteract disturbances due to the comings and goings of pilgrims, or as a "winter choir" to improve the level of comfort during the cold and wet times of the year, is unclear. The upper floor of the cloister begun at the same time provided direct access to the gallery.

The demise came with the commendatory abbots in the 15th century and the plundering of the monastery by the Huguenots in 1569. Dissolved shortly before the Revolution, the monastic buildings were sold after 1790 and partly demolished. A group of 12th-century capitals from the upper cloister found their way via an American collector into the Metropolitan Museum in New York, where today they form a central element of the "Cloisters."

Conques, France

◄ **The abbey church from the east** with the chevet surrounded by tall blind arcades.

◄◄ ◄ **Interior view of the church,** view from the nave eastwards towards the choir (left) and from the side aisle of the nave wall with the gallery openings subdivided by the twin arcades (right).

Conques Abbey was one of the most important staging posts on the pilgrimage to Santiago de Compostela. The monastery, founded by hermits at the end of the 8th century, received royal protection under Louis the Pious in 819 and followed the Rule of St. Benedict. In 863/83 the relics of Ste. Foy (Fides, Faith) of Agen were pilfered by monks from Conques, who brought them back to their abbey, where the cult of Ste. Foy quickly gained in significance and the abbey profited from numerous donations and a reputation extending well beyond the region. Conques maintained close relations with Spain during the 11th and 12th centuries. The Hundred Years' War sealed the abbey's fate. Dissolved in 1790, Conques has been a Premonstratensian priory since 1873.

The small but sophisticated church, which, with its vaulted, galleried hall with transept and ambulatory, is based on the "pilgrim route style", probably dates from the late 11th and early 12th centuries. It is especially renowned for its sculpted capitals and the large tympanum on the west porch. Its extensive church treasury includes the 10th-century statue of Ste. Foy, the oldest saint's statue surviving from the Middle Ages (see p. 113).

▲ ▼ **Tympanum on the west porch** (1120/30). Depiction of the Last Judgement in three registers on top of one another. In the middle register, Christ as Judge of the World in a mandorla, surrounded by the symbols of the Evangelists; to the left (i.e. his right) the Blessed, and to the right (his left) the Damned. Paradise and hell, each overhung by gables, are portrayed in the lower register. Above: **The depths of hell,** detail from the tympanum's lower register.

Pilgrimage and the Cult of Relics

"We are but guests here on earth, roaming restlessly with our sorrows in search of our eternal home," to quote the lines of an old hymn. This could well have been the motto for the pious wanderings of medieval pilgrims, although their journeys were sometimes also undertaken out of a thirst for adventure and for other motives, and their goal was not the eternal homeland but Christian holy places here on Earth. These "interim" destinations were very much linked to the eternal one because a pilgrim also aspired to be on the righteous path of a good Christian. According to the Apostle Paul (2 Cor 5,6), the life of a Christian is itself a pilgrimage and hence pilgrims were encouraged by the Church from early times.

Great Pilgrimage Destinations
At the top of the list of pilgrimage destinations were the holy sites in Palestine where Christ once lived and preached. In Late Antiquity, pilgrims were already setting off, following Helena's discovery of the Cross (326) and the erection of the Church of the Holy Sepulchre in Jerusalem and the Nativity Church in Bethlehem by Emperor Constantine.

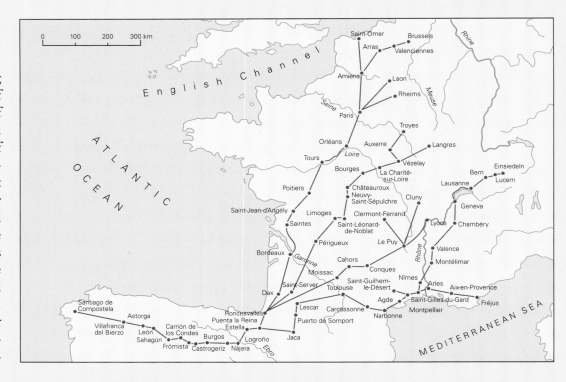

Pilgrims' roads to Santiago de Compostela: the four main routes through France.

Eight hundred years later crowds again surged in the same direction, this time during the Crusades, albeit mostly with warlike intentions. These "primary" pilgrimage destinations were followed by Rome (the Apostle Peter) and Santiago de Compostela in Galicia, further key places of pilgrimage that also enjoyed preferential status in the eyes of the Church. When, in the year 813, the tomb of the Apostle James was "discovered" near Santiago—an angel is said to have shown the hermit Pelagius the location—it took more than a century before the "epochal event" attracted a pilgrimage. It was only in the 11th century, following the suc-

▲ Depiction of a pilgrim from St. Juan de Ortega.

cesses of the Reconquista, that the situation changed: the pilgrimage to Santiago underwent a major revival that attained its first peak in the 12th century.

◀ Conques-en-Rouergue: former abbey church of Ste. Foy between the town and the countryside.

Veneration of Relics

The tremendous allure of Rome, Santiago, and Canterbury, to name just those places with the most famous tombs, was related to the enormous significance of relics in the Middle Ages. These are the mortal remains of deceased saints who enjoyed particular veneration due to their exemplary Christian conduct. This was especially the case if the early Christian paragons, as well as those of the early Middle Ages, were martyrs—people who had suffered torture and death for the sake of their faith—and so, once Christendom had become firmly established throughout Europe, the following centuries saw a multitude of other saints joining the ranks of those who were remembered and whose relics were sought out because they were believed to be the source of miracles. Contact with or proximity to them was considered to bring redemption, yet the relics were secured in precious shrines or reliquaries and could

◀ St.-Gilles-du-Gard, former abbey church and pilgrim hostel in southern France, porch detail with figurines, from mid-12th C.

▲ Statue of St. Fides, gold-plated sheet silver and precious stones on a wooden core, 985, monastery treasury of Ste. Foy in Conques.

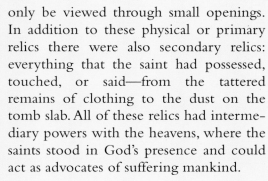

◀ Santiago de Compostela, cathedral. Upon reaching their destination pilgrims enter the cathedral of St. James through this porch (1168–88).

only be viewed through small openings. In addition to these physical or primary relics there were also secondary relics: everything that the saint had possessed, touched, or said—from the tattered remains of clothing to the dust on the tomb slab. All of these relics had intermediary powers with the heavens, where the saints stood in God's presence and could act as advocates of suffering mankind.

Role of the Monasteries

Medieval monasteries also played a significant role in the popularity of pilgrimages because, in addition to providing the theological foundations and the promotion, they also supplied the necessary infrastructure. The churches and charitable institutions along the main routes were largely run by the monasteries. Pastoral services in the form of physical care were desperately needed as the pilgrims included many people who had been forced to leave their homes due to economic need or other pressures, including the homeless and those undergoing an ecclesiastical punishment. The organization of pilgrimages therefore performed "a variety of social functions" (Droste).

113

Tournus, Saint-Philibert, France

While fleeing from the Normans on the Atlantic Coast, the monks from the Saint-Philibert monastery in Noirmoutier managed to reach Burgundy, where Charles the Bald gave them the Saint-Valérien monastery at Tournus. The new community made Tournus into a pilgrimage destination and the head of its own monastery network with properties throughout France. However, although Tournus was one of the largest French monasteries, it was always overshadowed by its mighty neighbor, Cluny.

The surviving and largely unchanged Early Romanesque church building is testimony to the abbey's importance in the 11th century. To the east a transept and an ambulatory with rectangular radiating chapels above a crypt of the same shape (consecrated in 1019) adjoin a high church with a nave and two side aisles; to the west is the narthex with a twin tower façade. The different types of vault in the narthex and nave are a magnificent display of the mastery of a technique that was still new in that period. The two-story narthex is the most impressive example surviving of this component of a monastic building, introduced in Cluny II shortly before Abbot Odilo's time.

▲ **View from the cloister of the nave and narthex with the towers.** The north tower was raised by two floors in the 12th century. The narthex, structured with pilaster strips and arched friezes, is the same height as the nave, which has large window openings.

▶ **Church interior looking east.** The tall, round pillars give the nave a hall-like character. The flying buttresses spanning the nave carry a series of transverse barrel vaults that support each other and make possible the complex of windows in the thrust-free clerestory walls.

▲ **Voussoir** with relief of a man's face, from the apsidal arch of the chapel on the upper floor of the narthex.

▶ **Madonna with Child** on pillared throne, 2nd half of the 12th century, wood with 19th-century paint work. Hollow sculpture as a depository for relics.

Paray-le-Monial, France

Founded in 973 as the Count of Chalon's house monastery, Paray became affiliated to Cluny in 999 and underwent a major revival in the 11th century due to endowments from the local nobility. A church erected in the early 11th century, based on Cluny II, which was discovered during recent excavations, acquired the existing west building with the twin tower façade towards the end of the 11th century. The rebuilding of the church with an extended layout based on the example and building styles of Cluny III was begun at the start of the 12th century but a lack of financial means prevented its completion. Instead, the monks had to be content with a short nave with only three recesses, which constituted the connection to the lower and much narrower west building, which remained one recess shorter.

The priory was plundered during the Wars of Religion in the 16th century and the development of the up-and-coming town that had arisen around it came to an abrupt end with the departure of the

◀ **View of the priory from the northwest.** The difference in size between the church and the older west building is cleverly disguised. To the right are adjoining 17th-century monastic buildings.

▶ **The church interior looking east.** The nave exhibits the layout known from Cluny III: arcades, blind triforium, clerestory, and pointed barrel vault. The lower apsidal dome compared to the choir vault is also a familiar feature from Cluny III.

Protestant population. The priory church served as a parish church after the Revolution. As the Basilique du Sacré-Coeur it has been an important modern pilgrimage destination since 1873, drawing many pilgrims to Paray every year. The priory buildings, renovated in the 17th century, house a museum. Despite the unsubtle restorations, as a scaled-down copy of the lost mother church Cluny III, Paray-le-Monial is a jewel of medieval architecture.

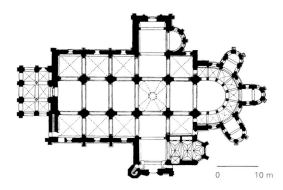

```
0          10 m
```

◀ **View of the choir from the northeast** with the characteristic staggered heights of the building elements: from the chapels to the ambulatory, choir aisles, chevet, long choir, and transept through to the crossing tower.

◄ **View of the hilltop town** with the former abbey church, Sainte-Marie-Madeleine at the highest point.

▶ **View from the narthex of the large sculpted porch and into the interior of the church.** The porch tympanum shows scenes from Pentecost with the descent of the Holy Spirit. In Cluniac tradition Christ himself appears in place of the dove representing the Holy Spirit.

Vézelay, France

Founded in the valley as a nunnery in the 9th century, converted to a monastery, ravaged by the Normans, and then moved to the ridge of the hill, the abbey, which enjoyed papal protection, was reformed according to the Cluniac model in the middle of the 11th century and assigned to the abbot of Cluny as its representative. The establishment of the cult of Mary Magdalene at the same time made Vézelay into one of the most important pilgrim destinations of the High Middle Ages. In 1146 Bernard of Clairvaux preached the Second Crusade in Vézelay in the presence of King Louis VII.

In the early 12th century an elongated abbey church with a large western narthex was erected, which is richly endowed with outstanding architectural sculptures. At the end of the 12th century it acquired an Early Gothic choir. The Gothic reconstruction of the façade was not completed: with the discovery of Mary Magdalene's "real" grave in Saint-Maximin in Provence in 1279 the pilgrimages to Vézelay came to end, bringing about the decline of the abbey's economic base. The Huguenots and the Revolution caused lasting damage to the buildings, the library, and the sculptures. At the start of the 19th century the church was a ruin close to collapse. Its survival in what is largely its original form is due to the young monument conservator Eugène Viollet-le-Duc, whose professional reputation is based on his work at Vézelay.

View through the nave to the Early Gothic choir. The simple, twin-zoned wall design is given a rhythmic character by the positioning of the pillar responds and a vibrancy from the color changes between the vault supports and the arcade lintels.

Caen, Cerisy-la-Forêt, Saint-Georges de Boscherville, France

Following the conquest of England, Normandy underwent an important revival under its Duke William II (1027/28–87; King William I of England). The founding of monasteries and the provision of endowments on the part of the ducal family and the local nobility allowed for the construction of elaborate new buildings from the 1070s. The abbeys of Sainte-Trinité (1059, for women) and Saint-Étienne (pre 1066, for men), founded in Caen by the ducal couple, acquired imposing twin tower façades and mighty crossing towers. The interior layout—comprising arcades on pillars with multiple responds, galleries (Saint-Étienne) or triforia (Sainte-Trinité) and a double-shell clerestory wall with a passageway between the windows and an arcature wall of freestanding pillars—was to become a hallmark of Norman architecture. It is also found in the abbey church at Cerisy-la-Forêt. The Caen abbeys acquired a vaulted nave at the start of the 12th century, and the Saint-Étienne choir was rebuilt in Early Gothic style c. 1200. The church at the abbey of Saint-Georges de Boscherville (post-1114) was vaulted from the outset; its layout with triforium is comparable with the Sainte-Trinité in Caen.

▲ **Caen, Saint-Étienne.** The interior looking east. View of the wall of the nave, the crossing, and the Early Gothic choir.

◄ **Caen, Saint-Étienne.** View from the southeast of the choir, with flying buttresses and towers, c. 1200. In the background are the façade towers with their Early Gothic spires.

▲ **Caen, Sainte-Trinité.** Twin tower façade. Both the monastic churches in Caen were intended as separate places of burial by the pair of founders: Saint-Étienne for William II, Sainte-Trinité for Mathilda.

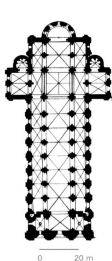

Caen, Saint-Étienne

◄ **Cerisy-la-Forêt.** View from the southeast of the small, compact abbey church with its wide, robust crossing tower.

▼ **Saint-Georges de Boscherville.** The 12th-century church, dominated by a high crossing tower, with the remains of modern era abbey buildings.

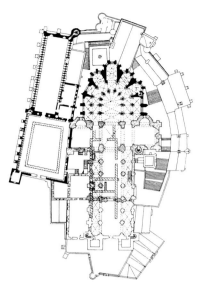

◀ **The abbey rock.** View from the southern land side. ▼ **Late Gothic choir.** View from the nave: a typical Norman Romanesque creation.

Mont-Saint-Michel, France

Following a vision of the Archangel Michael, in 709 Bishop Autbert of Avranches consecrated a church on the steep granite rock (260 ft/80 m high, 70 acres/28 ha area) located on the mudflats off the coast of Normandy, endowed it with the relics of Saint Michael from Monte Gargano and positioned 12 canons there. The community was converted into an abbey in 965/66. Its unique geographic location, which was both highly symbolic—as is expressed by its Latin name, *monasterium sancti Michaelis in periculo maris*—and also of particular military and political significance, made Mont-Saint-Michel into one of the most famous pilgrimage destinations in Europe. As of the 10th century pilgrims crowded to the site of the appearance of the Archangel Michael, some of them from far afield.

In the 11th century the church, with the support of the Duchess of Normandy, acquired a new building in a dominant position on the summit, the nave of which is a typically Norman Romanesque construction. However, repairs following the collapse of some parts of it and the construction of the monastic buildings, which were built on top of one another due to the lack of space, lasted until into the 13th century. The fortified rocky outcrop was the scene of combat in the Hundred Years' War at the end of the 13th century and the commendatory abbots, some of whom were deployed by the King, undertook military action. The choir, which collapsed in 1421, was rebuilt in 1446–1521 as a magnificent Late Gothic ambulatory. Mont-Saint-Michel was used as a prison after the Revolution. The appeal of the abbey with its cliff-hugging buildings was revived in the 20th century but tourists have now taken the place of the pilgrims.

▲ **Cloister** with the two alternating layers of arcades, completed in 1228.

▼ **Refectory,** spanned by an imposing wooden vault, 13th century. The small staircase on the right wall leads to the reading gallery.

Benedictines in the High Middle Ages   123

Westminster Abbey and Gloucester, England

Westminster Abbey, coronation site and place of burial, was the most prominent and one of the wealthiest of the English monasteries. Probably founded in the early 8th century by the Anglo-Saxon King Offa and converted to a Benedictine abbey by the English reforms of the 10th century, Westminster was extended by King Edward the Confessor (1042–66) to become England's most influential abbey, with adjoining royal palace. The church, which was erected by Edward and where his tomb was also located, is alleged to have outshone contemporary Norman buildings such as Jumièges. Two centuries later it was replaced by the present day building, considered to be one of the triumphs of English High Gothic architecture. In addition to the royal tombs the church—a secular collegiate convent since 1540—houses the shrine of Edward, canonized in 1161, which drew numerous pilgrims in the Middle Ages.

Saint Peter's Abbey in Gloucester was initially founded in the 7th century and, following its rebuilding in the 12th century, rose to become one of the greatest monasteries in England. As of 1331 the transept and the choir of the Romanesque abbey church acquired a new extension in exquisite Late Gothic, "Perpendicular" style, in which the old arcades and galleries were clad with a fine vertical and horizontal lattice. Only the clerestory and the large east window were rebuilt. Like all English monasteries, the abbey was dissolved in 1540, with the buildings and property going to the newly founded diocese of Gloucester.

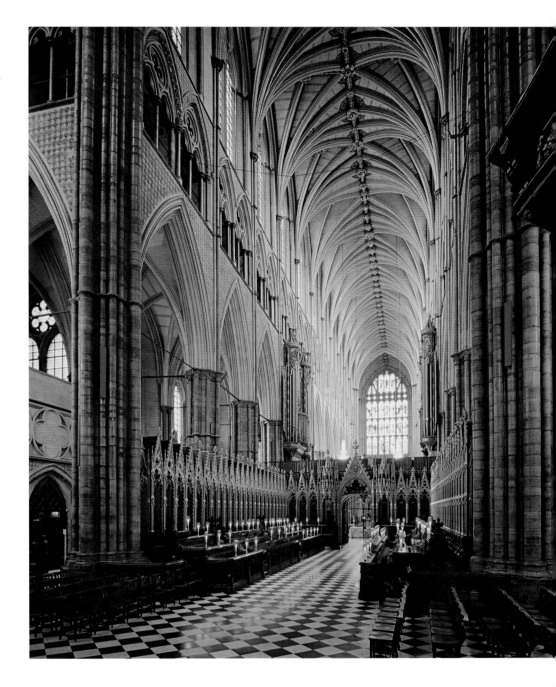

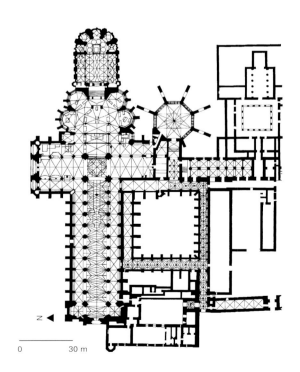

Westminster Abbey

▲ **Westminster Abbey, the nave looking southwest.** Based on the cathedral at Rheims, it exhibits a combination of French elements (pillar shape, high clerestory, thin, single walls) but also typically English features (galleries instead of a triforium, en-délit shafts and Purbeck marble columns, additional ribs).

◄ **Westminster Abbey, view from the west.** The façade with its huge 15th-century Perpendicular window was completed only in the 18th century.

◄◄ **Gloucester.** View of the choir, rebuilt in c. 1337–60. The east window—a glass pane divided and held in place only by tracery sections—was the largest of its era.

Hildesheim, St. Michael, Germany

This abbey was founded in 996 by Bernward, bishop of Hildesheim and tutor of Emperor Otto III. The church was consecrated in 1022 (the year of the death of the founder, who is buried in the west crypt) and completed in 1033. Bernward of Thierry had asked a monk from Saint-Benoît-sur-Loire to record the monastic customs at the famous Loire abbey as the basis for his monks' daily routine. The church, badly damaged during the war, was rebuilt in 1945 omitting later changes, such that, today, it largely corresponds to its original form and has thus come to be seen as the embodiment of Ottonian architecture. It is a twin choir basilica with matching transepts in the east and west, three flat east apses, and a deep west choir with a gallery level over an interior crypt and an ambulatory. The entire building is vaulted with the exception of the crypt. Important decorative elements have survived.

▲ **View from west to east**
through the vibrant church interior, with the alternating colors of the crossing arches and nave arcades, and the famous painted wooden ceiling (illustration of the Tree of Jesse, 1230/40; removed from storage in 1945).

▶ **View of the abbey church from the southeast**
with the two mighty transepts crowned with crossing towers, which, have lower octagonal and upper circular stair towers in front of them.

Cologne, St. Aposteln and St. Maria im Kapitol

Cologne is the city with more Romanesque churches than any other; many of these are former monastery churches. In the great century of Cologne church construction, from the middle of the 12th to the middle of the 13th century, 28 new churches were built, two churches were extended, and four underwent substantial alteration (H. Vogts). Largely destroyed in the Second World War, the most important churches have since been rebuilt: St. Andreas, St. Aposteln, St. Caecilien, St. Georg, St. Gereon, St. Cunibert, St. Maria im Kapitol, St. Maria Lys, Great St. Martin, St. Pantaleon, St. Severin and St. Ursula.

▶ **Cologne, St. Aposteln,** view of the roofscape of the east choir with its three conches, the corner towers of the choir, and the crossing tower, c. 1200; behind them the high west choir tower, 2nd half of the 12th C. and c. 1230. The main altar of the priory founded by Archbishop Pilgrim (1021–36) was in the west of the twin choir area, but the construction c. 1200 of the elaborate St Maria's choir in the east with its cloverleaf layout signaled the shift of the liturgical focus from the west to the east choir.

◀ **Cologne, St. Maria im Kapitol.** The famous door wings with carved reliefs portraying scenes from the life of Christ (completed in 1065) were originally in the city-side porch of the north conch.

▶ **Cologne, St. Maria im Kapitol,** the three conch choir, consecrated in 1065, from the northeast. The nunnery founded in the 7th century by the noblewoman Plektrudis and reestablished by Archbishop Bruno (953–65) acquired an unusual new building in the 11th century under Abbess Ida (died 1060), one of Emperor Otto II's granddaughters. The west part of the church with the monastic buildings in front of it was reserved for the nunnery, while the cloverleaf choir with its ambulatory in the east and crypt underneath with the same layout were also open to lay people.

Maria Laach, Germany

◀ **View of the interior of the church looking east.** The originally flat-roofed nave acquired groin vaults with banded arches during the construction phase.

▼ **View through the arcades** of the paradise erected c. 1220/30 in the forecourt (with the lion fountain 1936) and of the west apse.

▶ **The abbey church from the west** with the paradise, west apse, west transept, crossing tower, and circular towers at the sides. All the parts of the building are structured by blind arches resting on pilaster strips or (semi) circular wall responds (half-pillars).

The abbey church with its many towers and scenic location in the Eifel countryside around Lake Laach, is an early model of Rhenish High Romanesque architecture. Founded in 1093 by the Count Palatine Henry II and his wife Adelheid with monks from St. Maximin in Trier, the construction of the abbey came to a standstill following the death of its founder, was continued in 1127 following affiliation to the abbey at Afflighem (Belgium), and was only completed in 1230. The abbey was dissolved in 1802, used as a Jesuit college 1863–72, and resettled in 1892 by a Beuron Benedictine congregation who built it up into one of their most important bases.

The restoration work in the 19th and 20th centuries removed Gothic and baroque changes and returned the church to its original form. It is a twin choir construction with a basilica-like nave and two transepts with crossing towers. The main choir in the east is flanked by choir towers and the west transept is lined with high circular towers. The paradise extends from the west apse, its cloister-like arcades opening both to the outside and onto a small courtyard. Its capitals are considered to be masterpieces of German Late Romanesque sculpture.

Benedictines in the High Middle Ages

Hirsau, Alpirsbach, and Paulinzella, Germany

Two reform centers exerted considerable influence over the German monasteries in the second half of the 11th century: Cluny, whose practices Abbott William had recorded for his monastery at Hirsau; and Fruttuaria in northern Italy, whose *Consuetudines* were adopted in St. Blasien, from where the monks who settled the newly founded abbey at Alpirsbach in 1095 also came. The Alpirsbach church, erected in the first half of the 12th century, a basilica with a nave, two side aisles, a transept, three apses, and an atrium (instead of the planned two-story west building), is flat-roofed and has simple, straight lines. Nevertheless, the stonework with its precise alignment, the choir tower, and the porch sculptures are testimony to the high quality of the craftsmanship and cast doubt on the ostensible "simplicity" of the construction being an architectural expression of monastery reform. Due to a rare stroke of luck, the adjoining monastic buildings to the south have

▲ **Alpirsbach.** The interior looking west with a view of the twin openings to the planned upper floor in the west building.

◄ **Alpirsbach.** The abbey church from the east with the tower, raised in the 15th C., above the northern secondary choir and the main apse which was rebuilt in Late Gothic style.

▶ **Freudenstadt, town church.** The lectern is supported by figures of the four Evangelists, 12th century (wood with original paintwork), probably from Hirsau or another religious house in the region.

◄◄ **Hirsau.** View through the ruined cloister of the surviving north tower of the narthex.

◀ **Paulinzella,** south side of the church ruins and deanery, erected on the foundations of the west wing of the monastery following its dissolution in 1534, timber-framed construction on a stone base floor.

▶ **Paulinzella,** view through the narthex nave to the nave porch (left); side aisle to the east (right). The chequered frieze design edged at right angles with arcade arches is typical of numerous early 12th C. German buildings.

▼ **Paulinzella,** ruins of the monastery church from the southeast with the transept façades, nave, narthex, and south tower.

survived in their entirety. Despite extensive renovations in the Late Middle Ages these make possible a reconstruction of the abbey in the Romanesque and provide insights into the structural organization of a monastery c. 1200. The construction begun by William of Hirsau in 1082 is to be seen as a faithful reproduction of the Cluny II monastery complex—including the adoption of the dedication to Sts. Peter and Paul—according to the late 11th-century layout. The church consecrated in 1091 and the cloister rebuilt at the end of the 15th century were destroyed in 1692 but their original appearance can still be surmised on the basis of the remaining ruins.

The Paulinzella monastery, founded in 1102/05, was settled by monks from Hirsau. Dissolved in 1534, it fell into delapidation and was rediscovered in the early 19th century as a romantic ruin. The church, consecrated in 1124, has a more simple layout in the East section than that at Hirsau, but the large narthex, with nave and two side aisles, and the adjoining west towers exhibit the features of the ambitious Cluniac abbey churches that are familiar from Hirsau.

The recurrent classification of Paulinzella and other religious houses reformed by Hirsau as belonging to the "Hirsau school of building" is not to be understood in the sense of a troop of builders moving from abbey to abbey. The Hirsau features adopted by some monasteries were primarily typological and not stylistic. Their implementation was based on regional conventions and on respective contemporary construction layouts.

Comburg, Germany

◀ **Kleincomburg, church of St. Ägidius,** c. 1120/30. View through the nave to the northeast.

▼ **Comburg, abbey church.** Abbot Hertwig's altar antependium, c. 1140 (copper, gilded over a wooden core, enamel, filigree, precious stones). Christ in the mandorla with Evangelist symbols between the Apostles arranged in two rows and named in the inscriptions.

In 1078 Count Burkhard of Comburg founded an abbey at his castle near Schwäbisch Hall, which he entered himself and where he lived until his death in around 1098. The second Abbot of Comburg came from Hirsau. In 1488 the abbey was converted into a priory for secular canons. The church, consecrated in 1088 but only completed in 1108, was replaced by a new baroque building in 1707–15. This was a twin choir basilica with a tripartite east choir, west transept, and a main choir to the west crowned with towers, with the cloister and the conclave buildings adjoining it, on the church axis. There is a crypt underneath the east choir with the founder's tomb, which like the towers flanking the choir above the side apses, has survived the new building. The castle area also houses the surviving monastery gate from the first half of the 12th century, with St. Michael's Chapel on the upper floor, and the "Erhard Chapel," a centrally aligned, hexagonal building from c. 1220.

Two decorative pieces donated by Abbot Hertwig (c. 1103/04–1140) are of particular importance: a gilded altar antependium and a large wheel candelabrum—both key works of art by 12th-century South German goldsmiths that were made in workshops near the abbey.

The church of St. Ägidius, founded in 1108 under Abbot Hertwig, was erected in Kleincomburg; it was once a priory and has survived in its original form. It is unclear as to whether it later housed a nunnery mentioned in 1291.

◄ **Comburg.** Monastery gatehouse with round-arched entrance, a passageway above it, open at the front the whole width of the building via an arcature of short pillars. St. Michael's Chapel is on the upper floor between the two towers.

▲ **Comburg.** View of the castle from the southeast. In the foreground the castle walls, in the center the towering baroque priory church; the open floors of the two choir towers both date from the Middle Ages.

▼ **Comburg.** Former chapter house south of the west choir of the church, c. 1100; double portal and arcade openings to each side.

Verona, S. Zeno, Italy

View of the church from the west, with the tall, freestanding campanile. The gable under the 13th-C. rose window dominates the sculptured porch, which dates from c. 1130/40, and the bronze door.

The abbey founded in 805/06 outside the walls of Verona houses the relics of St. Zeno, a 4th-century Veronese bishop. It was one of the most important monasteries on the Po Plain in the Middle Ages. The present day building was started c. 1100 and, according to inscriptions, was completed in 1138; the freestanding campanile to the south was erected in 1120 before being clad on the exterior and raised in 1178. The three-aisled basilica-like church with high clerestory windows and wide, semicircular arcades, which are supported alternately by pillars and columns with semicircular responds, comprises two parts: the section accessible to lay people; the eastern third which leads via a wide staircase to the crypt containing the saint's tomb; and the east section reserved for the monks (above that with the choir and sanctuary), reached via a narrow set of stairs on the outside wall. The polygonal apse and the cloverleaf-shaped wooden nave vault originate from the 14th century. S. Zeno is famous for its Romanesque sculpted porch and its bronze door with 48 sections portraying scenes from the life of Christ, the Old Testament, and the life of Zeno.

▼ **Interior of the church looking east** with a view of the crypt and the monks' choir above it. The church walls are striped by alternating dark and light stone inlays.

▶ **Left wing of door.** Four bronze panels depicting the Flagellation, the Descent from the Cross, the Descent into Hell, and Christ in Glory; underneath are two panels with the Dance of Salome and the Beheading of John the Baptist; c. 1100 (bronze on wood).

S. Antimo and S. Pietro in Valle Ferentillo, Italy

The founding of the imperial abbey of S. Antimo dates back to the time of Charlemagne. Even in the 10th century its possessions were twice as extensive as those of the neighboring S. Salvatore abbey on Monte Amiata. The abbot and monastery of S. Antimo are also recorded in the Reichenau Book of Brotherhood from the 10th century. An extensive rebuilding of the abbey church was begun around or after 1118 but the abbey's financial situation declined from the second half of the 12th century. S. Antimo was assigned to the Williamite hermit order in 1291, before being dissolved in 1462. The remaining property and the abbot's title went to the newly founded diocese of Montalcino.

The S. Antimo church, a three-aisled construction, without a transept, but with galleries over the side aisles and an ambulatory with radiating chapels, is the most important Romanesque building in Tuscany. The architectural features exhibit influences from southern France, which are also evident in the sculpted capitals, these

▶ **S. Antimo.** View of the ambulatory.

▼ **S. Antimo.** View from the southeast of the abbey in the picturesque landscape.

▼ **S. Antimo.** View of the
interior of the church looking
east.

▲ **S. Pietro in Valle Ferentillo.**
View from the East of the church,
the tower, and the surviving
monastic buildings.

being stylistically very similar to those by the
"Master of Cabestany." The construction plans
were increasingly cut back—abandoning the
vaulting in the nave and galleries, reducing the
gallery openings, inclusion of only one porch
arcade—but the architecture and sculptures in the
east section are still of an especially high quality.

The Umbrian abbey of S. Pietro in Valle
Ferentillo developed from a hermitage and was
founded during the Lombard era in the early 8th
century. Destroyed by the Saracens at the end of
the 9th century, it was rebuilt c. 1000 at the instigation of Emperors Otto III and Henry II. The
abbey's revival in the 12th century, as documented
in its wall paintings, was short lived. Following a
variety of assignments it underwent a further
resurrection in 1478. Repairs were carried out,
the apse was painted throughout, and the façade
was renovated.

S. Pietro is a simple hall church with a high,
vaulted transept, two side apses, and a tower in the
north transept arm. The east parts of the church
are among the few Italian buildings with 11th-
century vaulting. Also of importance are the
reused Lombard reliefs in the tower and the
church, and the late 12th-century wall paintings
in the nave, where scenes, some severely damaged,
from the Old and New Testaments are visible in
three registers.

141

IV

Hermitic Lifestyles and other Reform Movements of the 11th Century

Group portrait of founders of orders. Fresco by the Dominican monk Fra Angelico. Standing: St. Benedict (left) and St. Romuald, founder of the Camaldulian order; kneeling (from left to right): St. Francis, St. Bernard, and St. John Gualbertus, founder of the Vallombrosans. (Bernard, Abbot of Clairvaux, was not himself a founder of the Cistercian order but was considered its greatest authority.)

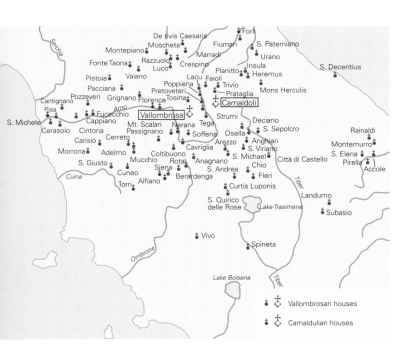

Hermitism

As in earlier times, during the whole of the Middle Ages other spiritual lifestyles also existed alongside monasticism. In particular, these include the way of life of the canons or capitulars, who combined communal choral prayer with mild forms of abstinence and a limited obligation to collective living, and the hermitic withdrawal from the world. While there were clear similarities between the canonical and the monastic lifestyles, and life in a canonical community was often a stepping stone towards monasticism, the link between hermits and monks or canons is not as obvious as it might at first appear. Nevertheless, many monastery founders did live initially as hermits, such as Benedict of Aniane and, especially, the Father of the Monks Benedict of Nursia himself. Hermits are also particularly prevalent in monastic reform center circles. So it was a group of canons and hermits who took over Gorze and made it into a reform monastery. Adhegrinus, too, the companion with whom Odo of Cluny had set out in search of true monastic life, did not later enter Baume or Cluny, but lived as a hermit in the surrounding countryside. During Abbot Peter the Venerable's time (1122–56), a monk named Gerard lived as a hermit on an isolated hill near Cluny, and another named Benedict withdrew into St. Michael's Chapel in a tower belonging to the abbey. In addition to such individual approaches to combining hermitism and monastic life, there were two successful attempts in the 11th century to unite hermitic and cenobitic lifestyles institutionally.

The Camaldulians

The life of Romuald (mid-10th C.–1027), the founder of the Camaldoli hermitage, was an unrelenting quest for a spiritual way of life that corresponded to his high moral and ascetic demands. Following the fatal outcome of a feud in which he was involved, Romuald entered the abbey of S. Apollinare in Classe near Ravenna. Disappointed by the lack of stringency there, he joined a hermit on the Venice lagoon, but was not content with his ascetic lifestyle, albeit one not subject to any rule, either. In Venice he met Garin, abbot of the Catalonian monastery Saint-Michel-de-Cuxa, who was returning from a journey to Rome, and joined forces with him, as well as Doge Pietro Orseolo and other aristocrats. In the library of the Pyrenean monastery Romuald found instructions on asceticism in the description of the life of the Egyptian Desert Fathers and in Cassian's *Collationes*. Following the Doge's death in 988 he returned to Italy and led a nomadic, hermitic life in the marshes around Ravenna and in the solitude of the Apennines. He came to the attention of Emperor Otto III, who assigned him the task of reforming the abbey of S. Apollinare in Classe. This attempt failed but Romuald remained in close contact with the Emperor for a while until he saw that Otto was not going to keep his promise to become a monk. Romuald began to found hermitages and small religious houses in the Apennines for his growing band of followers, including the Camaldoli hermitage in the province of Arezzo. He died in 1027 in another monastery in Val di Castro in Marche. Like the Desert Father Anthony, Romuald also retained contact with prominent secular personalities, despite his life *in eremo*, and like Anthony he had an influential biographer in the church reformer Peter Damian—himself prior of the Fonte

Avellana hermitage (Marche) as of 1043, he supported the cause of combining monastic and hermitic lifestyles.

The Camaldoli complex comprises two topographically and functionally separate parts: the Fontebuona monastery and the *Eremus* situated above it, 1.5 miles (2.5 km) away. The monastery was intended to prepare the monks for life in the *Eremus* and also served as a way station for pilgrims and guests, while the *Eremus* remained completely cut off from the world. It comprised a church, chapter house, library, and a series of individual dwellings for the hermits, each enclosed by a wall.

The *Consuetudines* recorded under the fourth prior (not abbot) Rudolfus in c. 1085 distinguish between the rigorous asceticism in the *Eremus* and the strict monastic discipline based on the Rule of St. Benedict in the monastery. All of the monasteries and hermitages incorporated within the subsequent network—over 40 of them in c. 1125—were subject to the prior of Camaldoli. In alternating dependency on the bishop of Arezzo and the Pope, the Camaldoli monastery network flourished in the 12th century especially. It experienced a further flowering in the 15th century in a climate of humanist erudition. Thereafter the network disintegrated into differing monastic and hermitic observances. The monastery and hermitage in Camaldoli still exist today as a hermitic Camaldulian center, a branch of the Benedictine order.

The Vallombrosans

The Camaldulians were not the only order of this kind founded in Italy in the first half of the 11th century. At the outset the abbey at Vallombrosa, founded in 1037, also exhibited clearly hermitic tendencies. In Vallombrosa, however, there was an even greater desire for a renunciation of the doubtful practices of the contemporary Church, where simony was the order of the day. John Gualbertus, the founder of Vallombrosa, had been a monk at S. Miniato in Florence, but had left the abbey after exposing the election of the

Fonte Avellana, founded by hermits c. 980. The early hermitic character of the monastery, situated in the mountainous Marche hinterland is still evident today. Peter Damian ensured the extension of the hermitage in the 11th century and endowed it with *Consuetudines*.

Camaldoli, Fontebuona Monastery, staircase up to the courtyard of the monastery, built on a hillside.

Camaldoli, Sacro Eremo with church and the hermits' cells in the form of small houses. Each house has its own walled garden. These mini-enclosures are set around a church and other communal buildings. The walled architectural ensemble is suggestive of the special lifestyle combining solitude and community. The Camaldoli hermitage is still inhabited by a number of anchorite monks today.

Camaldoli, Fontebuona Monastery, the courtyard enclosed by arcades. Camaldoli has been altered several times over the centuries. The complex of buildings acquired the strict appearance it has today in the 16th century.

abbot there on the basis of simony. Following a preliminary sojourn in Camaldoli, he and some of his companions retreated to the mountains east of Florence, where, on land that he had been given by the abbess of S. Ellero, he erected a remote monastery at an altitude of some 3250 ft (1000 m). Although certainly influenced initially by the experience of hermitic life in Camaldoli, the community ultimately adopted the Rule of St. Benedict. In order to put paid, from the beginning, to simony and the lure of material advantages, the monastic life was strongly oriented towards the poverty of each monk as well as of the community. Like numerous later reformers, John Gualbertus committed his monks to work hard in order to prevent idleness. The heavy physical toil was carried out only by illiterate lay brothers, however, who were not able to pursue any spiritual activities. The division of labor within a monastery, which later became common practice among the Carthusians and the Cistercians, had therefore already been anticipated in Vallombrosa.

Following the founding of Vallombrosa, which had made him well known within church reformer circles, John Gualbertus continued his commitment to combating the evil of simony. He even went as far as to support public revolts against this corrupt practice by the clergy. In 1090 Pope Urban II assigned the leadership of the monastery network that had developed as a result of assignments and new foundations to the abbot of Vallombrosa. Between the 12th and 14th centuries, what was then a network encompassing some 80 monasteries became an order with an abbot-general at its head (see "Order structures," p. 166), which continues to exist today as an independent congregation based in Vallombrosa.

▲ **Camaldoli, 'St. Romuald's cell'** with bed and prayer niche. The fittings in the entirely wooden room are reduced to the bare minimum.

▼ **Vallombrosa, abbey complex from above.** The Archabbey of Vallombrosa lies in the middle of a forest in the mountains east of Florence. After alterations in the 17th C., the large group of monastic buildings appears as a strict, inaccessible castle.

The Carthusians

While the Camaldulians had brought hermits and monks living apart from one another together within a monastery network, the Carthusians went a step further: they created a mixed observance that combined hermitism with elements of the monks' communal life.

The first hermitage was founded in 1084 by Bruno of Cologne (c. 1030–1101) with six companions in a remote valley in the Alps north of Grenoble, in the eponymous *Massif de la Chartreuse*. Bruno, a canon from Cologne, had studied in Rheims and had then run the Rheims cathedral school for a quarter of a century before he decided in favor of life as a hermit. Like Romuald and other ascetics who spent their lives seeking new challenges, Bruno did not stay at La Grande Chartreuse for long. In 1089 he heeded a summons from Pope Urban II, one of his former pupils, to Rome. He left the Curia again a few years later and withdrew to Calabria, where he founded a second hermitage, S. Maria dell'Eremo, where he died as abbot. It was primarily due to the support of Bishop Hugo of Grenoble that the hermit community at La Grande Chartreuse survived the difficult initial phase following the departure of Bruno, as he had provided the hermits with the location for their settlement in the first place.

According to the *Consuetudines*, in which Prior Guigo (1109–36) had recorded the customs at La Grande Chartreuse as they had been practiced from the outset under Bruno, the monastery comprised a prior, 12 monks and 16 lay brothers. In contrast to the monks, who were referred to as the *patres* (Latin for fathers) and who were clerics, the lay brothers (also known as conversi), were engaged in manual work within the monastery estate (or "domain") or as farm workers. The monastery domain, also called the *desertum* (Latin for desert), was a closed off area where there were no other property owners and to which outsiders could be refused entry. At La Grande

Bruno on a visit to Pope Urban II. Francisco de Zurbarán, (1598–1664), oil on canvas (Museo de Bellas Artes, Seville).

La Grande Chartreuse. Aerial view of the Carthusians' solitary mother house in a high, wooded valley near Grenoble. In the center is the church, on the left the long row of cells in the form of small houses for the monks. Many of the monasteries still inhabited by monks today are open to visitors, at least in part. This does not apply to La Grande Chartreuse, however, where visitors are kept at a distance so that they do not disturb the "Great Silence."

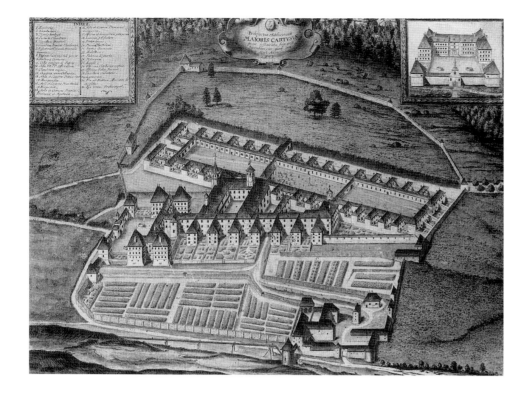

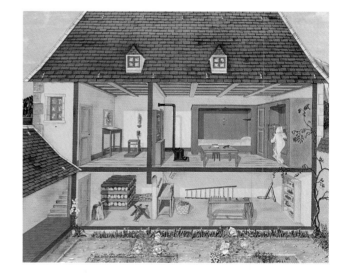

Chartreuse this was managed by means of a bottleneck at the entrance to the valley, behind which lay the lay brothers' house, the *correrie*, while the monks' hermitage was located much higher up the valley on the site where the Chapel of Notre-Dame de Casalibus is situated today. It was destroyed by an avalanche in 1132 and rebuilt lower down in the valley. The Carthusians owned no property outside the *desertum*.

The Carthusian hermitages were always grouped around two courtyards. Adjoining the church, a simple hall building, was the small cloister with the chapter house, refectory, and library. A second, larger cloister provided access to the individual monks' cells, which were in the form of small houses, each with a walled garden. Each cell comprised a workshop, a timber store, a living and study room, as well as a house chapel, and had running water. If the cells were two-story then the latter two rooms were on the upper floor. Next to the door to the cloister was a serving hatch for the monks' meals. The hermitic life of the monks in their cells followed a rhythm of communal activities. They all gathered in the church for vigil, matins (lauds), morning Mass and vespers. The monks spent the rest of the day in solitary prayer in their cells. They met in the chapter house in order to discuss monastery issues, ate together in the refectory on Sundays and Feast Days, and went for a walk once a week. In contrast to other hermits, the Carthusians were especially dedicated to studying the Holy Scriptures and to copying books, influenced by their founder, the scholastic Bruno. Even Guibert de Nogent, who visited La Grande Chartreuse at the beginning of the 12th century, praised its extensive library.

The first three hermitages for which Guigo had recorded the *Consuetudines* of La Grande Chartreuse and which subsequently affiliated themselves to the Carthusians were the start of a monastery network which grew slowly but consistently and in the 16th century numbered almost 200 houses. Charterhouses (Carthusian monasteries) initially arose in the Alpine regions, in the Jura, and in eastern France, later in Spain, Italy, England, and Denmark. In the 14th and 15th centuries Charterhouses were founded in German-speaking areas in particular, as well as in the areas surrounding important towns (including Paris, Dijon, Rome, Pavia, Venice, Cologne, Erfurt, Nuremburg, Basle, Burgos, Avignon).

Due to the manageable, even if later expanded, size of monasteries, the clear structure of monastic life, and the obviously successful balance between hermitic and cenobitic elements, the Carthusians never experienced a decline in discipline, as was often the case in other orders. Their stringency and detachment from the world ensured their appeal throughout the Middle Ages. Peter the Venerable saw the Carthusian way of life as the epitome of monastic practice. Once a year the abbot of Cluny withdrew from his grueling official functions to the seclusion of La Grande Chartreuse.

◄ **La Grande Chartreuse** after its reconstruction in the 17th century. Pen and ink drawing (private collection).

▲ **La Grande Chartreuse,** monks' procession in the large cloister from which the individual monks' cells are also accessible.

Cross-section of a Carthusian cell. Prayer, meditation, reading, and manual work (see lower floor) determine the daily life of a Carthusian monk. Every monk who is capable of doing so cuts the wood for the stove in winter with a large hand saw and an axe.

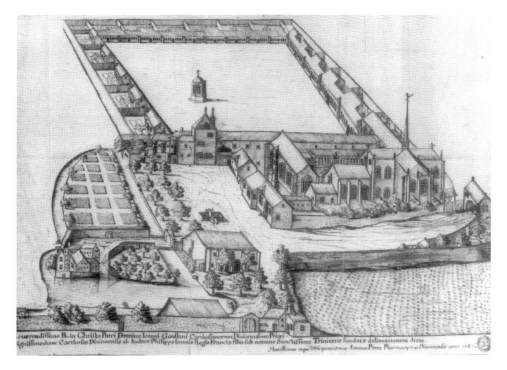

Dijon, the Chartreuse de Champmol.

▼ **Church porch** with the Madonna and the figure of the donor, Duke Philip the Bold of Burgundy, kneeling in adoration and his wife Margaret of Flanders, accompanied by John the Baptist and St. Katharine; 1389–1405/06, begun by Jean de Marville, completed by Claus Sluter.

▲ **Bird's eye view of the entire complex,** 1686, by Aimé Piron.

▶ **Well of Moses** in the large cloister, 1396–1405, by Claus Sluter, prophet figures on the pedestal.

Chartreuse de Champmol, Dijon

Duke Philip the Bold of Burgundy became benefactor of a charterhouse near Dijon, his ducal seat,
that was twice as large as usual (24 instead of 12
monks) in order to arrange the construction and
care of his burial place. The foundation stone was
laid in 1483. The composed, gilded ducal tombs
were placed in the center of the monks' choir. The
ducal couple's private chapel was on the north side.
The most important artists of the age were
involved in the decoration of the monastery. In the
15th century a pilgrimage took place with a detour
to Champmol, where the Well of Moses was the
attraction, in fact a portrayal of Calvary with a large
crucifix (lost) on the surviving pedestal with the
prophets. The large cloister and the church (all
except the porch) were torn down in the Revolution. The monastery and the surviving buildings
have since housed a psychiatric clinic.

Villeneuve-lès-Avignon

The charterhouse of Saint-Jean-Baptiste, founded
in 1356 by Pope Innocent VI in his former cardinal's palace, was further extended by his nephew
and enlarged to twice the normal size (24
monks). The complex comprised a hall church
with a polygonal choir, two adjoining benefactor's
chapels as a kind of southern side aisle with the
Pope's tomb, and two courtyards to the north surrounded by the monks' cells, separated by the
refectory—the former hall of the cardinal's
palace—and a chapel with wall paintings from
1354–55 north of that. The monastery owned the
large *Coronation of the Virgin* painting by Enguer-
rand Quarton (1453/54; today at the Musée
municipal). Sold and partly demolished during
the Revolution, the buildings have been reac-
quired by the state since the end of the 19th century and restored. Today they serve as an event
and cultural location.

▲ **Villeneuve-lès-Avignon, the
charterhouse of Saint-Jean-Baptiste,**
tomb of Pope Innocent VI in the Trinity
Chapel, c. 1362.

▼ **Villeneuve-lès-Avignon, the
charterhouse,** view of the large cloister with
the adjoining monks' houses, 1356–58.

Certosa di Pavia, Italy

▶ **South side of the church** with the crossing tower, from the small cloister. The color contrast between the red brick, the light-colored mini-galleries, the white crossing tower, and the gable supports, the terracotta-colored decoration, and the white marble columns increases the aesthetic and prestige value of the building's exterior.

Small cloister. The gallery arches, pendentives, and cornices are elaborately decorated with terracotta reliefs.

Overall view of Certosa with the forecourt, church, large and small cloisters (to the side of the church).

The endowment of the charterhouse at Pavia by the Milanese Duke Gian Galeazzo Visconti in 1396 is based on a provision in the will of his wife Caterina. Its construction involved architects and artists who had also worked on Milan Cathedral. Following the death of the benefactor in 1402 the building work repeatedly came to a standstill due to fierce disputes and continued until well into the 16th century. The church was completed in 1462, with the exception of the façade and the crossing tower, the mortal remains of the Duke were transferred there in 1474, and the completion ceremony took place in 1497, although the porch (1501/08) and the upper façade were not complete (until the mid-16th century). From 1460 the most famous Lombard artists of the era worked on the façade and the large and small cloister, including the architect Guiniforte Solari and the sculptor Mantegazza. The Certosa church with its three aisles, the nave lined with side chapels, its deep transept arms that, like the choir, culminate in tripartite conches, an elaborate crossing tower, and a façade with excessive sculptural decoration, does not correspond to Carthusian conventions at all and is instead indicative of the demands of its benefactor and his successor, which were oriented towards the key buildings of the region. Following the abolition of the contemplative order during the Habsburg Empire under Emperor Joseph II the charterhouse changed hands several times between the Cistercians, the Carmelites, and the returning Carthusians. It has been a Cistercian monastery since 1968.

Pavia, Charterhouse.

▲ **Monastery church,** view of the hall-like nave with its tall columns and low clerestory under the six-part, colored rib vaults, 1st half of the 15th C.

▶ **Charterhouse church,** monumental Renaissance-style screen façade with a pronounced porch axis and elaborate sculptural decoration; marble and multicolored incrustations, late 15th and 16th C.

▼ **Refectory** with lectern for readings during mealtimes. The vaulting and the architectural style originate from the 16th century, the decoration from the 17th century.

Buxheim, Germany

The charterhouse of Buxheim near Memmingen arose from the transfer of an older priory to the Carthusians in 1402. The church and the large cloister were developed, together with the monks' houses, up to the start of the 16th century. Following disputes with the Protestant town of Memmingen the monastery became subject to the empire in 1548 and was a charterhouse until secularization in 1803, after which it was in private ownership. Since 1926 it has belonged to the Salesians, who set up a high school there after the war. Buxheim is the best preserved charterhouse in the German-speaking world. The medieval monastery complex was converted to the baroque style in the 18th century by the Zimmermann family of stucco plasterers from Wessobrunn. Dominikus Zimmermann also decorated the parish church next door. Until 1955 the western cloister wing ran diagonally through the church and divided the room as if by a rood screen into the lay brothers' area and the monk's choir. The baroque choir stalls (1687–91 by Ignaz Waibl), which were sold in the 19th century, were restored and returned to their original location in 1992.

▼ **Large cloister** with the St. Anna Chapel in the northwest corner. The painted architectural features of the cloister and the chapel, and the strap work decoration in the interior (1738/39), are the work of the Zimmermann brothers.

▶ **Interior view of the charterhouse church** looking east, with the gallery of the cloister rood screen (removed in 1955–57), separating the lay brothers and the monks' choir.

▲ **Charterhouse church and large cloister** from the northeast; in the background the parish church.

▼ **Carthusian houses,** view of the garden and the sleeping quarters.

The Canons Regular

As members of the clergy, recipients of a regular income, and the holders of important church offices, canons (or capitulars) enjoyed social prestige and a prominent position in society. These aspects of life as a canon made a spiritual career attractive to members of the nobility, from amongst whom almost all canons were recruited, as it enabled them to have a lifestyle in keeping with their status. In contrast to the monks, therefore, the renunciation of private property and undertaking a communal life were out of the question for the majority of canons. Instead, simony and a plurality of offices were the norm. Exemption from the liturgical duties connected with a canonry, which also included spiritual guidance, was possible by paying deputies. For this reason, the ascetic life of the monks was always viewed more highly than the remunerated choir and altar services rendered by the canons. For a long time canons who sought greater spiritual discipline and asceticism had therefore converted to monasticism or, like Bruno of Cologne, had given up their canonry in favor of life as a hermit.

In 1039 four clerics from the cathedral of Avignon decided that it should also be possible, as a canon, to lead a communal, ascetic existence in adherence to the liturgical obligations and in renunciation of personal property. With the support of the bishop they moved into the abandoned pilgrimage church of Saint-Ruf outside the gates of Avignon, where they lived a semi monastic life. In 1059 the Lateran Synod under Pope Nicolas II imposed as a general requirement the *vita communis* (communal living) for the clergy and the renunciation of private property: aspects of the church reform efforts. Saint-Ruf suddenly found itself at the head of a reform movement that quickly gathered momentum and developed numerous regional characteristics and varieties. There was also the pressure to justify the reforms and, in order to support the canons' new way of life, those in Saint-Ruf, under the influence of reform personalities such as Hugo of Die and Bishop Hugo of Grenoble, relied on St. Augustine and the clerical monastery he founded, adopting the Rule of St. Augustine in 1080. This was of course a very general text, dealing with the apostolic life of the original community: without property, in chastity, and in mutual love. The rule therefore required more specification in the form of the community's own *Consuetudines*. These, once written, were exported from Saint-Ruf to the clerical monasteries subsequently assigned to it and to numerous other priories that adopted the way of life of the Avignon canons. While the religious houses assigned to Saint-Ruf were largely located in southern France and Catalonia, the influence of the *Consuetudines* extended far beyond the geographical boundaries to Marbach in Alsace and to Rottenbuch in Bavaria, both of which developed their own reform networks.

Despite the Roman reform efforts, most of the bishops, most of whom came from the same aristocratic circles as their clergy, were less interested in the reformation of their chapters. The reason for this reluctance was obvious: it would have greatly limited the comforts they enjoyed.

Only in the east of the German empire and in Catalonia did the reform of a large number of cathedral monasteries succeed. In 1092 the priory at Rottenbuch, originating from a hermitage in 1074, was awarded a papal privilege by Pope Urban II, based on the equal value of the *Vita canonica* and the *Vita monastica*, which accorded the canons their own spiritual tradition. The status thus bestowed on the canons could then only be justified by a lifestyle that could actually claim to be turning the writings of St. Augustine

◄ ▲ **Cardona, St. Vicenç,** priory church from the northeast; and nave looking southwest, 1019–40. The church at Cardona is one of the earliest entirely vaulted buildings in Romanesque architecture.

▼ **Serrabone,** former Augustinian canons (regular) priory: capital from the "choir tribune" (see pp. 142-143).

Lautenbach, former Augustinian canons (regular) priory, porch/atrium of the church, c. 1140/50. There is a chapel over the atrium which—like the upper floor chapels in Cluniac west buildings—was perhaps also used for intercessory prayer for the dead.

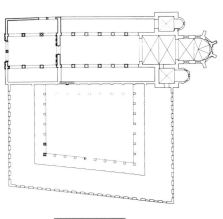

0   10 m

Marbach, ground plan. At Marbach the cloister extended as far as the narthex, located west of the façade; the narthex and cloister were directly connected to one another. (See below for the significance of these architectural findings.)

Commemoration of the Dead among the Canons Regular

The *Consuetudines* of the Marbach monastery, founded in 1089, provide greater insight into the rites practiced by the reform canons. Amongst other things, they describe practices for the commemoration of the dead that are very similar to the corresponding Cluniac provisions. The Marbach monastery church did in fact have a three-aisled narthex in the style of the Cluniac abbeys. The cloister in Marbach also extended to the narthex, west of the façade, thus exhibiting what was a characteristic motif of Cluniac monastery complexes: the direct connection of the narthex with the cloister. This correlation between text and architectural findings at Marbach is significant not least because the *Consuetudines* of other houses of canons regular such as Saint–Victor in Paris and Springiersbach contain comparable regulations for the commemoration of the dead. Clearly the canons regular followed the monks' orientation not only in spiritual and ascetic issues, but also in this regard. Like many religious communities before them, they too followed the successful Cluniac model of intercessory prayer for the departed, which, in addition to their outstanding reputation, had also brought the Cluniacs numerous donations.

into reality. This was subsequently followed by a dispute as to which of the two rule texts attributed to Augustine was better suited to fulfilling this claim: the *Praeceptum*, known as the Rule of St. Augustine, or the *Ordo monasterii*, which contained much stricter regulations, demanding silence, abstinence from meat, and manual work. While Saint-Ruf ultimately remained committed to its own traditions and, as was also the case in Rottenbuch and Marbach, continued to practice the so-called *Ordo antiquus*, a series of other religious houses adopted the stricter conditions of the *Ordo novus* at the start of the 12th century. These included Springiersbach (diocese of Trier), Klosterrath (Rolduc) near Aachen, Salzburg, Arrouaise (diocese of Arras), and finally Prémontré. This intensification of the ascetic attitude finally put the new observance of the canons regular on a par with the monks. Ultimately, the *Ordo novus* had more in common with the new 12th-century orders, the Cistercians and the Premonstratensians, than with the canonical tradition of the Early Middle Ages.

Hamersleben, former Augustinian canons (regular) priory. The priory church of St. Pancratius, view from the east (▲), remains of the northern rood screen with images of the Apostles (◄). The priory, initially founded in 1108 in Osterwieck by Bishop Reinhard of Halberstadt, was moved to Hamersleben in 1112. Construction of the church was completed in the middle of the 12th century, the rood screen relief early 13th C.

161

The New Orders of the 12th Century
The Cistercians

Cistercian (▲) and Benedictine monks (▲).
The Benedictine monks' clothing is all black, while white and/or light colors predominate with the Cistercians. (Illustrations from the Codex 420a of 1577, Stiftsbibliothek Zwettl, Austria.)

Cîteaux, the Cistercians' original abbey, according to a 17th-century engraving.

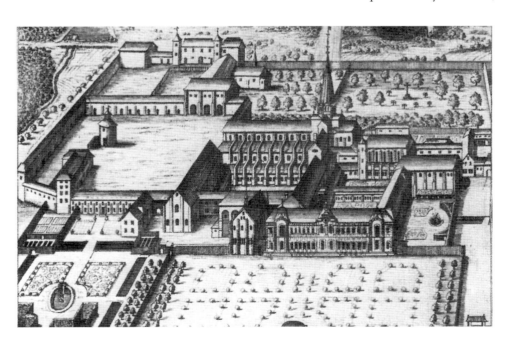

The Founding of Cîteaux

In 1098 Robert, abbot of Molesme, and 21 of his monks settled in a forest area south of Dijon with the intention of living there in deliberate solitude in strict accordance with the Rule of St. Benedict, without the slightest diminution or amendment. The purposive name they gave to their newly founded settlement, in a deliberate departure from older tradition, was *Novum monasterium* (Latin for new monastery). Unlike earlier reformers, who were concerned with "reestablishing" a lost status in terms of the rule, Robert and his followers were not aiming at this but wanted a new start. At *Novum monasterium* they wanted to lead a strictly ascetic life far removed from worldly agitation and activity, with the words of Benedict's text forming the only point of reference for its structure. Robert was not unknown among would-be hermits and monastery founders at the close of the 11th century. As a monk from Moutier-la-Celle and abbot of Tonnerre, in 1075 he had founded the abbey of Molesme in the Châtillon-sur-Seine (Burgundy) area for a group of hermits. Molesme became a focus of attraction for followers of a decidedly detached life. Bruno of Cologne, the founder of La Grande Chartreuse, spent a year as a hermit in the environs of the abbey. The widely traveled English monk Stephen Harding, who was familiar with the hermitic monasteries at Camaldoli and Vallombrosa, also joined the new community. Due to the generous donations of the nobility Molesme, within just 20 years, experienced such a boom that Robert regarded his original intentions as having been betrayed and he aspired to a return to the ascetic ideals of the early years. His reform plans failed, however, and so the abbot left his abbey together with those members who shared his fundamentalist approach.

The refusal of Robert and his followers to accept any interpretation of the rule in the form of monastic practices (*Consuetudines*) had a number of direct consequences in the new monastery. Some were extrinsic but highly symbolic—such as the renunciation of colored clothing, which distinguished the appearance of *Novum monasterium* monks from Benedictine monks; some required early revision, such as the attempt to practice Benedict's central Italy dress code in the Burgundian climate; and some were effective in the long term, such as the rejection of liturgical ceremony and ostentation in favor of the triad comprising *Opus dei* (Latin for religious service and prayer), *Lectio divin* (reading of the Holy Scriptures), and *Opus manuum* (manual work). While many traditional monasteries practiced a division between well-occupied priest monks and unoccupied, illiterate lay brothers, everyone at *Novum monasterium* was expected to work in accordance with his abilities. For clerical monks this meant straightforward manual or garden work in addition to the Liturgy of the Hours, while for the lay brothers this involved carrying out manual tasks or heavy field work alongside starkly reduced prayer times. Their new status was also reflected in their strict segregation from the monks in the church and the abbey.

Robert had to return to Molesme one year

Pontigny, former Cistercian abbey church. Pontigny was founded in 1114 as the "second daughter" of Cîteaux. The existing structure was erected in two stages between 1130/40 and 1160/70, the Gothic ambulatory between 1180/85 and 1205. Today the church, over 325 ft (100 m) stands tower-less in the Burgundian landscape; originally, there was a ridge turret over the crossing. The surrounding abbey buildings fell victim to the Revolution.

after the founding of *Novum monasterium* on the orders of the Pope. His successor was Aubri (Alberich, 1099–1108), who had already been a prior in Molesme. The rigor of the *Novum monasterium* monks soon attracted the local nobility, a tendency that continued to increase when the Duke of Burgundy's court outings to the monastery and hunting parties in its forests were subsequently banned. Popularity and donations enriched and enlarged the abbey, which soon became known well beyond the borders of Burgundy under the place name Cistercium (French Cîteaux).

First Affiliations and the Development of the Order

In order to prevent the abbey going down the same path as Molesme, Stephen Harding, the third abbot of Cîteaux (1108–33, died 1134), decided to send new entrant monks out to found daughter abbeys on the donated land. This was intended both to keep the size of the abbey manageable and also to solve the problem of distant, difficult to manage properties. Consequently, as of 1113, a series of new Cîteaux abbeys were settled in quick succession: 1113, La Ferté-sur-Grosne, south of Chalon; 1114, Pontigny, northeast of Auxerre; 1115, Clairvaux, northwest, and Morimond, north east of Langres. These initial daughter houses, the so-called "primary" abbeys, soon became the originators of their own affiliations.

The newly founded abbeys each comprised 12 monks and an abbot. Despite the spatial separation the monks at the new foundations were expected to form a "spiritual" union with the mother house and, usually, to follow the rule in the same way, to use the same liturgical books, and to keep to the same psalms and other rites. This is recorded in the *Carta caritatis et unanimitas* (Charter of Love and Harmony) compiled by Stephen Harding in 1114, a kind of Cistercian "constitution" that was officially acknowledged by Pope Calixtus II in 1119 as the articles of the Cistercian way of life. In 1116 was held the first general chapter, the annual gathering of the abbots at Cîteaux required by the *Carta caritatis et unanimitas*, where pending issues of rule observance, way of life, salvation, as well as lapses and disputes, were addressed under the chairmanship of the abbot of Cîteaux.

As a consequence of the spread of Cistercian abbeys, the inspection and control regulations of the *Carta caritatis* were revised during the 1120s and the mode of affiliation unified. The general chapter now took the place of the

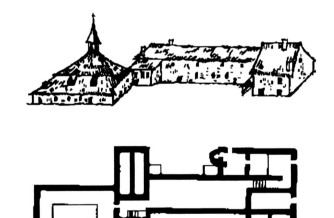

Clairvaux, *Monasterium vetus,* the first monastery, based on the layout by Dom Milley, 1708.

Stephan Harding (right) **and the abbot of Saint-Vaast** present their abbey models to the Mother of God. Miniature from Cîteaux: Book of Jeremiah—Commentaries of St. Jerome (Dijon, Bibliothèque municipale, Ms. 139, fol. 104).

The Adoption of the Order Structure by other Monastery Networks

The Cistercians' method, based on rational principles, for organizing the cohesion of abbeys living according to collective principles was adopted by both older and more recent monastery networks in the 12th century. The Premonstratensians were the first, replicating both the institution of the general chapter and the network structure in the form of affiliations. The Carthusians held their first general chapter in 1155 under the chairmanship of the prior of La Grande Chartreuse and introduced regular inspections. The canons regular of Saint-Ruf followed a two-yearly inspection cycle, but retained their centralized network structure with Saint-Ruf at the head. Only at the end of the 12th century did the Camaldulians adopt an order constitution with a general prior presiding over the general chapter, in which, in addition to abbots and priors, influential hermits also took part. As early as 1132 Peter the Venerable had gathered the abbots and priors of the *Cluniacensis ecclesia* together in a general chapter at Cluny. However, it was only c. 1200 that the monastery network was converted to an order with an annual general chapter, a system of inspections, and general statutes. The abbot of Cluny nevertheless retained a prominent position within the order.

abbot of Cîteaux as the central authority. The founding and management of a new abbey lay with the mother house, which appointed the abbot and the 12 monks, provided the necessary property, arranged the builder and manual workers for the construction of the monastic buildings and ensured that they were laid out according to regulations, and also made sure that the same liturgical books were used and the same rule observance followed as in the mother house. Although it was autonomous, the daughter abbey was not entirely independent but was subject to the mother house and underwent an inspection every year. The daughter abbey controlled the monasteries it had founded in the same manner. As the head of the network, Cîteaux was inspected by the abbots of its primary abbeys.

Even though the Cistercian abbeys were subject to a graded ranking in order of the founding dates entered on a panel at Cîteaux, unlike other monastery networks, theirs did not have a single abbot at the head making all the most important decisions. Instead, all important issues were addressed collectively in the general chapter, where every abbot—including the head of Cîteaux—was accountable to his fellow abbots. This fixed bond between the Cistercian abbeys, regulated by the *Carta caritatis* as if by a constitution, gave the structure of their network a new quality that distinguished it from all of the older monastery networks: general chapter, inspection to monitor the way of life, and their written constitution made the Cistercians the leading monastic order of the Middle Ages.

In order to ensure the use of uniform liturgical texts, at an early stage Abbot Stephen Harding had arranged the preparation of copies in the scriptorium at Cîteaux and had also commissioned a review and improvement of the Bible text. The Cistercian *Antiphonar* (liturgical songbook), was compiled by Harding; based on the 8th-century songbook by Bishop Chrodegang of Metz, which was seen as "Gregorian," it made deliberate use of archaic melodies and was revised after his death in 1134 on the instructions of the general chapter. From the outset the Cistercians had been vehemently opposed to the use of fixed, written monastic practices in addition to the rule but, given the escalation in the foundation of new abbeys as a consequence of the order's second wave of expansion from 1130, this dogma had to cede to the practical requirements of a uniform way of life. At the end of Stephen Harding's term in office, therefore, the *Ecclesiastica officia* for clerical monks and the *Usus conversorum* for the lay brothers were compiled in 1130/34 as the first Cistercian *Consuetudines*.

The decisions of the general chapter, only the most important of which had been recorded in writing at the beginning (First Collection of General Chapter Decisions on the Way of Life at Clairvaux 1123/24), were now recorded to an increasing extent. As of 1202 they were compiled systematically and forwarded to the abbeys for copying and reading in the chapter.

The Cistercian Way of Life: its Impact on Monastery Complexes and the Liturgy

Difference in Status between Monks and Lay Brothers
Despite all of their insistence that the Rule of St. Benedict be followed to the last, the Cistercians had from the outset deviated from the rule in one respect: while, in Benedictine monasteries, monks who were priests constituted an absolute exception and were therefore treated differently, under the Cistercians only priests or clerics on the path to being ordained as priests could be granted the status of monks. All others, irrespective of their social standing, were accepted into the monastery only as lay brothers. In contrast to Cluniacs and traditional Benedictine monks, "advancement" by learning to read and by acquiring Latin was not an option under the Cistercians; those accepted as lay brothers remained as lay brothers.

The monks and lay brothers in a Cistercian abbey lived in almost completely separate domains. While the monks were responsible for the Liturgy of the Hours and Mass services, and had their living quarters in the cloister and the surrounding buildings, the lay brothers were responsible for the manual labor in the monastery as well as for work in the fields or forests, and lived in the west wing of the abbey away from the cloister. They gathered in the church at sunrise and sunset for the Liturgy of the Hours, their place being to

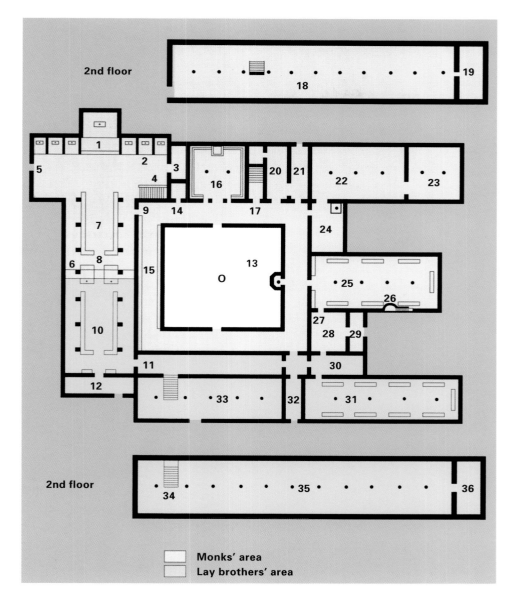

2nd floor

2nd floor

☐ Monks' area
☐ Lay brothers' area

the west in front of the stone rood screen separating the monks' choir from the rest of the nave—where, in a traditional Benedictine church, the lay visitors were accommodated. Provided the lay brothers were within earshot of the church bells, the other prayer times constituted brief breaks from work.

If the fields being worked were far away from the abbey, the lay brothers were often accommodated at individual farmsteads, called "granges," in order to avoid them traveling long distances. They lived and worked there under the management of a supervisor and only came to Mass at the abbey on Sundays. Due to the strict segregation of monks and lay brothers in Cistercian abbeys, rooms, of which only one normally existed, had to be duplicated. This applied in particular to the dormitorium and the refectorium, which for the monks were situated in their normal locations: on the upper floor of the east wing

Fontenay, cloister courtyard. Fontenay, founded in 1118 by Bernard of Clairvaux, is one of the best preserved Cistercian abbeys in France. It closely resembles the ideal plan depicted above. The good condition of the whole complex is the result of comprehensive renovations carried out with private funds in the first third of the 20th century. Fontenay is a UNESCO World Heritage Site (see also pp.184-185).

Bonnecombe, abbey complex. The abbey, founded in 1167 and with a magnificent setting in the undulating landscape 9 miles (15 km) south of Rodez, has lost none of its former beauty. It is now privately owned following a changeable history and houses a group of the Communauté catholique des Béatitudes.

Sénanque, east elevation of the abbey complex from above. Sénanque, one of the three "Provençal sisters" (together with Silvacane and Le Thoronet), is a classic example of the wildly romantic location of a Cistercian abbey in a remote valley. Its famous lavender fields and the good condition of the abbey merely add to its appeal (see also p. 194).

(dormitorium) and in the south wing of the cloister (refectorium). The west wing, separated from the cloister (or without any doors to it) by a characteristic alley, the "lay brothers' passageway," housed the lay brothers' refectorium and living room on the ground floor and their dormitorium on the upper floor. The lay brothers' passageway and the often very long west wing of the abbey—an indication of the large number of lay brothers in many monasteries, particularly in early times—are typical features that often enable a Cistercian abbey to be distinguished from a Benedictine one merely on the basis of the ground plan.

With their two-way split, based on social standing, into a monks' abbey, almost all of the members of which came from the lower and middle nobility, and a largely non aristocratic lay brothers' abbey, the Cistercian monasteries were a true reflection of contemporary society. It had been Benedict's requirement that, upon entry to a monastery all class differences should be set aside, but most of the traditional Benedictine houses had only complied formally to the extent that all of the monks in the community were treated equally, but the poor were not granted entry to the monastery at all. The Cistercians, on the other hand, clearly saw themselves as being above this requirement. Their success among the nobility and the many lay brothers who became affiliated to them shows that their argument, that everyone should serve God according to his own means, appealed to their contemporaries of both classes.

Detachment from the World

Differently from what was often later claimed, it was not the desire for the reclamation of new land but the quest for solitude that motivated the Cistercians to build their monasteries in forest areas or "deserts", i.e. remote areas empty of people. The Cistercian solitude was only relative, however: the magnificent Cîteaux was situated close to a road leading from Dijon to the Saône Valley, past a farm belonging to the Duke of Burgundy, which he made available to the monks. Pontigny, too, where the Cistercians took over an existing farm, was in an easily accessible location on the road to Troyes. In many instances the adoption of older infrastructures and transport connections were decisive factors in the selection of monastery sites. As was the case with all hermits and monks living in solitude, the Cistercians' main endeavor was also to keep the "disquiet" of the world at a distance, but under no circumstances were they prepared to forego their own external contacts. It was not a question of isolation, but of autonomous control of connections with outside. The hermits' biographies—from Anthony to Romuald and Bruno of Cologne—show that there was no-one better connected and that hardly anyone had more direct contact to society's big names than the monks living in detachment from the world.

Even though historians of the order at an early stage elevated the alleged solitude of the Cistercian abbeys to mythical status, their locations remote from other habitation did have significant consequences. Unlike conventional monasteries, the Cistercians did not allow the development of settlements in the proximity of their communities. This was facilitated by their substantial independence from abbey servants, as the work otherwise performed by lay servants was undertaken by the lay brothers. The lack of monastery settlements also meant that there were no paupers that they had to feed. At the same time, the Cistercians tried to keep the number of guests in the abbeys as low as possible. Although they were not able to exempt themselves completely from the obligation imposed by Benedict to accommodate pilgrims and travelers, guests did not constitute an integral part of abbey life, as was the case with the earlier Benedictines. Instead they were accommodated in lay hospices close to the outer abbey gates and had their own chapel for religious services. Only aristocratic male visitors were allowed to participate in Mass in the church, where they were usually seated in the transept arm away from the abbey. Women, on the other hand, were completely prohibited from entering the church or from access to the abbey complex beyond the guesthouse. The absence of any significant lay public, with the exception of the lay brothers, also changed the liturgical routine. Processions outside of the monastery, which also served to promote its external image, were not held by the Cistercians. The litanies of the Rogation processions prior to Ascension were recited in the choir. Only on Palm Sunday did abbey members emerge from the church porch in order to hold a station with singing in the atrium, before a celebratory return to the church, as Jesus entered Jerusalem.

Motivated by the endeavor to protect the abbey's solitude, these restrictions on the care of the poor and the right to hospitality also brought substantial financial advantages for the Cistercians. This is especially evident in comparison to Cluny, where, for the commemoration of the dead, 50 paupers' rations per day were handed out and on Feast Days several hundred guests and paupers had to be fed.

Staffarda, refectorium. In addition to the quest for detachment there were also other areas of life in which the early Cistercians sought to distinguish themselves from the Benedictines. Modest eating and drinking was an important aspect. With regard to Cluny, Bernard of Clairvaux criticized the fact that the meals there became ever more generous and that, instead of two cooked dishes as prescribed by the rule, three, four or five courses were served.

The Liturgy

One of the Cistercians' declared objectives was the return to a simpler liturgy. When compared to Benedict's era, the monastic religious service in the High Middle Ages was in fact hardly recognizable. Instead of a weekly Mass on Sundays, two Masses daily were celebrated in a monastery in the presence of the entire congregation, as well as a varying number of Requiem and private Masses, and the Liturgy of the Hours was extended with numerous series of psalms, intercessory prayers, and offices. The Cluniacs in particular had endeavored to embellish the monastery liturgy with additional offices and prayer obligations for benefactors, friends, and deceased with whom they had some kind of tie.

The Cistercians did away with most of these additions and thus drastically abbreviated the

Fontfroide, lay brothers' corridor. The vaulted lay brothers' corridor depicted here was parallel to the northwest wing of the cloister and afforded the lay brothers access to the rear area of the abbey church reserved for them. Unlike here, most lay brothers' passageways were open to the sky.

Monks chopping wood, Gregory the Great's *Moralia in Job* manuscript from Cîteaux, early 12th C. Heavy physical work such as the felling of wood was the responsibility of the lay brothers and not the monks. This book illumination shows the importance of *opus manuum* (manual work) for the Cistercians' self-image.

Cistercian church choir structures. The simple, straight choir end found in early Cistercian churches evolved over the course of time in line with changing demands. Altenberg (left) and Doberan (center) each have a round ambulatory with radiating chapels ("Cistercian cathedrals"), Riddagshausen (right) has a somewhat less differentiated rectangular ambulatory. The chapels also had sufficient room for altars.

Liturgy of the Hours. In particular the nightly *hore*, the vigil, was significantly shorter, except on Feast Days. They also abolished one of the two daily monastery Masses and held a second Mass only on Sundays, the main Feast Days, and on specific other Feast Days. The time saved as a result could be used by the monks for reading, the copying of texts, or for the *opus manuum*, daily manual labor.

The Monks' Opus Manuum

In addition to duties in the kitchen and other lighter activities within the monastery or in the garden this labor could sometimes include working in the nearby fields, especially if these adjoined the abbey complex. Only during harvest time did the monks regularly take part in field work. Up until the 14th century it was usual for them to be involved harvesting hay and in the grape harvest. Their contribution to the community's livelihood was never of economic significance, however. Physical work was first and foremost a matter of asceticism and contemplation. The frequent image of perspiring, toiling Cistercians applied only to the lay brothers, not to the monks. Despite the apparent contradiction to the reality of monastery life, the *opus manuum* played a key role in the order's corporate philosophy. The monks' annual participation in the harvest derives from the symbolic importance for the Cistercian self-image of working with one's own hands.

Commemoration of the Dead

The Cistercians took heed of the financial difficulties the Cluniacs faced as a result of their extensive practice of intercessory prayer for the dead. As of the second half of the 12th century the Cistercians entered only the abbots in the necrology; there was no longer an individual commemoration for monks, lay brothers, or monastery friends (*familiares*). Cluniac Requiem Masses held for the deceased during the 30 days after their death (*tricenar*) and on the anniversary (*anniversar*) of their death were done away with. Instead, following the death of a brother monk, every priest monk was obligated to read three Masses for him and 20 private Requiem Masses per annum for all of the orders' deceased over the past year. There were also prayers during the 30 day period and a private Mass every day in general commemoration of all deceased Cistercians. The handing out of paupers' meals was held three (!) times a day in each abbey in commemoration of the dead.

The new resolution to define the Mass obligation per monk priest instead of per deceased brought with it a fairer distribution of the liturgical

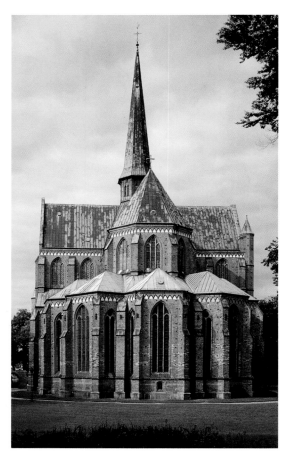

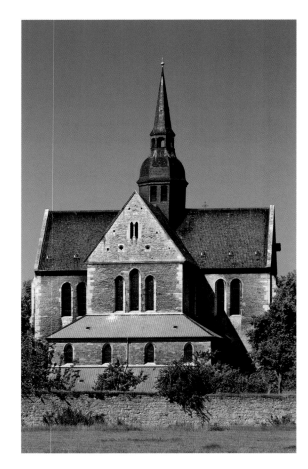

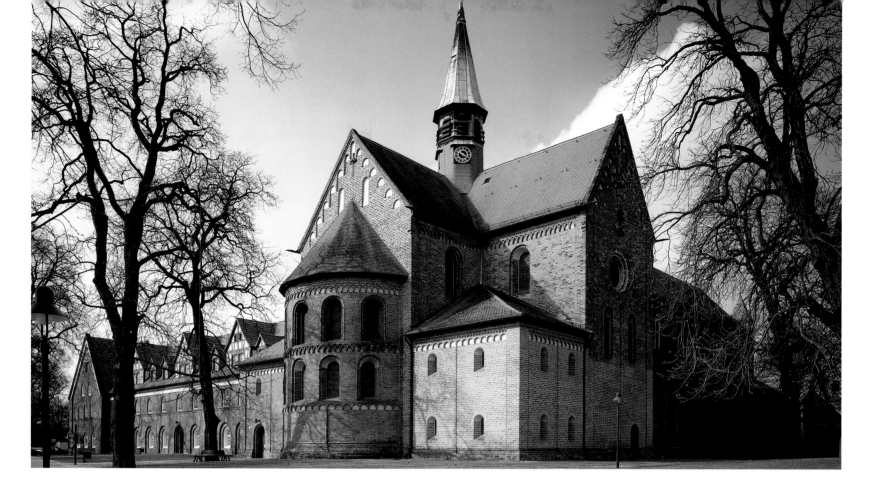

load and prevented the overburdening of smaller abbeys. At the same time, however, the close link between the individual deceased and the Mass read for them was relaxed: an abstract obligation was introduced instead of commemoration of the individual deceased during the 30 days following their death. Following this period there was just general commemoration; although deceased Cistercians were always included in their brothers' intercessory prayer, their individual names were never mentioned again. Not every simple Cistercian without a claim to entry in the necrology was convinced of the redemptory effectiveness of these new regulations; some endeavored to arrange individual commemoration outside the order by means of an endowment.

In addition to significant financial savings, as a result of introducing only a symbolic number of paupers' meals and the abolition of the individual commemoration of the dead, this also had consequences for abbey construction. Unlike the Cluniacs, the atria of Cistercian churches had no upper floor as the chapel for the reading of Requiem Masses had become superfluous. Instead, numerous altars were required in the eastern part of the church for the private Masses celebrated by the priest monks. In the earlier years these altars were often incorporated as rows of rectangular transept chapels on both sides of the rectangular sanctuary. The model for this type of construction, the so-called Bernard Plan, was the first large abbey church at Clairvaux (c. 1120/25). From the end of the 12th century many chapels were also erected in the ambulatory (first in Clairvaux, consecrated in 1174; other surviving examples include Pontigny, Longpont, Altenberg, and Doberan). There were also other, independent choir configurations such as the rectangular ambulatory with radiating chapels (Cîteaux, Morimond, Ebrach, Riddagshausen) and a double-story transept chapel that was especially widespread in Germany (Haina, Lehnin, Chorin). If there was not enough space for the altars in the eastern part, then they could be erected in the side aisle of the nave to the side of the monks' choir (Haina).

Lehnin, abbey church (▲) and view of the nave (▼). Founded in 1180, Lehnin was the first settlement by the Cistercian order in the Mark of Brandenburg. The Late Romanesque pillared basilica has a simple apsidal choir end. Two double-story chapels were built on the east side of the transept.

Bernard of Clairvaux (1090–1153), portrait of the famous Cistercian saint in a painting from the treasury of the cathedral of Troyes.

Bernard of Clairvaux

Bernard was a member of the lesser nobility in Fontaine-lès-Dijon and received a sound education in grammar, theology, philosophy, and literature at the canons regular priory of Saint-Vorles in Châtillon-sur-Seine. It was probably in 1113 that he entered Cîteaux, together with 30 relatives and associates whom he had himself convinced to take this step. As early as 1115 he was dispatched, with 12 monks including four of his brothers, to found a monastery in Clairvaux, where he remained as abbot until his death in1153. His charm, his rhetorical skills, and his magnetism drew to Clairvaux an unending flow of novices, with whom he founded some 70 daughter houses. Despite health problems caused by the extreme asceticism of his early years, Bernard undertook extensive writing from 1123. His handling of issues relating to monastic life and his numerous sermons, letters, and commentaries on contemporary church and secular events ensured that he was known well beyond the order's boundaries. He corresponded with scholars, men of the Church, and rulers, was approached from all sides for advice on spiritual issues and, for his part, became increasingly committed to the interests of the Cistercians: hence his support for the Templar Order, his active taking of sides in the Papal Schism, his fight against deviant theological opinions—including the instigation of Peter Abelard's denunciation—and his preparation of the 1147–49 crusade. His preaching tours took him across half of Europe. As the first and most important saint of his order, Bernard had a lasting influence on the spiritual life of the Cistercians and played a determining role with regard to the public image of the Cistercian order. Furthermore, his *Bridal Mysticism* (Sermons on the Song of Songs) and his reflections on the Passion and the death of Christ had considerable influence on the religious thought of the High and Late Middle Ages (religious women's movements and piety).

Chiaravalle Milanese, cloister courtyard, the first Italian daughter abbey (1136) founded by Clairvaux, from which it also takes it name. Today, the abbey, established close to the city by Milanese citizens who were ardent followers of Bernard, lies in the center of an industrial area.

The Expansion of the Order

The abolition of the individual Requiem Mass did nothing to halt the expansion of the Cistercians. The ten monasteries in existence in 1119 when Calixtus II acknowledged the *Carta caritatis* had grown to around 70 in 1134 when Stephen Hardings died and 343 in 1153 at the time of Bernard of Clairvaux's death.

The order's official history always links the beginning of the new foundations with the arrival of Bernard of Clairvaux and his 30 companions at Cîteaux. In fact, this started after the founding of the first daughter house in La Ferté. Nevertheless, the rapid expansion of the order after 1130 was closely linked to Bernard's influence: in the mid-12th century half of all Cistercian monasteries were affiliated to Clairvaux.

Older hermit settlements had already been incorporated into the newly established abbeys at Morimond (1115) and Fontenay (1119, Clairvaux daughter house). Such mergers were certainly not uncommon and entire monasteries often affiliated themselves with the Cistercians. The monks underwent a Cistercian training before being accepted into the order. Examples include the Benedictine monks from Fountains (England), who joined forces with Clairvaux in 1134/35, and the hermit monastery Silvanès (southern France), which made itself subject to the abbot of Mazan in 1135/36 (affiliation with Cîteaux, 1119). In the case of Savigny (Normandy, 1147), Obazine (Limousin, 1147), Dalon (Limousin, 1162) and Cadouin (Périgord, 1201) entire monastery networks entered the order. There were some 220 Cistercian monasteries in France c. 1200 and by c. 1300 these numbered about 250. The majority of them were in Burgundy, Champagne, and the Île-de-France.

The first Cistercian monasteries in Italy belonged to the La Ferté affiliation (S. Maria del Tiglieto, 1120, Liguria; S. Maria di Lucedio, 1123, diocese of Vercelli). Of greater significance, however, were the daughter houses founded by Clairvaux following Bernard's sojourns in Italy (Chiaravalle Milanese, 1136; Chiaravalle della Colomba near Piacenza, 1137) and the transfer of SS. Vincenzo e Anastasio alle Tre Fontane in Rome, 1140); these in turn undertook the founding of new houses themselves. Other important communities in the Clairvaux affiliation were the Benedictine abbeys reformed by the Cistercians, namely Fossanova (Latium, 1135), Casamari (Latium, 1140), and Monte Amiata (Tuscany, 1228), as well as the newly established S. Galgano near Siena (1201) and Sambucina in southern Italy (1144). Of the 114 Cistercian monasteries founded on German-speaking territory, 21 belonged to the Clairvaux affiliation, while all the others belonged to the Morimond line. The oldest German monastery, Kamp am Niederrhein (1123) originated an extensive network of 70 members.

The Ebrach (near Bamberg, 1127) network comprised 24 monasteries in Franconia, Bavaria, and Bohemia. The oldest monastery founded in Austria was Heiligenkreuz (1135), with daughter houses extending as far as Hungary and Moravia. The Clairvaux affiliation was concentrated on the Rhineland (Himmerod, Eberbach) and the Baltic Sea area (Kolbatz, Oliva, Eldena). In

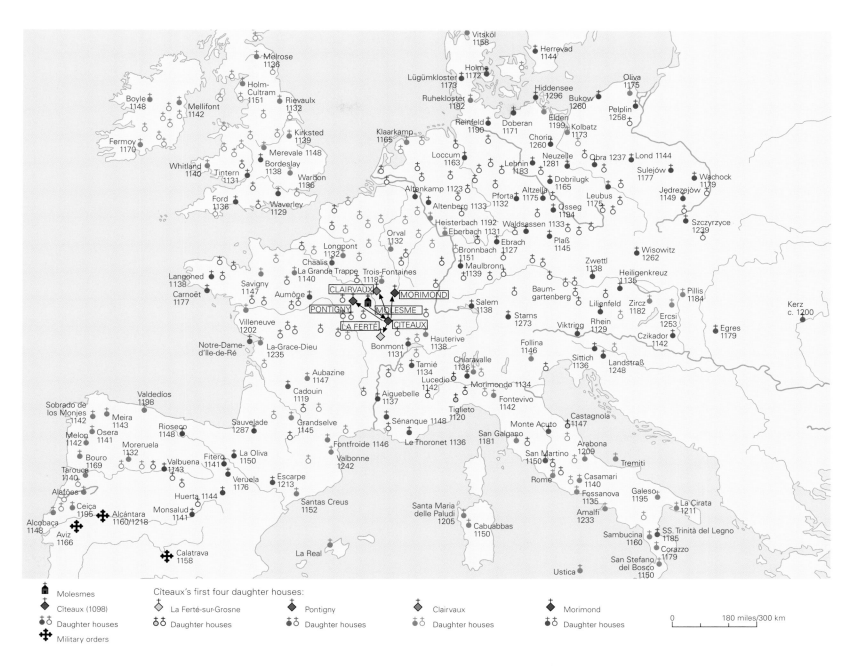

Map labels (north to south, roughly):

Vitsköl 1158
Melrose 1136
Herrevad 1144
Holme 1172
Lügümkloster 1173
Holm-Cultram 1151
Ruhekloster 1192
Hiddensee 1296
Oliva 1175
Bukow 1260
Boyle 1148
Rievaulx 1132
Pelplin 1258
Mellifont 1142
Reinfeld 1199
Doberan 1171
Elden 1199
Kolbatz 1173
Kirksted 1139
Klaarkamp 1165
Chorin 1260
Neuzelle 1281
Qbra 1237
Lond 1144
Fermoy 1170
Loccum 1163
Lehnin 1183
Dobrilugk 1165
Sulejów 1177
Wachock 1179
Whitland 1140
Merevale 1148
Bordeslay 1138
Pforta 1132
Altzella 1175
Jedrzejów 1149
Tintern 1131
Wardon 1136
Altenkamp 1123
Leubus 1175
Ford 1136
Waverley 1129
Altenberg 1133
Ossegg 1194
Szczyrzyce 1239
Heisterbach 1192
Waldsassen 1133
Wisowitz 1262
Orval 1132
Eberbach 1131
Ebrach 1145
Plaß 1145
Longpont 1132
Bronnbach 1151
Maulbronn 1139
Zwettl 1138
Heiligenkreuz 1135
Chaalis
La Grande Trappe 1140
Trois-Fontaines 1118
Kerz c. 1200
Langoned 1138
Savigny 1147
CLAIRVAUX
MORIMOND
Salem 1138
Baumgartenberg
Lilienfeld
Zircz 1182
Pillis 1184
Carnoët 1177
Aumône
PONTIGNY
MOLESME
Stams 1273
Ercsi 1253
CITEAUX
Viktring
Rhein 1129
LA FERTÉ
Czikador 1142
Egres 1179
Villeneuve 1202
Bonmont 1131
Hauterive 1138
Follina 1146
Notre-Dame-d'Ile-de-Ré
La-Grace-Dieu 1235
Tamié 1134
Chiaravalle 1136
Sittich 1136
Landstraß 1248
Aubazine 1147
Lucedio 1142
Morimondo 1134
Fontevivo 1142
Cadouin 1119
Aiguebelle 1137
Sénanque 1148
Tiglieto 1120
Castagnola 1147
Valdedios 1198
Grandselve 1145
Monte Acuto
Arabona 1209
Sobrado de los Monjes 1142
Meira 1143
Rioseco 1148
Sauvelade 1287
Le Thoronet 1136
San Galgano 1181
Tremiti
Melon 1142
Osera 1141
Fontfroide 1146
San Martino 1150
Casamari 1140
Galeso 1195
Bouro 1169
Moreruela 1132
La Oliva 1150
Valbonne 1242
Rome
Fossanova 1135
La Cirata 1211
Tarouca 1140
Valbuena 1143
Fitero 1141
Veruela 1176
Escarpe 1213
Amalfi 1233
Alafões
Huerta 1144
Santas Creus 1152
Santa Maria delle Paludi 1205
Sambucina 1160
SS. Trinità del Legno 1185
Ceiça 1195
Alcántara 1160/1218
Monsalud 1141
Cabuabbas 1150
Corazzo 1179
Alcobaça 1148
Aviz 1166
Calatrava 1158
La Real
San Stefano del Bosco 1150
Ustica

Legend:
🜨 Molesmes
◆ Cîteaux (1098)
♂♀ Daughter houses
✠ Military orders

Cîteaux's first four daughter houses:
◇ La Ferté-sur-Grosne   ♂♀ Daughter houses
◆ Pontigny   ♂♀ Daughter houses
◆ Clairvaux   ♂♀ Daughter houses
◆ Morimond   ♂♀ Daughter houses

0   180 miles/300 km

Brandenburg, on the Oder, and in Silesia the Cistercians were actively involved in agricultural development of large areas; they founded towns (including Eldena Greifswald, Dobrilugk Kirchhain, Leubus Müncheberg, among others) on the Baltic coast and in other areas beyond the Elbe. The majority of the Cistercian houses in Poland and Bohemia were founded by monasteries in German-speaking areas; it was only in Hungary that monasteries were settled by French monks. As of 1132 Cistercian communities were founded in Belgium and the Netherlands in rapid succession, some of them

Expansion of the Cistercian order. The map shows that the majority of the affiliations originated from Cîteaux, Clairvaux, or Morimond, and that the activities of the primary abbeys were focused on key points in specific regions.

Bad Herrenalb, double arcades of the paradise.
Frauenalb (1138) and Herrenalb (1149/50) were founded by Berthold III of Eberstein, a participant in the Second Crusade, and his wife Uta von Sinsheim. He handed over his second monastery, which was intended as his burial place, to the Cistercians. The most attractive part of the picturesque Late Romanesque church ruins is the paradise in front of the nave porch with its many columns.

endowed with extensive lands (Orval, Vaucelles, Villers, Aulne, Ter Doest). Some of them focused on land reclamation and development through irrigation and dyke construction (Ter Duinen, Clairmarais).

In Spain and Portugal, from 1140, the settlements were primarily motivated by the royal families. The monasteries belonged to the Morimond and Clairvaux affiliations and were situated in favorable locations that had been regained during the *Reconquista* and were to be resettled. Monasteries such as Stes. Creus and Poblet in Catalonia, as well as the Las Huelgas nunnery near Burgos in Castile, which were intended as royal burial places, were endowed with large properties and wealth. The most significant Portuguese monastery was that in Alcobaça, founded in 1153 by King Alfonso I. The layout of the monumental church at the monastery, settled directly by Clairvaux, was based on that at the mother house. All the Cistercian monasteries were situated north of the Santarém–Valencia axis. Only Calatrava, headquarters of the military order of the same name (affiliated to the Cistercians in 1187), is located south of this axis.

Due to Stephen Harding's contacts in his homeland, news of the new order had already reached England prior to the founding of the first Cistercian abbey at Waverley (Surrey, 1128). However, the expansion of the Cistercians in England is largely due to the initiative of Bernard of Clairvaux, who dispatched a group of monks to the court of King Henry I in 1131. They settled at Rievaulx Abbey and instigated a comprehensive monastic revival in Yorkshire with the establishment of numerous other monasteries (including

S. Galgano, side aisle (▲) and nave (▶) of the ruined church. The solitary former Cistercian abbey set in the unspoilt Tuscan landscape southwest of Siena was founded in 1201, initially as a priory. The *Abbatia nova* buildings below Monte Siepi were erected c. 1224. The construction of the church lasted until the end of the 13th century. On the east wall the arrangement of windows dominated by the circular aperture is especially impressive.

▶▶ **Moreruela, choir of the ruined church,** post-1168. Its picturesque walls still give a good impression of what the former Cistercian church looked like: the cruciform structure with a three-aisle nave extending over nine spans had an ambulatory with radiating chapels on the other side of the transept. The direct models for this were the ambulatory choirs at Veruela and Fitero in Aragón, built at around the same time and based on French buildings. Other architectural details also provide evidence of French influence, in particular the Burgundian Romanesque in imitation of Cluny III.

▲ **Melrose Abbey.** This former Cistercian abbey situated in the south of Scotland, founded in 1136 by David I and settled by monks from Rievaulx, is one of the largest monastery ruins in Britain.

▼ **Jerpoint Abbey.** This Irish Cistercian monastery was founded in 1180 by Donal MacGillapatrick, King of Ossory. The impressive complex has remained a ruin following an attack in the 16th century.

▶ **Rievaulx Abbey.** Founded in 1131 by Lord Helmsley and settled by monks from Clairvaux, this abbey in North Yorkshire—at times comprising 140 monks and up to 500 lay brothers—grew to become one of the largest monasteries in the kingdom.

Byland and Kirkstall). At the beginning of the 13th century the number of English Cistercian monasteries had reached its peak with 75. There were a further 11 monasteries in Scotland as a consequence of the efforts of Melrose Abbey (a Rievaulx daughter house), founded in 1136 by King David I, and another 40 monasteries in Ireland, where, with Mellifont north of Dublin, the first monastery was set up directly by Clairvaux in 1142. The English abbeys were famous for their efficient land management, which was based on a manorial system. Their frequently high numbers of lay brothers also enabled them to cultivate badlands. In Scotland the focus was on sheep rearing and wool trading. The founding of Cistercian monasteries in Scandinavia was also due to Bernard of Clairvaux. In 1143, at the request of the archbishop of Lund, he dispatched monks to Sweden for two royal monasteries (Alvastra, Varnhem); before this time there had been neither monasteries nor monks in Sweden. Further monasteries were founded in Sweden (Nydala, Julita), Gotland (Roma), and especially in Denmark (Esrom, Sorø, Øm, Vitskøl) during the course of the 12th century. Two Norwegian religious houses were settled from England, while Esrom dispatched communities to Dargun (1172; moved to Eldena in 1199) and Kolbatz (1174).

The Founding of Cistercian Monasteries: Methods, Organization and Buildings

Reports of the rapid expansion of the order belie the fact that the founding of a Cistercian abbey required more than religious enthusiasm and 12 monks. Careful planning was essential in order to avoid the 12 monks and their abbot being faced with destitution at the onset of the first winter. The material livelihood had to be ensured before a community could be sent out. This applied both to the buildings required for the monks' accommodation—such as living and dining rooms, dormitory, chapel, and guest house—as well as to the community's source of support during the initial phase before the monastery was able to cater for its own needs. It was usually incumbent upon the abbey's aristocratic founder to provide these basic requirements: it was not the monks who came and cleared the forest and built the monastery and church; it was the benefactor who arranged the clearance and construction of the first buildings.

There were two possible approaches to this: either the benefactor erected stone monastic buildings prior to the arrival of the monks, or he provided for the construction of initial, temporary wooden structures and commissioned the erection of stone buildings thereafter or at the same time. As the wooden buildings had to accommodate monastic life until the completion of the final abbey they were usually situated somewhat apart from the site of the later complex so that the church services were not disturbed by the building noise and the monks were afforded a certain degree of detachment. These initial wooden buildings are only seldom identified during excavations because they were not located within the later monastery confines.

The founder abbey dispatched an experienced monk to inform the benefactor of the intended plan for the new monastery; this monk made all of the important decisions and monitored their implementation. This "instructor" advised the benefactor on the selection of the construction site, provided details of the monastery complex and the design of the buildings, supervised the building work, and in addition managed the regulated way of life in the new community.

The lay brothers had as little to do with the erection of the monastery buildings as the monks had with the clearing of the building site. Instead, existing sources indicate that the construction work was very much in the hands of a professional building team. Individual lay brothers who possessed the required skills were sometimes involved but this was the exception. The activities of the monks and lay brothers were usually restricted to the management and organization of the building work. As the not insubstantial building costs of the stone monastery buildings almost always exceeded the economic means of the recent foundations, such costs were usually borne by the monastery's founder.

The involvement of professional, secular building experts also explains why there are recognizable regional differences between Cistercian churches. While established specifications existed for the ground plan of the church and for the layout of the entire monastery complex, which were usually based on the mother house, their implementation was bound by the relevant material conditions on site as well as by regional traditions with regard to masonry, technique, building practices, and architectural styles.

Cistercian monks building a church, left exterior of the two-sided foundation panel from 1450, Maulbronn Monastery museum. The white robes of the working monks are an indication that this is clearly an idealization. Such activities were usually carried out by a professional team of builders, at the most with the occasional help of the lay brothers.

Regulations on Art and Architecture

Contrary to what is often assumed, the much-vaunted simplicity of the Cistercian churches is not due to the order's established building regulations. It was only the decoration of the church and not the architecture that was the subject of a few and, what's more, very general conditions. According to the order's first chronicle, the *Exordium parvum* (pre-1119), Cistercian buildings are prohibited from exhibiting any indications of *superbia* (pride, arrogance) and *superfluitas* (opulence). The general chapter resolution of 1123/24 also prohibited sculptures and images in churches and monastery rooms, with the exception of painted crosses. The reason for this ban was given as the fact that sculptures and paintings disturb and distract the monks' contemplation and thus threaten austerity and monastic solemnity. What was being referred to was primarily figural, three dimensional depictions and large images. This did not include book illumination, as commissioned by Abbot Stephen Harding in Cîteaux in the same year (the illumination of a manuscript of *Moralia in Job* by Gregory the Great). Bernhard of Clairvaux's text *Apologia ad Guillelmum*, in which the negative impact of sculpture in particular is portrayed in detail, also makes no mention of manuscript images. Only in 1149/50 did the general chapter also draw attention to the issue of monochrome initials and also

banned stained glass windows with images. High stone towers—the epitome of *superbia*—were explicitly forbidden in 1157.

The exclusion of figural sculptures on buildings, wall paintings, altar tables with reliefs or images of saints, and stained glass led to the Cistercians placing even more emphasis on the meticulous execution of the architecture within the entire monastery area. Long, vaulted dormitories and refectories, as well as ever larger, vaulted churches, met with no resistance, due to the

◄ **Le Thoronet, chapter house,** c. 1200.
▲ **Obazine, grisaille (grey monochrome) window,** 12th C.
Both the chapter house and the colorless but nevertheless elaborate glass window are representative of the austere beauty of early Cistercian art, which was based on the principle of *simplicitas*, simplicity.

Silvacane, west façade of the abbey church, completed c. 1230. This façade is an impressive example of the Cistercians' meticulous architectural execution. Few decorative elements in the porch and window areas and an impressive solidity are what characterize the building.

increasing number of monks and provided that the church displayed a simple ground plan with arcades and a clerestory, but not an elaborate gallery or triforium floor with its additional height. Wall paintings were replaced by a colorfully balanced interior that emphasized the composition of the wall with columns and responds (half-pillars). Such spatial designs are to be found not only in Cistercian churches, however. The Cistercian renunciation of sculpture is also related to a general rejection of figural decoration of capitals in early Gothic architecture. The rejection of stained glass was ultimately compensated for by a revival in costly stained glass windows.

The various regulations were relaxed during the 13th century. The general prohibition on images and sculptures in the church had already disappeared by 1220. Flooring comprising multi-colored tiles, often censured between 1205 and 1235, became widespread after 1240. The general chapter continued to issue a rebuke on occasion, repeated the old resolution, and sometimes issued a reminder that the established principle of *simplicitas* be followed, but the old bans were no longer implemented from the end of the 13th century. The Cistercian approach to images and (architectural) art no longer distinguished itself from contemporary attitudes.

The Monastery Economy and the Expansion of the Order

Within no time at all, the rapid boom, the proliferation of abbeys, and the resultant rapid expansion of the order had turned its initial ideals upside down. Having started out wanting to lead a life of strict asceticism detached from the world, by c. 1120 the Cistercians had become substantial landowners. Their refusal to do business in the conventional manner with tenants and paid workers brought them the approval of their contemporaries and increasing donations; however, the new methods of husbandry using the monastery's lay brothers led to immense cost savings and thus to a direct increase in wealth—which the Cistercians had in theory renounced. While they had initially turned down the possession of parish churches, villages, mills, and returns from interest, these sacrifices were offset in 1119 by the granting of exemption from the payment of tithes on goods produced themselves and, at the end of the 12th century, the lifting of ownership restrictions because they stood in the way of the benefactors' endowment practices. The organization of the monastery economy with granges as subordinate centers for remote monastery lands, where the lay brothers working there lived under the supervision of a "grange master," was in complete accordance with the rational justification for, and the functional implementation of, the procedures that had also become evident in the commemoration of the dead reform. The farmstead system was supplemented by urban settlements ("town yards"), which were responsible for the selling of goods in the markets. These bases, serving as merchant establishments, enabled some Cistercian monasteries to enter into wholesale and long distance trading, especially in wool, salt, or wine. Other monasteries carried out a trade such as tile production, or were involved in mining. Due to

▼ ▶ Ter Doest, granary, 13th C. This granary near Lissewege in Belgium is a good example of the Cistercians' farm building architecture, of which a number of other examples have survived (including at Froidmont and Maubuisson). With its ridge turret the barn could almost be seen as a Cistercian church. This barn aesthetic was the dominant design element of the Benedictine monastery church at Saint-Wandrille in the 20th C. (see p. 412).

their location in largely unpopulated areas, the Cistercians were often the owners of large areas of forest. They were therefore more frequently and more intensively involved in forestry than the Benedictine monks, which again provided a significant source of income. Wood was the most important raw material in medieval society, being essential for crafts, construction, and as fuel, and trading in wood was therefore more lucrative than the monasteries' traditional cultivation of grain and wine.

Together with cutting the costs of the commemoration of the dead, limiting hospitality, and reducing relief for the poor, the Cistercians' economic practices soon led to the increasing prosperity of their abbeys, most of which significantly outperformed religious houses with a traditional economy. Unlike these, however, the way remained barred for the Cistercians to invest their acquired wealth in elaborate construction projects and costly church decoration, as the semblance of *superfluitas* had to be avoided in accordance with the order's principles. The resultant contradictory situation of the wealthy ascetics in their exaggeratedly poor robes impaired the image and esteem of the Cistercians in the Late Middle Ages. Despite crises and significant problems—a decline in the willingness to make endowments, starkly reduced numbers of lay brothers from the 14th century on, and a decline in discipline—the order did not manage to achieve any radical reforms. It was only in the 17th century that the abbey of La Trappe initiated a serious attempt at reformation.

Clay tiles in Cistercian abbeys.
1, 2, 3: Buildwas Abbey, Wales; 4, 5, 6: Byland Abbey, England; 7, 8, 9: Rievaulx Abbey, England. Some of the Cistercian farmsteads specialized in the processing of clay and produced bricks, roofing tiles, and clay tiles. Largely fulfilling just their own requirements initially, the tiles and clay products were later distributed among other Cistercian abbeys and, ultimately, were even sold locally.

The Success of the Cistercians

With their propagation of a strictly ascetic life in solitude the Cistercians had their finger on the pulse of the spiritual ideas characterizing their founding era. The concept of finding a way back to a concentration on the true meaning of life through the spatial separation of communities and an emphasis on strict rules was as well received by their contemporaries as was the renunciation of liturgical pomp and excess. For the Cistercians and their followers simplicity of design was considered a sign of depth of devotion and the contraction of the church service as proof of the focused clarity and purity of prayer. Corresponding to the pattern of a typical reform debate, the renunciation of ostentation in the liturgy and in church decoration was backed by a call for greater and more genuine piety.

However, the Cistercians' way of life met with approval because it corresponded not only to the spiritual but also to the social concepts of its time. With the clear hierarchical segregation of the monks and lay brothers, the reality outside the abbey was reflected in the living and working arrangements inside. The religious community was no longer a world of its own, beyond social segregation, where the law of service to God sometimes forced a rethinking. Instead, anyone who entered the monastery remained in his familiar domain and served God according to his status and his abilities acquired in secular life. Only upper class laymen who deliberately chose the status of lay brother diverged from this arrangement, thereby also confirming its validity: the change of social class became an act of humility and one of renunciation.

Ultimately, the widespread proliferation of the Cistercians was only made possible by the clear structure of the order. The mother house's responsibility for its daughter houses created a system of direct dependency within the affiliation, though with distinct development prospects for newly founded monasteries. This arrangement provided security for benefactors and was therefore successful. Far more important, however, was the role model function of the Cistercian order's constitution for other monastery networks, with its manifesto, general chapter, and inspections. The systematic approach and the pragmatic rationality expressed in the order's constitution and structure, and which also characterized all other areas of monastery life, was what was so innovative about the Cistercian model and explains its paramount importance for the development of monastic orders.

Casamari, refectorium. For the Cistercians in Bernard's time, anything exceeding that expressly allowed by the rule was intemperance. That also applied to mealtimes. Regular fasting was a given. Even this aspect of the sought-after austerity, which, in addition to food, also applied to other requirements of *cura corporis* (bodily care: sleep, clothing, hygiene etc.) is considered to have contributed to the Cistercians' success.

Fontenay, forge waterfall. The Cistercians also developed a mastery of water-driven technology, which was important for every religious house. Diversions, drains, canals, underground pipes, waterways, and mills are to be found in numerous monasteries.

◄ **Dormitorium,** 15th-C. roof construction. The Cistercians adhered for a long time to communal sleeping quarters as prescribed by the Rule of St Benedict. Wooden partitions between the beds were introduced as of the 13th century and individual cells from the 15th century.

▶ **Interior of the church looking east.** The thrust of the long barrel vault in the nave is supported by the transverse barrel vaults in the side aisle spans. The lack of a clerestory in the nave gives greater emphasis to the windows above the choir arch and on the east wall.

▼ **The abbey complex from the east.** Left is the east wing of the monastery; right is the church with transept chapels and choir, which is the same height as the transept arms and significantly lower than the nave.

Fontenay, France

Fontenay, Clairvaux's second "daughter," was founded in 1119 in the Chastelun Forest northwest of Dijon, at the site of a hermitage belonging to Molesme Abbey, to which the Lords of Montbard, relatives of Bernard of Clairvaux, had assigned the neighboring lands. This monastery became the burial place for several noble families and for members of the ducal family. Its important economic position was based on its wealthy estates, where, in addition to wine, primarily high quality wool, and iron were produced and sold via the town yards in Dijon, Montbard, Tonnerre, Auxerre, and Autun. The abbey church is perhaps the best preserved example of the so-called Bernard Plan—a cruciform ground plan with a rectangular choir and transept chapel—the Burgundian version of which had pointed barrel vaults in the nave and transverse barrel vaults in the side aisles, low transept arms, and no clerestory. The more elaborate individual deviations of later constructions—two storied wall responds extending to the floor, spans divided by barrel vault supports, the use of pilaster strips (in addition to semicircular responds) and capitals—are indicative of construction having started c. 1130. The church was consecrated in 1147 by Pope Eugene III.

Noirlac, France

Following a difficult start, Noirlac Abbey in the Cher valley near Saint Amand, settled in 1136 by monks from Clairvaux, went on to enjoy steady progress. The construction of the abbey complex began in the middle of the 12th century with the eastern part of the church as well as the east and west wings of the abbey, was continued in the 13th century with the nave, the south wing of the abbey and the cloister galleries, and ended in the 14th century with the renovation of the east gallery. The abbey was fortified during the Hundred Years' War following occupation by English troops. Factional fighting in the 17th century led to damage that was repaired in 1724–26 during a general renovation of the complex. Following the Revolution, in 1820–86, the church and the abbey buildings served as a porcelain factory. Noirlac was acquired by the Département of Cher in 1909, and renovation and restoration work, starting in the 1950s, lasted until the 1980s.

Noirlac's church matches the Bernard Plan, with its cruciform-shape, rectangular choir and transept chapel but, in contrast to Fontenay, the pointed barrel vaulting planned initially was executed only in the choir. Although the choir is significantly lower, the transept arms are the same height as the nave and also have rib vaults. The nave has a two-zone elevation with clerestory windows and buttresses on the outside. Therefore, not only does Noirlac exhibit a more modern (Gothic) architectural design than the older Fontenay, it also has an elevation extended by the clerestory.

▼ **View from a hillside** to the northwest: the church and the abbey buildings restored in the 18th C.

▶ **View through the crossing** into the north arm of the transept, 2nd half of the 12th and beginning of the 13th century (vaulting).

◄ **Chapter house,** 2nd half of the 12th C.
▼ **Refectory,** 1st half of the 13th C., a two-aisled room with rib vaults and narrow central pillars. The window groups comprising two lancet windows with a circular window above them are a variation on the choir and front transept wall motif.

▲ **Church from the east.** The choir is much lower than the transept and nave. The openings in its east wall (three lancet windows with a circular, filled-in window above them) match those in the northern transept wall.

Fontfroide, France

◀ **Nave pillar** with a high pedestal and nave responds that end in consoles below the pedestal edge.

▶ **Nave** with view towards the choir.

▼ **The abbey complex from the east.**

The abbey founded in 1093 by the Viscount of Narbonne belonged to the Grandselve monastery network, which joined the Cistercian order in 1144/47. Fontfroide acquired great wealth and, as an abbey commissioned by the Pope to combat the Cathars, it also benefited from the land redistribution in Languedoc after the end of the Albigensian war in 1209–29. Nevertheless, with the exception of the Catalan monastery at Poblet, no significant daughter houses were founded. The abbey church, the construction of which began in

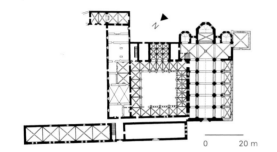

the second half of the 12th century, complies with the Cistercian principle of avoiding superfluous decoration but, despite its cruciform layout, does not match the Bernard Plan. The choir and exterior of the transept chapel end in polygonal apses, with small rectangular chapels between them. The steep proportions of the nave, with clerestory windows in the north only, are illuminated by a window group in the wall above the very low choir; the nave has a pointed barrel vault and there are quarter circle barrel vaults in the side aisles; the transept and crossing have rib vaults. The nave pillars on high, narrow pedestals with bulging base cornices are without parallel in other Cistercian churches.

◄ **Cloister arcades,** c. 1300, with fine foliage capitals.

▶ **Chapter house** (c. 1200). View from the east gallery of the cloister (c. 1300).

▼ **Cloister.** East and south galleries with courtyard.

Le Thoronet, Silvacane, Sénanque—France

▲ Le Thoronet. The monks' dormitorium with reconstructed pointed barrel vaults. In the middle, the opening for the staircase leading to the cloister.

▼ Le Thoronet. Cloister, dormitorium and church from the northwest. The frame of a belfry with its steep spire rises above the eastern span of the nave.

As with the Burgundian Fontenay, the three Provençal Cistercian abbeys are famous for the austere simplicity of their churches and abbey complexes. The lack of embellishment in the empty church buildings is a consequence of the complete avoidance of liturgical decoration and the purging restorations of the 19th century. All three abbeys, founded in the first half of the 12th century, remained small and without interregional significance. Their churches, constructed in the second half of the 12th century, have short naves with pointed barrel vaults and inclined quarter circle barrel vaults in the aisles.

The abbey of Le Thoronet was founded in 1136 by Ramón Berenguer IV, Count of Barcelona and Provence, and was transferred to its present day location in 1147. In a state of decline as of the 15th century, the abbey structures were in a precarious condition following its abolition. Prosper Mérimée's efforts to save Le Thoronet resulted in renovation by the architects Révoil (from 1878) and Formigé (post-1906), who restored the church and the abbey buildings, made additions and changes, and completed extensions. Stabilizing measures have continued to be necessary right up to recent times due to underground geological movement. The church begun c. 1160 has a nave extending through to the choir and low transept arms. The choir and the transept arm chapels end in semicircular apses, which are combined behind a straight wall on the exterior.

◄ Le Thoronet. Church interior looking east.

Le Thoronet

0   10 m

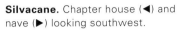

Silvacane. Chapter house (◄) and nave (►) looking southwest.

▼ **Sénanque.** The church and east wing of the abbey from the east.

Like Le Thoronet, Sénanque Abbey, founded in 1148 by Bishop Alfant of Avignon and whose ground plan displays almost identical east sections with semicircular apses, is a daughter house of Mazan (near Viviers), its construction having begun before 1160. Unlike Le Thoronet, however, Sénanque has transept arms as high as the nave and an imposing domical vault rises above the crossing.

In contrast, and in accordance with the Bernard Plan, Silvacane Abbey, which developed from a hermit settlement, has east sections with rectangular sanctuaries. Settled in 1147 by monks from Morimond, construction of the church was only begun later and lasted into the 13th century. As at Sénanque, the transept at Silvacane is the same height as the nave but the crossing has a rib vault instead of a dome.

The cloister and monastic buildings of all three abbeys have been preserved. They exhibit the same simple but architecturally high quality designs as the church (including a precisely worked ashlar assembly, dormitories with pointed barrel vaults, and hexagonal fountain houses). The only rooms that are elaborate in design are the chapter houses, which have rib vaulting on a variety of supports.

Royaumont, France

● Beauvais
Paris ●
Dijon ●
● Lyons
● Bordeaux
Toulouse ●

▲ **Baroque park.** View of the abbey's east wing.

▶▶ **Monks' refectory,** mid-13th C., a two-aisled Gothic hall design supported by narrow, round pillars.

▶ **Pulpit in the monks' refectory.**

Louis IX, later *St. Louis*, founded the abbey of Royaumont in 1228 near the royal castle at Asnières-sur-Oise under a provision in the will of his father Louis VIII; the monks came from Clairvaux. The abbey's generous endowments enabled rapid building progress such that the church could be consecrated as early as 1235. Several members of the royal family were buried there. In 1258 the number of monks was increased from 60 to 114 due to a further endowment from the King. The abbey was sold during the Revolution and the church torn down. Only the southern side aisle and the southern transept walls remained standing, adjoining the almost completely preserved but heavily restored 13th-century monastic buildings, as well as the northeast corner of the northern transept. The church, known through excavations within the ground plan, had a three-aisled nave with a west atrium, a three-aisled transept and an ambulatory with seven radiating chapels. The elevation had three zones with a triforium and was executed in the contemporary rayonnant design. This unusually elaborate arrangement for a Cistercian church corresponded to the layout and construction of the somewhat older abbey church at Longpont and three related buildings in northern France, and was therefore obviously not the result of royal intervention.

Ora et labora—a Day in the Life of a Monk c. 1200

The day begins in the middle of the night. The monks are woken by the ringing of a bell so that they can make their way to the church for the vigil (night watch). The dormitorium is dimly lit by a lamp that burns the whole night. So as to reach the church as soon as possible, the monks sleep fully clothed, both in summer and in winter. It is only the Cistercians, however, who also keep their outer garments on over their shirt or tunic. The *cucullus* (hood or cowl) is thrown on after getting up. In winter there are also leg warmers, stockings, boots, and padded cloaks for periods spent outside. Each monk makes his bed, which comprises a mat or a cloth-covered paillasse (straw mattress), one or two blankets and pillows, in the North also furs or feather-filled quilts. Anyone who needs to visit the latrines, which are behind the dormitorium, connected via a passageway angulated to prevent bad smells. The monks then all descend to the cloister. They wash their hands and their faces in the fountain house before entering the church via the transept porch and taking their places in the choir. The older monks sit in the back rows so that they have a good view of the younger monks and the novices in the front rows. The vigil begins with the Lord's Prayer and the profession of faith, which are followed by psalms and hymns; then come the readings from the Bible or the Church Fathers. There are hymns, psalm recitations and a prayer at the end. The vigil can take a long time on Feast Days, with particularly extensive readings. On such occasions the monks may then all go back to bed until dawn, or else this time is spent in prayer and meditation in the church.

Psalms are sung at morning prayer (matins) in particular. In many Benedictine monasteries matins is combined with a small procession in a chapel behind the chapter house, where an All Saints prayer is said, with prayers for the dead.

Thereafter it is time for the morning ablutions. The Rule of St. Benedict prescribes the regular washing of body and clothes. Hands and face are washed in the morning and before Mass, the hands also after using the latrine, before eating, and before working in the kitchen, the feet once a week and after barefoot processions. The monks are expected to comb their hair every morning. Among the Cistercians, reciprocal shaving, during which the hair is also washed and cut and the

Monk with a book: sculpture from the Dominican church in Neubrandenburg. As guardians of the true faith the Dominicans had a special affinity to books right from the outset, not least due to the scholarly background of their founder, Dominic.

In the monastery school. A novice is instructed by an older monk. The teaching of reading, writing, and other disciplines from the ancient canon of the Septem Artes Liberales largely took place in monastery schools until the High Middle Ages.

tonsure redone, takes place six or seven times a year, otherwise every two to three weeks. Bathing, frowned upon as a luxury, is allowed only after heavy physical labor or in the event of illness. Benedict of Aniane restricted bathing to a minimum and set Easter and Christmas as bathing times, but not all abbeys were as ascetic. Following their ablutions, in summer the monks can read in the cloister until the sun has risen and the bells summon them to prime, prayers during the first hours of the day. Prime is immediately followed by morning Mass and then by the daily gathering in the chapter house. The chapter serves to regulate both internal and external monastery affairs. It is led by the abbot or his deputy, the prior. First of all a chap-

Sénanque, former Cistercian abbey church. The monks gather for communal prayer in the church several times a day and even during the night. In many monastery churches there was a staircase leading directly from the dormitory to the church.

ter from the canon is read and displayed. Organizational matters are then discussed, such as the schedule for the celebration of Mass, readings, work in the kitchen, etc. The names of deceased monks and members of the order are then read out on the anniversary of their deaths, and the prayers to be repeated for them at vespers and matins are said. The "punishment chapter," where lapses are addressed, takes place at the end. Punishment can mean physical chastisement or confinement.

After the chapter and the nones (prayers said in mid-afternoon), the monks may then speak to one another. The cloister, otherwise a place of absolute silence, now reverberates with quiet but audible conversations. This is the time allocated to the day's work, the *opus manuum* (manual labor) and upcoming enterprises are discussed. During the rest of the day communication is by means of sign language, which all of the monks have to learn.

Even with the Cistercians, manual labor for the monks, who can read and write, seldom extends beyond work in the kitchen and garden. Instead, their efforts are required for the management of the monastery or for the copying of the texts needed for the church services. With the Cistercians, the monks who perform choir services are clearly segregated from

The community in the refectory. Scene from the life of St. Benedict by Antonio Bazzi, known as Sodoma, 1505–08, Abbey of Monte Oliveto Maggiore. The reader monk performs his duties in the pulpit above the dining monks.

the lay brothers, who are called upon to work in the fields and to perform other forms of physical labor. Unlike the monks, they do not attend the daily prayers in the church: they say their prayers out in the fields. It is only for morning praise and compline (last prayers of the day) that they take up their places in the church nave, in front of the rood screen separating the monks' choir from the lay brothers' area.

Work in the monastery is interrupted at regular intervals by the bells summoning the monks to the Liturgy of the Hours: at the third hour, i.e. 9.00 a.m. (terce), at midday (sext), in the afternoon (nones), and in the evening (vespers). Among the Benedictines there is also a second Mass, the "main Mass," while the Cistercians keep it to just one Mass per day. In summer, when the days are long, the main Mass is held in the morning, a meal is eaten after the sext—the first meal of the day—and the monks retire to the dormitory at midday to rest. They then eat again in the evening after vespers. In winter, when there is only one meal a day, the main Mass takes place after the *sext* and the monks and their grumbling stomachs have to wait until the nones before they are summoned to the next meal in the refectory. The range of food in the monastery is in no way modest but it is somewhat monotonous. The main meals usually comprise two cooked dishes, of which one might be poultry and the other fish. The other dishes are usually beans or other kinds of pulses, which constitute the staple food. Vegetables are also

Monks chopping wood. Miniature from Cîteaux: *Moralia in Job*, Gregory the Great, early 12th C. (Dijon, Bibliothèque municipale, Ms 170, fol 59).

served, especially cabbage in winter and fruit and salad in summer. Each monk receives, per day, a pound (half a kilo) of bread and about two thirds of a pint (a third of a liter) of wine, which is drunk diluted with water. During the meals a monk in the refectory's specially constructed, elevated pulpit reads from the lives of the saints, accounts of miracles, or the Holy Scriptures.

Vespers also includes a procession in the chapel behind the chapter house or at the altar of the saint who is to be celebrated the following day: following the Jewish tradition, the liturgical day begins the evening before. Processions through the cloister are held on all of the main Feast Days and on Sundays. Benedictine monks leave the monastery only on Palm Sunday and for Rogation processions, while the Cistercians never leave the monastery.

Before nightfall the monks gather in the cloister wing adjoining the church for the evening reading, the collation, named after the *Collationes* of Egyptian Desert Father John Cassian (end of the 4th century), a work very popular in monasteries. The day draws to an end in the church with compline, the prayer before going to bed. Following the usual psalms and prayers, the Lord's Prayer and the Creed, with which the day began are said together by the monks, who then go directly from the transept via the staircase to the dormitory, to enjoy their well earned rest.

S. Maria de Poblet, Spain

East gallery of the cloister, 13th C.

Poblet was the second Cistercian monastery, after Le Thoronet in Provence, founded by Count Ramón Berenguer IV of Barcelona. It was settled in 1151 by monks from Fontfroide and went on to become one of the order's most important monasteries. As the burial place for the kings of Catalonia–Aragón it was closely linked to the Crown—the abbot officiated as the royal alms administrator—and was therefore exempted from episcopal control. The royal tombs erected in the crossing by King Pere IV in the 14th century were destroyed following the dissolution of the monastery in 1835. Under Franco, up to 1952, the tombs were reconstructed, using the original fragments, as monuments to the monarchy.

As with the contemporary Spanish Cistercian monasteries Veruela and Fitero, the church, begun in 1166, had an ambulatory with radiating chapels. The elevation has two zones, with the high blind arches towering over the clerestory windows. The nave and transept have pointed barrel vaults, while the ambulatory, side aisles, and the crossing have rib vaults. Following the completion of the monastery buildings and the cloister in the 13th century, a row of chapels along the southern side aisle, an octagonal crossing tower with large tracery windows, and a monumental monastery gate framed by two robust towers, the Porta Reial, were erected in the 14th century.

◄ **Chapter house,** mid- to end of the 13th C.

▲ **Walled monastery complex from the southeast.** South of the church, with the crossing tower of the imposing baroque sacristy.

▼ **Restored monument with the royal tombs,** 2nd half of the 14th century and 1952.

The Cistercians   203

Stes. Creus, Spain

Founded in 1150 as a daughter house of Grandselve by the noble Montcada family, this Catalan monastery soon gained the support of aristocratic rulers as well. The construction work at Stes. Creus began after 1168 following two changes of location. The richly endowed abbey became a royal burial place temporarily with Pere III of Catalonia-Aragón (died 1285) but was superceded by Poblet in 1340. In 1297 Jaume II appointed the then abbot of Stes. Creus as royal chaplain and in 1319 entrusted him with selecting the prior for the newly founded military order of Montesa, which was under the authority of Stes. Creus. The church of the monastery, which was dissolved in 1835, became a parish church in 1843, while the buildings were accorded protected status in 1844. The church, most of which was built between 1174–1225, adheres to the Bernard Plan. The two zones of its elevation, with high clerestory windows and the transept and choir the same height as the nave, are characterized by solid, plain columns, robust walls, and the heavy edged rib vaults throughout the building. The monastery buildings were not completed until the 14th century (the crossing tower and a new cloister with elaborate tracery work were begun in 1313/14). Pere IV had the abbey fortified in 1376–78.

Monastery complex from the southwest, only about 19 miles (30 km) away from Poblet and set in the undulating hinterland of Tarragona.

Cloister courtyard looking east with the elegant tracery arcades of the east gallery. In the foreground the plainer, hexagonal fountain house from the first cloister, dating back to the early 13th C.

▲ **Church interior looking east.** The wide half-pillars on their step-shaped consoles are especially conspicuous.

▼ **Capitals and consoles from the cloister** with figural decoration, 1331–41, by the English master Reinard de Fonoll.

▲ **The tombs** in the crossing, of King Pere III (died 1285, front) and King Jaume II (died 1327, with his wife Blanca of Anjou, back) in their elaborately decorated, colored, tracery shrines.

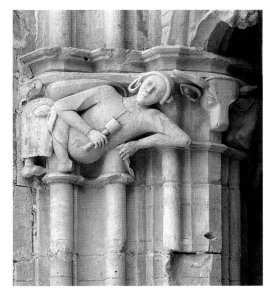

Rievaulx and Fountains Abbey, England

Founded in 1132 as the first abbey in the Cistercian "offensive" in northern England, Rievaulx soon established further houses. The stone buildings were erected under the third abbot, Aelred of Rievaulx (1147–67), the most famous English theologian of the 12th century, and the abbey extended to become one of the largest in the country. The church's side aisles had pointed vaulting, while the central nave had a wooden ceiling. In the early 13th century the church acquired a long, three-nave, vaulted choir with a precise eastern alignment, the tripartite outline of which, with its elaborately decorated columns and arcades, is highly unusual for Cistercian architecture.

Fountains Abbey, founded in 1132 by former Benedictine monks under Rievaulx's influence, became the wealthiest English monastery due to its trade in wool. After the first hall church burnt down, a new structure was begun in 1147: a long building extended during its construction to include three naves, as per the "Bernard plan." The three-nave choir was built in 1203 with diagonal crossings to the altars. Both abbeys were dissolved in 1538–39 and have remained as ruins ever since.

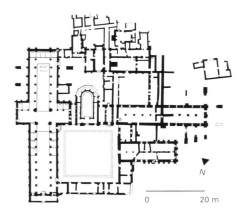

0   20 m

▲ **Rievaulx.** Central nave arcades of the choir, c.1220, from the north. The side aisles are missing, the vaults having collapsed.

▼ **Rievaulx.** Early Gothic choir and southern transept, built from 1215, from the southeast. In the foreground are the half-height remains of the former infirmary walls (later the abbot's house).

▲ **Fountains Abbey.** The church's diagonal eastern alignment (Chapel of the Nine Altars), early 13th C., and Late Gothic tower in the northern transept, 1495–1526, from the east.

◄ **Fountains Abbey.** The porch comprising several rows of columns, entrance to the refectory, c. 1180.

Alcobaça, Portugal

This abbey, situated halfway between Lisbon and Coimbra, was Portugal's most prominent Cistercian monastery, significant in religious, cultural, economic, and social terms, and boasting a very sophisticated architecture. Alcobaça was founded in 1153 by the general chapter in Cîteaux upon the request of the first King of Portugal, Alfonso I, and was settled by monks from Clairvaux. The abbey enjoyed a privileged position with the royal family and its abbots often came from within the ruler's circle. In the Late Middle Ages the abbot was a member of the royal council and the *cortes*, was the king's head chaplain and had statutory supervision of the military order of Avis and the Order of Christ as successors to the Templars.

Construction of the abbey began in 1178, but was interrupted for a while due to attacks by the Almohads. The monks' choir in the eastern nave spans was completed in 1223 and the consecration of the church took place in 1252: a monumental three-aisled hall church, with transept arms lower in the east and chapels as high as the aisles in the west, making the ground plan appear three-aisled, and an ambulatory with radiating chapels, the exterior of which is enclosed by a continuous wall. The ground plan is a copy of the church at Clairvaux erected in 1148–74, and orients itself to the latter's dimensions. The elevation differs from Clairvaux in the hall-like nave, without a clerestory and illuminated by the aisle windows only, a design of which no other Cistercian examples exist. The impression of monumentality is further emphasized by the height of the nave arcades and the pillar positioning, which is narrow in comparison to Clairvaux.

◀ **Burial place of the Portuguese kings** on the southern transept arm.

▶ **The church nave looking east.**

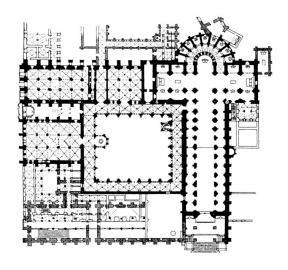

▼ **Fraternei.** The monks' living room with numerous pillars supporting rib vaults. The size of the church and of this room indicate that the monastery must once have accommodated many monks and indeed according to legend the largest number of monks at the abbey was 999.

◄ **Paradise.** View of the interior of the Early Gothic church's atrium, looking north.

► The Early Gothic **"Gentlemen's Refectory"** (monks' refectory), c.1220/30, an elegant, two-aisled room supported by round pillars of differing sizes.

▼ **The church and abbey from the west.** The abbey gate and lay brothers' refectory have been altered in modern times. Between the paradise in front of the west wall of the church and the gatehouse is the lay brothers' passageway, providing them with access to the church.

Maulbronn, Germany

This Morimond-affiliated abbey, established by the nobleman Walter von Lomersheim in Ecken-weiher in 1138, was transferred to Maulbronn in 1147. The emperors took on the role of abbey *Vogt* (governor/protector) as of 1156. Its expanding property made the abbey one of the largest and wealthiest in Württemberg. It was dissolved in 1537 with the onset of the Reformation. From 1556 the buildings housed a Protestant monastery school and it has been a Protestant seminary since 1806. Maulbronn is one of the best preserved Cistercian abbey complexes and, in addition to the

monastery, it also comprises the farm buildings and the abbey wall with its gate and towers. The church, begun soon after 1147 (consecrated 1178), has a basilica-like nave, which was once flat-roofed, and a vaulted eastern part with an unusual design. There are three transept chapels to the side of the rectangular choir but the transept arms themselves are merely low, narrow passageways with unused empty spaces above them, in order to give the exterior of the church a familiar appearance. The large tracery window in the choir was built in 1340/50; the nave vaulting and the

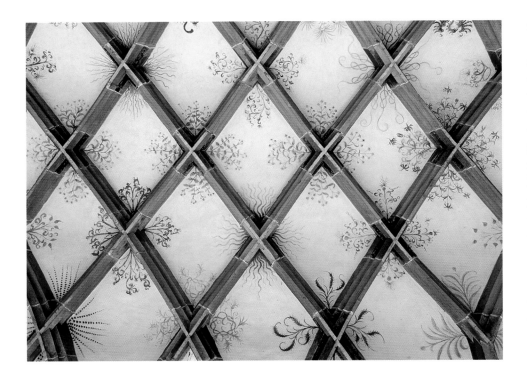

row of chapels on the southern side aisle date to 1424. The stone rood screen with round archways, dating to 1170/78, which separates the lay brothers' section of the nave from the monks' choir in the four eastern spans, is one of the very few surviving examples of its kind. While the east wing of the abbey (chapter house, parlatorium, living room, and above it the monks' dormitory) was renovated after 1300, the west wing with the cellar and the lay brothers' refectory dates to the period c. 1200/10 (the lay brothers' dormitory above it was altered in the 19th century). Of particular historical and architectural significance are the church atrium (paradise) and the southern cloister wing with its characteristic Early Gothic design, both erected c. 1210/20: the ribs of the vaults were mounted on supports and divided with whorls, with their capitals always indicating the impost of the arch, which is the reason why their heights vary.

▲▲ **Reticulated vaulting in the parlatorium,** 1493.

▲ **Madonna with Child Enthroned,** c. 1300.

▶ **Church interior looking east** with the large tracery window on the east wall of the choir, the nave vaulting from 1424, the rood screen dominated by a Late Gothic crucifix, and two baldachins by the nave pillars, under which altars used to be located.

▶▶ **South wing of the cloister** with the Early Gothic rib vaults mounted on numerous supports.

Bebenhausen, Germany

Founded c. 1185 by the Count Palatine of Tübingen as a Premonstratensian monastery, then occupied by Cistercians from Schönau (daughter house of Eberbach) in 1191, the abbey was abolished during the Reformation, in 1535. From then on it served, amongst other things, as a Protestant monastery school, hunting lodge, and seat of the regional parliament; today it is used by forestry management. With the exception of the nave, torn down in 1566–68 (the three east spans were rebuilt using Late Gothic masonry), the abbey complex with its walls and towers has survived in its entirety. The basilica-like church with its rectangular choir and narrow transept chapels was consecrated in 1228. The choir acquired a large tracery window c. 1335/40, the filigree tower with the open work spire was erected over the crossing in 1407–09, and the reticulated vaulting in the east sections followed in 1466/1522. The early 13th-century abbey buildings were modernized with the rebuilding of the refectory (c. 1340) and the cloister (end of the 15th century).

Cloister court yard and church with shortened, renovated nave (16th C.), south transept arm, and crossing tower.

▼ **Enclosed abbey complex.** Archaeological investigations have revealed that the abbey, situated on an open plateau, encompasses the site of an older village settlement with a parish church. The elevated location must therefore have been seen as beneficial, because otherwise the newly built abbey would have been sited at the bottom of the valley.

▲▲ The west wing, rebuilt in 1500/30 with the cloister (c. 1500), which used to be glazed, and the large timbered gable on the upper floor, dating from the hunting lodge era.

▲ The chapter house (c. 1225), with rib vaults on four round pillars; in the place of a capital there is a wreath of individual sepal capitals on short, collared, truncated pillars.

Fountain Houses— the Significance of Water

Since time immemorial, places where water gushes from the ground or from rock faces have not merely been valuable for the usefulness of the water but have been considered holy, as sources of life, for which a higher being is to be thanked. Spring water has always been of special value compared to water from other sources. Often "a healing center (hot springs, baths, etc)" developed "at the holy site of the spring," or else a form of water-related architecture served the cult-like veneration of the spring. Archaeological finds have confirmed this as fact for periods going back 8000 to 10,000 years.

Traveling forward several periods in history, to ancient Roman Nîmes, we find an elaborate complex also dedicated to the veneration of the nymphs arising around the Celtic holy site of Nemausus at the foot of Mont Cavalier, evidenced today by the so-called Temple of Diana from the early 2nd century. The Temple of Diana was converted into a nunnery in the early Middle Ages.

Such privileged proximity to fresh water as enjoyed by the nuns at Nîmes was an exception for religious houses. Most had to make do initially with a bucket well and a basic raising technique. In some places even a decent, marble water trough and a properly functioning hoisting mechanism suspended in a tripod frame was a rarity. However, a bucket well did not provide cascading, bubbling water. Where fresh water was not directly available great efforts were undertaken to procure it by means of pipes. The Romans were masters of aquifer systems, sometimes covering considerable distances. The benefits of their aqueducts, which were significant engineering achievements, continued into the Middle Ages. The monasteries also played a significant role in the maintenance and transmission of this tradition.

The Athos monastery Chilandar, the ciborium fountain. The outer structure, called a ciborium, served the purpose of visual and sacral elevation, as with a dais. With its freestanding fountain houses, Athos is reminiscent of the fountains in the atria of the early Christian basilicas.

The Christian fountain houses had their Biblical example in the "bronze sea," a water vessel in the outer courtyard of the Temple of Solomon, which was the inspiration for a number of early Christian basilicas in the 4th century. There too the fountain was built in the outer courtyard, often referred to as a paradise. It was used for ritual hand washing, thus being sacralized from the outset, and was linked with the notion of the fountain of life (*fons vitae*). Its exterior design was characterized by an upper section comprising a small dome supported by pillars. A number of this type of fountain have been preserved in the Athos monasteries. From such ciborium fountains it took only a small architectural change, namely the enlargement of the pillars' radius, to achieve the fountain pavilion a design that

Vallmagne, a former Cistercian abbey. Only the arcade gallery remains of the 13th-century fountain house. The rebuilt ribs of the collapsed vaulting today serve as supports for a graceful leafy structure.

◄ Monreale, cathedral. The fountain in the middle of the cloister has a fountain pillar decorated with a zigzag pattern and a bud-like crown above the shallow circular basin. Like the cloister pillars, the arcade pillars around the fountain also display unusually elaborate mosaic and sculptural decoration.

is still to be found in many monasteries. The Late Romanesque and Gothic fountain houses shown here differ greatly in their design. Polygonal ground plans were predominant in this era but there were also circular—in Magdeburg (p. 234) and Maulbronn (only the Late Romanesque base)—and square outlines. The fountain houses became ever more opulent in the Gothic era. Chapels such as that at Maulbronn are no exception; the fountain chapel at Heiligenkreuz has even more magnificent windows which were in fact glazed at an early stage; the Portuguese fountain houses at Alcobaça and Batalha (see p. 324) truly deserve to be called "water temples." The shape and size of the fountains also vary widely. The large three basin fountain at Poblet is still preserved

in its entirety; many others are reconstructions or later models. It is not certain whether the fountains were originally reserved solely for ritual washing but this is unlikely. The fact that access to the fountains was from the refectory wing of the cloister was also for practical reasons. At least the washing of hands and face before meal times took place there. Separate basins and tubs were available for the washing of feet and for shaving, however, and were located in special washrooms for this purpose (lavatoria). Unfortunately the regulations relating to washing and to bodily hygiene in the body of rules (Consuetudines) are not particularly detailed or precise with regard to the places where these practices were carried out.

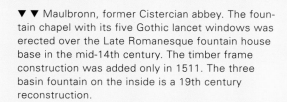

▼▼ Maulbronn, former Cistercian abbey. The fountain chapel with its five Gothic lancet windows was erected over the Late Romanesque fountain house base in the mid-14th century. The timber frame construction was added only in 1511. The three basin fountain on the inside is a 19th century reconstruction.

▲ Poblet, former Cistercian monastery. The fountain house of the Catalan royal monastery still houses the original fountain with three basins, the bubbling water a joy to both eye and ear.

Eberbach, Germany

Interior of the abbey church. View from the crossing through the nave to the west.

In 1136, following an encounter with Bernard of Clairvaux, Archbishop Adalbert I of Mainz founded a Cistercian abbey in Eberbach in Rheingau, at the site of a priory of canons regular he had previously established. The first monks came from Clairvaux. The abbey soon grew into a large community, itself founding daughter houses (including Otterberg and Arnsburg/Wetterau). A series of nunneries in the region, as well as town yards in Cologne and Mainz where its wine was sold, belonged to Eberbach. In 1190/1220 the Eberbach monk Konrad compiled an extensive

▶ **The abbey church from the southeast** with the baroque ridge turret over the crossing and the row of chapels built into the south side aisle after 1313.

▼ **The monks' dormitory** on the upper floor of the east wing, moved to the north and vaulted in the mid-13th century. To the right of the central pillars are the stairs leading up to the dormitory from the east wing of the cloister. The console blocks between the windows are the remains of the individual cells which were added in 1501.

history of the order (*Exordium magnum*). Following the Peasant Wars (1525) and the Swedish occupation in the Thirty Years' War (1631), to which the abbey library fell victim, Eberbach enjoyed a period of renewed prosperity in the 18th century. The former lay brothers' wing was converted into a baroque abbot's residence based on plans by Ludwig Dientzenhofer, the refectory was renovated, and a baroque garden with an orangery was created. Following its dissolution in 1803 the monastery served as a psychiatric institution 1813–49 and as a prison until 1912. It has accommodated a government-owned vineyard since then. A succession of restorations since 1929 have freed the church and abbey buildings of later alterations and additions.

The church is an elongated basilica with groin vaults, a rectangular choir, and three conspicuously low and straight closed chapels per transept arm. Construction was begun before 1160, it was consecrated in 1186, and completed c. 1200. With the exception of baroque alterations and the destruction of the south and east wings of the cloister after 1803, almost all of the medieval abbey buildings have been preserved. Eberbach is therefore one of the best examples of a Cistercian abbey complex dating largely from the 12th and 13th centuries.

Chorin, Germany

The abbey founded in 1258 by the Margrave of Brandenburg on an island in Lake Parstein was transferred to its present location in 1266/73. As the burial place for a line of the Askanian dynasty it acquired extensive lands and was located within an almost self-contained abbey domain. Secularized in 1539 with the onset of the Reformation, Chorin became an office of the elector. The Thirty Years' War and the changes in use led to the church falling into disrepair and to the abbey buildings being torn down. Its rediscovery as a romantic ruin by Karl Friedrich Schinkel at the start of the 19th century

ensured the survival of the complex, which has since undergone several phases of systematic restoration, excavation, and survey. Between 1861 and 1990 it housed a forestry management office.

Begun prior to 1273, the main sections of the church and abbey complex had been erected by the end of the 13th century; the nave was completed at the start of the 14th century. Despite the loss of the church vaulting, the southern side aisle, the transept chapel, and the south wing of the cloister with the refectory, and calefactorium, the abbey gives the impression of a self-contained complex that, with the guest house (in front of the abbey gate) and the kitchen, has two buildings that have not usually survived elsewhere. The ground plan and style of the church (elongated, vaulted basilica with a double-story transept chapel and a tripartite façade supported by substantial buttresses) are based on the mother house at Lehnin, although the styles are much more refined here than at Lehnin.

Its elegant, balanced proportions, the elaborate west façade, and the abbey buildings with the different types of tracery work on the decorative gable make Chorin a masterpiece of High Gothic brick architecture.

▶ **East wing of the cloister** with the door to the church.

▶▶ **The "Princes' Room" in the west wing,** once a heated living room for the lay brothers (with doors to the lay brothers' refectory and cloister) as well as a connecting room to the church for lay visitors (west façade portal, door to church).

Abbey from the south with the guest house ("brewhouse"), the west wing of the cloister, the south side of the church, and the east wing of the cloister.

Nave of the church looking east. The high, narrow, and very low reaching windows in the choir polygon give the space a sense of both depth and height.

▶ **West façade.** With its narrow lancet windows and apertures, divided into the lower side sections and a higher middle section, which is framed by substantial tower-like buttresses, the west façade is as splendid in style as it is harmonic in its proportions.

Staffarda, Italy

Staffarda Abbey was founded south of Turin in 1135 by the Marchese of Saluzzo and settled by monks from Tiglieto, a daughter house of La Ferté. The abbey's extensive lands, acquired through endowments from the local nobility, extended as far as the gates of Turin. It was the burial place of the marchesi of Saluzzo and the focal point of their regime. The church was begun in the middle of the 12th century and completed c. 1200. It does not display any typical Cistercian features at all. A short, three-aisled basilica-like nave adjoins a non-protruding transept, which is followed by a straight choir bay and three semicircular apses with a vaulted front bay. The nave and the choir have heavy, banded rib vaults and the transept

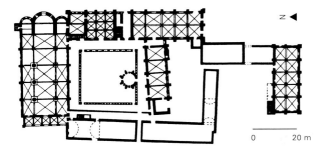

▲ **Abbey church.** Interior view to the east.

▼ **Abbey from the east** with its tall campanile.

arms are barrel vaulted. Both the exterior with its brickwork and arched friezes on the choir, transept arms, and apses, and the interior with its arches of alternating color, from the bricks and lighter ashlars, and robust pillars with voluminous semicircular responds are indicative of 12th–century Piedmontese-Lombard architectural style. Neither the position nor the height of the four story tower erected in the Late Middle Ages above the front bay of the southern side apse correspond to Cistercian building practices. Following the building of the church, the abbey buildings, most of which survive, were erected on the southern side of the church in the 13th century.

▲ **Cloister courtyard** with a view of the southern transept arm, tower, and east wing of the abbey.

◄ **Church façade** with the western atrium.

Fossanova, Italy

This abbey, founded in 1135 by Pope Innocent II through the conversion of an older Benedictine monastery, was the most important Cistercian monastery in Italy. The name (which means "New Ditch") refers to a system of canals for draining the marshes around the abbey, situated northeast of Terracina. The first monks came from Hautecombe (Savoy), a daughter house of Clairvaux. Gerard, the first abbot of Fossanova, was elected abbot of Clairvaux in 1170. His successor was Gottfried of Auxerre, Bernard of Clairvaux's secretary and biographer. In the 12th and 13th centuries the connections with France were just as close as those with the emperors and popes. Thomas Aquinas died at Fossanova in 1274. The abbey came into its own in the 15th century but was dissolved in 1810. Conventual Franciscans have been living at Fossanova since 1936.

The ground plan of the abbey church, begun prior to 1172/73, adheres to the Bernard Plan. The elevation—nave arcades with lintels, narrow, pointed arch-like clerestory windows, groin vaults with supports, and the use of cornices for height differentiation—closely resembles the primary abbey at Pontigny (completed in 1160/70), but has an additional opening to the attic above the side aisles. The individual elements—semicircular responds, capitals, cornices around the responds, and rectangular span divisions—are very reminiscent of 12th-century Burgundian structures and are therefore indicative of the involvement of Burgundian stonemasons. The cloister and the abbey buildings of the later 12th century and early 13th century have survived almost in their entirety.

◀ **South wing of the cloister,** c. 1200. Local elements such as the decorated double columns, popular in central and southern Italy, were combined with Early Gothic styles from France (arcades and banded arch shapes, bud-style capitals).

▼ **Abbey church from the northwest** (consecrated 1208). The elaborate style with the Gothic rose window and the two story, stone crossing tower with its lantern are what make Fossanova stand out from other Cistercian churches.

▲ **The monks' refectory,** c. 1170/80, with the pulpit on the right. The inclined, timbered ceiling is supported by floating arches connected to the walls by means of collared, truncated columns.

▼ **The nave wall,** end of the 12th C.

Casamari, Italy

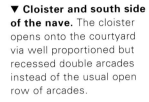

▶ **Church and abbey** in the Campanian countryside.

▼ **Cloister and south side of the nave.** The cloister opens onto the courtyard via well proportioned but recessed double arcades instead of the usual open row of arcades.

Like Fossanova, Casamari, in Campagna, was derived from a Benedictine abbey that Pope Eugene III assigned to the Cistercians in 1151. In accordance with Cistercian custom the Pope dedicated the existing church to the Mother of God and reconsecrated it. Thereafter the abbey's possessions increased dramatically as a result of endowments from popes, emperors, and kings of Sicily. The rebuilding of the church and abbey buildings commissioned by Pope Innocent III began in 1203, and was completed under Honorius III, who consecrated them in 1217. The abbey prospered between 1430 and 1850. Since 1929 it has been a

◄ **East gallery of the cloister** with the openings to the chapter house.

▼ **Chapter house** with elegant rib vaults on pillars formed from a cluster of mounts, 1st half of the 13th C.

self-contained congregation within the Cistercian order, of which 19 other monasteries, notably in Italy and Eritrea, also form part. Like the closely related building at Fossanova, the abbey church, begun in 1203 and built quickly and uniformly, adheres to the Bernard Plan but supplements it with open chapel spaces on the west side of the transepts, which therefore appear as three-aisled on the ground plan. The elevation corresponds to that of Fossanova with the exception of the lower nave arcades and the use of rib vaults. The cloister and the abbey buildings have also been preserved, in addition to the church and its western atrium.

The Premonstratensians

Norbert receives the Rule from St. Augustine. Norbert of Xanten (c. 1080/85–1134), founder of the Premonstratensian order, gave his newly founded order a canonical constitution based on the Rule of St. Augustine. Medieval book illumination (Munich, Bayerische Staatsbibliothek).

Brandenburg, cathedral, gable cupboard. The Brandenburg cathedral priory was settled by Premonstratensians around the middle of the 12th century. This gable cupboard (c. 1300), part of the Gothic furnishings, was used to store liturgical robes, amongst other things.

Like the Cistercians, Carthusians, canons regular, and others, the Premonstratensians derived from a movement of spiritual renewal based on poverty and asceticism. Their origins, however, lie not in the "escapism" of established monks or clerics, but in the public preaching activities of their founder, Norbert of Xanten. His call for spiritual change and a life in emulation of Christ was aimed at both clerics and laymen and at women as well as men.

Norbert, a canon at the Xanten priory church, was ordained as a priest in 1115 following a conversion experience and thereafter tried a number of spiritual lifestyles: he lived for a while in the reformed Benedictine abbey at Siegburg, in the canons regular priory at Klosterrath, and as a hermit in Xanten. It was there that he began to give penitential sermons. In 1118 he gave up his possessions and his canonry, and, with papal approval, began a life as a wandering preacher moving between northern France and the Lower Rhine. This erratic, migrant life met with the displeasure of the Church, however, and so Pope Calixtus II instructed the bishop of Laon to assign Norbert a monastery where he could settle down. In 1120 Prémontré was founded in the forest of Coucy, west of Laon, where, at the end of 1121, a community numbering some 40 clerics and lay brothers, men and women, took their vows. As a former canon Norbert gave his foundation a canonical constitution based on the Rule of St. Augustine and introduced living practices according to the model of the *Ordo monasterii*, with the strict silence, abstinence from meat, and manual labor, with which he was familiar from Klosterrath. Other than for himself personally, sermons and preaching did not initially play any role in the monastery, which was primarily intended to enable its members to lead an exemplary spiritual life.

Within a few years Norbert was assigned a series of properties for the foundation of monasteries (Viviers near Soissons; Floreffe near Namur; Cappenberg and Varlar in Westphalia; Ilbenstadt in Wetterau), as well as older priory churches to be reformed following the Prémontré example (Saint-Martin in Laon; St. Michael in Antwerp). In 1126 he had the Premonstratensian way of life and the possessions of Prémontré and the other priories acknowledged by Pope Honorius II. In the same year, however, he implemented a complete change in his reform strategy. He applied for the office of bishop and was made archbishop of Magdeburg. The preacher of reform "from below" thus became a churchman who endeavored to implement the lifestyle he advocated "from above."

Development and Expansion of the Order

Norbert's departure left his supporters disillusioned and his priory network without a leader or a written basis for their way of life. It was only from 1128 that he appointed abbots in the individual monasteries. His pupil Hugo of Fosse became abbot of Prémontré and immediately set about consolidating the network, which was threatened with disintegration. He ensured the compilation of written statutes based on the *Consuetudines* of Springiersbach-Klosterrath and, in a long drawn out process, converted the monastery network into an order based on the Cistercian example. In addition to literal borrowings from the *Carta caritatis*, the order's constitution introduced the principle of affiliation as well as the annual general chapter. The choir prayer of the *Ordo monasterii*, which was so significant at Springiersbach-Klosterrath and which was adopted by Norbert, but which was not consistent with the Roman Rite, was adapted to the customs of other canons regular following papal intervention.

The priories that were reformed or newly founded by Norbert in Magdeburg (Liebfrauen, Gottesgnaden) and the cathedral priories of the dioceses of Havelberg, Brandenburg and Ratzeburg, whose bishoprics were

Brandenburg, cathedral, triumphal cross (◄) and chapter house (▲). The chapter house is Gothic, while the triumphal cross dates from 1426; the other furnishings (altars, retables, etc) are largely Late Gothic. Only in the "Painted Chapel" have the remains of the earlier wall paintings (c. 1235) survived.

occupied by his pupils, ensured the expansion of the Premonstratensians in the east of the German Empire (Leitzkau, Jerichow, Gramzow) and beyond. These priories, however, followed less ascetic living practices, ones similar to those of the old canons regular (*Ordo antiquus*), and also retained local liturgical customs. In the eastern missionary areas, where the organization of parishes was still being developed, preaching was of particular importance. While it was only in exceptional cases that the Premonstratensians in the west carried out parish duties themselves in the churches with which they were endowed in the 12th century, in the east this involvement at the parish level made them an expedient alternative to monks or secular canons. Thus the founding of a Premonstratensian priory gave the benefactor not only a monastery-like priory,

Ratzeburg, cathedral, 1160/70–1215/20. The majority of the approximately 500 Premonstratensian monasteries date from the Romanesque period (in Germany up to 1250). Despite all of the destruction, important buildings such as the cathedrals at Brandenburg, Havelberg, and Ratzeburg have survived, in addition to numerous other priory churches. The cruciform basilica at Ratzeburg has an imposing west tower flanked by transept-like buildings. This arrangement, like the gracefully structured gable, are common features of Gothic brickwork.

▲ ▲ **Cappenberg, former priory church of St. Johannes,** former Premonstratensian priory founded in 1122 by Count Gottfried von Cappenberg. The count, following a radical renunciation of his previous lifestyle, joined forces with St. Norbert of Xanten and converted his castle into a monastery. With the exception of the Gothic vaulting, the present day parish church still retains its original Romanesque style.

▶ **Choir stalls,** 1509 and 1520, the greatest extravagance in the former Cappenberg priory church. Drolleries with depictions of devilish grimaces, hobgoblins, dragons, etc. and themes from the story of salvation combine to impart the message that man has to resist the evil in this world in its many forms.

▼ **Three apostles,** wall painting, c. 1170/80, Knechtsteden, former Premonstratensian abbey church. In 1801/02 the Knechtsteden monks fled from Napoleon's troops; the abbey was secularized during this period, as were many others.

but also clerics ordained as priests who could be deployed as parish priests, of which the newly Christianized regions were especially in need. Accordingly, the Premonstratensian expansion took place primarily in areas where parish structures were still to be established or expanded, such as in Bohemia (Strahov near Prague, Tepl), Hungary (Jászó, Csorna), Poland (Breslau/Wroclaw, Hedbow), Scandinavia (Børglum, Tommarp), in the Baltic States (the Riga chapter), and in the areas of the Spanish *Repoblación*, i.e. repopulation after the reconquest (La Vid/diocese of Burgos, Retuerta/diocese of Valladolid, and their daughter houses). In addition to their original territory in northern France, the Premonstratensians expanded in Flanders, Brabant, the Rhineland, and in Saarland in particular (including Knechtsteden, Arnstein/Lahn, Wadgassen), where their numbers were also increased by monasteries from the Springiersbach network, which disintegrated early on (including Steinfeld/Eifel). Important priories were also founded in southern Germany 1130–40 (Ursberg, Schäftlarn, Rot a. d. Rot, Steingaden, Obermarchtal, Windberg). The expansion of the order had largely been concluded by c. 1200. The significant geographic fragmentation led to the arrangement of the order into provinces, "Circaria," which held their own chapter, resulting in the general chapter already having lost its relevance by the 13th century.

Premonstratensian Characteristics

Unlike other reform networks of the 11th and 12th centuries that viewed the inclusion of nunneries with a great deal of skepticism, all early Premonstratensian priories were originally double priories comprising a male and a female community. This was due to the influence of Norbert of Xanten, who had always expressly addressed himself to women as well. The segregation of the communities decreed in 1140 was a result of the ban on communal choir prayer pronounced by the Second Lateran Council in 1139, and not disciplinary difficulties. Over the decades that followed, many monasteries split into two separate but neighboring priories, which usually, although not always, meant the evacuation of the female community. However, there were also cases such as Wadgassen, where double monasteries existed until well into the 13th century. As a result of the separation from the women and the stark decline in the numbers of lay brothers after 1200, the Premonstratensian priories for men became solely cleric and priest monasteries.

Nothing is known about the physical organization of the double priories since, with the exception of a number of churches, no monastery buildings from the early era have survived. Most of the Premonstratensian churches exhibit regional styles. There were both large, unvaulted church structures with simple pillar shapes (Cappenberg) and impressive buildings with twin tower west façades (Ilbenstadt), located next to each other from the outset, at times even commissioned by the same benefactor (Count von Cappenberg). Architectural features specific to the order are not apparent. Also, the much postulated adoption of Cistercian building styles, in particular the similarity of the ground plan to the Bernard Plan, is rather a result of the endeavor to build chapels with altars than a deliberate imitation of Clairvaux.

▼ **Two story Romanesque cloister** with the double story fountain house in the east wing, 1129–60.

▲ **Interior of the fountain house.** Fountain houses with a circular ground plan were the exception (others only at Clairvaux and Maulbronn).

Magdeburg, Germany

Following his appointment as archbishop of Magdeburg (1126–34), Norbert of Xanten, the founder of the Premonstratensian order, transformed the Liebfrauen monastery into the first eastern German Premonstratensian priory by converting the collegiate priory set up in 1017/18 into a canons regular priory adhering to the Premonstratensian Rule. The priory was Protestant from 1591 until its abolition in 1832 and incorporated a school as of 1698. In the reconstruction following its destruction during the war, in 1944/45, the monastery rooms were set up as an art museum and the church as a concert hall.

The church is a basilica erected in the late 11th century with a transept and a long choir with an apse. There is a crypt underneath the choir. The exterior of the church is dominated by the two round stair towers flanking the high west tower, which was probably only erected after 1129. The vaulting comprises the superimposed pointed-arch blind arcades and the shield arches of the 1188/1222 nave and transept walls which support the Early Gothic rib vaults. Of the monastery buildings erected in the 12th century only the cloister, the "High Column Chapel" to the north of the choir, and the refectory in the north wing survive.

▼ **Church from the southeast.** The group of towers to the west are well-endowed with windows.

▶ **Crypt under the choir,** 2nd half of the 11th C. Columns with cushion capitals support the groin vaults with their pronounced transverse arches.

Jerichow, Germany

The Premonstratensian priory of St. Marien and St. Nikolai was founded in 1144 by Count Hartwig von Stade and transferred to undeveloped land outside the town in 1148/49. Following secularization in 1552 the priory and its lands became a Brandenburg demesne, becoming agricultural cooperative property after 1945. The monastery buildings were cleared out 1964–90, subjected to archaeological survey from 1984 and then restored. The church, used and redecorated in baroque style by the reformed community as of 1685, underwent exemplary refurbishment by Ferdinand von Quast in 1853–56 and was restored to its original design. The church, erected in the 2nd half of the 12th century, is one of the most important brick buildings in Germany. The design and features—the elevated choir tribune over the crypt, which is open to the nave, round pillars with trapezium-shaped capitals—display the influence of northern Italian architecture. The three-aisled brick basilica has a transept and a square choir with an apse which is flanked by narrower side choirs, and a high west section, the wider middle part of which

Capital from the "summer refectory," c. 1230.

protrudes slightly from the towers to the side. With the exception of the groin vaults of the crypt under the choir and the crossing, all areas of the building are flat-roofed. With the exception of the west wing of the priory and the church-side cloister wing, the monastery buildings and the cloister, erected from the end of the 12th century to the middle of the 13th century to the south of the church, have survived.

◀ **Church interior looking east** with a view of the choir tribune and the crypt beneath it, 2nd half of the 12th C. The warm red color of the brickwork contrasts with the pale sandstone imposts of the pillars and the white plastered wall surfaces (the circular areas between the arches, the undersides of the arcade lintels, the apse dome).

▼ **The church from the northwest,** dominated by the high, west section crowned by the towers; the open stories date from the middle of the 13th century, the narrow spires from the 15th century.

▼ **The "summer refectory,"** in the south wing of the monastery, c. 1230: the freestanding columns of the two-aisled room with sculptured chalice block capitals.

▲ The church and priory buildings. The south and west wings of the priory are directly adjoining, with stepped gables at right angles.

▼ West wing of the cloister. The west wing was the last section of the priory complex to be erected, in the last quarter of the 13th C.

Havelberg, Germany

Following the Slav uprising of 983, the bishops of the diocese of Havelberg, founded in the 10th century, resided in Magdeburg. The construction of the Romanesque cathedral was begun c. 1150 at the same time as the now Premonstratensian cathedral priory and was consecrated in 1170. Alterations in the Gothic style took place from the end of the 13th century through to c. 1330; the rood screen was added after 1396. In 1506 the Premonstratensian priory was converted to a secular chapter and in 1561 to a Protestant cathedral priory, which existed until 1819. The restoration work of 1885–90 removed the baroque elements from the interior and uncovered the brickwork structure. In 1907/08 the height of the west block was raised with the addition of a belfry floor with five open arcades, and the present day west porch was added. The Romanesque cathedral was a long, flat-roofed basilica with no transept and with two double storey chapels on each side of the choir and at the top of the west block, protruding over the nave exit. The apse was replaced with a choir polygon during the Gothic conversion, while the nave was heightened and rib vaulted using brick wall responds that were linked via pointed-arch blind arcades. Significant sections of the medieval church decoration have also been preserved in addition to the monastery buildings.

◄ **Gothic triumphal cross group in the nave,** 1270/80.

▼ **Relief from the south side of the rood screen:** the Flagellation of Christ, c. 1400.

▼▼ **Rood screen** with side archways, lay altar and (above) pulpit, elaborately decorated with reliefs and statues of the saints (apostle cycle).

VI

The Military Orders

The Pilgrimage to Jerusalem and the Crusades

Christ as head of the Crusader army, early 14th C. (London, British Library, Ms. Roy. 19BXV, fol. 37). Theologians developed a new theory on violence in the 11th century—with a view to promoting the Crusades as an enterprise according to God's will. When Pope Urban traveled through France in 1095/96 with a summons to join the Crusade he made reference to Christ's own summons: "If any man come after me, let him deny himself, and take up his cross, and follow me."

Since its conversion to a Christian city under Emperor Constantine (306–37) Jerusalem had been the paramount, noblest of destinations for Christian pilgrims. Here they sought out the Church of the Holy Sepulchre and numerous other Christian cult sites related to the Life and Passion of Jesus. These journeys took place less frequently following the conquest of Jerusalem by the Arabs in 638 but never ceased completely: the pilgrimage to Jerusalem retained its outstanding significance in the Christian imagination. The motivation of the pilgrims did change, however. While the expedition to the places of Jesus' work was undertaken in Late Antiquity for reasons of personal piety, from the Early Middle Ages onwards the long and dangerous journey was increasingly seen as an act of penitence for the atonement of sins. The number of Christian pilgrims to the Holy Land rose sharply again from the end of the 10th century, despite the military conflicts in the region. The Fatimid caliph al-Hakim occupied Jerusalem in 1009 and ordered the destruction of the Church of the Holy Sepulchre, which was rebuilt by 1048 on the instigation of the Byzantine emperor. The Turkish Seljuks conquered the city in 1071 but this had no long lasting detrimental effect on the pilgrimages, and in 1098 the city again fell to the Fatimids.

Jerusalem, Church of the Holy Sepulchre, 4th and 12th C. (Engraving by L. Deifel. 1st half of the 19th C.) The Church of the Holy Sepulchre was the most important of all the holy sites in Palestine and Jerusalem and Bethlehem the primary pilgrimage destination, next to which all other pilgrimage locations took second place.

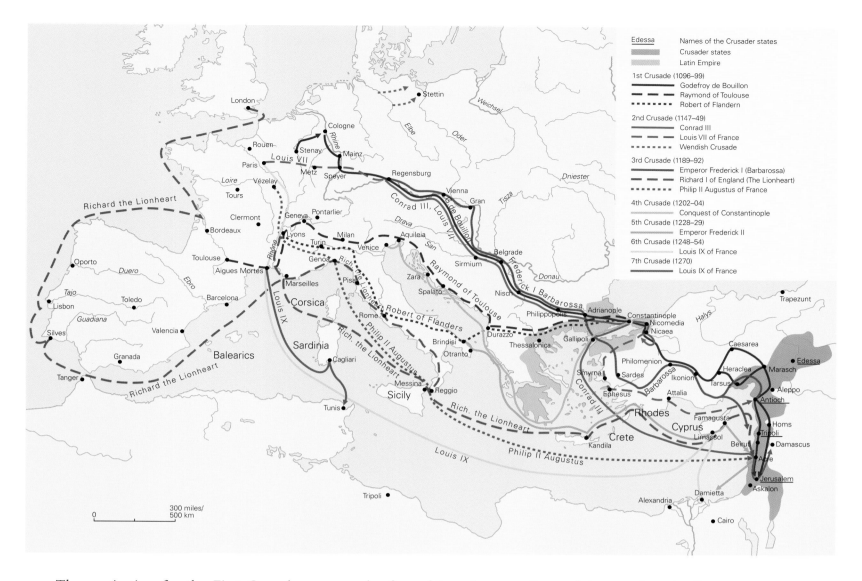

The motivation for the First Crusade was not the fate of Jerusalem, however, but the loss of further parts of the Byzantine Empire to the Seljuks. In an appeal to the Pope the Byzantine emperor had asked the western Christians for help in the fight against the Muslim conquerors. Pope Urban II issued a summons for the Crusade at the Council of Clermont and at other locations during a round trip through France lasting several months in 1095–96. It was intended as a military expedition for the liberation of the holy sites and of the eastern Christians in the east from Muslim rule. Following papal approval the fight against the "enemies of the faith" was not only justified but was also required for the love of God and for the fellow-Christians in the east, thus making it a duty for every Christian. Based on Jesus' example, every Christian had to "bear his cross" and do penance. The expedition as a form of "religious battle" thus became an act of repentance for weapon bearing laymen. At the same time, the Pope positioned himself at the head of this enterprise, incorporating the whole of western Christianity, and manifestly underpinning the claimed primacy of spiritual over secular power in the investiture controversy with the emperor and kings.

The Pope's summons was well received in the society at the end of the 11th century, in which many laymen sought religious meaning: three waves of Crusaders made their way to the Holy Land between 1096 and 1101. The disordered military contingent of the first wave never did reach its destination but attacked the Jewish communities of numerous towns en route, in France, the Rhineland and Bohemia, where they carried out massacres and forced baptisms. Their understanding of "religious battle" established a lasting association of "Crusade" with the murder of Jews, one that remained virulent until well into the Late Middle Ages. The Crusader army of the second wave reached Palestine after a long haul lasting several years and captured Jerusalem on July 15, 1099. The Crusaders wreaked a bloodbath among the "non-believing" residents—Muslims and Jews—during the subsequent plundering and destruction of the city. The Third Crusade's army suffered a crushing defeat in Asia Minor at the hands of the Seljuks. This deprived the conquerors of their urgently needed reinforcements for, despite the euphoria over the capture of Jerusalem, the majority of the Crusaders had no intention of set-

Routes of the seven Crusades. The First Crusade departed in waves from a variety of different places in France, some of the groups taking different routes. The army contingent of the first wave paused en route to the Holy Land, indicated on the map as a change of direction near Nicaea.

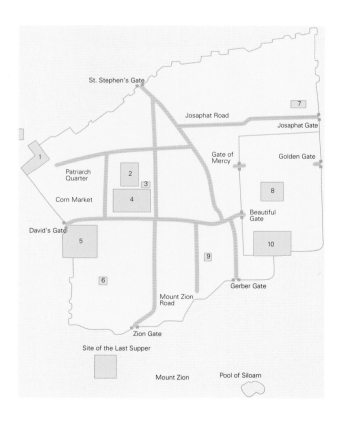

Jerusalem during the Crusades: 1 Tancred's Tower, 2 Church of the Holy Sepulchre, 3 St. Maria Latina, 4 Knights of St John Hospitaller, 5 David's Tower, 6 St. James the Great 7 St. Anna, 8 Dome of the Rock/Templum Domini, 9 St. Maria Alemannorum, 10 Al-Aqsa Mosque/Templum Salomonis

Heavenly Jerusalem and *Majestas Domini,* ceiling paintings in the double church of St. Maria und Klemens, Schwarzrheindorf, c. 1180.

Map of Jerusalem, St. Bertin (?), c. 1170/80, parchment, colored pen drawing (The Hague, Koninklijke Bibliothek, Ms. 76 F5). In the Middle Ages, Jerusalem, centre of holy events and "navel of the world," was not just a real place on the map (with the addition of Christian pilgrimage sites), it was also a symbol of the apocalyptic paradise. The open view from the lower to the upper church in Schwarzrheindorf makes this heavenly reference obvious.

tling in the newly created "Kingdom of Jerusalem" or in the dominions of Tripoli, Antioch, or Edessa, and returned to their homelands. The result was that the Crusaders were the military rulers of the Holy Land but they were not in a position to protect from attack the pilgrims who, attracted by the good tidings of the capture of Jerusalem, came in droves—unarmed. The pilgrims' safety was as precarious as it had been before.

Under these circumstances the amalgamation of Crusaders with fighting fraternities who made it their job to protect the pilgrims was more than welcome. The Templars, the Knights of St. John and other smaller military orders were immediately drafted to defend the Crusader states and quickly received papal acknowledgement as orders. They were directly answerable to the Pope and were soon exempted from tithe payments. In contrast to the traditional spiritual communities they were dominated not by clerics but by fighting laymen—noble knights and the nonaristocratic brothers who served them.

The military orders consolidated their position as national defenders using means procured in Europe and newly recruited Crusaders. After the 1140s they were assigned strategically important castles, which they extended to become large fortresses. With the Crusaders stationed in their castles they maintained the first standing army of the Middle Ages. Nevertheless, the occupation of the Holy Land never really extended beyond a system of military bases and fortified towns. The territory, inhabited by relatively few European settlers in addition to the local residents, resisted real control by the Crusaders.

Following the lost battle of Hattin and the capture of Jerusalem by Saladin in 1187, there remained only a narrow strip of coast for the Crusaders. The harbor town of Acre was captured in 1191 with the help of forces hastily despatched from Europe and became the new capital and seat of the military orders. Although the Christian sphere of control was further extended as a result of subsequent Crusades, to which there were unremitting papal summons, as well as via a number of military successes, a great deal of diplomacy, and Jerusalem making a brief return to Christian control, the basis of the Crusaders' rule remained fragile. Reliant on funds and troops from Europe, which was only accessible via the sea, and weakened by internal conflicts as well as the rivalry between the Templars and the Knights of St. John (which extended as far as open conflict), the Crusaders were ultimately unable to prevent the recapture of the Holy Land. Jerusalem was lost for good in 1244. In 1268 the Egyptian Mamluk sultans, who had inherited the legacy of Saladin's descendents, undertook the systematic conquest of the Crusader states, which came to an end in 1291 with the capture of Acre.

The Templars

In 1120 Hugues de Payens, a nobleman from Champagne, and a number of like-minded knights joined forces as a brotherhood and made a pledge before the Patriarch of Jerusalem to lead a life of poverty, abstinence and obedience in the service of God. King Baldwin II of Jerusalem entrusted them with protecting the Christian pilgrims in the Holy Land from attack and made premises available to them in his palace on the Temple Mount. The new knights took their name from this "palace"—the secularized Al-Aqsa Mosque—which, according to legend, was the site of Solomon's temple. The early years were difficult for the Knights Templar despite the income granted them by the King and his followers. Hugues de Payens went on a promotional tour through Europe in 1127, which brought the Templars a multitude of new members and their first possessions in France and England, to help with the financing of their responsibilities in the Holy Land. The Templars were officially recognized as an order at the Council of Troyes in 1129 and were assigned a rule compiled with the help of Bernard of Clairvaux. In the written version, *De laude novae militiae*, completed shortly thereafter, Bernard celebrated the link between an ascetic lifestyle and the knightly battle for Christianity as a new means of forgiveness for one's sins and for achieving salvation. He thus made the Templars known, secured their widespread social acceptance, and, in doing so, laid the foundations for the European nobility's ongoing willingness to make donations to "God's Warriors." The Templars were granted papal acknowledgement as a military order in 1139 and thereafter were directly answerable to the Pope.

The order was divided into fighting conventual brothers and brothers entrusted with commercial responsibilities. The conventual brothers comprised knights, servant brothers (*sergents*), and chaplains—priests responsible for the Liturgy of the Hours and celebrating Mass—and their vows committed them to obedience, chastity, and poverty. Then there were also those knights who belonged to the order only "temporarily"—during their sojourn in the Holy Land, for example. The members of the order were required to observe the Liturgy of the Hours except when they were traveling or fighting. The "Master" stood at the head of the order, supported by the council and high ranking dignitaries. Each of the order's provinces in the west was

The Al-Aqsa Mosque. Two buildings in Jerusalem had a particular link to the Templars: the Church of the Holy Sepulchre and the Al-Aqsa Mosque. The first Templar knights were recruited from armed brothers in the area around the Church of the Holy Sepulchre, forming a kind of lay or tertiary brotherhood for the protection of the site and its possessions. The Al-Aqsa Mosque, alleged to be the site of Solomon's Temple, became the eponymous first seat of the Templars.

Crusaders riding out from a fortified town, fresco from the Templar chapel at Cressac, last third of the 12th C. (copy from the Musée des Monuments Français, Paris). The chapel at Cressac is one of the few surviving buildings from a former French commandery of the Knights Templar. Modest in its outside appearance, the interior of the chapel is surprisingly rich in wall paintings; it is the most important Romanesque fresco cycle commissioned by the Templars.

Segovia, church of the Holy Cross, consecrated in 1208. The *Vera Cruz* of Segovia is not only a contemporary of the Charola, the Templar church at Tomar (see pp. 250-51), it is also similar in style. The noticeable increase in copies or references to the Church of the Holy Sepulchre in Jerusalem from the late 12th century is probably related to the loss of Jerusalem to the Arabs in 1187, which resulted in an increased desire for commemoration.

Cambridge, Holy Sepulchre, begun c. 1120, west elevation. The reasons for the construction of this round church are not known. During restoration work in 1841 the Gothic tower was rebuilt in Norman Romanesque style, which corresponds to the year in which the church was built. It is a very early imitation of the Church of the Holy Sepulchre.

also run by a Master. The order's individual settlements, or commanderies, which were responsible for the administration of the order's possessions, were presided over by a commander. The majority of the Templar settlements were in France; there were also commanderies in England, northern Spain, Portugal, and Italy, but only a few on imperial territory. As the commanderies were primarily responsible for the administration of possessions but did not accommodate a community, they resembled farmsteads more than they did monasteries. In addition to farm and administration buildings there was also accommodation for a limited number of brothers and chaplains as well as a chapel. The majority of the chapels were plain hall-like buildings with an apse or straight choir end, but in some instances the Templars did erect centrally oriented buildings in imitation of the Dome of the Rock, which was adjacent to the seat of their order on the Temple Mount and served as a church between 1099 and 1187. Such centrally oriented buildings have been preserved in Laon, Segovia, London, Cambridge, and Metz, for example; the Paris "Temple" was destroyed.

From the 1130s an increasing number of castles in the Crusader states were assigned to or purchased by the Templars. These castles were then extended according to what were then the most modern principles of fortification. They comprised a double moat as a rule, always a large dungeon, cisterns, and a chapel. Accommodation, dining rooms and kitchens, storerooms and stables were sized according to the extent of the complex and the intended occupants, who could number from a few dozen to several thousand warriors. There were approximately three *sergents* per knight as well further, more lightly armed local mercenaries. The important Templar castles included Baghras north of Antioch, Chastel Blanc, the Citadel of Tortosa, Sefad, and Atlit (Chastel Pèlerin), where there was also a centrally aligned chapel.

While the Templars' possessions in the west grew, so did their significance in the east. Together with the Knights of St. John, at the end of the 12th century they comprised some 600 knights, half of the forces in the Kingdom of Jerusalem. At the same time, their far flung network of settlements and their continual requirement for financial transfers from west to east made them into the pioneers of cashless monetary transactions, services that were also utilized by others. Following the end of the Crusader states the Templars were quick to take on the role of financially well placed money lenders, upon whom even the King of France was reliant. This was to become their downfall: in October 1307 Philip IV had all of the Templars in France arrested under suspicion of heresy and their possessions confiscated. The Pope abolished the order in 1312 and the order's Master, Jacques de Molay, was burnt at the stake as a heretic in 1314. Despite what was clearly an unjust accusation nobody came to the defense of the Templars: the order's transformation into a powerful financial institution with an army of holy warriors in the background had been a source of unease not only for the French King. The Templars' possessions outside France passed to the Knights of St. John.

The Knights of St. John

The Knights of St. John derived from a spiritual brotherhood for the care of the poor and the sick at the hospital of the St Maria Latina Abbey in Jerusalem. Following the conquest of Jerusalem this hospital, which had been founded by Italian merchants from Amalfi prior to 1080, received numerous property endowments in Palestine and in the west. It was divided into a variety of medical departments, employed eight doctors as well as nurses and clergy, and in the 12th century provided a high quality of care for an astonishing total of up to 2000 sick people of both sexes.

In c. 1120, or even earlier, the hospital brothers were joined by Crusaders, who formed a military wing based on the example of the Templars and gradually let the care of the sick fade into the background. The first of a series of castles in the Kingdom of Jerusalem were assigned to the Knights of St. John in 1136 (including Belvoir in the Jordan Valley); in 1144 they received the Crac des Chevaliers from the Counts of Tripoli, which they extended into an enormous fortress that could accommodate up to 2000 occupants. Another important Knights of St. John castle in the north was Margat.

Acknowledged by the Pope in 1154, the order comprised knights, servant brothers for looking after the hospital and the weapons, as well as priests, and followed a rule combining the Rule of St. Augustine with elements of the Templar rule, and which placed the emphasis on help for the poor. There were also female members living in the communities in accordance with the Rule of St. Augustine. The order was led by a Grand Master. The settlements in the west were divided into commanderies, "priories" (regions), and great commanderies (provinces of the order), as well as into "langues," i.e. language groups. In addition to large possessions in France there were also settlements

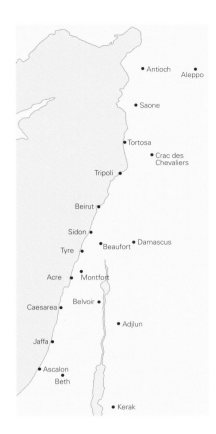

Crac des Chevaliers, Syria, 12th C. This famous Crusader castle is one of the most important medieval fortresses. It had been the site of a small "castle on the slope" as early as the 11th century but the expansion into what is still today an impressive display of size and architectural compactness only took place after the Knights of St. John had taken over the castle in 1144.

in Italy, Spain and Portugal, England, in the German Empire as well as in Denmark and southern Sweden. Unlike the Templars, the Knights of St. John commanderies usually included a sick room with an apse for erecting an altar or with an opening to the church, which was either adjoining or below.

The Knights of St. John withdrew to Cyprus following the loss of the Holy Land. From there, in 1306, they conquered the island of Rhodes, which they then ruled until its capture by the Turks in 1522. Thereafter they moved their "order state" to Malta (which is why they are also called the Knights of Malta), from where they were later expelled by Napoleon. A naval power with a strong fleet between 1306 and 1798, today the Knights of St. John have reverted to their origins and dedicate themselves to the care of the sick.

The Teutonic Knights

The Teutonic Knights were initially founded during the siege of Acre in 1190 by Crusaders from Bremen and Lübeck as a hospital brotherhood for the care of the German-speaking sick and wounded. The community was quickly supplemented by a military wing and was acknowledged by the Pope as a military order in 1199, yet despite support from the German Staufer dynasty in the Holy Land it did not achieve the same significance as the older military orders on whose example their observance and order organization was based. The knights followed the Templar rule while the hospital brothers adhered to the rule of the Knights of St. John. A Grand Master stood at the head of the order and the settlements were organized regionally in bailiwicks. Apart from those within the German Empire, the order also had possessions in southern Italy, Lombardy, Venice, and Greece.

While the Teutonic Knights possessed only a few castles in Palestine, including the seat of the order at Montfort, at an early stage they turned to other challenges in other regions. After all, the popes had not restricted the religious battle to the holy sites but had also issued calls for Crusades against the Muslims in al-Andalus and the heathen peoples of northeast Europe. Asked by the Duke of Masovia for help, the order took up the fight against the heathen Prutzens (later Prussians) in 1231 and then developed the captured land, with settlements and the founding of towns, into an autonomous

Aquamanile in form of knight, Hildesheim, 13th C., bronze, height 27 cm (Oslo, Universitetets Kulturhistoriske Museer). Such water containers for hand washing before meals were increasingly common in courtly households in the High Middle Ages.

Knightly figures in historical costume,
height approx. 74 in (190 cm): Templar, c. 1150 (left); Knight of St. John, c. 1200 (center); Teutonic Knight, c. 1280 (right). (Mainz, Bischöfliches Dom- und Diözesanmuseum; produced 2003 by Ars Militia, Bad Wünnenberg).

territorial power. Two local military orders (Swordbrothers, Order of Dobrin) had been incorporated by 1237. The Teutonic Knights had thus created an "order state" prior to the loss of the Holy Land and before the Knights of St. John, one that went on to be extended up to the start of the 15th century through the conquest and purchase of parts of Livonia, Pomerania, Estonia, and the Neumark. Having become too powerful for the liking of its neighbors, the order was defeated by the Polish-Lithuanian army in the Battle of Tannenberg in 1410 and had to cede the core areas of its territory to Poland in 1466. Prussia became a Polish duchy in 1524.

The Teutonic Knights developed a specific form of settlement in Prussia, namely the fortified monastery (or convent castle). These were enclosed and fortified four-winged complexes accessed from a central courtyard via multi-storey galleries, with the most important rooms (chapel, chapter house, dining and living rooms, dormitory and sick room) on the upper floor. The most famous of these Teutonic Order castles was Marienburg (now Malbork), east of Gdansk (erected c. 1290–c. 1400), which was the seat of the Grand Master as of 1309. There the square fortified monastery was successively expanded with an outer fortification and the Grand Master's palace, both of which are surrounded by moats. The chapel too, usually included within the fortified square of the convent castle, protrudes far out to the east at Marienburg.

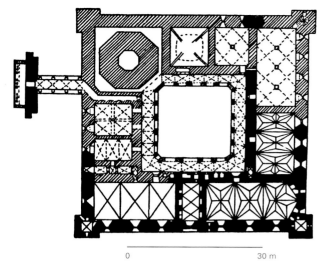

The Teutonic Knights' Castle at Rehden, ground plan. The castle of the commander of Rehden was erected in 1300. The complex exhibits the orderliness characteristic of the Prussian order's castles. Only the dungeon (above left) breaks away from the layout of the courtyard enclosed by four wings of equal size.

Military Orders on the Iberian Peninsula

It was the will of the Pope that Hispanic Crusaders should not take part in the Crusades to the east but should fight the Muslim rulers in the south of the Iberian Peninsula. The Spanish kings quickly recognized the significance of the military orders as ever available warriors and encouraged the settlement of the Templars and the Knights of St. John, as well as the formation of local orders. Like the Templars, the Hispanic orders, with the exception of that from Calatrava, derived from brotherhoods of knights. They were at their height in the 13th century but before the end of the *Reconquista* had already worn themselves out with internal and political conflicts. Subject successively to royal management between 1492 and 1501 and to the control of the king as Master of the Order, they became irrelevant as a political factor.

Calatrava Castle (northeast of Ciudad Real), from 1147 the southern-most Christian outpost in Castilian possession, was abandoned by the Templars stationed there in 1157 and assigned to the abbot of the Fitero (Aragón) monastery in 1158 upon the initiative of a Cistercian and former knight. The Crusaders recruited to defend it pledged themselves to a life of poverty, chastity, and obedience, according to the *Carta caritatis*. They were recognized by the General Chapter in Cîteaux in 1164 and acknowledged by the Pope, becoming affiliated to Morimond in 1187. The order participated in all of the important *Reconquista* military conquests of the late 12th and the first part of the 13th century.

The Brotherhood of the Knights of Santiago was established in 1170 by King Ferdinand II of León to defend the city of Cáceres and was entrusted with the defense of archiepiscopal towns by the archbishop of Santiago de Compostela. Acknowledged as an order by the Pope in 1175, the Knights of the Order of St. James, like the canons to whom they were linked, followed the example of the Rule of St. Augustine. In addition to military services, they also ran pilgrims' hospices and carried out land development in conquered territories.

The Order of Alcántara derived from a brotherhood of knights founded in S. Julián del Pereiro (north of Cáceres) and acknowledged by the Pope in 1176. It was assigned the castle and town of Alcántara, as well as other possessions, in 1218. In return it adopted the Cistercian Rule and was made formally answerable to Calatrava. In addition to the *Reconquista*, the order also took part in land development in Extremadura and in battles against Portugal.

The Order of Avis dates from a brotherhood of knights founded in 1166 in Évora (Portugal), which was part of the Order of Calatrava. The knights were given the town of Avis as a fief in 1211 and they made this the seat of their order. Following the end of the *Reconquista* in Portugal in the middle of the 13th century they tried to do away with the Castilian influence. The order's Masters were Portuguese princes as of 1363 and disassociation with Calatrava followed in 1438.

Four Santiago knights from the *Libro de Los Caballeros de la Cofradia de Santiago.* Spanish book illumination, 14–17th C. (Burgos, Museo Catedralicio).

◀ ▶ **Templar church,** 2nd half of the 12th C. The exterior of this Romanesque church comprises a sixteen sided centrally oriented building crowned with battlements, in the center of which is a freestanding octagonal chapel. It once stood at the protective walls, where it served as a fortified tower. In contrast to the solid walls of the exterior construction, the central chapel has narrow arcades underneath and an upper story with tall, narrow windows.

Tomar, Portugal

▶ **The Knights of Christ monastery,** early 16th–17th C., window of the chapter house (above) and main porch (below). The imaginative, naturalistic, and emblematic decorations are characteristic of Portuguese art on the threshold of the modern age: the imagery of the era of Manuel I was influenced by the experiences of the voyages of discovery.

During the height of their power in the 13th century the Templar Order owned a large number of commanderies in various European countries. With every new member having to make a donation to the order, the Templars consequently acquired significant properties as well as the associated social influence. The allegation that the commanderies were usually castles is a romantic myth; most of them were in fact farmsteads or administrative centers. Those that were true fortresses, however, included Tomar. This Templar castle was built after 1160 under the order's Master in Portugal, Gualdim Pais, who had fought with the Templars in the Second Crusade to the Holy Land. Its multiple ringed enclosures made possible the successful defense of Tomar against attacks by the Almohads in 1190. Besides the remains of the fortified towers, the church, called the Charola (rotunda), is all that has survived of the former fortified monastery. Following the abolition of the Templar Order in 1312, their possessions passed to the Knights of Christ, newly founded in 1318. The fact that, after 1350, the latter order was led by members of the royal family ensured the expansion of Tomar into a magnificent monastic residence in the 15th and 17th centuries.

Holy Sepulchre Buildings

Circular buildings surviving from the High Middle Ages are often seen as being based on the Church of the Holy Sepulchre and/or the Holy Sepulchre in Jerusalem. The actual architectural references do vary considerably, however, as these examples from Germany indicate. Only the Holy Sepulchre Chapel in Eichstätt is a true copy of the model in Jerusalem, reproducing the state of the original in the High Middle Ages with numerous details. The Holy Sepulchre with 19th century additions is all that remains of the Middle Age monastery complex. Neither the Holy Sepulchre in the Mauritius rotunda of the Minster in Constance nor the room at the core of the St. Matthias castle chapel in Kobern, both 13th century, have any architectural connection to Jerusalem. They need to be seen as Holy Sepulchre replicas only in the widest sense.

▲ ▶▶ **Kobern/Mosel,** St. Matthias castle chapel, c. 1220/30, built by the Crusader Henry II of Isenburg.

▼ **Eichstätt,** Holy Sepulchre, built prior to 1182/88, Capuchin Church of the Holy Cross and the Holy Sepulchre.

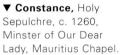

▼ **Constance,** Holy Sepulchre, c. 1260, Minster of Our Dear Lady, Mauritius Chapel.

◄ **"Summer refectory",** reception room on the upper floor of the Grand Master's Palace with magnificent fan vaulting supported by an octagonal centre column, 1382/99.

▼ **Marienburg from the southwest,** seen from the opposite bank of the Nogat. In the front, the outer fortified wall with the drawbridge (left); the adjoining Grand Master's Palace in the west wing of the Middle Castle, end of the 14th C.; and the High Castle, end of the 13th–mid-14th C., with the chapel bell tower (above, back) and, by the wall, the protruding keep (the "Dansker").

Marienburg, Poland

A typically Prussian monastery castle was built as the commandery of the Teutonic Knights, established in Prussia shortly before 1280: a fortified four-winged complex facing inwards, the upper floor of which housed the church and the monastic premises, and which had an outer castle with farm buildings to the north. Following the loss of the Holy Land and the transfer of the Grand Master's seat to Marienburg in 1309, successive expansion work was undertaken to convert the castle into a

▲ **East wing of the High Castle** with St. Mary's Chapel and the bell tower, 1st half of the 14th C.; in front, the double protective wall; right, the "priests' tower" (rebuilt in the 19th C.) and the east wing of the Middle Castle.

well-fortified governmental and administrative center, which lasted for the whole of the 14th century. The fortified monastery, the High Castle, was equipped with new living quarters for the order's members, in keeping with the importance of Marienburg, and it also acquired a large chapel extending over the eastern flank of the building. A spacious, three-winged complex, the Middle Castle, was erected in the grounds of the outer bailey, with administrative and meeting rooms, a guest wing, and the Grand Master's Palace. The reception rooms at Marienburg are among the most elaborate of contemporary secular architecture. Their preservation is due to the comprehensive restoration carried out by the Prussian government in 1882–1923 and by the Polish monuments authorities since 1961.

"Winter refectory" on the upper floor of the Grand Master's Palace, 1382/99. The remains of wall paintings depicting the Grand Master can be seen under the shield arches of the vaults.

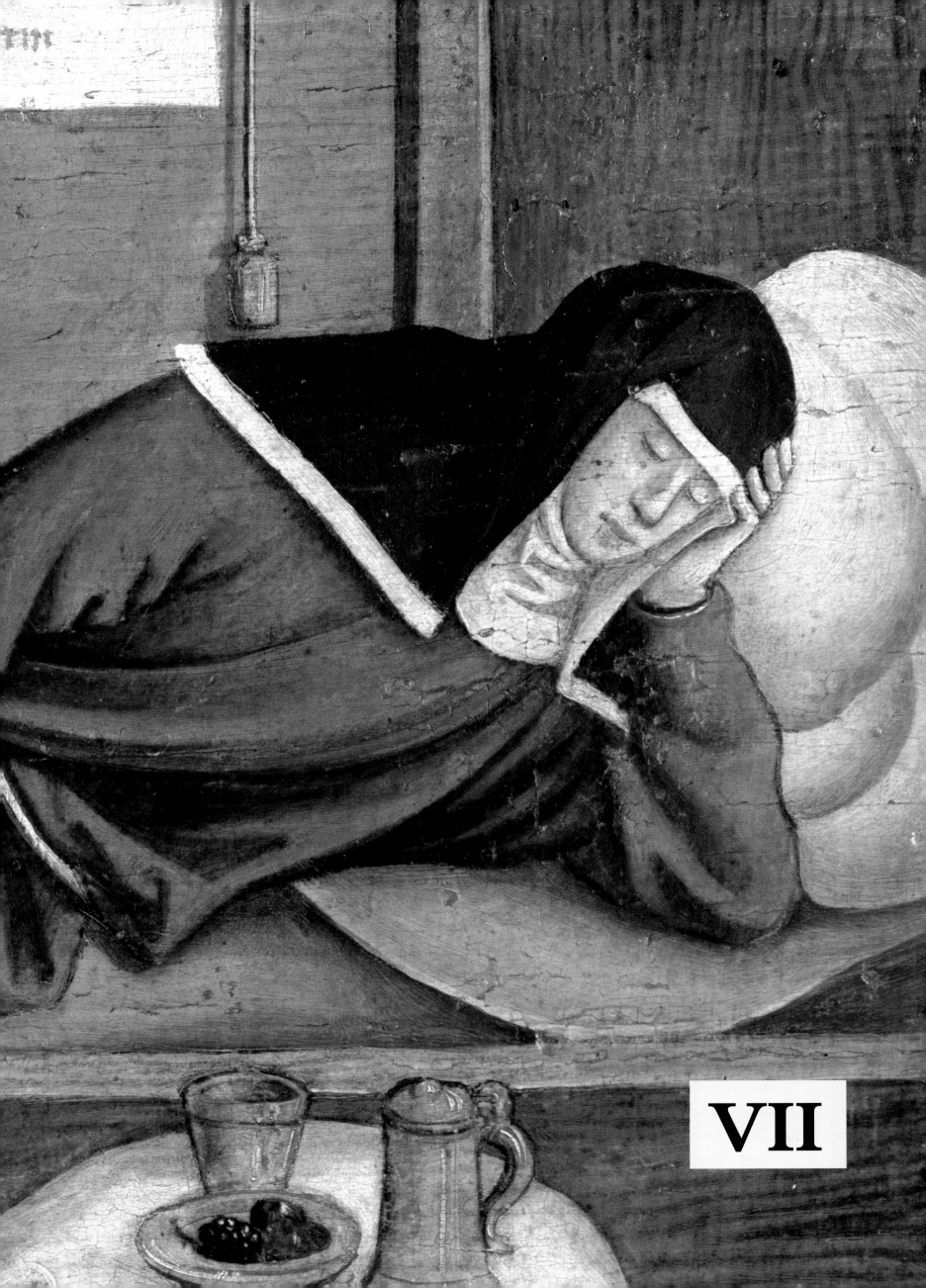

VII

Female Orders

Nuns' communion, initial in a songbook from the Cistercian convent of St. Marienstern (Hs. 4, fol. 125r), Altzella, 1522–23. The fact that nuns were forbidden from celebrating Mass but regular participation in Mass was nevertheless considered necessary for them resulted in a certain dependency on the priests. In addition to this devotional dependency, nuns also had to pay for such clerical services.

Procession with nuns and clerics, lower section of an opening miniature of *La Sainte Abbaye*, Maubuisson (?), pre-1294 (The British Library, London Add. Ms. 39843, fol 6v.) Even this portrayal, which does at least accord the nuns an active role in the staging of the procession (as carriers of candles and illuminated manuscripts), places the emphasis on the role of the male participants by means of the separate positioning of the monks between the two pillars, the dimensions of the figures, and the nimbus.

Dependency on Male Clerics

Like men, women, too, have always undertaken religious withdrawal from the world. Nevertheless, there was always a significant difference between monasteries (for men) and nunneries in that women could not become priests—circumstances that remain unchanged in the Catholic Church today. Unlike monasteries, nunneries were, therefore, always dependent on male clerics from outside their own community for the key aspects of Christian religious practice—confession, performing Mass, and giving communion. This meant that they were never able to achieve the spiritual autonomy enjoyed by male communities and always remained dependent on the help and support of male clerics. This dependency had important consequences both for the status of nunneries within the Church and for the internal organization of the convents and their construction.

While in the early stages the impossibility of being ordained as a priest was of little significance—after all, the Rule of St. Benedict saw the monks as laymen and their having a priest among them was the exception—this did change once intercessory prayer and especially the reading of Requiem Masses became the monks' main tasks. Even though the prayers of the nuns and canonesses, especially those of the virgins among them, were considered to be especially pure and effective, in the long term this esteem was not enough to compensate for the inability to perform Mass. In order to be able to meet their obligations towards the family of the convent's patron as well as the expectations of their own convent members with regard to an appropriate commemoration of the dead, the female communities had to employ clerics whom they had to pay to fulfill the appropriate Mass obligations. The spiritual dependency thus gave rise to an economic disadvantage in comparison to the monasteries, where the celebration of Mass did not result in additional costs.

Like the monks, the nuns, of course, also had to practice sexual abstinence. The safest means of ensuring this was considered to be the strict exclusion of the nuns from the outside world. However, as the presence of priests was required for performing Mass, communion, and confession this meant

that the nuns could not be completely shielded from contact with men. This resulted in the paradoxical situation whereby the women living in strict enclosure were dependent on the presence of men for performing their spiritual life and it was this very contact that harbored the danger for both sides of being tempted and violating the chastity requirement. It is generally accepted that those who were supposed to provide spiritual guidance for the nuns were the ones who posed the greatest threat to their spiritual status. The practical organization of life in a nunnery, from the provision of a screened location for choral prayer through to the elaborate confession regulations, constituted an attempt to deal with this ambivalence.

Nunneries and Female Priories

Making a distinction between nuns and canonesses, the first attempt at which was made at the Council of Aachen, remained difficult for a long time after 817. In principle, canonesses, unlike nuns, do not take a vow and do not have to abstain from eating meat; they may possess property and can even leave the convent for longer family visits. As with monasteries, however, the actual lifestyles during the 9th and 10th centuries are not always easy to determine. It was only as a result of the Gregorian Reform in the second half of the 11th century that monasteries were "regularized," which meant that they were given the alternative of following either the Rule of St. Benedict or that of St. Augustine.

Eibingen, abbey of St. Hildegard, Benedictine nuns. This abbey, near Rüdesheim, was founded in 1165 by Hildegard of Bingen as a daughter house of the convent at Rupertsberg. Hildegard had founded Rupertsberg near Bingen in 1147, despite resistance from the Benedictine monks of Disibodenberg and moved into it c. 1150 with a group of nuns over whom she presided. The significant influx of women from the upper nobility into Rupertsberg soon necessitated the founding of the Eibingen convent. Rupertsberg was destroyed by the Swedes in 1632; the Eibingen convent was rebuilt at a different location from 1900. The Benedictine nuns living there form part of the Beuron congregation.

▲ **Essen, Minster, former female priory church,** end of the 10th C., begun by Abbess Mathilde, consecrated in the middle of the 11th C., west choir, based on the example of Aachen. "Due to the Ottonians' immunity privileges the female priory at Essen was assured of direct royal protection; this transfer of jurisdiction strengthened the priory's economic performance." (Rösener).

▶ **Cologne, St. Maria im Kapitol,** wooden door, 1049 and/or 1065, detail with scenes from the New Testament: the Annunciation, the Visitation, the Annunciation to the Shepherds, the Nativity Scene with Mary and Joseph beside the crib (see also p. 128).

▶▶ **Quedlinburg, interior view of the former female priory church of St. Servatius,** post-1070–1129. Quedlinburg Priory was founded in 936 by Queen Mathilde, wife of Henry I of Germany. The female priories of Quedlinburg and Essen are prominent but not isolated examples of the power and esteem that female religious houses were able to enjoy in the 11th and 12th centuries.

The Social Functions of Nunneries

The female priories founded in the 9th and 10th centuries by prominent families and sometimes even by the imperial court, particularly in Westphalia and Lower Saxony— including Essen, Freckenhorst, Gandersheim, Gernrode, Quedlinburg, and St. Maria im Kapitol in Cologne—are a German anomaly. They gave the aristocracy the possibility of providing for their younger daughters in a manner befitting their social standing and also of ensuring that they did not bear any legitimate heirs. The priories also served as educational institutions for aristocratic daughters. Since the canonesses did not have to take a vow they were able to return to secular life at any time once their education was complete or if the family wanted them to marry. A priory enjoyed close ties with the founding family and the abbess usually came from that family, as did the *Vogt*, a secular overseer whose responsibility it was to protect the convent and to represent it in all legal matters. Some female priories managed to retain their nonregulated "secular" status beyond the 11th century and to remain in existence as aristocratic ladies' priories until the end of the Middle Ages (e.g. Gandersheim, Möllenbeck, Wunstorf).

The Cluniac convent of Marcigny-sur-Loire represented another kind of caring environment for women. Founded shortly before 1055 by the Abbot Hugo of Semur, Marcigny was intended to fulfill two roles: as a place of religious life for women, especially for those whose husbands had entered Cluniac monasteries as monks, and also as a place of retreat for widows, so they could live out their lives in both spiritual and material security. The fact that the mothers of Hugo of Semur and Peter the Venerable, as well as numerous other prominent widows from European ruling houses stretching between England and Spain, spent their later years in Marcigny, underlines this convent's function as a religious old-age home. Even more so than Cluny itself, where, in addition to the sick ward, the *conversio in extremis*—entering a convent in old age—led to the development of a kind of residence for the elderly, for aristocrats who had just entered the order and spiritual dignitaries, Marcigny became the preferred retreat for prominent women, a role that remained undisputed despite the subsequent founding of a series of convents in northern Italy, the Black Forest and the Massif Central.

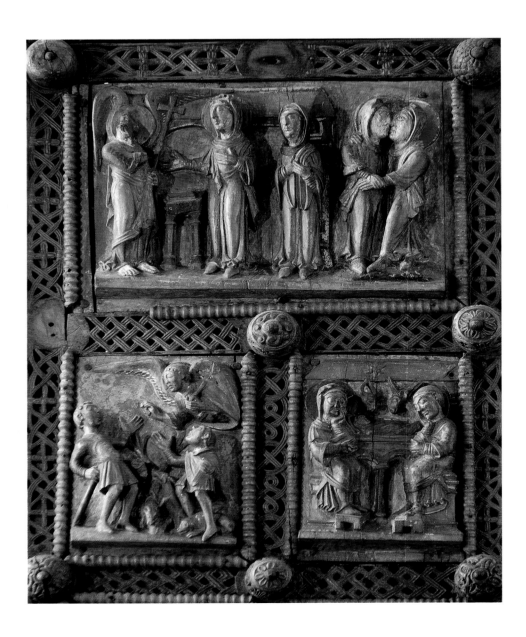

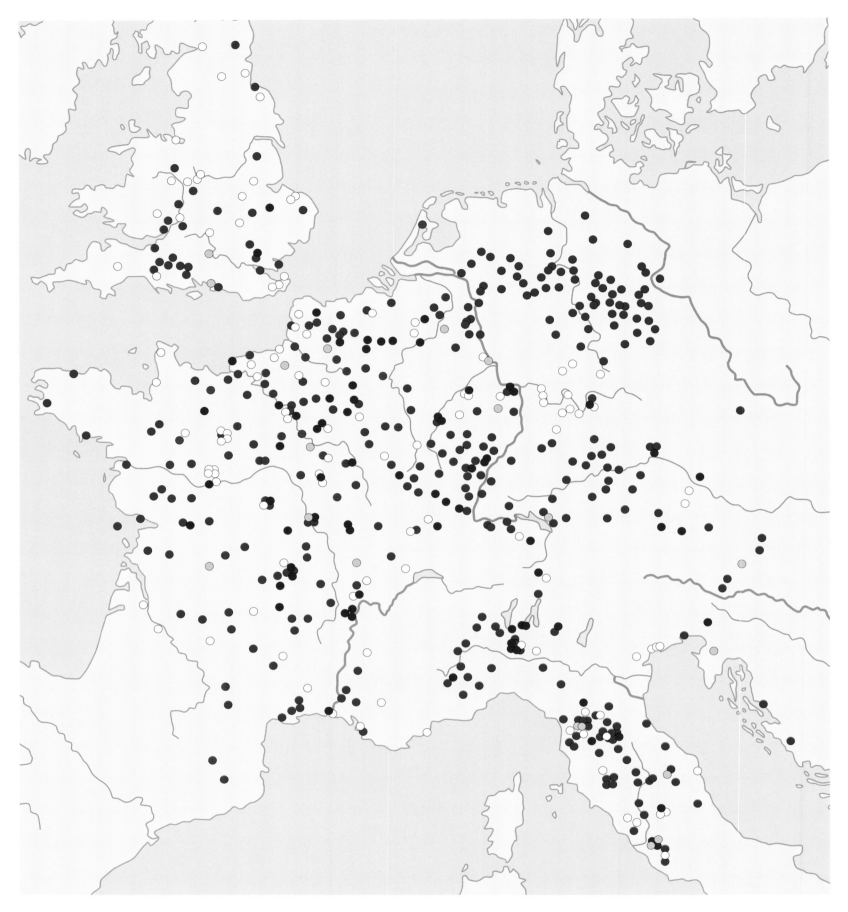

Map showing the distribution of nunneries founded prior to 1100 (Western Europe excluding Spain and Ireland), after K. Bodarwé and N. M. Barner

- ● Founded before 800, still in existence in 1100
- ● Founded before 800, monastery prior to 1100
- ○ Founded before 800, dissolved prior to 1100

- ● Founded between 800 and 1100, still in existence in 1100
- ● Founded between 800 and 1100, monastery prior to 1100
- ○ Founded between 800 and 1100, dissolved prior to 1100

The New Orders

It was only c. 1100 that the founding of nunneries for primarily religious reasons came to the fore. The increased proactivity on the part of women committed to a religious lifestyle and who were within the newly founded orders of that era was indicative of this development. Nevertheless, the establishment of female branches was frowned upon in the majority of orders and could be implemented only in the teeth of resistance. This applied to the Cistercians, for example, where nunneries such as Le Tart and Las Huelgas did stand in tandem with the primary abbeys at the head of extensive affiliations, while others adhering to the Cistercian way of life sought affiliation to the order in vain. The general chapter tried to prevent the incorporation of new convents during the wave of newly founded nunneries between 1200 and 1250 in particular. Consequently, not all nunneries that saw themselves as Cistercian actually belonged to the order. The mendicant orders also frequently resisted the affiliation of convents and the related spiritual guidance responsibilities. At times papal intervention was required in order to oblige the orders to commit to providing for their convents in spiritual matters and to support them in secular issues.

Double Monasteries

Norbert of Xanten, on the other hand, had established all of the Premonstratensian communities that he founded as double monasteries. The segregation of men and women introduced after 1140 corresponded to the widespread reservations on the part of the Church with regard to double monasteries, but certainly not to the intentions of the order's founder.

The wandering preacher from Brittany, Robert d'Arbrissel (c. 1050–1116), went a step further with the founding of Fontevraud (1101). The abbey erected for his many followers of both sexes was a double monastery that was led by a woman. The large female community, initially divided into virgins and the rest—widows, previously married, concubines, and prostitutes—and later according to background into aristocratic virgins and widows, nonaristocratic women as well as the sick, was equal to the male monastery in spiritual matters, but was otherwise subordinate. The differences between men and women at Fontevraud were also evident from the various rules that both parts of the monastery followed: the Rule of St. Benedict applied to the women leading a strict convent life, while the Rule of

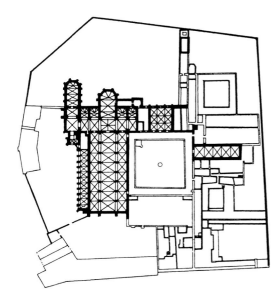

Burgos, Las Huelgas Reales, abbey of Cistercian/Trappist nuns. Ground plan showing the large cloister and the small cloister (*claustrillo*). Las Huelgas was a mother house with 14 daughter houses.

Fontevraud, chapter house. Parts of the high medieval building underwent considerable renovations and/or rebuilding in the 16th C., including the magnificent chapter house with its elegant central columns. The wall paintings were created by Thomas Pot in 1563: they are scenes from the Gospels, the largest portrayal being the Crucifixion.

St. Augustine applied to the men who served them as clerics. The division of labor at Fontevraud was therefore similar to that of traditional nunneries or female priories which, as of the end of the 11th century, often had a fixed number of canons regular living according to the Rule of St. Augustine assigned to them for their spiritual guidance.

The fact that, for spiritual services, convents were often affiliated to a smaller male monastery that was comprised neither of members of the same order nor of canons regular frequently led to rivalry between the two parts of the community. Despite the men's superiority in spiritual matters, the abbesses nevertheless usually managed to maintain their leadership role as well as the leading position and rights of the female community.

Beguines

In addition to entering a convent, another form of female *conversio* (Latin for religious conversion, reversion) became established as of the 13th century, particularly in Belgium, the Netherlands, and the Rhineland, in the form of the so-called Beguines: women who led a pious life of withdrawal without a set rule or a vow but in affiliation to an urban monastery, usually of a mendicant order, and who settled in individual houses or "Beguine courtyards" nearby. The withdrawal of women from the (upper) aristocracy to their own houses in direct proximity to esteemed male monasteries, where they took part in the religious services in the monastery church, was not unknown previously but the new movement included a greater number of non aristocratic women from the urban middle and upper classes who, in addition to prayer, contemplation, and charitable work, also pursued a handicraft or gave reading and writing lessons in order to secure their livelihood. Although they were not bound by a vow, upon entering the community the women did commit themselves to a life of chastity and voluntary poverty based on the Gospels; property and social privileges were repudiated. Beguine courtyards were convent-like complexes comprising novice houses with individual cells, small cottages with a garden for the longstanding residents, an infirmary and out buildings; some of them also included a simple church. The Beguines' considerable freedom in comparison to the members of the female orders was a thorn in the side of the bishops and prompted ongoing suspicions of heresy as well as persecution at times. The Beguines enjoyed a renewed influx of members as a consequence of the piety movements of the Late Middle Ages and the Counter-Reformation.

▲ ▶ **Bruges, Beguine courtyard.**
Beguine courtyards such as this one are today restricted to the territory of present day Belgium. They are enclosed by a wall and comprise a simple church, one or more houses for the novices, who live in their own cells within the house, and a number of smaller, individual houses for advanced Beguines, usually with a small garden. There are also outbuildings and an infirmary.

Convent and Enclosure

The location of the female choir, the separate area shielded and protected from the view of outsiders—including the priest celebrating the Mass—where the nuns or canonesses performed the Liturgy of the Hours, was not initially a regulated feature. In Irish or Anglo-Saxon religious houses the church was sometimes divided into areas for nuns, priests, and lay members, using wooden room dividers. In Germany, on the other hand, galleries, which were easily visible due to their elevated position, were widespread. From the Carolingian era, such nuns' galleries were more evident in the transept than in the west section of the church (Meschede, Gernrode, Freckenhorst). The gallery situated in the convent-side transept arm provided direct access to the convent buildings, in particular the dormitory, so that its location in the transept clearly had practical advantages. Only where the church was reserved for the female community alone and did not fulfill any additional parish functions was it possible for the nuns' choir to be located at ground level in the east of the nave, as was the case with the monks' choir in the monasteries. This was especially the case in France and Switzerland.

It is only since the 12th century that nuns' choirs were frequently located in or moved to a west gallery. Where possible the nuns' living room and the dormitory were then located not in the east but in the adjoining west wing of the convent (Lippoldsberg, Nottuln near Münster). Some of the mendicant order churches display a special arrangement: there the nuns' choir is in a separate room behind the sanctuary with the main altar and is connected only by means of small openings intended more for listening to the Mass than for seeing it (S. Chiara in Naples, for example). Strict observance of the enclosure was adhered to. The room at the interface between the outside world and the enclosure, where the nuns were allowed to receive visitors, the parlatorium or locutorium (Latin for conversation room), was fitted with a grille that prevented direct physical contact and allowed communication only through a small, barred window.

The altar where Mass was read was outside the nuns' or canonesses' choir so that the priest was not able to make direct contact with the women. Nevertheless, as of the 13th century there was often an altar in the nuns' choir but this was solely for the display of the Eucharist—the consecrated host—in the monstrance for worship and meditation purposes. It is also no coincidence that the introduction of the feast of Corpus Christi, devoted to the veneration of the Eucharist, was prompted by a nun.

In addition to the nuns' choir, both nunneries and monasteries had other locations where the Liturgy of the Hours was held on specific occasions or where Mass was celebrated. These included a sometimes available west choir in the monastery church (e.g. Freckenhorst, Gernrode, Drübeck), chapels in the monastery area that are used on the main saints' days, the chapter house, and patrons' graves if they existed. Furthermore, processions through the church and convent also took place in nunneries on different occasions but

Grille, former Clares convent at Pfullingen, c. 1300. The nuns' outside contact was strictly regulated. The grille with its long metal spikes was very effective in preventing too close a proximity to visitors.

◀ **Gernrode, the former canoness priory church of St. Cyriakus,** erected in 959 by Margrave Gero, the nave looking east. Gero's daughter-in-law Hathui became the first abbess. The priory church is an important Ottonian period building and also Gero's burial place. In the center to the left are parts of the "nuns' gallery" in the transept; the gallery had direct access to the dormitory.

▼ **Frauenchiemsee, abbey of Frauenwörth, Benedictine nuns.** This abbey, founded by the Bavarian Duke Tassilo III c. 722 is one of the oldest religious houses in Germany. Most of the structure was rebuilt in 1722–30. The line of abbesses extends from the Blessed Irmengard (831/33–66) to the present incumbent, her 56th successor, Johanna Mayer OSB (from 2006).

Eibingen, St. Hildegard's Abbey, St. Mary's Garden, in one of the two courtyards. Contrary to what one might expect in a nunnery founded by St. Hildegard (1165), the convent did not have a herb garden. St. Mary's Garden is not a produce garden but is used by the convent's nuns for relaxation in their free time.

these did not usually leave the enclosure. It was only very seldom that processions were held outside the nunnery, for example for Corpus Christi in the Late Middle Ages.

Convent Life

As in the monasteries, daily life in the nunneries was strictly regulated by the Liturgy of the Hours. The remaining time was used primarily for personal meditation, convent organization, and practical tasks, as well as for education and training. Apart from the omission of the *armarius* responsible for the liturgy, the distribution of functions in the nunneries was much the same as in the monasteries. Since the nuns' freedom of movement was restricted, however, the administration of the convent's properties was usually entrusted to a male member of the order, often a lay brother. Following the decline in the numbers of lay brothers in the Late Middle Ages, the nunneries employed lay administrators in their place.

In addition to the usual convent work in the kitchen or the garden, the nuns and canonesses often pursued textile handicrafts as well. They produced embroidered and woven articles for liturgical use but also as a means of personal meditation. These included altar cloths or antependia embroidered with ornamental motifs or figural illustrations, woven, multicolored, and embroidered wall hangings or tapestries with individual portrayals or image cycles from the Bible or the lives of the saints. These were used to decorate the church on Feast Days or were commissioned by other monasteries or priories. They also produced handicrafts reflecting the particular situation of women themselves, such as images of Mary depicting the deep bond between mother and son, as well as figures of the Christ Child and the crib. Sculptures and graphic images in general played an important role in convents as they made the theological content accessible, sometimes even bringing it to life, in that they provided an interpretation of salvation from a specifically female perspective. In this sense the renowned southern German Christ-John groups, for example, are to be seen as the adoption of the biblical story and its theological significance on the part of the nuns, who saw themselves as the "brides of Christ" reflected in the figure of the favorite disciple.

Sculptures and images in convents served not as a replacement for reading, therefore, but they aided its interpretation. Reading and writing were essential skills for convent life, from choral prayer with psalm recitations and readings from the Bible and the writings of the Doctors of the Church to the daily reading during mealtimes in the refectory, as well as for administrative purposes and written correspondence with the outside world. The education of young girls and women therefore consisted in particular of reading and Latin lessons. In the early Middle Ages female priories such as Gandersheim were reputable educational centers where the works of the classic authors

Women with books in conversation, relief panels from Werden, 2nd half of the 11th C., height 10 in (32 cm) (Schatzkammer der Kath. Propsteikirche St. Ludgerus, Essen-Werden). The women sitting under the blind arches with nothing besides books in their hands (the whole ensemble numbers 12 women) face each other in pairs. The dialogue situation is emphasized by the communicating gestures of the hands.

were read in addition to spiritual reading matter. The writings of the poetess Hrotsvit of Gandersheim (c. 935–c. 975), which included dramas and historical works, are an eloquent testimony to the high educational level of women at the time.

The nuns' activities also included copying work and book illumination but in no way did they limit themselves to transcribing the work of others. Especially in the Middle Ages and against the background of an increasing tendency towards mysticism, they frequently recorded their own spiritual experiences, dreams, and visions, and compiled their own works. There are also many indications of scholarly exchange and written correspondence with educated male members of their order. In some cases notes were made about their reading on the edge of the pages and theological discussions among the sisters are likely to have been frequent occurrences.

Hildegard of Bingen (1098–1179) constitutes an exceptional case. Having had visions since her childhood, she was entrusted for her upbringing to the women living at the Disibodenberg convent, where she received a theological education. Following her election as head of the female community she transformed it into an independent convent (Rupertsberg near Bingen). Her extensive works, in which she described her visions and gave them a theological interpretation, made her a legend in her own lifetime. She not only corresponded with emperors, popes and other church dignitaries, she also undertook three preaching trips in her later years: papal recognition of her as a visionary exempted her from the Church's ban on preaching and teaching by women.

Colmar, cloister courtyard of the former Dominican nuns' convent, 13th C. During the Middle Ages the convent was one of the centers of Christian mysticism. Today the ancient walls house the Unterlinden Museum, whose greatest treasures include works by Martin Schongauer and Matthias Grünewald's famous work, the Isenheim Altar.

Lectern cloth from Ebstorf, silk, gold and silver embroidery, end of the 15th C. The embroidered image on the cloth, from the female priory of Ebstorf, combines the theme of the Annunciation with the motif of a mythical unicorn hunt. The legendary creature buries its head in the lap of the Virgin Mary—a pose which was seen as an allegory for the incarnation of Christ.

Nuns' Mystical Visions

Since nuns and monks have dedicated their lives to God it is therefore to be assumed that they also have a predisposition for a special relationship with God. After all, prayer and meditative concentration are part of their daily activities.

To such special relationships with God belong mystical visions and experiences, in other words: a knowledge of God based on inner experience. In such cases, faith is not only communicated in the traditional manner or accessed philosophically; it is a direct, practical experience. The culmination of such mystic encounters is the *unio mystica*, the union of God with the human soul. Not all those with mystical leanings

The Circle of Creation, from: Hildegard of Bingen, *Liber Scivias*, created post-1141, received approbation in 1147/48 from Pope Eugene III (Lucca, Biblioteca Statale).

were party to such peak experiences, however; most of them also required specific preparations and precursors. This section deals with the spectrum of mystical relationships with God, based on the experiences of three famous nuns.

Hildegard of Bingen (1098–1179)

The Benedictine nun Hildegard, the tenth child of a nonaristocratic family, was handed over to the female hermit Jutta of Spanheim at the age of eight, took her vows at 15, and was elected abbess at 38. According to her own testimony, since her childhood she had possessed the gift of experiencing "the power and mystery of cryptic, prodigious stories," but she

kept this to herself for the most part. Only when she was 42, when "a fiery light with lightning came down from the open skies," unlocking the meaning of the Holy Scriptures to her, did she hear "a heavenly voice" telling her of her calling as a prophet and messenger of godly tidings. Thereafter Hildegard told people about her visions, including the Church and secular leaders. In the convent she founded at Rupertsberg near Bingen, which she entered as a nun in 1150 at the age of 18, she was sought out by numerous people requesting advice and guidance. Yet she also undertook numerous journeys herself in order to preach publicly. What had resulted in accusations of heresy for other women was carried out by Hildegard with unchallenged authority after Pope Eugene III, on the recommendation of Bernard of Clairvaux, reviewed and acknowledged her prophetic gifts.

Hildegard's revelations, recorded in her great prophetic works, *Liber Scivias* (Know the Ways!), *Liber vitae meritorum* (Book of the Rewards of Life), and *Liber divinorum operum* (Book of Divine Works), are not the direct recordings of her experiences, "but a long lasting analysis of the visions". This is an argument in favor of calling her a "visionary theologian" because, unlike later people with mystic experiences, she "did not bring herself into these visions"; instead, she reproduced what the Lord showed and said to her (Dinzelbacher). In this regard the miniatures in her works, which she designed herself, at least in part, and whose production she monitored, are also significant, as is indicated by their context within the text. The illustration below deals with the interconnec-

The Birth of Christ with Bridget of Sweden, c. 1415, panel of winged retable (Constance, Rosgartenmuseum). Bridget's saintly attributes are the pilgrim's accessories depicted next to her: staff, hat, and bag.

tion of microcosmos (man) and macrocosmos (world)—typically for Hildegard—in a kind of didactic visualization (with Vitruvius' renowned proportional figure). The verification of the vision through an illustration by the visionary herself, who captures it directly on her wax tablet, corresponds in text to starting every piece with "I." Each experience then retreats behind the quasi-"objective" content of the vision. Hildegard, who disavowed her learning, nevertheless proved to be the type of scholarly mystic whose writing style is often reminiscent of the Old Testament prophets.

Bridget of Sweden (1302/03–1373)

The visions of the only known mystic from medieval Scandinavia are also reminiscent of the Old Testament prophets. They often relate to prophecies and the threat of divine punishment. Bridget Birgersdotter of Sweden initially led a life in accordance with her aristocratic background. Her marriage produced eight children, including St. Catherine of Sweden. The married couple, who undertook pilgrimages together—and also came into contact with European politics due to their close connections to the Swedish royal court—became more intensively religious over the years. However, it was only after her husband's death that Bridget's life underwent its decisive change. Her earlier visionary gift began to play an increasingly prominent role as she saw

The interconnection of the microcosmos (man) and the macrocosmos (world), from: Hildegard of Bingen, *Liber divinorum operum*, created in the decade following 1163 (Lucca, Biblioteca Statale).

Man of Sorrows, c. 1360 (Kulturhistorisches Museum Görlitz). In the Late Middle Ages the suffering of Christ was frequently an object of meditation and the subject of mystic visions.

herself as "God's bride and mouthpiece" and tried to exert an influence on the world in this role. She founded a new order (the Birgittines)—the mother house was in Vadstena castle at Vättersee—and traveled to Rome in 1349 with a small group of followers, as she was instructed to do by her revelations.

A model of pious asceticism and charitable acts, she purposefully used her visionary talents to hold popes and rulers to a life that would please God. In 1372 she undertook a pilgrimage to the Holy Land, returning at the beginning of 1373 to Rome, where she died in July of the same year. She was canonized by Boniface IX 18 years after her death.

Bridget's confessors collected the visions she dictated to them, reviewed them from a theological perspective, and translated them into Latin, later also revising the language. The *Revelationes celestes*, compiled in seven books, contain hundreds of revelatory texts on a variety of topics. Scenes of apocalyptic judgment occur with a noticeable frequency, at times with dramatic content. For the portrayal of agony when applied to the crucifixion of Christ and to the pain of his mother,

Bridget favored the dolorism (cult of suffering) typical of the Late Middle Ages. Only seldom, however, are Bridget's own sentiments heard, which distinguishes her from other mystics of her era.

Bridget's vision of the birth of Christ, which includes a detailed description of Mary's circumstances in childbirth, influenced the composition of the nativity scene in paintings and changed the traditional models to: Mary in a kneeling position (instead of lying down or sitting), the Child lying on the floor (instead of in the crib) surrounded by a nimbus (instead of giving blessings), etc. The panel at the top of the opposite page showing Bridget kneeling behind Mary is a detailed graphic interpretation of her vision.

Teresa of Ávila (1515–82)

The intensity of the experiences and suffering of the great Spanish mystic Teresa of Ávila are dealt with very differently in comparison to Hildegard and Bridget. With Teresa the reporting distance that is noticeable even with Bridget's dramatic accounts of the suffering of the Lord, gives way to an "entrancing inebriation of the soul." Teresa is separated by 400 years from Hildegard, by 200 years from Bridget, but it is not only the centuries that make the difference: it is a completely different way of being "spoken to" by God. For her part, Teresa sought the dialogues with God with all her might.

While her two predecessors were largely

"mouthpieces", bearers of God's tidings, the Spanish Carmelite nun experienced truly ecstatic encounters. In the account of her life Teresa talks in depth about how she had a vision of an angel "with a long, golden arrow, and the tip of the arrow seemed to be on fire. It was as if he bored right into me several times with the arrow, through my heart, and when he withdrew the arrow again it was as if the most inner part of my heart was drawn out. He finally left me, on fire with a fervent love for God. The wound was so great that it caused me to moan in pain; but the joy caused by this great pain was so effusive that it was impossible for me to want to be free of it, or that I should be content with anything less than God."

The great Italian Renaissance sculptor Gianlorenzo Bernini endeavored to produce a passionate representation of this scene in a celebrated, much acclaimed (and criticized) work of art (see left).

St. Teresa of Ávila, 1576, portrait by an unknown painter (Convento de S. Teresa, Carmelitas Descalzas, Valladolid). Teresa founded the first reformed convent of Discalced Carmelite Nuns.

Ecstasy of St. Teresa of Ávila, marble sculpture by Gianlorenzo Bernini (1647–52). (Rome, S. Maria della Vittoria).

Wienhausen, Germany

Duchess Agnes of Brunswick founded a convent for women living according to the Cistercian rule in 1221/29 on the site of the old priory church and it was officially incorporated into the order in 1244. The well endowed nunnery prospered until the 15th century. In 1469 the strict convent life was renewed by the Windesheim Reform. Instead of leading to the abolition of the nunnery, the introduction of the Reformation enforced by the Duke of Celle in 1528/29 led it to be converted into a Protestant-Lutheran female priory that is still in existence today. The extensive nunnery complex is grouped around two inner courtyards, with the church on the south side. The church comprises an older hall church to the east (the former parish church that underwent a Gothic extension in 1330) and four narrower spans to the west added in around 1330 with the nuns' choir on the upper floor. Parts of the nunnery buildings, originally built from brick, were renewed with timber frame constructions in the 16-17th centuries. Their arrangement does not completely comply with the "classic" Cistercian layout (cell dormitory in the north wing, middle north-south gallery in the cloister). The nuns' choir and the convent rooms have retained much of their elaborate artistic decoration in its original position.

◄◄ **Nuns' choir,** c. 1330, with walls and vaulting completely covered with paintings, c. 1335, and the choir stalls along the nave walls, c. 1280. In the foreground the wooden shrine of the Holy Sepulchre, donated by Abbess Katharina of Hoya, 1448, with the recumbent figure of the dead Christ and painted scenes from his Life and Passion.

◄ **South wing of the cloister and the church.** View of the convent's western courtyard.

► **Cell dormitory** on the upper floor of the north wing, renewed as timber frame after 1531: a nun's cell with landscape paintings from the second half of the 17th C.

▼ **Nunnery complex from the southwest** with the tiered blind arches of the gables of the church (right, c. 1330) and the west wing of the convent (left, c. 1310).

Fontevraud (formerly: Fontevrault), France

The monastery founded in 1101 for the wandering preacher Robert d'Arbrissel's large numbers of followers housed several communities next to one another: the aristocratic women's convent under the abbess, the penitents (former concubines and prostitutes), and the lepers, as well as the clerics who provided liturgical services. Under the second abbess, Mathilde of Anjou, who was related to the house of Plantagenet, Fontevrault was the burial place of the English kings for a time. The churches and the buildings of these neighboring religious houses were partly destroyed following the dissolution of the abbey in 1790. Extensive research on the buildings has taken place recently.

The large abbey church erected in the 12th century has an ambulatory with radiating chapels, and protruding transept arms, each with a chapel and a wide hall-like nave roofed by a series of domes. The royal tombs with their recumbent figures of the deceased (including Henry II of England and his wife Eleanor of Aquitaine) are among the oldest examples of this type of tomb.

▼ The abbey church from the east with the three chapels of the ambulatory and a chapel in each of the transept arms.

▲ Tombs of Isabelle of Angoulême, wife of King John I of England, mid-13th C. and of Richard I of England (the Lionheart), early 13th C.

Fontevraud, Kitchen Buildings

The Romanesque kitchen in the southwest corner of the cloister is the one remaining building from the 12th century abbey complex, which was largely rebuilt in the first half of the 16th century. The kitchen has an octagonal ground plan and is surrounded by semicircular, chapel-like extensions. The central room, above four tall arcades, has a steep domical vault on niches, the apex of which has a chimney opening. The exterior is dominated by the high, tapered pavilion roof, which, like the conical roofs of the extensions, is crowned by a vented lantern. The kitchen at Glastonbury Abbey in England is of a similar construction, being a centrally aligned building with a distinctive, pointed roof.

Gabriele Uerscheln
Monastery Gardens in the Middle Ages

The edict issued in 311 by Emperor Galerius (284–311) and by Lizinius (306–37) led to Christianity being considered a permitted religion (*religio incita*). In 313 Emperor Constantine added the Edict of Milan, which gave Christianity the same rights as other religions, before it finally became the imperial religion under Emperor Theodosius (347–95). This applied to both the eastern and western Roman Empire. The bishop of Rome and patriarch in the west was subsequently acknowledged as Peter's successor, against the claims of the patriarch in Constantinople, and Latin came to supersede Greek as the accepted language of the Church.

Early Middle Ages
The first monastic communities had originally come together, before the time of the western Roman Empire, as places of retreat from the world but, within a relatively short period of time, they developed into the originating headquarters of far-reaching missionary movements, accompanied by the founding of new monasteries. The followers of what was once the religion of resistance themselves now encountered people who fought with all their might against what was often the violent destruction of their natural sanctuaries, albeit ultimately in vain. "Holy trees" were cut down, and ancient sacred springs were covered with wells and other structures, which, in the Christian sense, symbolized the four biblical rivers of paradise or water as a source of the purity of a believer's life.

The buildings which the new communities of monks erected were surrounded by high walls, marking the boundary between the ordered world on the inside and the menacing world outside the monasteries. With the increasing consolidation of monasticism the layout of the monastery gardens, with their symmetrically organized and geometrically shaped beds, developed into the reflection of divine order; the monasteries became the nursery of science and education.

It took about 200 years after the retreat of the Romans for the later generation of priests, as a consequence of the missionary expeditions of the early 7th century, to set about founding monasteries, which then developed into centers of religious culture. Names such as Waldkirch (forest church) and Klosterwald (monastery forest) are indicative of the early existence of such foundations, which, in the transition

▲ The St. Gallen monastery plan: excerpt with different green areas for various uses.

▶ The *Hortulus* by Walahfrid Strabo, compared with the plants in the St. Gallen monastery plan herb garden: light green areas (e.g. lilium) = identical plants; dark green areas (e.g. papaver) = plants from the St. Gallen monastery plan vegetable garden; medium-green areas (e.g. abrotanum) = plants added by the *Hortulus* (after D. Hennebo).

zones between cleared and wooded areas, laid the basis for later creatively designed gardens. Initially, however, work in the fields and gardens as part of the monks' activities were strictly focused on their own subsistence needs. The differentiation of the gardens into vegetable and herb gardens, fruit orchards, hop fields, and vineyards developed only gradually, and depending on the respective local conditions and requirements.

Carolingian farmsteads and monastery gardens have antique origins. The monastery garden surrounded by a cloister, with beds laid out in an orderly fashion, and with a well, derives from the classical peristyle garden and became the source of a new art of gardening. The text *Capitulare de villis vel curtis imperii* (c. 800), the St. Gallen monastery plan (c. 830), and the *Hortulus* by Abbot Walahfrid Strabo of Reichenau (c. 830) provide contemporary accounts of gardening culture in the Early Middle Ages. The first of these sources is testimony to Charlemagne's considerable interest in farming and gardening, which was obviously shared by his son, Louis the Pious, who compiled the *Capitulare*, with its comprehensive list of plants. Texts by the imperial biographer Engelbert also provide evidence of Charlemagne having a flower garden established at his imperial palatinate in Aachen, the magnificence of which was partly due to gifts of plants from the caliph Harun al-Raschid. Although this is the first early court garden for which written evidence exists, it can be assumed that the creative medieval gardens had their origins in the monasteries of the Early Middle Ages. The small "paradise garden," which was not a produce garden at all, was to be found in the middle of the open space surrounded by the monastery's cloister: four garden sections, clearly demarcated by a longitudinal and a lateral path, with a fountain at their intersection to provide water for the garden, and which symbolized the source of life and/or the spring in Paradise, were arranged as a well ordered whole. Despite their original use being the cultivation of vegetables and herbs, as well as flowers for altar decoration, cloister gardens clearly developed into places of contemplation.

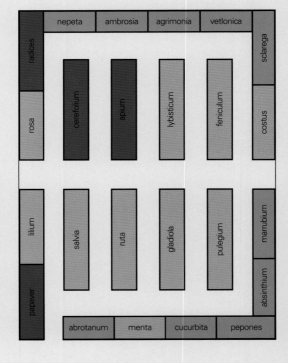

The Fountain of Life, the Gospels from Saint-Médard in Soissons, pre-827 (Paris, Bibliothèque nationale de France, Ms. Lat. 8850, fol. 6 v). The circular temple, enclosing an octagonal well and surrounded by animals, symbolizes the spring in Paradise and is also an allegory of the four Gospels.

There were no cultivation instructions for the large cloister garden (see overall plan, p. 52) but the plan does illustrate the obvious combination of architecture and garden. The cloister garden brings the colonnades closely together in its center. As a young monk and later abbot of the Benedictine monastery at Reichenau, Walahfrid Strabo (808/09–49) composed poems about the plants in the garden there in his *Hortulus*, which clearly followed the *Capitulare*. He gave his didactic poem to Abbot Grimaldus of St. Gallen as a gift between friends. As in the St. Gallen monastery plan, there are two rows each comprising four middle beds, but the side beds are halved in order to make space for the further eight plants contained in Walahfrid's garden. The beds for the 23 plants were to be raised and surrounded with wooden borders (usually wattle from young chestnut trees) so that the earth did not slide away. There is no central section as there is in the cloister of the St. Gallen plan, for example.

Walahfrid extols both the beauty and the medicinal properties of the plants in his garden and also links the individual plants with traditional symbols and the Christian doctrine of salvation. For him clary sage is a symbol of virtue, while the lily is the image of the purity and chastity of the Virgin Mary. The rose, too, used to be considered a medicinal plant, with its beauty and pleasant aroma being enjoyed, while its thorns, symbolizing the Passion of Christ, earned respect.

Some of the plants listed prefer warmer temperatures but their cultivation in the favorable climate of the island of Reichenau in Lake Constance is indeed possible. The young abbot's poems are testimony to the well informed compilation of the Benedictines' natural healing skills, handed down since the end of the antique Roman culture. The ingredients of the very varied monastic medicines soon also included exotic plants such as nutmeg and ginseng, which were introduced to the monks via Arabian sources. The objective was always to combine the healing powers of indigenous and exotic plants in the optimum ratio. The high standard of medical knowledge among Arab physicians was also utilized such that medieval medicinal books combine their experience with the knowledge handed down via the monasteries.

One example of such a garden is given in the St. Gallen monastery plan, which contains a variety of garden types with specific details on their cultivation with useful plants. The plan indicates the layout for the ideal monastery complex. It was probably compiled c. 830 by Reginbert, the librarian on the island of Reichenau, for Gozbert, abbot of the Benedictine monastery at St. Gallen. This plan, drawn on a roll of parchment using the natural pigment red lead, provides the first evidence of the plants being arranged in separate types of gardens: the vegetable garden (detail on the opposite page, below) with its symmetrically arranged rectangular beds was for growing vegetables and spices such as onions, leeks, celeriac, cilantro, dill, poppy seeds, radish, chard, garlic, parsley, chervil, lettuce, summer savory, parsnips, cabbage, and black cumin. Fruit such as apples, pears, plums, sorb trees, bay leaves, quinces, peaches, hazelnuts, almonds, mulberries, walnuts, and chestnuts were recommended for the orchard (section in the middle), which was also a place of remembrance of the monks whose graves were located there. With the fruit crop chosen the trees' natural rhythm became a striking allegory for the Resurrection.

The herb garden was located in close proximity to the apothecary and the physician's house (detail on the opposite page, above). Like the vegetable garden it had a strictly symmetrical layout and was used for the cultivation of medicinal plants. Angelica, fenugreek, rosemary, peppermint, sage, rue, irises, pennyroyal, mint, cumin, lovage, and fennel were among the components of healing medicines from "God's apothecary."

Wine harvest in autumn, *Autumnus*, miniature from *Tacuinum Sanitatis in Medicina*, a medicinal book of Arabian origin (based on a 13th-C. Latin translation), produced in northern Italy shortly before 1400.

High Middle Ages

In addition to such stores of knowledge and the profound respect for the divine gift of nutritional and medicinal plants, mechanical skills also continued to improve. Sophisticated irrigation systems helped to produce a wealth of blooms and a good harvest. The water conduit plan for the Christ Church cathedral monastery (c. 1160) in Canterbury, England, makes the advanced development of water technology clear. The excerpt from the plan shows the fountain house in the form of a small tower in the large cloister. The herb garden (*herbarium*) with its rows of plants enclosed by trellises, lies to the north of the cathedral (c. 1165). The vineyard (*vinea*) and the orchard (*pomerium*) are in a separate area between the town wall and the open fields. The 12th-century abbey chronicle from Fontevraud in the Loire Valley, France, states: "The different vegetable and herb gardens serve as living books. Based on their example we cultivate large quantities in the fields outside the monastery walls."

The additional use of land outside the walls was possible in the case of monasteries that enjoyed royal and/or papal protection and had been endowed with abundant lands and other valuable property. This applied in equal measure to both nunneries and male monasteries. In the High Middle Ages, both the agricultural and the medicinal plant descriptions contained in the *Capitulare* and the *Hortulus* followed the first comprehensive work on plants, by Abbess Hildegard of Bingen (1098–1179), who founded her own convent in 1147/48 at Rupertsberg close to

Bingen. The abbess paid the same amount of attention to the use and the symbolism of the plants in the vegetable and herb beds as did her fellow monastic gardeners and, for her part, contributed to the fact that, in addition to the exemplary Benedictines, other communities also dedicated themselves to the development and cultivation of gardens. The number of sources on the art of gardening increases steadily with the High Middle Ages: illuminated Books of Hours, texts on the layout of gardens, diagrams, and paintings reflect the development from the produce garden to the creatively designed pleasure garden as a place of cultivated relaxation, of play, of hunting, of earthly amours, and of divine love in the enclosed paradise garden (*hortus conclusus*). The transition from produce to pleasure garden was a slow one and was dependent on social and political conditions. The title of the *Hortus deliciarum*, by the abbess of the convent at Hohenburg, is evidence of the concept of gardening pleasure existing in the 12th century. Count Albert of Bollstädt (c. 1200–1280), known as Albertus Magnus, universal scholar, naturalist, a theorist of garden layout, and also teacher of Thomas Aquinas, wrote his work *De Vegetabilibus* in around 1260. In winter 1249 his much acclaimed monastery garden was the venue for a celebration for Wilhelm of Holland, who, so the legend has it, was surprised with fruit and flowers that had obviously been grown with the help of greenhouses. This possibly expressed merely the dream of a greenhouse but it is known that Albertus Magnus spoke not only of the produce garden but also of a paradisiacal place on earth, for a garden of "delight," i.e. one for pleasure purposes.

Ground plan of the abbey at Canterbury, 12th C., section with water supply system around the fountain house. The plan was drawn up because new water pipes needed to be laid. (Cambridge, Trinity College Library, Ms. R. 17 1).

Late Middle Ages

Like Albertus Magnus, the knowledgeable scholar Pietro de Crescenzi (1233–1321) from Bologna, in his work *Ruralia Commodora*, written between 1304 and 1306, also argued in favor of the pleasure garden, which he saw as divided into: smaller gardens with herbs; large and medium sized gardens for middle class citizens, which might include sloe and rose hedges, fruit trees, rows of vines, and meadow areas; as well as pleasure gardens for the nobility and the wealthy, which, given the land available, Crescenzi would settle with wild animals and birds, as well as providing fish ponds and special garden

Diagram of a pleasure garden based on the instructions of Albertus Magnus (after D. Hennebo).

① meadow
② herb garden with flowers
③ bench with flowers on the side
④ water source
⑤ trees

buildings. Crescenzi's descriptions in fact extend well beyond the medieval art of gardening and verge on the ideas, like "green paradises" of the Renaissance epoch, which also brought the monastery gardens into full blossom.

The history of the Certosa di S. Lorenzo monastery began in 1305 when the Carthusians were given a property with rudimentary buildings in the Diano valley, then still a marsh. The Carthusians reclaimed the valley. The buildings of the monastery complex, which was nationalized in 1866, were constructed in several phases. The four sided, two story structure, which has a generous, rectangular courtyard with the arcade passageway enclosed by 48 columns is characteristic. Three flanks of the building house the 25 *cellas*, private apartments for the monks

The Paradise Garden, c. 1410, originating from a workshop in the Upper Rhineland (Frankfurt am Main, Städelsches Kunstinstitut). The numerous plants in this *hortus conclusus* are depicted in great detail.

from noble families, each with a garden and an arcaded passageway to the side, and adjoin the exterior of the complex. The layout of the monastery reflects a form of hermitism focused on contemplation and spiritual work but not bound to the original ascetic lifestyle.

It was to divine love, and not the jovial erotic games of the nobility in a hidden garden, that the 1410 painting *Paradise Garden* by an Upper-Rhine master was dedicated. The walled paradise garden (*hortus conclusus*) symbolizes the virginal body of Mary the Mother of God. Borage, primroses, rose campions, daisies, irises, hollyhocks, madonna lilies, lilies of the valley, peonies, sweet rocket, violets, myrtle, snowdrops, and blossoming and fruiting strawberries are growing in the meadow. But the elaborate portrayal still indicates the dangers that are to be found even in the paradise garden. An ominous, dark form lurks at the foot of the tree; a dragon lying on its back is depicted to the lower right of the picture, its position and diminutive size indicating that it has been conquered. Even the most beautiful of earthly gardens should not belie the fact that paradise lost is not to be found on earth but only in the Heavenly Jerusalem, according to St. John (Revelations, 21, 16–27).

Philip II of Spain had one of the largest cloisters in the world erected in the middle of one of the Renaissance's most extensive feudal complexes as a monumental echo of past medieval monastery and oriental garden design. The surface area of the monastery garden in the Patio de los Evangelistas in the Escorial (1563–84) is divided into four compart-

ments by two axes. At the intersection of the axes stands an octagonal temple, around which four square basins with stone borders are grouped above ground level, while the plants within the compartments are planted more deeply in accordance with oriental guidelines.

The high degree of knowledge about the uses and symbolism of plants and how the monastery gardens' design symbolized divine order provided role models for the postmedieval apothecary gardens and urban botanical gardens. It was the ruling families and the feudal dynasties, however, who were to go on to write the great history of garden masterpieces at the beginning of the Italian Renaissance.

▼ This illustration from Crescenzi's text *Ruralia Commodora* shows a classic example of the layout of a country estate, with the manor house, dovecote, orchard, vegetable garden, and the yard enclosed by a wattle fence.

▲▲ Maisonnais, Prieuré Notre-Dame-d'Orsan. The layout and the plants grown here are part of an attempt to reproduce the elements of a medieval garden.

VIII

The Mendicant Orders

Vita Apostolica

Since Late Antiquity monasteries have always been erected *in eremo*, in the actual or the self-proclaimed desert, but certainly away from settlements and towns. Their declared objective was withdrawal from the world and a life of prayer and asceticism. Monasteries had also always owned at least the land on which the church and monastery buildings stood; from the Early Middle Ages they were often the owners of extensive properties. Like the agrarian society around them, the monks lived solely from what was yielded by the land belonging to their monastery. Although donations and endowments made them increasingly wealthy, against their original intentions, it seemed unthinkable (with the exception of individuals who withdrew to the forests and lived as hermits) for religious communities to forgo property ownership as the basis of their livelihood or to exchange the countryside for the towns as their living environment.

This is precisely what the mendicant orders did, however: instead of a withdrawn life of prayer in the country they chose the up-and-coming towns of c. 1200, with their fast growing populations and dynamic economies, as the field of operation for their religious message, the sermon; instead of a self-sanctifying *vita contemplative* (Latin for concentration on prayer and the Holy Scriptures) they applied themselves to an active *vita apostolica* (in succession to Christ) focused on their fellow men, for which the Gospels themselves provided the model. What's more, they made the absolute lack of possessions of the two major orders, the Franciscans and the Dominicans, their principle not only for individuals but for the whole community. This was based on a radical interpretation of the life of the original Christian community, as outlined in the Acts of the Apostles and in the Gospel of Matthew, where it says: "And as you go, preach, saying, 'The kingdom of heaven is at hand.' ... Provide neither gold nor silver nor copper in your money belts, nor bag for your journey, nor two tunics, nor sandals ..." (Matthew 10, 7-10). Even though the origins and the religious backgrounds of the two major mendicant orders differ greatly from one another, the new monastic ideal that they propagated and lived concurred on the following key points: lack of possessions and active work as preachers in the towns.

Town Life and Lay Piety

Towns had grown all over Europe during the 12th century. Ancient towns that had shrunk since antiquity had expanded again and new towns had arisen out of monastery settlements or had been founded by the landed aristocracy. Manual labor and especially trade formed the basis of urban development and produced a new elite whose activities usually meant that they were able to read and write the popular language. Parallel to the economic revival, the urban elite also increasingly sought religious fulfillment that the parish clerics with their rudimentary education, and to whom the elite considered themselves to be equals or superiors, were not able to provide. Since only very few people knew Latin, however, they were barred access to the religious ranks. Excluded from an active spiritual life via recognized channels, the urban elite began to organize themselves independently. They saw the Bible

Late medieval town scene, detail from Filippino Lippi's *Madonna with Child and Saints*, 1488, in S. Spirito, Florence. View of the city gate and the street near S. Frediano, a district on the other side of the Arno river. The 14th-C. city gate, which still exists today, used to serve as a watch tower over the road to Pisa.

itself as the model for their religious way of life, in which the Gospels and the Acts of the Apostles outlined the life of the disciples of Jesus and the original Christian community—a community that, like themselves, comprised married and unmarried lay people who had surrendered their personal possessions and dedicated themselves solely to their faith and its proclamation. Their independent quest to present what they recognized as the truth in public sermons, and the direct reference to the New Testament without a detour via the earlier monastic tradition, challenged the existing monopoly of the monks, canons regular, and secular clerics in matters of religious truth and redemption. The institutional Church reacted with the ostracism of the urban lay activities and the charge of heresy.

Such lay movements were especially widespread in the towns of northern Italy, where they went under the name of the Humiliates (from the Latin *humiliare*, humiliate), but also arose in Lyons (the home of the Waldensians), Provence, and Piedmont, as far as central Italy. While the Humiliates continued to accept the orthodoxy of the Church, the Waldensians were split between an orthodox faction and one increasingly opposed to the institutional Church. In the Midi region of southern France and in Languedoc, a heretic sect was indeed spreading, namely the Cathars, who preached a dualist world divided between good and evil. All were condemned as heretics in 1184, but the Humiliates were acknowledged by Pope Innocent III in 1201 and were thus—as was later the case with some of the Waldensians—brought back into the Church. By institutionalizing them, the Pope acknowledged the Humiliates as the first religious movement to be (alongside the canons regular and nuns, and the lay monastic communities of men and women) a third branch of married order members, the "tertiaries," who, despite their religious status, remained in the secular world and continued to live with their families. The question of the "second way" within Christianity, which had in fact been decided since Late Antiquity in favor of celibacy and the renunciation of worldly ties, was put back on the agenda by the lay movements and thus suddenly became a key issue again.

Scenes from the life of St. Francis, Giotto (?), 1295/1300, Assisi, upper basilica. The defection from his father (left) is portrayed here as a dramatic event in an urban setting. Charged by his father before the bishop's court with squandering the paternal assets, Francis hands his clothes to the irate head of the family and renounces him. Innocent III's dream (right) shows the Lateran Church, in danger of collapse, being supported by a simply dressed man. The Pope saw Francis as the savior of the church and admired him from then on.

The Franciscans

St. Francis preaching to the birds, fragment from a psalter, c. 1230–40 (Karlsruhe, Badische Landesbibliothek, cod. 410 (b)).

Confirmation of the Rule of St. Francis by Pope Honorius III, Giotto (?), 1295/1300, Assisi, upper basilica.

Francis, born in 1181 as the son of a wealthy textile merchant in Assisi, received a typical, upper class urban school education comprising reading and writing as well as Latin, and French from his father as the language of trade at that time. He moved in the circles of young people from good families and took part in military actions against the neighboring town of Perugia. In 1205 he found himself en route to a military expedition against the Staufer dynasty in Apulia, when he turned around in Spoleto, following a dream in which Christ had appeared to him. Back in Assisi he renounced his inheritance, left his family's house, and began a hermitic life of penitence in the Umbrian mountains. Three years later he decided to follow a life closely based on the *Vita apostolica*, based on the Acts of the Apostles, of which the main focus was on missionary work preaching changing one's ways and penitence. Together with the followers who had joined him in the meantime— primarily the sons of wealthy Assisi residents—Francis traveled through the towns of central Italy and preached in the market places and in the churches. The "friars minor," as they called themselves, wore a tunic of rough, plain fabric, held together by a cord at the waist, and went barefoot. They earned their livelihood through temporary employment or manual labor, resorting to begging only in emergencies.

In 1209 Francis took his group to Rome in order to attain papal recognition of their way of life as wandering preachers based on the Gospels, without possessions and without a fixed abode. With the mediation of advocates such as the bishop of Assisi, they received a verbal approbation from Innocent III. In order to avoid problems involving licenses to preach and to improve the Church's self-image, relating to the formation of an order dominated by

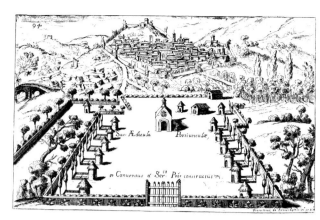

The Portiuncula Chapel at the time of St. Francis. Engraving from 1704 (▲), outside view of the chapel in S. Maria degli Angeli Church near Assisi (◀). Francis made this chapel the focal point of the new order: this is where his life of poverty came to an end.

(▼) **St. Francis and 20 episodes from his life,** 13th C., Florence, S. Croce, Bardi Chapel. Such panels with the saint and scenes from his life were very popular. Less elaborate examples contain only six or eight scenes; their arrangement and the depiction of the saint are all very similar, however.

laymen Innocent decided to allow them to have the tonsure and thus officially incorporated them into the clerical ranks.

Back in Umbria Francis recognized that the new brotherhood needed a fixed headquarters and a church for celebrating religious services. The Benedictines made a disused church of St. Mary close to Assisi available to him, which he and his followers renovated themselves, adding an infirmary and living quarters. From them on this place, referred to as Portiuncula, became the focal point of their communal life. The brotherhood continued to acquire new followers. Anyone who disposed of his possessions, distributing the proceeds among the poor, and who took up the life of a wandering preacher was accepted as a member. In 1217 Francis decided to replace the preaching activities in regions both near and far with a universal mission. The years that followed saw the definition of provinces and the dispatch of groups of brothers to the countries north of the Alps and on the Iberian Peninsula.

Francis himself opted for preaching to the Muslims. In 1219 he traveled by ship to Egypt, where, during the siege of Damietta, he tried in vain to convert Sultan al-Kamil. He returned suffering from malaria and an eye disease. Francis resigned his leadership of the order in favor of his longstanding companion Petrus Catanii and, following his death, Elias of Cortona; he had the office of Cardinal Bishop Ugolino of Ostia, whom he had already appointed as protector of the order prior to his journey, officially confirmed by the Pope. He then largely withdrew from the order's activities and led an ascetic existence characterized by illness, increasing blindness, and also, after 1224, stigmatization—the scars of Christ appearing on his body. With his contribution to the final rule confirmed by Pope Honorius III in 1223 (*Regula bullata*) and his "Testament" he tried again to impress on the expanding order, for whom the ideal of poverty was becoming more of a problem, the initial intentions. Francis died in the infirmary at Portiuncula on October 3, 1226 and was canonized only two years later.

▼ ▶ **Crucifix,** Giunta Pisano, 1236-40, Assisi, S. Maria degli Angeli. Of the numerous well known figures who appeared as successors of Christ, St. Francis is the most popular of the medieval saints.

Development of the Order and the Poverty Dispute

Organizing the development and life of the rapidly growing order without infringing upon the rule soon proved to be impossible: the requirement of an absolute lack of possessions, the ban on accepting money, and the traveling life with no fixed abode was not practical for a community divided into numerous provinces and with a continually increasing number of members. Consequently, an assimilation of the organizational forms of older orders was introduced, supported by the Church but viewed with distrust by many Franciscans. The poverty requirement was obviated by a privilege from Innocent IV in 1245 declaring all Franciscan possessions to be the property of the pope, who then assigned the use of the land and buildings to the brothers. Buildings erected by patrons could also remain as their property, which the Franciscans merely had the use of. The ban on accepting money in any form whatsoever was annulled by the appointment of trustees who accepted donations and endowments on behalf of the brothers and undertook all payments and related activities for them.

Furthermore, a revision of the internal order structure was undertaken that was intended to clarify responsibilities and achieve greater efficiency, but led above all to a radical clericalization. While Francis was still alive (1220), the Pope had revised the rules regarding acceptance into the order to make them consistent with canonical law: accordingly there was a one year novitiate and a binding vow to be taken. The act of preaching, which had initially been accorded to all brothers, increasingly became an office related to education and theological knowledge that could only be practiced following review and nomination by the order's dignitaries. Following the removal of the general minister Elias of Cortona, a layman, it was decided at the general chapter of 1239 that, in the future, positions with a leadership function should only be filled by clerics. The community in which laymen and clerics had lived side by side as equals, and in which laymen had in fact made up the majority and had performed the most important functions, thus became a clerical order that excluded the laymen from codetermination and responsibility. The strengthening of the clergy was accompanied by a revaluation of theological education and training, which reflected the success of the order among the educated and scholarly. In 1260 the general chapter in Narbonne

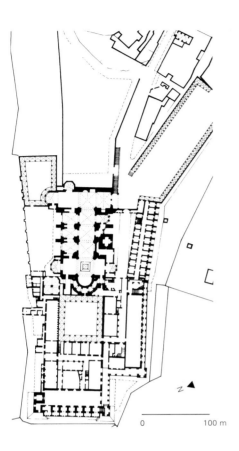

Assisi, S. Francesco, overall complex and ground plan of the basilica and monastery; 1228 saw the laying of the foundation stone for the lower basilica, 1230 the transfer of the saint's mortal remains, 1253 the consecration. A less ostentatious resting place would have been more in keeping with Francis' ideal of poverty.

0   100 m

decided to accept only theologically trained clerics and prominent lay personalities into the order. A brotherhood familiar with the Gospels in the language of the people and for whom the possession of books was in fact forbidden thus became an order of scholarly clerics that maintained large communities in university towns such as Paris and Oxford and built its own study centers for the training of preachers.

The conflicts resulting from this new direction kept the Franciscans on edge until well into the 16th century and led to ostracism and divisions. The advocates of absolute poverty, the "Spirituals," saw the acceptance of money and the elaborate buildings as an infringement of the rule and rejected the formal transfer of property to the pope and the appointment of trustees as legal gimmicks. They saw their position as being confirmed by the testimony of the first generation of brothers and by Francis' "Testament". The decade-long conflicts came to an end with the oppression of the spirituals, who were excommunicated by Pope John XXII in 1317. Four of them were burnt at the stake in Marseilles in 1318. In order to end the dispute once and for all, in 1323 the Pope declared Christ's and the Apostles' absolute lack of possessions to be heterodoxy, which led to the secession of even the more moderate Franciscans and to the election of an antipope. The increasing departure from poverty and preaching caused a decline in discipline, which the "Observants" tried to counter from 1368 with a return to the ideals of St. Francis and an adherence to the rule. Their reform movement received the support of Pope Martin V, who revoked Pope John XXII's radical position in the poverty dispute. As the result of a papal decree the Observants were accorded their own representative within the order in 1438 and autonomy in 1446, which was a prelude to their final separation in 1517. While the Observants' intention was the pursuit of the Franciscan ideals, the "Conventuals" became a traditional monastic order.

Nothing illustrates the virulent discrepancies between spiritual ideals and the order's practice in the case of the Franciscans more clearly than the basilica erected in Assisi in honor of the order's founder. One day after Francis' canonization in the Assisi market square, Pope Gregory IX, the former cardinal protector Ugolino of Ostia, laid the foundation stone for a

monumental sepulchral basilica comprising two floors: an open lower basilica for pilgrims, with St. Francis' tomb; and an upper basilica for the order, with the pope's seat in the apex of the apse, which was based on the French Gothic style, then the most modern form of design. The transfer of the saint's mortal remains took place in 1230 and the basilica was consecrated in 1253. The most famous artists of the age were commissioned to create the wall paintings for the liturgical decoration and the embellishment of the building. Thus the "poor brother" Francis found his resting place in one of the most prestigious and exquisitely decorated new buildings of the 13th century, which today remains an attraction for both pilgrims and art lovers alike. He thus met with the same destiny as other successful patrons of the order: the perpetuation of his memory and his veneration as a saint took on dimensions that were the very antithesis of his intentions during his lifetime.

Assisi, S. Francesco, façade of the upper basilica. The façade, divided into three sections of equal height but otherwise with few divisions, whose only decoration comprises the large rose window and the porch, gives no hint that the interior of the church is so lavishly endowed with frescoes. The façade type adheres to that of older Umbrian tradition.

Assisi, S. Francesco,
◄ interior view of the upper basilica.
► Crypt with the tomb of St. Francis.
▼ Nave of the lower basilica.

The transfer of the saint's remains to the still incomplete
basilica on May 25, 1230 took place one day ahead of the
planned date—in great secrecy, as it was feared that the
treasured relics might be stolen. The precise location of the
grave was also kept a secret for the same reason. It was
only in 1818 that one of the many searches met with
success. A crypt was erected in 1822–24 on the site where
the grave was found.

S. Francesco in Assisi is unique in terms of decorative
church frescoes.

The Dominicans

Unlike the Franciscans, the Dominicans were a clerical order from the outset and placed their emphasis on the profound theological education of their members right from the beginning. Although they opted for the lifestyle of the follower of the apostles, they were closer to traditional monasticism and in their monasteries tried to combine the Liturgy of the Hours with study and preaching work.

Dominic was born c. 1170 in Caleruega in Castile and completed his training as a priest in Palencia. In 1195 he was a canon regular at the cathedral of Osma. He became aware of the widespread heretical beliefs while accompanying his bishop on a journey through southern France. Following his return from a visit to the Danish court in 1206 he decided, together with the bishop, to become involved in actively combating the Cathars. Unlike the Cistercians, whom the Pope had entrusted with preaching against the Cathars, Bishop Diego and Dominic adopted a life as simple traveling preachers, which gave them the same aura of austerity as the leaders of the Cathars, the "perfecti" (Latin for perfect), and brought them into direct contact with the people they wanted to convince. Their success soon became apparent. In 1206 they were already able to found a convent in Prouille (Aude) for women who had reverted from heresy. Following Diego's death at the end of 1207, Dominic continued his preaching activities from neighboring Fanjeaux, work which he also continued during the Albigensian war.

Following the end of the war he moved his base to Toulouse, where, together with a group of helpers, he founded his first clerical monastery in 1215. In the same year he traveled to Rome with the bishop of Toulouse in order to obtain papal recognition of his community's objectives and lifestyle. However, although the Pope supported Dominic's efforts in combating heretics, he was not willing to approbate a new rule and was reluctant to grant the monks a general mandate for spiritual guidance and preaching. After consulting his brothers, Dominic opted for the next best solution: he gave them the rule that he himself followed, namely the Premonstratensians' Rule of St. Augustine in a version focusing on the sermon, which then made the members of his order canons regular who were allowed to provide spiritual guidance.

Dominic meditating, fresco by Fra Angelico in the former Dominican monastery in Florence. The founder of the preaching or Dominican order, born c. 1170 in Caleruega, Old Castile, and who died in Bologna in 1221, led a contemplative life initially. His lifestyle changed when he became a wandering preacher against the Cathars from 1206.

Occitan cross from Fanjeaux, 12th C. An edict from Bishop Fulco of Toulouse in 1214 described Dominic as the priest of Fanjeaux. Dominic lived there for a few months until early 1215.

▶ **Montségur,** "Le Pog" (cliffs) with fortress. Around 200 Cathars met their death here in 1244.

The Albigensian War

Following the murder of the papal legate Pierre de Castelnau in 1208, Innocent III called for a crusade against the Cathar heretics (named "Albigensians" after the town of Albi). The expedition, comprising aristocrats from the north of France who had heeded the summons, soon developed into a political battle between the Count of Toulouse and the French Crown over the domination of Languedoc. It lasted, with interruptions, until 1229 and ended with the removal from power of the Count and the annexation of southern France. The senseless brutality on the part of the military leaders is illustrated by the bloodbath wrought among the residents following the crusaders' capture of Béziers in 1209.

St. Dominic's cell, Bologna, S. Domenico. From Toulouse, where Dominic had founded a community of preachers in 1215, he dispatched several of his brothers to Paris and Bologna to study and found monasteries. He converted this community into an order in 1217 and summoned the first general chapter to Bologna in 1220. He died in Bologna in 1221 and was laid to rest in S. Domenico.

In the summer of 1217, shortly before Francis began his universal mission, Dominic decided to expand his community into a general order. He sent the majority of the Toulouse brothers off to Paris to study and to found monasteries, others went to Spain, and he himself left for Bologna with a third group shortly thereafter. The deliberate choice of the two university towns for the foundation of monasteries was based on the recognition that intellectual debates on the correct doctrinal interpretations took place at the important schools of theology and that was where they needed to be won. This meant that the preaching brothers not only had to be well educated, they had to be on site as well.

In the years that followed Dominic undertook preaching journeys in Spain, Languedoc, and Italy, visited the newly founded monasteries and concerned himself with the organization of the order. In 1221 the general chapter decided to extend activities throughout Europe and the Middle East. Dominic died on August 6, 1221 in Bologna.

Order Structure and Life

In contrast to the Franciscans and the older orders, the Dominicans had an order constitution strongly characterized by the principles of representation and the responsibility of the office bearers. The entire order was divided into individual monasteries, which were allocated to provinces. The members of the individual monasteries elected their superiors, the priors. The prior also had an elected *socius* (Latin for companion) at his side, who provided a report on the state of the monastery and the work of the prior to the annual provincial chapter. The provincial prior was elected by the prior and two representatives from each of the monasteries and was answerable to the provincial chapter. Four "diffinitors" elected at the start of the chapter meeting acted as his controllers, received complaints, and could remove him from office. The order's highest authority was the general chapter, which met annually with differing participants, alternating between Paris and Bologna, and later also in other cities. While for two years, in addition to the head of the order, it comprised the master general and one diffinitor per province sent as a representative by the provincial chapter, in the third year it was the provincial priors who met instead. New statutes could be issued only by three consecutive general chapters. The master general was elected by an extended general chapter. He was answerable to the chapter and could be censured and

The Test of Fire, Pedro Berruguete, c. 1500. This scene shows books being tested for their validity in the presence of St. Dominic. The book hanging in the air, a Bible, passes the test. Following the death of their founder, the Dominicans, known for their scholarly religious zeal, were entrusted with the Inquisition and were deeply involved in its machinations.

The Path to Salvation, Andrea Bonaiuti (Andrea da Firenze), c. 1365–67, fresco, Florence, S. Maria Novella, Spanish chapel. This work illustrates the claim of the Dominican order to possess directional authority over the path to salvation. This is precisely the role played by one of the order's saints in the center of the fresco: as a signpost to the gates of Paradise. The group gathered in front of the large domed church, which represents the community of the faithful, headed by the spiritual and secular authorities, shows a cardinal in a Dominican habit on the left (looking at the painting) of the elevated, seated pope. He is seated at the same level as the emperor to the right of the pope. His book indicating that he is keeper of the official doctrine, the cardinal embodies the power claimed by his order. The type of power in question is illustrated by the black and white dogs, the *Domini canes* (dogs of the Lord). Two of them are guarding a group of four sheep located at the feet of the pope and the emperor, an allegory for the Christians needing to be watched over. The pack of hounds to the right rounds up the errant sheep and mauls the wolves. The meaning of these allegories is then explained by the sermons of the Dominican saints.

removed from office by the diffinitors. Annual inspections of the individual monasteries were carried out by the representatives of the provincial chapter for two years and by those of the general chapter in the third year. All members of the order made their vows to the master general, this guaranteeing unity and making possible the brothers' mobility. Key features of this very "modern" constitution, based on the principles of representation and control of the office bearers at all levels, and unparalleled in its time, are attributable to Dominic himself and his extraordinary talent for organization, even though it was passed by the general chapter only in 1228 and 1238. It served as a model for others, including the Franciscans, who adopted the basic features of the Dominican order structure but replaced the election of office bearers in many instances with nomination. In contrast to the Franciscans, the Dominicans never experienced a division of their order.

Like Francis, Dominic also chose the *vita apostolica*, renouncing all possessions for himself and his brothers. The decisive factor was the reluctance to provide a target for the widespread criticism of the luxurious lifestyles of the spiritual ranks in the conflict with the heretics, and to be able to measure up, in terms of modesty, to the Cathars' perfecti, who disdained worldly goods. This decision was also influenced by the example of Norbert of Xanten, who had himself practiced apostolic poverty following Christ's example as a wandering preacher. Unlike the Franciscans, however, the Dominicans never had problems with the possession of churches and monastery buildings. The issue of whether the transfer of property to the pope was no more than a legal trick provoked no dispute among them.

With the adoption of the Premonstratensian rule the Dominicans were faced with the challenge of integrating the preaching and spiritual guidance requirements into monastery life. The day was structured around the Liturgy of the Hours in an abbreviated form and without any additions. The monastic code of silence applied in the monastery, the usual fasting times were adhered to, and a general abstinence from meat prevailed. Manual labor by monks was abolished in favor of study. All of the brothers were required to attend the daily chapter, but there were numerous dispensations from the Liturgy of the Hours on weekdays for the purposes of preaching and studying, with the exception of compline. The Dominicans celebrated this evening officium before retiring for the night as a public church service in order to draw the faithful into their churches at the end of their working day. It ended with the celebratory singing of the *Salve Regina*, a hymn to the Virgin Mary, and a procession by the brothers from the choir to the lay people in the nave.

In addition to clerics, the Dominicans did sometimes accept laymen as members who performed the manual labor in the monastery, served as sacristans, and accompanied the preachers on their travels. They were barred from a training as clerics but, unlike the Cistercian lay brothers, they did not live apart from their fellows but together with them and also took part in the Liturgy of the Hours in the choir.

Since not all of the preachers could be sent to Paris or Bologna to study, the monasteries set up their own schools. There *lectores*, educated brothers appointed by the order's hierarchy as teachers, gave lessons in Bible studies, issues of faith, and moral theology, as well as in the confession and penitence. In each province there were monasteries with *studia solemnia*, larger schools where a comprehensive education in the *artes liberals* was possible. Finally, there were also the *studia generalia*, high level schools of theology based in the university towns. The first and for a long time the only *studium generale* was in Paris. Until the end of the 13th century such centers of study were also set up in the monasteries at Oxford, Cologne, Bologna, Montpellier, Florence, and Barcelona. In comparison to the rapid expansion of the Franciscans, which took place even faster than that of the Cistercians a century previously, the

The Path to Salvation (detail). The two guard dogs facing in each direction indicate that Christians are threatened by danger from the side of the clerics (left) and from the side of the laymen (right). Heretical heterodoxies can arise in all classes of society.

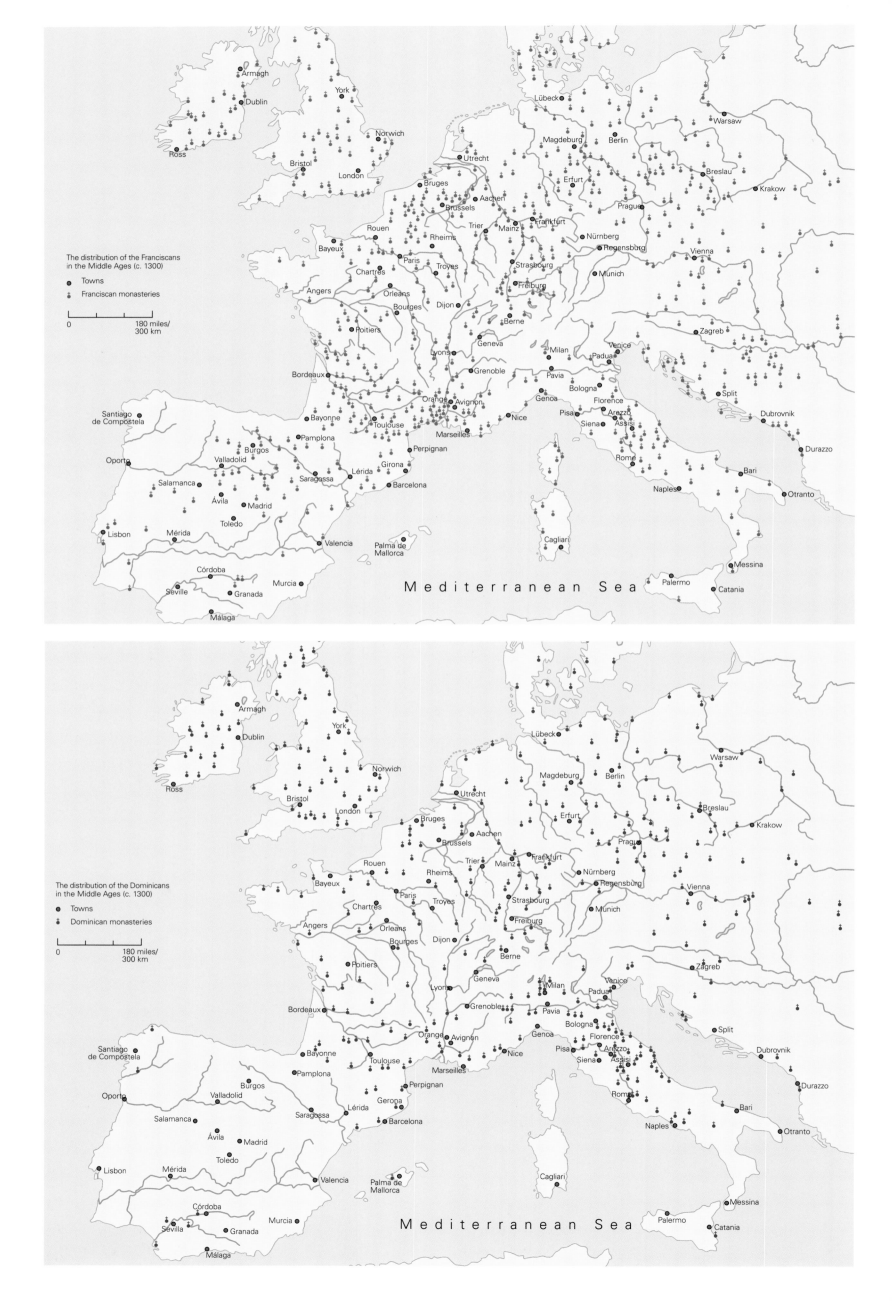

The distribution of the Franciscans
in the Middle Ages (c. 1300)

● Towns

♟ Franciscan monasteries

0 ——— 180 miles/
300 km

Upper map labels:

Armagh
Dublin
Ross
Bristol
London
York
Norwich
Utrecht
Lübeck
Magdeburg
Berlin
Warsaw
Erfurt
Breslau
Krakow
Prague
Bruges
Aachen
Brussels
Trier
Mainz
Frankfurt
Nürnberg
Regensburg
Vienna
Rouen
Rheims
Bayeux
Paris
Troyes
Strasbourg
Freiburg
Munich
Chartres
Angers
Orleans
Bourges
Dijon
Berne
Poitiers
Geneva
Lyons
Milan
Padua
Venice
Zagreb
Bordeaux
Grenoble
Pavia
Bologna
Split
Orange
Avignon
Genoa
Florence
Arezzo
Assisi
Dubrovnik
Nice
Pisa
Siena
Durazzo
Santiago
de Compostela
Bayonne
Toulouse
Marseilles
Rome
Bari
Oporto
Burgos
Pamplona
Perpignan
Naples
Otranto
Valladolid
Saragossa
Lérida
Girona
Barcelona
Salamanca
Ávila
Madrid
Toledo
Valencia
Palma de
Mallorca
Cagliari
Lisbon
Mérida
Córdoba
Murcia
Messina
Palermo
Catania
Seville
Granada
Málaga

Mediterranean Sea

The distribution of the Dominicans
in the Middle Ages (c. 1300)

● Towns

♟ Dominican monasteries

0 ——— 180 miles/
300 km

Lower map labels:

Armagh
Dublin
Ross
York
Norwich
Bristol
London
Lübeck
Magdeburg
Berlin
Warsaw
Erfurt
Breslau
Krakow
Prague
Utrecht
Bruges
Brussels
Aachen
Trier
Mainz
Frankfurt
Nürnberg
Regensburg
Vienna
Rouen
Rheims
Bayeux
Paris
Troyes
Strasbourg
Munich
Chartres
Angers
Orleans
Bourges
Dijon
Freiburg
Berne
Poitiers
Geneva
Lyons
Milan
Padua
Venice
Zagreb
Bordeaux
Grenoble
Pavia
Bologna
Split
Orange
Avignon
Genoa
Florence
Arezzo
Assisi
Dubrovnik
Nice
Pisa
Siena
Durazzo
Santiago
de Compostela
Bayonne
Pamplona
Toulouse
Marseilles
Perpignan
Rome
Bari
Oporto
Burgos
Valladolid
Saragossa
Lérida
Gerona
Barcelona
Naples
Otranto
Salamanca
Ávila
Madrid
Toledo
Valencia
Palma de
Mallorca
Cagliari
Lisbon
Mérida
Córdoba
Murcia
Messina
Palermo
Catania
Sevilla
Granada
Málaga

Mediterranean Sea

Dominicans' development followed a more sedate pace. Since they had only accepted clerics from the outset and also directed themselves primarily at the educated classes, they were never able to compete with the Franciscans in terms of monastery numbers, even though they had bases in all European countries. In 1358 there were 635 Dominican monasteries in comparison to the 1400 of the Franciscan order.

Female Branches of the Franciscans and the Dominicans

Both Francis and Dominic had female followers and were involved in the establishment of female religious houses, and yet both orders later opposed the incorporation of convents. The extra time required for the women's spiritual guidance would keep the brothers from their real responsibilities, namely preaching, was the reasoning. In addition there was also apprehension about the financial obligations involved in the adoption of poorly endowed convents and of discipline problems with self-confident and opinionated nuns, as well as the permanent fear of sexual approaches between the brothers and the women.

The first foundation by Dominic, together with Diego of Osma, was the nunnery at Prouille. The customs at Prouille, based on the Prémontré model, were in accordance with the normal monastic tradition and required a strict enclosure. It was unthinkable that women should share the poverty and mendicant lifestyle of the brothers, or that they should pursue activities outside the convent. When, in 1219, Dominic founded a convent in Rome, at S. Sisto, at the request of the Pope he gave its members the *Consuetudines* from Prouille. Consequently, several convents and also Beguine communities wanted to be incorporated in the order but those that were accepted were ostracized and the brothers forbidden from providing them with spiritual services. It was only after longstanding conflict that this restrictive approach was relaxed, under pressure from the Pope and aristocratic monastery patrons, and a female branch of the order was established, for whom the type of enclosure prescribed was as in the convent at S. Sisto.

Francis had also excluded Clare of Assisi (who, following his example, had lived her life as a successor of Christ) from the life of a traveling preacher and assigned to her and her sisters the church and convent buildings at S. Damiano near Assisi. Clare, however, rejected the rule compiled by Ugolino of Ostia for S. Damiano, not because of the strict enclosure, but in order to enforce the absolute poverty of her community. Thus the nunneries that had affiliated themselves to the mendicant order lived a traditional *vita contemplativa* behind the high convent walls, entirely in accord with older monastic tradition.

Prouille, convent of Dominican nuns, founded in 1207 by Diego of Osma and by Dominic, and equipped by the archbishop of Narbonne. The women converted by Dominic were among those accepted into Prouille, which was initially also a Dominican preaching center. The male and female communities did not form a double monastery, however. The present day buildings date largely from the middle of the 19th C.

The Tertiaries

Following the inclusion of lay people by the Franciscans, the establishment, during Francis' own lifetime, of a third branch of the order, similar to the Humiliates, for members still living in the secular world, some of whom were also married, provided an alternative solution for lay followers. Such "tertiaries" also existed among the Dominicans. Tertiaries also sometimes affiliated themselves to monastery communities and gained the status of Conventuals. The best known Dominican tertiary is Catherine of Siena (1347–80), who maintained contact with Popes Gregory XI and Urban VI, as well as with other prominent personalities of her time, and who fought for the return of the popes from exile in Avignon to Rome.

Assisi, S. Chiara, Order of the Poor Clares' church and convent, 1257 start of construction, 1260 burial of the relics of St. Clare who had been a pupil of St. Francis and founder of the order, 1265 consecration. While the exterior, with its layers of red and white masonry, differs from S. Francesco, the interior of S. Chiara is to a large extent a repetition of S. Francesco's upper basilica.

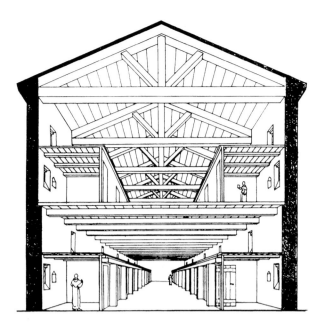

The Hermits of St. Augustine and the Carmelites

In addition to the two major orders, there was also a series of small mendicant orders, which were abolished in 1274, with the exception of the Hermits of St. Augustine and the Carmelites. Both these orders derived from hermit communities who took on spiritual guidance work only later. The Carmelites had their origins in a hermit community on Mount Carmel that left the Holy Land following the Muslim conquest in the 13th century in the direction of Western Europe, thus changing their way of life. In 1247 Pope Innocent IV gave them a rule that prescribed monastery life and a *vita activa* providing pastoral care with preaching and confessional in place of the hermit existence. The Hermits of St. Augustine were formed in 1256 through the amalgamation, ordered by Pope Alexander IV, of various Italian hermit communities with a poverty movement from Waldensian circles in southern France; they adopted the Rule of St. Augustine. As with the Carmelites, the organization of their order was based on the example of the Dominicans, and like them they dedicated themselves primarily to study in preparation for becoming preachers. Both newly founded mendicant orders had their fields of activity in the towns and both were endowed with communal property.

Bologna, S. Domenico, cells in the dormitory building (▲), cloister (▶). The monastery was founded in the first half of the 13th C. An elongated, two storey wing was built close to the southeast city wall, with sacristy, chapter house, parlatorium, and dormitory. The dormitory extended to the south of the parlatorium over both floors and was comprised of individual cells in which the monks could study as well as sleep—a decisive new development in European monasteries.

Monasteries/Convents and Churches of the Mendicant Orders

At the end of the 13th century there were mendicant order settlements in all of the large and in many of the medium-sized and smaller towns, often with two or more monasteries at different locations in the same urban area. The Franciscans in particular often undertook more extensive tasks within the life of the town. Their monasteries were often meeting places for the town's citizens and the focus of political life. However, the fact that the mendicant orders provided the towns with a second spiritual guidance network independent of the parishes sometimes led to sharp conflicts with the town clergy as well as to stiff competition between them. From the middle of the 13th century, and more especially in the 14th and 15th centuries, the donation of altars or chapels by private individuals became an important source of income for the monasteries and also constituted a unifying factor between the mendicant orders and the urban elite.

Brescia, S. Francesco, cloister. The three-aisled basilica. with no transept, was constructed in 1245–65 and redesigned in 1274–1335. The master builder of the cloister, completed in 1394, was Guglielmo Frisone da Campione.

▼ **Florence, S. Croce,** aerial view of the Franciscan church and monastery, founded in 1226 by St. Francis. The order's rapid development meant that both the first church and the second one built in 1252 were too small. Completion of the 373 ft (115 m) long third church, begun in 1294–95, took more than 100 years. The huge dimensions of this church were due not only to the rivalry between the Franciscan and Dominican orders, but also to the fact that the Franciscan churches became especially popular as final resting places among the middle classes who, in death at least, wanted to pay homage to the Franciscan ideals.

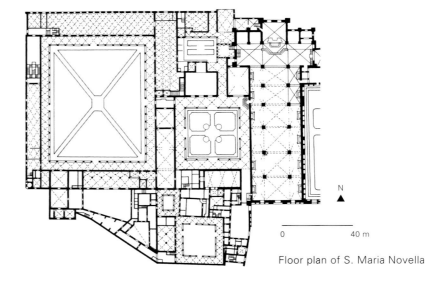

N
▲

0   40 m

Floor plan of S. Maria Novella

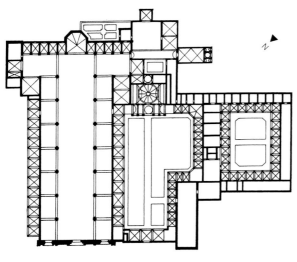

Floor plan of S. Croce

0   75 m

Monastery Layouts

The orders had to build their settlements on the pieces of land assigned to them in the city or outside its walls, or else on land that they were able to acquire. Due to the lack of space within the city walls, therefore, monasteries often took on unusual shapes and attempts were then made to round them off by acquiring additional areas of land. Traditional construction continued to be based on the standard model of a quadrangular cloister with the church on one side and the monastery buildings on the other three sides, but the layout of the rooms did not follow any established plan as it did with the Cistercians. Hence, unneeded storerooms in the west wing could make way for school rooms and the library or the refectory, and the chapter house could be located in the south wing instead of the east wing. Extensions to the conclave wing or the inclusion of a second courtyard were also not uncommon.

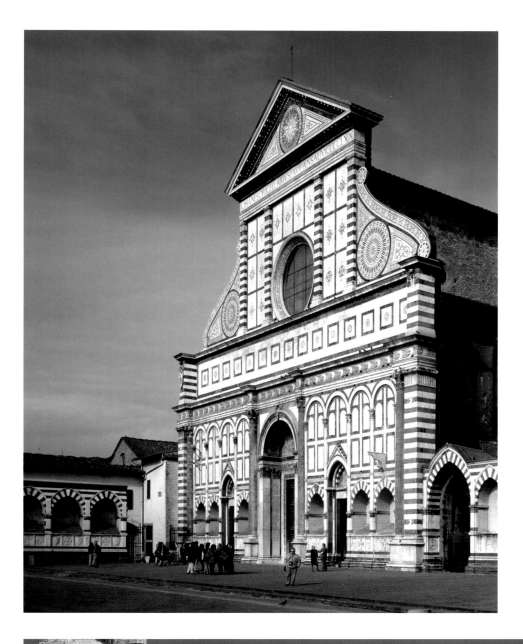

Florence, S. Maria Novella, façade and detail. The present day building, with the choir facing north and the façade south, was probably built in the 1370s according to a new plan. The lower part of the façade dates to before 1360; it was completed after 1458 based on the plans of the great scholar and architectural theorist Leon Battista Alberti: a masterpiece of Renaissance architecture.

Florence, S. Croce, exterior and interior view of the Pazzi Chapel, Filippo Brunelleschi, plan 1430, construction 1442–70. The characteristic architectural motif on both the exterior and the interior of the Pazzi Chapel, once the Franciscan chapter house of S. Croce, is a triumphal arch-like serliana (specially designed window with three openings).

303

Florence, S. Maria Novella. The Florentine Dominican monastery was founded in 1221 on the site of an older church of S. Maria outside the town. Whether the construction of the basilica was begun in 1240/50 or whether it was first erected in 1279–1300 is a matter of dispute. The vaulting is unusual: it is possibly the first vaulted construction in a mendicant order church in central Italy. The ground plan—a basilica-like nave and transept arms, each with two chapels to the side of the main apse—is based on the Bernard Plan of Cistercian churches, such as S. Galgano. The walls, as they rise, are dominated by high, wide arcades, with the low clerestory wall and the rather small round windows receding behind them. The numerous altars, which were donated in the Late Middle Ages, and the artworks created for them, were not housed in separate chapels but in the side aisles.

Florence, S. Croce. The Florentine Franciscan church was rebuilt after 1294, replacing a small building dating from around 1250, and became the largest mendicant order church erected in the Middle Ages. It had to do without vaulting in order to attain a nave width of 65 ft (20 m) and a height of 112 ft (34.5 m). The monumental aspect of the east section, with each of the five transept chapels to the side of the polygonal, closed, and vaulted apse, is also expressed in the triumphal arch motif of the choir wall: the large choir arch is flanked by low, thin openings to the inside of the side chapels, with the narrow lancet windows rising above them. The high, wide nave arcades give the room a hall-like appearance. As in S. Maria Novella, the altars and donated artworks here are also located in the side aisle spans.

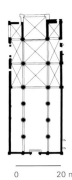
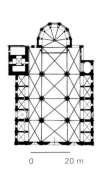
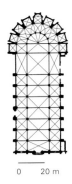

0   20 m   0   20 m   0   20 m

Ground plans (from left to right) S. Giovanni in Canale, Dominican church in Piacenza; S. Fortunato, Franciscan church in Todi; S. Francesco in Bologna. The comparison makes the different choir layouts especially noticeable.

▶ **Bologna, S. Francesco,** 1236–56. While many Franciscan churches in central Italy were based on S. Francesco in Assisi, Bologna's Franciscan church, with its basilica-like nave and ambulatory, is representative of a different tradition.

▶▶ **Todi, S. Fortunato,** 1292–1328. The three-aisled interior is constructed as a hall. Bathed in light and seemingly without direction, it is spanned by rib vaults. The design of the space, with the transverse arches in the side aisles, was influenced by examples from the west of France such as St.-Hilaire in Poitiers.

▼ **Cologne, Friars Minor Church,** second half of the 13th C. Like S. Fortunato in Todi, the Cologne Franciscan church also has a polygonal choir. Unlike S. Fortunato, however, here the elongated tracery windows are positioned like the high nave windows of the inner choirs in Gothic cathedrals.

Churches

The prevalent adoption, style, and appearance of mendicant order churches were determined primarily by their function as preaching venues, as well as by the obligation of simplicity deriving from the poverty ideal, but in no way does this account for all of their features.

The first Franciscan and Dominican churches were usually very simple hall churches—rectangular rooms without vaulting, often purposely built with a straight choir end instead of an apse. This style corresponded to the Dominicans' building regulations passed in 1220 and supplemented several times up to 1263. In accordance with these regulations the buildings were to be modest and not too large, nor should the height of the church exceed 30 ft (about 10 m). Only the choir and the sacristy could be vaulted and the decoration was not to comprise any spectacular or superfluous sculptures, paintings, flooring, or similar as this was irreconcilable with the preaching brothers' poverty. In addition to the general wording, which had already been used by the Cistercians, here the restriction on the height provided the first concrete requirement regarding the shape of the building. After 1300, however, this very requirement was abolished in order to avoid conflicts that had evidently arisen between regulations and practice.

With the exception of ridge turrets, the mendicant order churches were without towers and usually had simple façades without sculptured porches or elaborate tracery decoration. Outside Italy the churches usually had no transept. None of the mendicant orders developed a preferred architectural style or one that was typical of the order. Instead, the individual churches usually show the clear influence of regional building traditions and shapes. Nevertheless, characteristic ground plan and elevation types did develop, largely owing to the quest for simplicity, the clear segregation between lay areas and the choir, and the need to erect as many altars and chapels as possible. One of these architectural types was the "chapel hall"—a hall church (or two-aisled hall) that was lined with flanking chapels, not only in the east section but also along the sides of the nave, in a chain between the buttresses. This style of building was especially widespread in Languedoc and in Catalonia but was in no way limited to these regions. The other prevalent architectural type was a

Toulouse, Les Jacobins, Dominican church, late 13th C.–1385.
◀ ▶ Interior with vault detail: "palm tree".
▼ Cloister and chapter house.
Since the Dominican order was founded in Toulouse in 1215 (as a community of preachers), Les Jacobins is considered to be the order's mother church. The French Franciscans were named "Jacobins" after their first gathering place in Paris, which was near a church consecrated to St. James (Jacob in Latin).

church with a three-aisled nave and a long, single-aisled choir; this could include basilica-like buildings as well as hall churches. Simple pillar shapes and wide arcades with plain profiles, as well as, in the case of basilica-like elevations, a high, unstructured wall area between the arcades and the clerestory windows, are features of this building style. In many instances there were no separate chapel constructions, meaning that the side aisles had to accommodate the altars and the chapels. In contrast to older traditions of church architecture, there were numerous two-aisled constructions, most of which derived from the extension of a hall church with an additional aisle. Overall there was an increasing tendency towards technically and aesthetically demanding building types—such as the hall with high, narrow pillars—as well as towards more complex structures with elaborate respond profiles, tracery work, and, especially, the vaulting of the entire building.

The alignment of the mighty circular pillars in the middle of the wide, high room, the magnificent stained glass windows above the low side chapels, together with the "palm tree" apse vault give the Dominican church in Toulouse an extraordinary beauty.

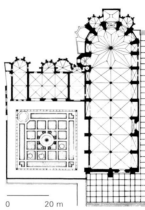

0   20 m

Sts. Clare and Elizabeth, Assisi, S. Francesco, lower basilica, Chapel of St. Martin, Simone Martini, c. 1320/25. An opportunity to study an entire epoch in Italian painting, featuring names such as Cimabue, Giotto, and Simone Martini.

▼ ▶ **Erfurt, Dominican church,** the choir was completed in 1172/73, the nave in 1360–80. Interior view towards the east; and a view of the choir stalls in the monks' choir. The rood screen divides the church into two sections, which used to be reserved for different functions.

Interior Decoration

The rood screen divided the church into two parts, each with different functions: the monks' or canons' choir where the Liturgy of the Hours took place; and the lay area where sermons and confessions were held. While the rood screen platform served as a pulpit for the sermon, the often vaulted lower section of the rood screen housed the public altar(s). Access to the monastery buildings was in the rood screen span or to the east of it, while the sacristy was to the side of the choir.

Due to their reliance on donations and the resulting competition between the different religious establishments in the town, the mendicant orders were the forerunners in the provision of private chapels. Altars donated for private purposes were placed either in front of the nave pillars, or in their own chapels, or in side aisle spans separated by barriers. Their decorative artworks included painted panels, retables, sculpture, and wall paintings; cloths and curtains were used as room dividers. Stained glass was often also used in independent chapels in France and Germany, while wall paintings were preferred in Italy. The donation of an altar or a chapel always included the provision of the altar equipment, liturgical books, and embroidered altar cloths, sometimes even the priest's robes.

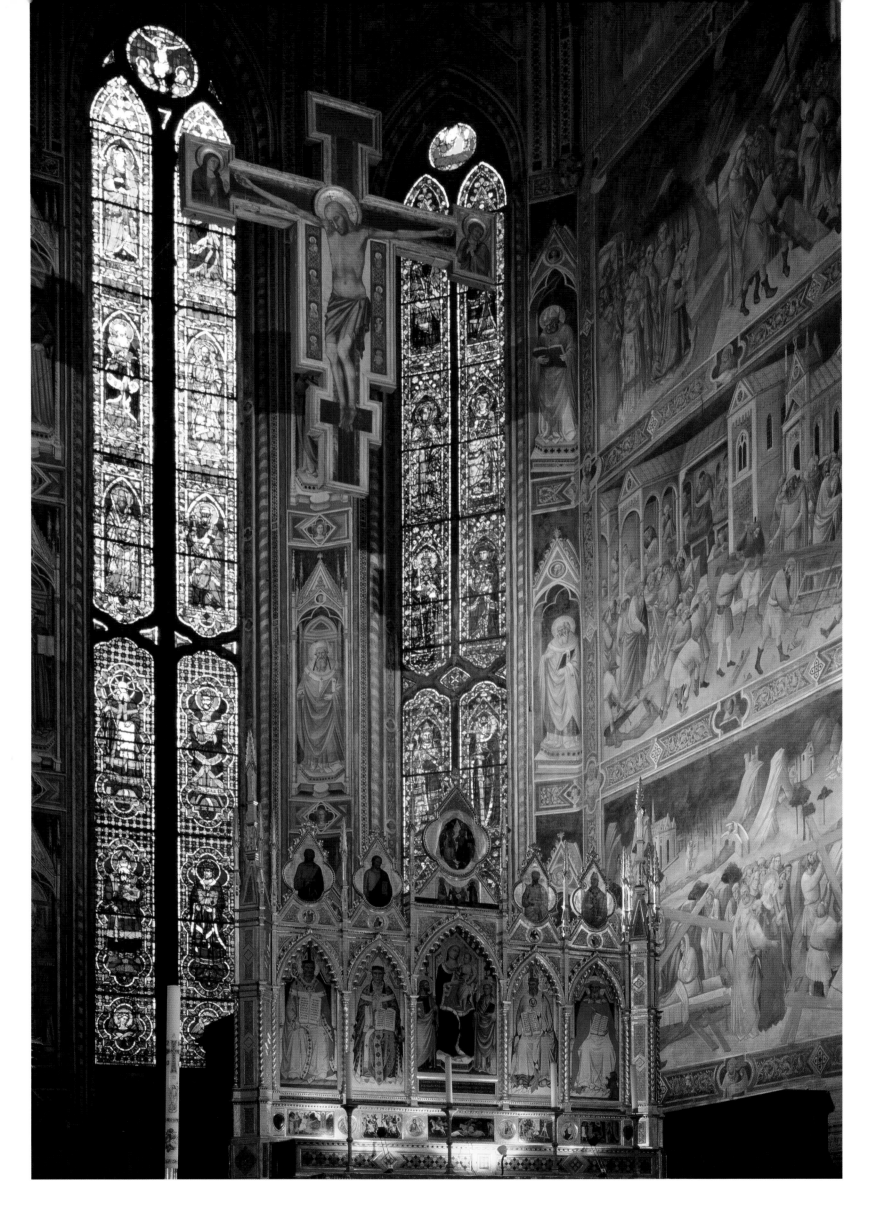

◀ **Florence, S. Croce,** chapel in the main choir. This choir chapel was painted in 1380 by Agnolo Gaddi and his workshop. The cycle of frescoes depicts the *Legend of the Holy Cross*, thus making reference to the name of the church. The painted triumphal cross is considered to be the work of the Master of Figline. The polyptych with the central image of the Madonna by Niccolò di Pietro Gerini, the four Church Fathers by Giovanni del Biondo, and other elements were only combined in their present form in the 19th C.

▲ *Annunciation* **of the Cavalcanti Tabernacle** (detail) by Donatello, 1430/35, Florence, S. Croce. The sandstone relief with the annunciation scene is richly decorated; the portrayal of the two figures, in particular the manner of their encounter, is selectively realistic and the entire ensemble is a Renaissance masterpiece. S. Croce is rich in works of art paid for by wealthy patrons. It was primarily the banking families of Bardi, Peruzzi, and Alberti who donated the chapels, providing monuments to themselves with painting cycles by famous artists.

Visual Propaganda

In addition to the sermon, the mendicant orders made significant use of the visual media in order to illustrate their ideals and the positions they represented. Although their reticence with regard to sculptures was similar to that of the Cistercians, the Franciscans made particular use of images from an early stage in order to promote the cult of St. Francis—and especially his similarity to Christ as a result of his stigmatization. In Tuscany and in central Italy the tendency towards older, three-dimensional figures of the saints created a new type of painted panel showing Francis framed on both sides by miniature miracle scenes; these panels were mass produced from c. 1230. From c. 1260 more extensive image cycles are to be found as wall paintings in the chapels adjacent to the choir or in the main choir of Italian Franciscan churches. The culmination in the development of this "Franciscan iconography" is the frescoes of the legend of St. Francis in the nave of S. Francesco in Assisi, created shortly before 1300 and attributed to Giotto.

With the Dominicans, the early approval of private chapel donations, which always included extensive imagery, functioned as a catalyst for the use of pictures as propaganda for the order.

The Healing of John of Ilerda, Assisi, upper basilica, Giotto (?), c. 1295/1300.
Badly injured by a nocturnal attacker, the physicians had already given up hope for John when Francis appeared at his sickbed, accompanied by two angels, touched his wounds, and healed him. The performing of this miracle by Francis followed the example of Christ, and its attribution, in the words and image, to the great founder of the order was an important authentication for the Franciscan preachers.

St. Francis panel, Pescia, S. Francesco, Bonaventura Berlinghieri, 1235. The six images flanking the saint emphasize his miraculous powers.

Treviso, S. Nicolò, Italy

Under the Dominican Pope Benedict XI (1303/04) the church at his home monastery of S. Nicolò in Treviso, founded in 1221, received a large new building. Completed as far as the third nave span by 1318, the construction work was then continued after 1348 and completed with a wooden ogival arched roof in the nave instead of vaulting. As with many mendicant order churches, the long building was an adaptation of the so-called Bernard Plan for the early Cistercian churches: a cruciform ground plan with a choir as wide as the nave and two chapels in the transept. The lack of apses on the outer chapels did, however, create a variety of apse in the sense of a hierarchical tapering of the sanctuaries up to the high choir apse in the middle. At the same time, the high, circular pillars supporting the wide arcades, and the east section illuminated by a close succession of narrower, higher windows arranged on two levels, produce a monumental impression, with regard to both the exterior and the interior. S. Nicolò is thus illustrative of the mendicant orders' widespread break with the simplicity and architectural reticence of the early period in favor of the prestige-laden effect of ostentatious buildings.

◄ **Wall paintings by Tomaso da Modena** on the second nave pillar on the north side, mid-14th C.: St. Agnes (center), St. John the Baptist (right), and a small, kneeling figure of a donor at the side of St. Romuald Enthroned (left).

▼ **Church interior looking east.** The high, circular pillars and wide arcades characterize the monumental impression made by the space.

▼ **Main apse, campanile, and transept** with the prominent inner transept chapel, from the northeast.

▲ **Wall painting in the chapter house** by Tomaso da Modena, mid-14th C.; detail: the scholarly Dominican and bishop, Albertus Magnus.

▲ **Courtyard and east gallery** of the cloister with the chapter house arcades and porch.

▼ **Chapter house with wall paintings** by Tomaso da Modena, mid-14th C.: portrayal of some famous Dominicans as scholars at their writing desks.

▶ **Writing scholar with glasses.** This depiction of the Dominican cardinal Hugh of Provence shows a figure wearing reading glasses for the first time in the history of art.

Florence, S. Marco, Italy

From 1437 Cosimo I de Medici had a new building constructed for the Dominicans of S. Domenico in Florence, on the site of an older monastery. In addition to the church, the monastery complex, with Michelozzo as architect until 1452, comprised a rectangular space with a square choir and a 5/8 polygonal apse, two large cloisters with monastery rooms, and two small courtyards surrounded by arcades. The church was redecorated in the baroque style after 1679 and acquired a monumental façade in 1777. Those sections of the original Michelozzo construction still remaining include the (walled in) apse, the sacristy, the two cloisters, and the small arcaded courtyard in the style of the early Florentine Renaissance. Michelozzo's three-aisled library dating from 1444 was to set a trend: narrow columns with Ionic capitals supporting wide arcades separate the vaulted central passageway from the wider, groin vaulted side aisles (with the bookshelves and the pulpit), which are lit by the windows on both sides.

S. Marco is famous for the painted decoration of the monastery and the monks' cells with frescoes by the Dominican monk Fra Angelico (1400–55) and his fellow workers (including Benozzo Gozzoli). Today the monastery rooms house a Fra Angelico Museum.

Annunciation. Fresco by Fra Angelico in the northern corridor of the upper floor.

◄ **Corridor of the Fra Angelico Museum** (former monastery corridor).

▼ **The library of the former monastery built by Michelozzo,** 1444, with Ionic capitals on narrow columns and wide arcades.

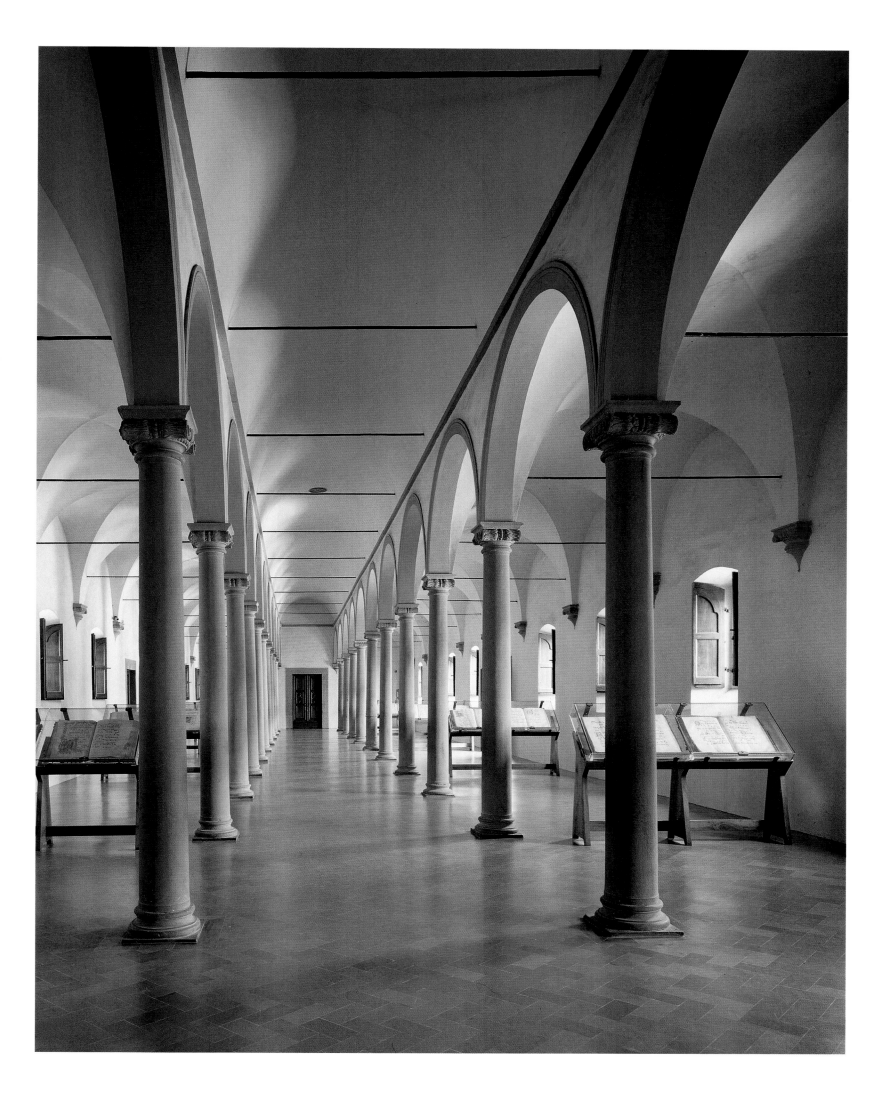

S. Maria da Vitória da Batalha, Portugal

The monastery church of Batalha is a magnificent royal building serving the purposes of dynastic prestige, which was designed to compete with the older Cistercian church at Alcobaça, a little further south. The monastery was built as the result of a vow by King João I of Portugal to commemorate the battle at Aljubarrota in 1385, where Portugal had defended its independence from Castile. The king handed the newly founded monastery, appropriately named "St. Mary of Victory in Battle," over to the Dominican order in 1388. Construction work began in the same year.

The monastery, grouped around the cloister to the north of the church and other courtyards, was planned as a unit and the construction of the church, cloister, and monastery buildings on the large area of land was started simultaneously. The high degree of dimensional accuracy involved in the construction indicates that the complex was built on undeveloped land and is also evidence of the quality and professionalism of the leading architect, Afonso Domingues. His successor, Huguet, was responsible for the completion of the church and for the successive construction of two royal sepulchral chapels after 1402. The artistic decoration of the monastery lasted through to the start of the 16th century. Work on the not yet

◀ **View down the nave** to the apse lit by two rows of windows, end of the 14th C.

▼ **Monastery church from the south west.** In the foreground King João I's sepulchral chapel, Capela do Fundador, pre-1426–c. 1434.

▲ **West porch of the church,** pre-1434. Flamboyant blind tracery work dominates the middle section of the west façade.

completed second sepulchral chapel was halted in 1534. The church is a monumental version of the three-aisled basilica-like mendicant order church with a transept and a closed, polygonal east chapel in a variation of the Cistercians' Bernard Plan. The extremely high clustered piers give the building a hall-like character. The clerestory took second place as a source of light in the face of the two levels of windows in the apse. Both of the royal sepulchral chapels are centrally oriented constructions.

The chapel at the southwest end of the nave, donated by João I prior to 1426, is an elegant, well lit structure on a square ground plan, featuring a towering central octagon with its own clerestory and fine stellar vaults. Still one dimension greater is the construction in the apex of the choir, begun in 1433 under Duarte I, namely a centrally oriented space surrounded by eight closed, polygonal chapels that remained without any vaulting, hence the name Capelas Imperfeitas.

◄ **Fountain house in the cloister,** 1st half of the 15th C.

▼ **Cloister arcades with tracery work** by Diogo Boytac, 1495/1521.

► **Capelas Imperfeitas,** begun under Duarte I, 1433–37.

IX

Rainer Warland

Byzantine Monasticism

Karl Suso Frank, magistro et amico

Comparison of Western and Eastern Monasteries

Meteora monastery of Hagios Nikolaos. For a long time the "monasteries floating up in the heavens" in northeastern Greece were accessible only by means of hanging ladders or hoisted baskets. The founding of the monastery of St. Nicholas dates back to the late 14th C.

Monasticism in the West and in the East derives from the same Late Antique roots. Nevertheless, Latin and Orthodox monasteries differ considerably in their outside appearance. The reason is that their common Late Antique origins were followed by two entirely different Middle Ages. The specific characteristics of an eastern, Byzantine monastery are noticeable at first glance: monastery fortresses with walls and towers dominate the picture. In the West, on the other hand, the monastery provides a tightly structured organization comprising church and cloister with adjoining communal living quarters, blending into the landscape without fortified walls. The ground plans are dominated by a rectangular crosslinking based on the square of the cloister. In contrast, the ground plans of Byzantine monasteries are subject to the topography alone. They assert themselves with at times breathtaking constructions on narrow needle cliffs, on ravine slopes, or in impassable territory. No one ground plan is the same as the next. The focal point of the inner monastery courtyard is solely the freestanding monastery church, which faces the liturgical direction of the East. This *katholikon* and the *trapeza*, the communal dining room, are the indispensable core of a Byzantine monastery. The other parts are subject to continual rebuilding, renovation, and subsequent adaptation following famous models.

Monasticism does not derive from the Bible alone. The misogynistic, ascetic utterances of an anonymous Jewish Christian author in the letters of Paul have long been acknowledged as postscripts. It was far more the populist, philosophical ideal of stoicism that had paved the way in late imperial society for diverse forms of asceticism. The exchange and interpenetration of pagan and Christian concepts led to the formation of a Christian form of asceticism—now serving the will of God. The Christian ascetic movement had its origins in Egypt and Palestine of the 3rd–4th centuries and grew at an astonishing pace. By Late Antiquity, however, the historical parameters of the East and the West diverged, allowing the respective traditions to develop and become established.

In the West, the differing monastery landscapes of the Rhône, the Jura, and Italy agreed on the binding Rule of St. Benedict, which came to supersede the competing Rule of the Master. The Rule of St. Benedict thus became the standard monastic rule in the West. Strictly organized monastery networks developed in the midst of the political transformation processes of the Early Middle Ages, carrying out missionary work in the name of Christianity, furthering the advance of the clergy, as well as exercising political and cultural power. The unique significance of Western monasticism proved to be its reform potential for the Latin Church and its opening up to medieval urban society, in particular through the new kind of preaching and mendicant orders arising from the poverty and pietistic movements of the 13th and subsequent centuries. The monasticism of the East, on the other hand, in the long term remained attached to its origins: charismatic, self-sufficient, and elitist. Since Byzantine imperialism and Orthodox religion developed uninterrupted into Late Antiquity, there was no historical need for a rule at all. During Late Antiquity the eastern Mediterranean seaboard from Syria via Asia Minor to Greece was the most Christianized. The Christian towns of this period were the

An Overview of Byzantine Monasticism

Hermits Anchorites Hesychasts	Cenobites	Monks in monastery settlements (laura)
Paul of Thebes, died 341	Pachomios 294–346 Monastery in Tabannese c. 320 Eight Monastery Network "Angel Rule"	Combination of cenobites and anchorites, particularly in Palestine
Anthony the Hermit, died 356 The Life of Athanasius of Alexandria		Euthymios in Palestine, died 473 Life of Cyril of Scythopolis
Apophthegmata, *The Wisdom of the Fathers*, collected by Evagrios Pontikos 246–99	Basil of Caesarea c. 330–79	
	Theodore Studites 759–826	Sabas in Palestine, died 523 (Monastery of Mar Saba, founded 483)
Monastic settlements of the Nitria, the Sketis (Wadi Natrun) and the Kellia	Iconophile John of Damascus	
Simeon Stylites		

328   Byzantine Monasticism

Athos monastery of Stavronikita. This monastery fortress, dating from the 16th C., towers above the Aegean Sea on a spur on the northeast coast of Mount Athos.

concern and responsibility of the bishops whose dioceses were organized entirely in accordance with the layout of urban metropolitan networks. Their supervision of the respective monasteries and hermitages, however, was soon annulled by special imperial privileges or marginalized. It was not missionary work, education, or monastery authority but radical retreat from the world that opened up the separate path of Eastern monasticism. There was no strict monastic observance according to a binding rule, even though Basil, in Cappadochian Caesarea had paramount authority for the East. His "Great Rule," however, which clearly advocated communal, cenobitic monasticism, never gained the status achieved by the Rule of St. Benedict in the West. Instead, how the relevant obligations of the liturgy and monastic observance were to be fulfilled was stipulated in detail and sealed for all time in the *typikon*, the founding and endowment deed of each monastery. Wealthy patrons who commissioned a pious work for the sake of intercessory commemorative prayer and hoped-for salvation strengthened medieval and late Byzantine monasticism in its progress towards becoming a central authority in Orthodoxy, charity, and piety. Some of the monasteries that benefited from prominent endowments soon came to resemble a treasury of mosaics and marble paneling, containing liturgical treasures as well as precious relics and icons.

In Byzantium the promotional texts about monastic life, monastic wisdom (*Apophtegmata patrum*), and monastic spirituality, such as the widely known *Stairway to Heaven* by John Klimakos, for example, took the place of the Western monastery rule and the order networks. The narration of monastic life, a literary medium of subtle propaganda since its Late Antique origins, remained an enduring genre in Byzantium. The success of the Byzantine concept of the monastery was made or broken by the example of the spiritual teacher. The model of the hermit, like the abbot (*hegumenos*), the monastic wisdom embodied in his biography and his personality, remained the basis of Byzantine monasticism. Without networks and hierarchies, Eastern monasticism thus retained a significant degree of independence and diversity. It is therefore understandable that Byzantine monasteries and monastic colonies were subject to very changeable, barely controllable influxes and influences. The sense of living the epitome of Christian existence, achieved by only a small minority, continues to predominate right up to the present day.

The Stairway to Heaven, after John Klimakos. This 12th-C. icon in St. Catherine's Monastery in Sinai depicts the 30 steps of the monks' ascent as an allegory of the ascetic doctrine of virtue which triumphs over evil.

Early Byzantine Monasticism

Early monasticism in the eastern Mediterranean region. The origins of Christian monasticism lie in Palestine, Syria, Egypt, and Asia Minor.

Sabas Monastery. Situated on the slopes of the Kidron Valley near Bethlehem, this famous monastery in Palestine is built on a mountainside with cave hermitages. Founded in the 6th C., it was gradually extended with substructures as well as being enclosed by defensive walls and fortified refuge towers.

During the Dark Ages, ascetics, hermits, and anchorites from all corners of the world were attracted to the Egyptian desert and the solitude of Palestine. As a broad generalization this diverse group can be seen as the dropouts of antique society. The Greek term "anchorites" literally means people who move out of the *chora* (Greek for locality), who renounce the regulated life of the village and the town. Their ideal was the aspiration to perfection beyond physical needs, forces, and impulses. The philosophy of stoicism required the liberation of the pure spirit from the base, weak body and paved the way for an antiphysical rigorousness. In the Christian version it was the angels—the *asomatoi* (Greek for bodiless entity)—who rose to become the ascetic model for an "angelic" life, who sing their eternal praise in the presence of God.

The monastic life of the Egyptian Father of the Monks, Anthony (c. 251–356), rapidly brought knowledge of the new ascetic way of life to public attention in the Roman Empire. A promotional text written by Athanasius of Alexandria was passed from hand to hand, and even in Late Antique Trier it was a topic of daily discussion. Pachomius' (292–346) monastery in Tabennisi was said to have already numbered more than 3000 monks. Archaeological evidence of these early monastic colonies is becoming increasingly available today. The Kellia, an excavated monastic settlement in Lower Egypt, exhibits independent housing units with chapels that form a loose association. Such monastic settlements, also called lauras or lavras, are also known from Palestine and from the Judean desert.

An Early Byzantine monastery with living and farming areas, a *trapeza* (literally, Greek for table, so dining room), and an apse room as a church was excavated during the building of a new suburb on the outskirts of Jerusalem, in Ma´ale Adummim. All of the rooms were contained within a walled square. The recently exposed mosaic floor near the Megiddo prison, one of the inscriptions of which mentions a trapeza, is also likely to have been part of such a monastery. The most important monastery in Palestine is that of Abbot Sabas (died 532), founded near Bethlehem, which continues to exist today as a hermitage and monastic colony center.

As early as the 5th century the north Syrian mountains also provided an imposing monastery landscape. There were at least 57 monasteries in the Gebel Barisha area alone, in the hinterland of Antioch. Since the buildings were made of stone blocks that were cut directly from the surrounding area and the resulting caverns then used as cisterns, as in Deir Breig for example, these testimonies of Early Byzantine architecture are astoundingly easy to reconstruct. Some of the buildings continue to stand as high as their eaves today. There was no specific type of monastic construction during this early

period, however. Instead, the regional conventions of stone masonry and nomadic shelters characterized the appearance of these churches and monasteries, some of which exhibit impressive ornamentation and exterior structures with decorative banding around the whole building and apses decorated with dual zoned, square-edged pillars.

Syria attracted attention with an extreme form of asceticism in Late Antiquity: *Stylites* (Greek for pillar saints) fasted and prayed, lived and slept on the narrow confines of pillar capitals. These ascetics soon attained the status of living saints among the rural population and were sought out for advice and blessing in decisions of political importance as well as in times of need due to failed harvests. Much like the local eastern tradition of elevated holy shrines with stair towers and roof altars, the high pillars emphasized the holy man's proximity to God. The pilgrimage center of Qualaat Seman is one of the largest monastery complexes in the Christian East. The plateau comprises extensive open areas with hostels and monasteries; an inclined processional road with a triumphal arch-like gate monument leads up to the holy mount, which is dominated by a cruciform building revealed by excavation work, with substructures beneath it, which has an octagonal dome at its center. An Early Byzantine imperial monastery such as this could only have been built by an efficient construction team and with imperial support. The central octagonal dome enclosed the pillar monument to Simeon Stylites, who lived here on the pillar as an ascetic. The base of the pillar, carved out of the surrounding rock, is still visible today. Simeon was undoubtedly a hero among the early Christian ascetics and, consequently, there is evidence of many imitators in Syria and Byzantium.

Just as celebrated is St. Catherine's Monastery on Mount Sinai, which was rediscovered as a treasury of Byzantine and Crusade-era literature following the manuscript finds by Konstantin von Tischendorf in the 19th century, as well as the results of more recent icon research by Kurt Weitzmann. Its location at the foot of the holy mount is evocative of Moses, in Exodus 19, receiving the Ten Commandments on Sinai. The topography of the holy site was added soon thereafter with the veneration of the burning thorn bush (Exodus 3, 5), behind the apse of the monastery church. Only in the Middle Ages were these Old Testament references superseded by the veneration of the relics of St. Catherine of Alexandria, but the Early Byzantine mosaics in the apse (the Transfiguration on Mount Tabor) and on the front wall of the apse (the handing down of the Commandments, the burning thorn bush) keep alive the original concept of the holy mount of divine encounters. The St. Catherine's monastery is protected by a high ring of walls. According to the inscriptions on the roof beams, the monastery church, as well as parts of

Qualaat Seman (northern Syria). The rambling pilgrims' center, dating from the 5th C., encloses, with its cruciform church and central octagon, the living rock where the base of St. Simeon Stylites' column survives.

Icons of the Stylites. Syria's pillar saints, who lived, fasted, and prayed in the space on top of a pillar, in order to be close to God, continued to be subjects of veneration into the modern age.

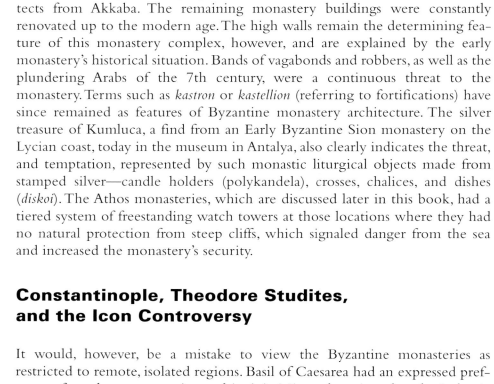

► **Monks at prayer in a church.** This portrays monks in liturgical prayer gathered together in a church, indicated by the ciborium, pulpit, and icons. 12th-C. manuscript, Sinai, St. Catherine's Monastery (Ms. gr. 418, fol. 269r).

►► **St. Catherine's Monastery on Mount Sinai.** Situated at the foot of Mount Sinai, the monastery acquired a high wall in the 6th C. as protection against bands of marauders. The enclosure includes a church with important mosaics surviving from the Justinian era.

John Klimakos with monks. This miniature portrays the 7th-C. Father of the Monks as a prophetic teacher, with both himself and a scroll enlarged and at a sacred distance from the contemporary monks of the 11-12th centuries. It indicates the authority possessed by the author of the *Stairway to Heaven* among the Mid-Byzantine era monastic communities. (Biblioteca Apostolica Vaticana vat. gr. 1754, fol. 3r.) End of the 11-12th C.

the tower in front of it, date from the 6th century. The inscriptions make reference to the imperial couple Justinian and Theodora as well as to local architects from Akkaba. The remaining monastery buildings were constantly renovated up to the modern age. The high walls remain the determining feature of this monastery complex, however, and are explained by the early monastery's historical situation. Bands of vagabonds and robbers, as well as the plundering Arabs of the 7th century, were a continuous threat to the monastery. Terms such as *kastron* or *kastellion* (referring to fortifications) have since remained as features of Byzantine monastery architecture. The silver treasure of Kumluca, a find from an Early Byzantine Sion monastery on the Lycian coast, today in the museum in Antalya, also clearly indicates the threat, and temptation, represented by such monastic liturgical objects made from stamped silver—candle holders (polykandela), crosses, chalices, and dishes (*diskoi*). The Athos monasteries, which are discussed later in this book, had a tiered system of freestanding watch towers at those locations where they had no natural protection from steep cliffs, which signaled danger from the sea and increased the monastery's security.

Constantinople, Theodore Studites, and the Icon Controversy

It would, however, be a mistake to view the Byzantine monasteries as restricted to remote, isolated regions. Basil of Caesarea had an expressed preference for urban monasteries, and in Asia Minor there is archaeological evidence of countless monasteries in the midst of settlements. Constantinople in the 6th century is said to have had more than 70 city monasteries. Perhaps the most significant of these was the Studios monastery, an Early Byzantine community dating from 452, located close to the Golden Gate. The ruins of the church are now in danger of collapse following the last earthquake and are no longer accessible. The remaining monastery buildings have long since disappeared. During the Mid-Byzantine era this monastery was respected throughout the empire for its Orthodoxy and monastic status. Its scriptorium was especially famous. Magnificently illustrated manuscripts and liturgical texts such as psalters bear the colophon (the closing inscription) of the Studios monastery, where both monks and laymen were at work.

At that time, however, the monastery's lasting reputation was largely due to the work of its abbot, Theodore Studites (759–826), with whose name the most enduring reform of Byzantine monasticism since Basil of Caesarea is associated. He committed the monks to a strict life of poverty and labor, based on a fixed daily routine and on the discipline of a monastic community. The freedom and idiosyncrasies of the hermits and hesychasts were reduced

Iconoclasts inflict damage on an icon of Christ. The polemical emphasis of this illustration of Psalm 21 from the 9th-C. Chludov Psalter equates the havoc wreaked by image destroyers on the icon's image of Christ with the physical suffering of Christ on the Cross, who has a sponge of vinegar held to his face. (Moscow, Hist. Museum Ms. 129 D, fol 67r)

Cross decoration in a Cappadochian cave church. The veneration of the precious, life-giving Cross remained a central subject for imagery in the cave churches of Cappadochia, even after the icon controversy. Painted ceiling in the chapel of St. Basil near Sinassos, c. 9th C.

Theodore Studites in monks' robes. This 11th-C. mosaic in the large monastery church at Hosios Lukas portrays the abbot of the Studios monastery in Constantinople, who was a great authority within Byzantine monasticism and a defender of image veneration.

to a cenobitic, monastic life under the hierarchical supervision of the abbot. Yet this new orientation did not come about through the compilation of rules but through short, intense sermons, catecheses, and exhortations that Theodore Studites directed at his monks three times a week. These "short catecheses" comprise a collection of 134 speeches, which, judged by the multitude of copies made of them, had an enormous influence. An overview of duties, directed at each of the monastery officials, which also addressed issues of repentance, neglectfulness, and lapses, the catecheses strengthened the spiritual countenance. Poverty, modesty, and manual labor as the goals of spiritual perfection became the focal points of monastic life.

Theodore Studites, an educated writer and poet as well as a monk, was also one of the most important icon theologians in Early Byzantium. The icon controversy of 726–843, which divided *ikonodules* (in favor of icons) and *iconoclasts* (opposed to icons), was ultimately the extrapolation of the old Christian doctrine versus the Christological decisions by the Councils of Nicaea and Constantinople. The basic argument of those opposed to icons was: does a portrait-like representation not contradict the divinity of Christ and is the symbol of the Cross not the only appropriate representation? The well-founded arguments of the icon opponents are noticeably absent from historical sources. Instead, all of the positive utterances from Christian tradition in support of icons were collated by monks such John of Damascus. In the aftermath, barbed, polemical versions of the posticonoclastic psalter illustrations equated the former icon opponents with Christ's tormentors at the Crucifixion. Historically the dispute was settled in favor of icons, and monks such as Theodore Studites played a significant role therein.

Theodore saw icons as the visible proof of the incarnation of Christ. As in the Platonic philosophical tradition, it was not the effigy but the archetype that was venerated, just as an image of one's mortal parents is not the object of respect but rather those who are remembered in the image. According to Theodore Studites, therefore, the veneration of images corresponds to the

same respect that the iconoclasts paid to the symbol of the Cross. He insisted that, for historical purposes, the images should be named via inscriptions. All icons, wall paintings, or reliefs since the Mid-Byzantine era have an inscription that clearly indicates the Christian subject. Following fluctuating victories and setbacks, the icon controversy was finally decided in 843. Icons have since risen to become the guarantors of Orthodoxy and of the profession of

The triumph of Orthodoxy. This liturgical feast day icon depicts a procession of the most important representatives of icon theology as the guarantors of the true faith. The Empress Theodora and her underage son, Michael VIII, who ended the icon controversy in 843, are flanked by monks and nuns. c. 1400. (London, British Museum).

◄ ▲ Monastery church in Mistra in the Peloponnese. This Brontochion monastery, with the church of the Hodegetria, also referred to as the Aphentiko church, built after 1310, established the "Mistra style", the combination of a long, basilica-like building and a cross-dome church.

▼ Monastery church in the Lycian mountains (southern Turkey). This remote 5th-century monastery ruins at Asarcik in the Myra/Demre hinterland has a reliquary chapel, with a cross window, where the monastery's abbots were buried.

God's incarnation. In posticonoclastic art, nuns and monks are almost the only representatives of Orthodoxy depicted.

Monastic Landscapes and Monastery Settlements on the Mountains and Islands

The 9th and 10th centuries were characterized by the blossoming of monastic landscapes and settled monastery colonies on holy mountains. Mount Athos, on the Chalcidice Peninsula, the best known present day instance of a Byzantine monastic landscape, was able to gradually assume this exemplary role only because it was consistently able to assert itself in the midst of political spheres of influence. Other monastic landscapes, which have since disappeared, were just as significant in Byzantium. Mount Ida at Hellespont, Latmos near Miletus, Mount Papikion in Thrace, and particularly Mount Olympus in Bithynia, were densely inhabited monastery areas. The topography of the Bithynia monastery area, for example, remains unresearched until now. The mountains above Bursa, where Theodore Studites once garnered his initial monastic experience, is today covered by forests and leisure areas for the nearby city.

On the other hand, Mount Latmos and Lake Bafa in front of it, are still illustrative of dense monastic settlement. The mountain monasteries, protected by walls and with their diverse cells, churches, and dining rooms, are matched by numerous island monasteries at the foot of the mountainous slopes. There is evidence of an early 9th- and 10th-century phase and a later flowering in the 13th century, the era of Lascarid rule in Byzantium. The break in the 11th century is explained by the devastating defeat of the Byzantine troops near Mantzikert in 1071, after which the Seljuks advanced as far as the west coast of Asia Minor. In 1079 Christodoulos, abbot of the famous Paulos monastery, felt forced to leave Latmos. With imperial support, in 1088 he founded a new monastery on the island of Patmos. The monastery fortress of St. John on Patmos, which is visible from far afield and where Christodoulos was buried, in turn houses important art treasures: 13th-century wall paintings in the chapel and trapeza, as well as valuable manuscripts, including rare liturgical rotuli (scrolls), and Late Byzantine icons.

Cappadochia, too, is considered to be a Byzantine monastic landscape, although there is no literary evidence of this at all. The monastic landscape myth prevalent in Europe since the 19th century is based on the presence of countless cave-like chapels and churches. There were undisputedly hermitages and monasteries in this territory of volcanic stone and bizarre rock formations caused by erosion. Inscriptions provide evidence of hermits living in the needle cliffs, believing themselves to be the new Stylites. The concentration of monasteries at Göreme, including three cross-dome churches painted throughout, is

▲ ▼ **The monastery of St. John on the island of Patmos.** The monastery was built in the late 11th C. on the site where, according to tradition, John the Evangelist wrote the Book of Revelation. The 13th-century chapel and refectory (trapeza) are grouped around the courtyard. The monastery possesses a unique inventory of manuscripts and icons.

◀ **The Latmos mountains at Lake Bafa** (western Turkey). The rocky mountain slopes and the islands off the coast house an impressive number of monasteries and hermitages. The monks who were grouped around Abbot Christodoulos retreated to the island of Patmos when the Seljuks entered the area after 1071.

Mosaic icon of St. Nicholas in St. John's Monastery on Patmos. The 11th C. saw the appearance in Byzantium of icons made from the tiniest of glass shards. These icons are reminiscent of the antique technique of fine emblema (small section made separately) mosaics and are very rare.

▶ **St. John's Monastery on Patmos.** The imposing monastery fortress with its ring of battlements crowns the whitewashed houses on the island of Patmos, creating a unique image. View from the northeast.

▶ **St. John's Monastery on Patmos,** Gospel book of 1334/35. The miniature with Mark the Evangelist writing is part of the monastery's significant treasure of icons and manuscripts. (Patmos, Cod. 81 fol.98v–99r).

▼ ► Monastic landscapes in Cappadochia and Anatolia.
The craggy regions of Göreme and Nevsehir, created by the
erosion of the volcanic stone, are the site of chapels,
necropolises, monasteries, and hermitages, most of which
date from the 10–13th centuries. Ascetics lived in the steep
needle cliffs in imitation of the pillar saints.

also certain to have been a spiritual center in this region. Based on the paintings in its Tokale Kilise, it could have been the site where the relics of Basil of Caesarea, Father of the Monks, liturgist, and celebrated Cappadochian, were kept. However, based on present day research, the majority of the Cappadochian cave churches are likely to have served as necropolises and monument chapels for the local elite. Experts are currently focusing on a different, new perception of this landscape in the context of Mid-Byzantine settlement history.

The basis for the concentration of monasteries on Mount Athos is provided by the special natural conditions, the legally guaranteed privileges, and the intensive influx of ascetics of all nationalities and languages. The more than 28 mile (45 km) long but extremely narrow and high ridge of mountains on the Athos Peninsula was linked to the mainland only by means of a narrow strip of land. This natural retreat for the early hermits and ascetics experienced a new concept when the Great Laura was founded in 963 by Athanasios of Athos (the monks soon to become the Athonites). A cenobitic typikon was compiled with the support of Emperor Tzimiskes, the *Tragos*, named after the buckskin on which the deed was written. Based on the reforms of Theodore Studites, this typikon became the model for the new Athonite monasticism. The founding of further monasteries soon followed: Iberon, Chilandar (renovated as a Serbian monastery in 1198), Esphigmenu, Panteleimon, Vatopedi, Xenophontos, and many more. The monasteries are alleged to have numbered 45 by c. 1000. The collective leadership of the monastery network by an elected representative, a *protos* (the first), who had his administrative base in Karyes, was soon replaced by a form of council. The monastic principle of the "poor" monastery also fell by the wayside soon after the founding fathers' generation, initially due to the insistence on imperial financial donations and tax privileges, but even more so due to the immense and growing possession of property in neighboring areas. The monasteries became economically active organizations involved in trade and shipping, as well as substantial landowners. Self-determined lifestyles arose as a result of hereditary private ownership and private living areas, undermining the cenobitic monastic ideal. Nevertheless, in the Late Byzantine era, Athos always remained a place of Byzantine theology and spirituality (Palamism). Bishops and patriarchs continued to be recruited from among the Athonite monks. Following the downfall of Byzantium in 1453 Athos managed to maintain its sovereignty by means of clever tactics and the payment of tribute to the Ottoman rulers. The autonomy of the monastic republic of Athos was recognized in the 1923 Treaty of Lausanne, with Greece as its protector.

The Athos monasteries were treasure houses of liturgical donations but not centers of artistic creation. The liturgical objects came from the best ateliers in Constantinople. In 1313 the Protaton church in Karyes was decorated by a painting workshop that also worked for King Milutin in Serbia. The monastic brother as painter is also a comparatively recent concept. The iconographic section of the *Painters' Book of Mount Athos*, which became famous in the 19th century, is less a source of practical advice and more a systematic depiction of scenes, figure types, and their epigrams.

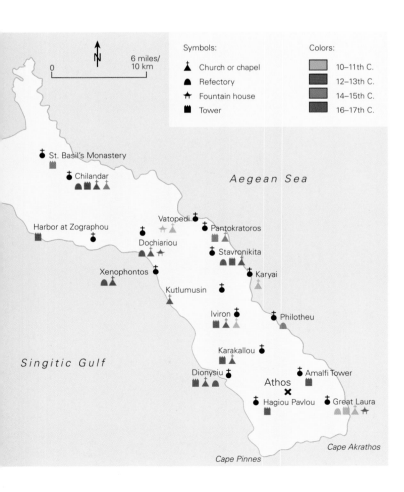

▶ **Athos, Chilandar Monastery.** The monastery church exhibits the typical design of an Athonite cross-dome church: with the transept arm ending in an apse and with a large atrium in front of it to the west for the monks' prayers. The early 13th-C. church (katholikon) is an example of the historically significant building style of the Palaeologus Renaissance.

▶▶ **Athos, Great Laura.** The freestanding fountain house (*phiale*) with Mid-Byzantine panels (10th C.) and a monolithic fountain basin, located to the west in front of the monastery church, evokes Christ and the Gospels as the source of the water of life.

▲ ◀ **Views of the Great Laura on Mount Athos.** The main monastery at Athos, based on that founded by St. Athanasius in 963, established a new form of communal monastery life that was to become the model for the whole of Athos. It is situated on the barely accessible far eastern tip of the Athos Peninsula.

▼ **Athos, Xenophontos Monastery.** Located on the west coast of the Athos Peninsula, this monastery, founded in the 11th C. was restored in its current form following a fire in the early 19th century.

Finally, the Meteora monasteries of northern Greece also deserve a mention in this section on the "holy mountains" of Byzantine monasticism. "Meteora" means "floating high" and these monastery buildings do indeed crown their spectacularly high, column-like, and almost inaccessible cliffs, which provided only very limited space for groups of buildings. For a long time, baskets hoisted by winches were the most comfortable, and also the only, means of access. The magnificently scenic landscape was inhabited by hermits from the 12-13th centuries onwards. It was in the 16th century, however, that the Meteora monasteries experienced their true flowering, evidenced by the Warlaam monastery, for example, with its painted church decoration and iconostasis (screen bearing icons and separating the sanctuary from the nave).

▶ **Meteora monastery of Hagia Triada.** Founded in 1476, with modern extensions. Situated at a dizzying height on a rocky plateau, it symbolizes complete withdrawal from the world and the radicalism of an angel-like life.

Meteora monastery at Roussanou. 16th C. Of the 24 monasteries in extremely steep locations, only six are still inhabited. The monastery group is today protected as a UNESCO World Heritage Site.

▲ ▼ **Athos, Chilandar Monastery.** For centuries the monastic republic of Athos has been a reflection of the different region and peoples of the Byzantine Empire. Chilandar Monastery, which is dominated by the imposing tower of St. Sava dating from 1198, was and continues to be the Serbs' main monastery.

Byzantine Monastery Architecture, Memorial Foundations, and Cultural Identity

The picturesque Athos monasteries offer a wide spectrum of Byzantine monastery architecture. Each is a unique example, committed only to its written typikon. The countless extension buildings, the changing building materials, and saddling of upper floors on existing wall decks obscure the planning and construction processes. The numerous repairs following fires, which were almost unavoidable and which, due to the negligent construction of attics extending over several buildings, had devastating consequences, also contribute to this image.

Despite the irregularities, however, there are also common features that can be determined. The most precise architecture was always used for the freestanding church or katholikon, the exterior of which had a decorative character, contrasting all too often with the other buildings. Then there were the solid fortification and refuge towers (*pyrgos*) which introduced their own architectural accents, and which are positioned at the highest point as close as possible to the monastery access. The majestic St. Sava tower dating from 1198 has continued to dominate the exterior view of the monastery of Chilandar up to the present day. Numerous individual finds indicate the functions of the monastery buildings, these being just a few examples: dining rooms (trapeze), sometimes freestanding buildings with painted decoration throughout, independent kitchen buildings (*hestia*) with a central chimney stack in Chilandar, bathrooms (*lutra*), sick wards, and sepulchral chapels. Finally, what applies far more than in the West: Byzantine monastery architecture is primarily church architecture.

The churches of the Athos monasteries are the only ones to have developed their own monastic building typology. Based on the outstanding example of the Great Laura, the Athonite cross-dome churches have transepts ending in apses. This modification of the otherwise flat, closed shield walls to the side was not entirely new but was seldom used and therefore significant. In the case of the Athos monasteries this seemed to have had a functional basis. The opposing open apses aided the antiphony of the two monks' choirs standing opposite one another, as the Byzantine liturgy is a sung, eulogic, and commemorative liturgy with precentors and succentors. The monastery churches also had spacious atriums (lite) located in front to the west, sometimes flanked by chapels. These halls served the purposes of the monks' non-liturgical prayer obligations. Upper floors above the interior atrium (or narthex) or tower compartments on the side could be used as libraries. Only Athos, with its freestanding fountain houses (phiale) in front of the façade remained reminiscent of the fountains in the atriums of the early Christian basilicas. Water as the source of life was generally seen in Byzantium as a symbol of God's blessing. The panels connecting the eight columns of the ciborium-like fountain house in the Great Lavra are among the best works of the Mid-Byzantine era, c. 1060. Based on the example of the Great Laura, *trikonchoi* (triconch, three apsidal domes), *lite* (atrium), and *phiale* (fountain house) make up the specific building conventions of the network of the Athonite monastery.

The period following the icon controversy, and especially the 10th and 11th centuries, were extraordinarily creative periods in Byzantine architecture. Different dome designs competed with one another in the attempt to render visible, under the vault of heaven, the symbolism of the liturgy and its promises of salvation. In the monastery church of Hosios Lukas in Phokis, west of Athens and not far from Delphi, the main structure of a cross-dome church appears in a new guise, the "eight pillar construction." It is named

Hosios Lukas Monastery, small monastery church.

◀ ▲ **Hosios Lukas monastery** (Phokis, central Greece). The large 11th-C. monastery church represents a version of the cross-dome church on eight supporting wall pillars (eight pillar construction). The remains of a mosaic feast day cycle depicting the main festivals of the Church year survive on the vaulting under the dome cornices.

Hosios Lukas Monastery. Exterior view of the apses of the large and small monastery churches, from the east.

▶ Hosios Lukas Monastery, Mosaic on the vaulting above the sanctuary of the 11th-C. large monastery church. On the throne is the Mother of God with Child, to whom the church is consecrated, dominating the main apse, while the other dome depicts the ascension of the Holy Ghost at Pentecost.

Nea Moni Monastery on Chios, exterior view of the monastery church from the east. Founded by the Byzantine Emperor Constantine Monomachos in the mid-11th C., the monastery has an extraordinarily steep, tower-like dome based on the architectural examples in the capital, Constantinople.

after the eight wall pillars that support the space's dominant dome. The historical background and the identity of the patron of the Hosios Lukas Monastery remain unknown. Following the death of a monk named Lukas, about whom nothing else is known, his grave was the object of great veneration, and the monastery, situated in an unfavorable sloping location, underwent a construction boom. A second, larger katholikon was soon erected next to the older one. The several storied eight pillar construction also houses a series of mosaic images decorating several zones. Covering the entire church interior, the mosaics combine the circular salvation cycle of Christ's life with the vertical steps of the divine hierarchy of monks, saints, prophets, apostles, and the angels. The depiction of the Pantocrator (Almighty) in the center has been lost. The dome mosaic of the Almighty in the monastery at Daphni (late 11th C.), on the western outskirts of Athens, provides an alternative. Recent restoration work has shown, however, that this mosaic is a restored version from the 19th century. The violent earthquakes of this period have had devastating consequences in Hosios Lukas and Daphni, both on the mainland and on the Greek islands.

In its remote mountain location the Nea Moni Monastery on Chios houses the boldest example of eight pillar construction. The domed space of the monastery church is built like a tower above the square *naos* (aisle). Tower galleries and arcades are entirely absent. The eight wall pillars have been reduced to a minimum number of responds, so that the dome is supported directly by the outside walls. The corners are bridged by four diagonal conches (apsidal domes), bringing the story of salvation told in the mosaics strikingly close to the viewer. The precious marble panels also add rhythm and a rounded form to this elaborate, square room. This is not the work of ascetics on a remote island but the design of one of the best architects of the period. Contemporary sources indicate that Nea Moni is a copy of a monastery building in the capital. Constantine Monomachos (1042–55) confirmed the founding of Nea Moni in the imperial *chrysobull*, the deed of endowment written in gold. It was the fulfillment of a commitment: the hermits of the neighboring island of Mytilene had predicted his return to imperial power while he had been in exile. This pious and somewhat contrived legend does, however, support the observation that both the building and the mosaic work at Nea Moni are testimony to the lost art of 11th-century

Church procession carrying the cross from the *Menologion* of Basil II (976–1025);. Rome (Biblioteca Apostolica Vaticana, vat. gr. 1613, p. 142).

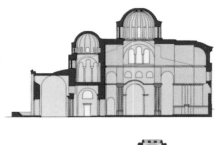

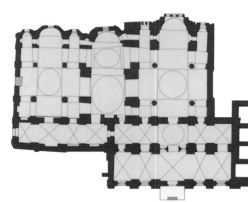

▼ ▶ Istanbul, Zeyrek Camii, former Pantokrator monastery. The 12th-C. Comnenian emperors erected this double church as a house monastery and had their dynastic burial place here. Although the other monastery buildings, including a hospital with specialist departments, have been lost, Zeyrek Camii still constitutes a spectacular showplace of Mid-Byzantine history.

Constantinople. The mosaics in the atrium (Mary Going to the Temple, the Washing of the Apostles' Feet) as well as the conch mosaics in the octagon (Baptism of Christ, Crucifixion, Resurrection) document a drawing style that was replaced by a more vivid, colored painting style during the course of the 12th century.

In Constantinople itself, of the three most famous Mid-Byzantine monasteries: Blachernai, Hedegon, and Pantokrator, only the last survives. Even following the recent restoration of the present day Zeyrek Camii, the significance of the group of buildings, which were erected successively between 1118 and 1136, becomes clear only with reference to the typikon of 1136. The monastery complex originally comprised three churches, a hospital, an old-age home, as well as other social facilities. The typikon lists details of the departments and the number of beds in the hospital used for surgery, pathology, ophthalmology, and gynecology. The imperial monastery was therefore more advanced than the Ottoman monasteries (*külliye*), which were able to cover an entire suburb with their mosques, Koran schools, hospitals, and soup kitchens, as is shown by the impressive example of the Sulemaniye (16th C.) in Istanbul.

John II Comnenos (1118–43) erected the burial place of the 12th-century Comnenian imperial dynasty in the Pantokrator monastery. A final section in the form of a chapel for the imperial tombs was built between the south church of the Pantokrator and the north church of the Theotokos (Mother of God). This was dedicated to the Archangel Michael, the general of the undefeatable divine army, as protector of the tombs. The sepulchral chapel with the archaic name of the Heroon (shrine to a hero) was a new type of mausoleum and it was entirely incorporated into the liturgy. In the group of churches it constituted an exclusive, sacral sphere between the earthly Autocrator and the divine Pantocrator. At the same time, it combined monastic commemorative prayer with the special blessing of the icons. The liturgical typikon of 1136 went into great detail about the precatory church procession rites and the displays of icons around the tombs in the Heroon. A procession was held every Friday and for the annual commemoration, during which the icon of Mary was transferred from the neighboring church of Christ and remained overnight during the monks' precatory prayer. On the night of a requiem the icon also appeared as the emperor's advocate. The wrath of God over the sins of Man meant that there was one intercession that the Pantocrator could not refuse: that of his Mother, the Theotokos. The staging of different candle illuminations and the transfer of the icon, as laid down in the Pantokrator monastery typikon, also activated the spiritual power designated by the honorary titles of the icon of Mary in a variety of ways: Mary as Episkepsis (protector), Paramythia (comforter), and Boethia (helper). However, the most important icon in the Hagia Maria Church in the Comnenian Pantokrator monastery and in its ritual memorial liturgy was the Eleousa (merciful).

Hence the provision of an institutionalized liturgical requiem soon became the dominant concept behind the constantly increasing founding of monasteries with sepulchral chapels by the local elite of the 12th and 13th centuries. Both Cyprus and Cappadochia exhibit dense topographies of such sepulchral churches, which were equipped with monasteries for the monks. In Byzantine terms three monks can constitute a monastery, meaning that the outlay and ongoing expense of donations, amounting to the harvest of a vineyard, were calculable. The Cappadochian pillar churches of Göreme and especially the monastery at Karanlik Kilise conducted complex funeral programs from c. 1200. A popular subject in the apses of these cave churches was the *Deesis*, the intercession of Mary and John the Baptist in front of the Pantocrator Enthroned. These apse compositions were not solely a provincial feature,

Karanlik Kilise near Göreme/Nevsehir, Crucifixion of Christ. The "dark" church with its wall paintings of c. 1200 houses a complex series of liturgical images. The cave church is part of a larger monastery complex in the highlands of Anatolia.

▲ ▼ **Istanbul, Kariye Camii,** formerly Chora Monastery. The extensive surviving mosaics were donated by Theodore Metochites (1260–1332) who, as scholar and chancellor, was a prominent figure in Late Byzantium. He spent the last years of his life as a monk in the rebuilt monastery, intended as his burial place. The mosaic below shows him as patron.

however. In 1304–08, next to the Theotokos Pammakaristos monastery in Constantinople, a sepulchral chapel was built with the full regalia of a cross-dome church. It was built for the Byzantine General Michael Glabas by his widow, who herself entered the monastery as a nun. In the apse Christ is depicted in the Deesis, and the epigram describes him as Hyperagathos, the Very Gracious One. This epigram has been shown to be a quotation from the requiem liturgy, thus completing the circle. Also worthy of mention is that the Theotokos Pammakaristos monastery was the seat of the ecumenical patriarchy from 1455 to 1587.

The illustrations so far show that monastery buildings in Late Byzantium were individual concepts that were not characterized by traditional building styles but by the features provided by painted decoration, the main icons of the *templon* (separation of the sanctuary), or other specific facilities. The architectural styles of the cross-dome church, domed naos, or pillar basilica were suited to the construction of monastery churches without the need for adaptation. The rebuilding of the Chora church in Constantinople, completed by 1321, is an exemplary display of how an older, probably dilapidated, cross-dome church could be converted into a very individual monastic retreat and individual burial place by means of clever cladding and the addition of a sepulchral chapel. The patron, Theodore Metochites, was chancellor to Emperor Andronicus II (1282–1328). Following his retirement he withdrew as a monk to the monastery he had been preparing over the years. A small suite of rooms above the northern corridor, accessible via a narrow staircase, enabled him to hear the liturgy from this upper floor and to prepare himself for death in theological study and prayer. The monastery's decoration has a leitmotif based on Psalm 116, 9, which is depicted above the entrance: Christ, the Land of the Living—and as Mary's

Rila Monastery near Sofia, Bulgaria. It was rebuilt in the 19th century based on the example of the Athos monasteries to become a center of Orthodox and national identity.

counterpart, the home of God who cannot be claimed by any land. This monastery's reference to the aspirations of the afterlife and of Paradise, as well as of the incarnation and of salvation serves an obvious purpose.

The Mary and Christ mosaic cycles in the Chora church provide typological references to the actual construction of the church when viewed closely in the context of the images and spatial axes, as well as with reference to the hymns and singing of the daily liturgy. In the imagery the church space is interpreted as a new Temple and as the home of God. In the wall painting the spacious sepulchral chapel to the side is typologically and metaphorically comparable to the judgment and intercession of Mary. It is through these decorative discourses, recorded in a contemporary monastic church, that a Late Byzantine monastery gives a voice to its patron and its individual intercessors. It is not the typology and affiliation of the architecture, but the imagery of the painted decoration and the rhetoric of the icons that prove to be the determining features of the Byzantine monastery church.

The fall of Constantinople in 1453 brought Byzantine monastic architecture to an abrupt halt. Worthy of mention in conclusion and as a representative of the other revival movements of the 18th and 19th centuries is Bulgaria's Rila Monastery, the founding of which in the 10th century is best commemorated by the dominant Chreljo tower dating from 1335. The monastery's present day appearance, however, the compactness of the imposing fortress-like complex, and the strict aesthetics of the layered black and white masonry, is the result of building work in the 19th century. The imposing, high wings of the monastery courtyard were erected between 1816 and 1850. The models for the monastery church, however, were Athos buildings, in particular the katholikon of the (Bulgarian) monastery at Zograph and that of the Esphigmenu monastery, both dating from the start of the 19th century. The reconstruction of Rila is representative of the return to its own Orthodoxy and national identity, and the monastery therefore predates the 1879 demise of Ottoman rule in Bulgaria by decades.

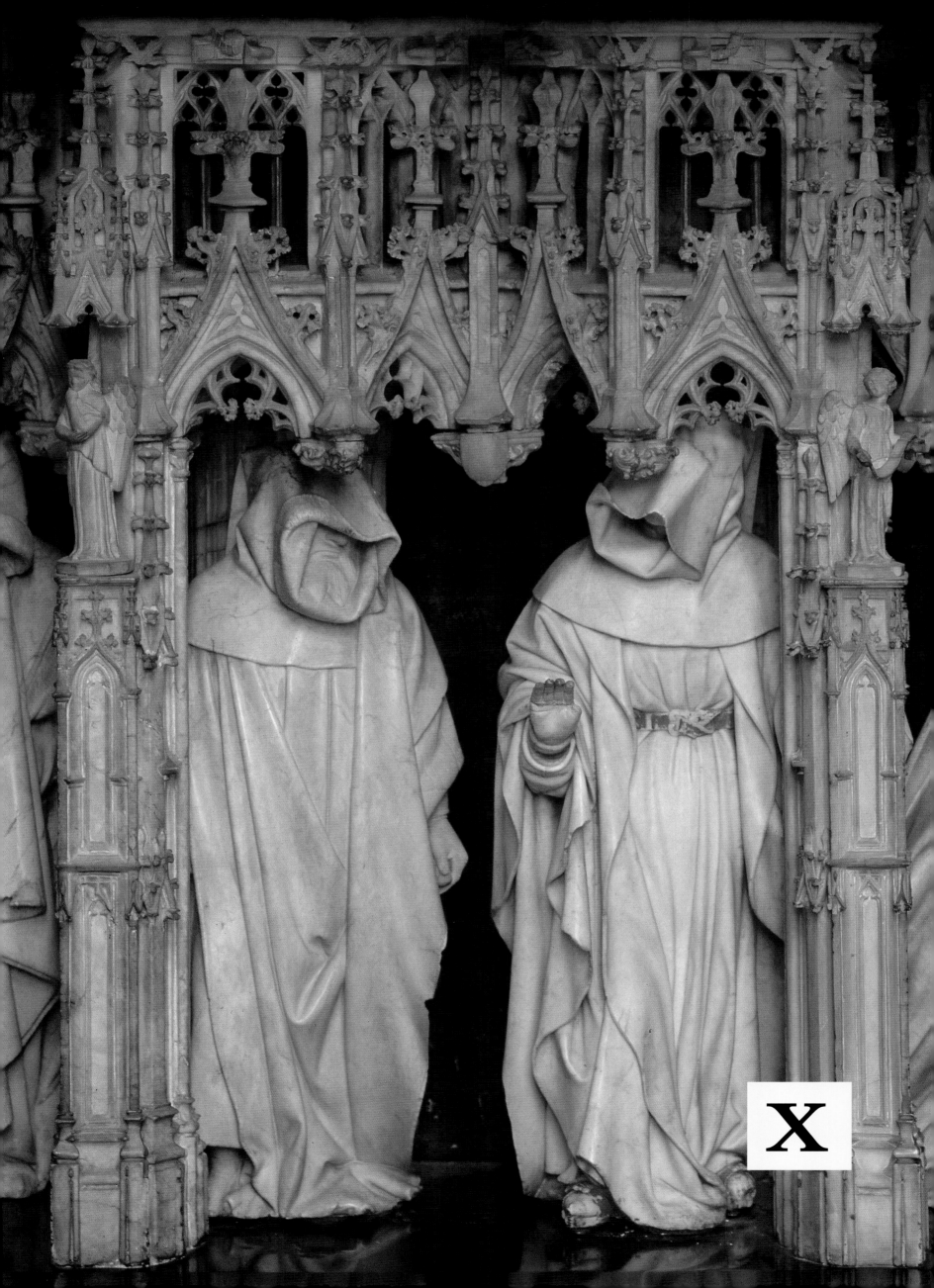

X

The Late Middle Ages, the Reformation, and the Counter-Reformation

Monastic Reform in the Late Middle Ages

St. Odilie frees her father from the fires of hell, Alsace, c. 1450, painted woodcut print (Staatliche Graphische Sammlung München, Inv.-Nr. 10667). Woodcut printing and the simultaneous spread of paper as a printing material brought with them a wealth of illustrations from the late 14th C. Woodcut printing was initially used mainly for single pages. These often included sheets with religious motifs—only in exceptional cases were they of a high artistic level—which were used for personal meditation purposes. This woodcut print emphasizes the significance of nuns' prayer. Just as the Alsatian abbess Odilie was once able to use prayer to free her suffering father from the fires of hell, so can monastic prayer be a source of salvation at any time.

The periodic cycle of monastic decline, dissolution, and revival continued in the Late Middle Ages as well. The late medieval reforms were not merely an attempt to return to the "original ideals," however; they also exhibit a series of independent features.

In the Late Middle Ages the aspiration towards a spiritual life characterized by extensive frugality, which continued to be found in all of the orders and monastic reform movements, no longer meant the same as it had in earlier centuries. Material culture had developed since the 13th century and new standards relating to daily living comfort had been set, which no-one wanted to give up. The austerity and harshness of monastery life in the Early and High Middle Ages was no longer sought in the 14th and 15th centuries. Heating and appropriate clothing in winter were expected, while furniture and utensils that had previously been considered luxuries, a variety of fabrics for bed linen and clothing, as well as comprehensive tableware, became everyday features. In the observance of the poverty rule, the distinction began to be made between "superficialities" that were no longer considered relevant to the contemporary era and the actual inner attitude that was to be aspired to.

The space accorded to each individual was also extended. Dormitories with rows of beds side by side were replaced by single cells and existing communal sleeping quarters were divided into individual compartments using wooden crates and curtains, enabling withdrawal into a private sphere, albeit a modest one. At the same time, the concept of lack of personal possessions also acquired nuances: in addition to toiletry articles, monks and nuns often owned devotional objects, like crosses, pilgrim insignia, small commemorative pictures they had sometimes created themselves, personal and spiritual correspondence, as well as books. Manuscript production increased dramatically in the Late Middle Ages. Books were found not only inside monasteries, but increasingly often outside them. In addition to the clergy there were also numerous laypeople who could read and who owned books. Individual monks in the monasteries no longer obtained their reading material solely from the monastery library, but acquired manuscripts corresponding to their particular interests and for their own use. The way for such interests had been paved by increased and more intensive education. A basic theological education for monks or even more advanced study for talented new entrants came to be seen as desirable not only by the mendicant orders but also by the others, although not to the same extent everywhere. Travel and the exchange of information, over greater distances, ultimately became a natural component of spiritual life, as they had been in early centuries, only now on a much wider front.

A direct consequence of the changed external living conditions was the construction of numerous new monastery buildings in the 14th and 15th centuries. Cloisters, chapter houses, dormitories, refectories, and living rooms were rebuilt or converted according to contemporary tastes and in line with the increased standards of comfort (ovens, individual cells). The cloister—with the exception of the east wing, which had always comprised two stories—was often extended with an upper floor to accommodate monks' cells and library rooms and, in some places north of the Alps, the cloister galleries were also glazed. The conversion of the monastery churches also often included the installation of large glass windows, e.g. in the choir or the west

section of the nave, and many previously unvaulted buildings in Germany and Italy acquired Late Gothic vaulting.

The reforms of the Late Middle Ages were not directed against these developments but against what went beyond them, threatening to blur the boundaries between spiritual and secular life. The symptoms of a decline in discipline often quoted in historical sources include the possession of large sums of money or personal incomes by office holders or individual monks or nuns, the adoption of secular fashions in clothing or mens' beards, the partaking of worldly pleasures, the staging of feasts in monasteries, and, finally, living openly or semi-openly in marriage-like relationships. Such "concubinages" were especially prevalent where individual or groups of monks—such as monks from smaller monasteries in the countryside and lay brothers at Cistercian granges—lived at remote distances from their community.

In addition to the abolition of grievances, the main focus of the reforms was aimed at the creation of a new form of religious introspection. These endeavors were a result of the influence of the *Devotio moderna* (Latin for new piety), a lay pietistic movement that developed in the Netherlands at the end of the 14th century, placing emphasis on the personal faith of the individual, the effects of which were felt far inside clerical circles as well. The model of Christian life around which the followers of the *Devotio moderna* oriented themselves had long been familiar (the original community of the Apostles and the first Christians), but the hoped for goals and the methods used were new. Unlike in the 12th and 13th centuries, these reforms were not concerned with the most "authentic" way of emulating the Apostles, but with a spiritual relationship with the life and suffering of Jesus and the example of the original Jerusalem community; the inner attitude thus achieved was to be applied to the life of the individual, and in the contemporary language. The means to this end was a new form of spiritual reflection: individual meditation. Following the accounts of the Gospels and the writings of the Church Fathers, it was intended that individuals should visualize spiritual issues, incorporating events from the Life of and, especially, the Passion of Christ, for example, reconstructing them spiritually in their minds. Pictures, preferably those depicting the crucifixion, Christ's suffering, or of St. Mary, could therefore be used in addition to texts as a starting point for meditational practice. Prints that were quick and cheap to reproduce as well as easy to transport—

Brou, monastery church, 1513–32, interior with rood screen. Commissioned by the Regent of the Habsburg Netherlands, Margaret of Austria, this church was constructed by the Brussels architect Loys van Boghem and is resplendent with multicolored tiled roofs and high quality ornamentation. Late Gothic elements of the *style flamboyant* decorate the church's rood screen and the famous tombs.

Vallombrosa, monastery courtyard. The open, wrought iron gate provides a view of the elegant, Renaissance-style courtyard façade of the archabbey (the mother house of the congregation of the same name).

Bursfelde, Benedictine abbey, interior view of the west section of the Romanesque abbey church. The wall paintings of the nave arcades date from the mid-15th C.

Farfa, Benedictine abbey, church and large cloister. In the Late Middle Ages, the abbey came into the possession of the aristocratic Orsini family, who forged an alliance between Farfa and the reformed monastery at Subiaco, leading to the settlement of German monks. The rebuilding of the abbey complex at the end of the 15th century was also thanks to the Orsinis.

woodcuts, engravings, and later also etchings, were used for such purposes and, accordingly, were produced in great quantities as well as sometimes in large batches.

The reform efforts implemented in traditional Benedictine monasticism on both sides of the Alps during the last decades of the 14th century led during the 15th century to the formation of monastery networks—so-called congregations—among the reformed houses of one observance. The first to start reform was the Upper Palatinate abbey of Kastl, from 1380. By the time of its decline in the second half of the 15th century, the Kastl Reform had been adopted by the abbeys of Reichenbach, St. Ägidien in Nuremberg, Weihenstephan, Michelfeld, Prüfening, and others, who in turn spread it further within Franconia, Bavaria, Swabia, and Switzerland (St. Gallen).

In Italy the abbeys of Subiaco, Farfa, Camáldoli, and Vallombrosa were active reform centers. Subiaco, in particular, also attracted monks from the countries north of the Alps. These brought what were seen as the "authentic Benedictine" living habits of their host monastery back to the Austrian abbey of Melk, adapting them to the conditions there, such that a further reform movement based at Melk was formed after c. 1410. With the support of the landowners this was initially successful, in Austria in particular, but extended to Bavaria and Swabia, where the abbeys of Blaubeuren and St. Ulrich in Augsburg, for example, were reformed. These in turn also become the sources of new reform impulses that extended to the north as far as the St. Bonifazius abbey in Fulda.

From the start of the 15th century, the further development of the Benedictine Reform in Italy was determined in particular by the reformed abbey of S. Giustina in Padua, which rose to become the head of a large reform congregation. In the early 16th century its influence extended as far as Spain, where the congregation of S. Benito de Valladolid adopted its constitution. First founded in 1389, the S. Benito monastery had reformed numerous Castilian religious houses since the start of the 15th century, reintroducing strict monastic standards there.

The most important late medieval reform movement, however, was the Bursfelde Reform. The abbey at Bursfelde, on the Weser west of Göttingen, was reformed in 1433 by abbot John Dederoth and subsequently developed intensive reform activities of its own. Initially restricted to the immediate proximity, the Bursfelde Reform soon extended to the whole of Lower Saxony, Thuringia, Westphalia, and the Rhineland, ultimately reaching as far as the Netherlands, Belgium, and Denmark. The monasteries reformed by Bursfelde followed a common liturgical regime and were acknowledged as an independent congregation at the Council of Basle in 1446, with chapters and regular inspections carried out by the abbot of Bursfelde. In 1461 the Pope commissioned Bursfelde with the reform of all German Benedictine abbeys. The way in which the reform was communicated corresponded to the old system already practiced by the Cluniacs in that small groups of experienced monks were dispatched from a reformed monastery to one that was to be

reformed, where they were expected to serve as living examples of a life conforming to the rule.

A reform congregation was also formed under the canons regular at the end of the 14th century. The lay movement *Devotio moderna* established in 1375 by Geert Grote in Deventer led not only to the combination of groups of pious laymen and women, who then lived as "Brothers and Sisters of the Common Life" in a semireligious manner similar to that of the Beguines and the Tertiaries of the mendicant orders, but also to the founding in 1387 of the reformed canons regular monastery of Windesheim. The Windesheim Reform included canons regular monasteries throughout the German-speaking region. Their Italian counterpart was the contemporary Lateran Congregation, whose influence also extended to eastern central Europe.

While the development and ultimate secession of the Observants among the Franciscans in the 14th and 15th centuries saw the implementation of a reform process similar to that in Benedictine monasticism, there was among the Cistercians no reform movement encompassing the entire order and, in particular, none that affected the French core of the order. Nevertheless, the Cistercian monasteries did undergo limited regional reform processes, which ensured the continuity of discipline and regular monastery life; these included monasteries located in the Netherlands, in the Rhineland, Westphalia, Bohemia, and Moravia.

In addition to the reform of existing monasteries there were also numerous new foundations in the Late Middle Ages. In particular, the number of mendicant order communities continued to grow and for the Carthusians the 15th century was the main period of their order's development, especially in German-speaking areas. The reason for this is considered to be the Carthusian philosophy, which, with its combination of withdrawal, individual prayer, and communal life, left ample space for each member and so met the late medieval requirement for greater individualism.

▲ ▼ **Bursfelde, Benedictine abbey**, overall view with the abbey church and surrounding buildings; interior of the east section (formerly the monks' choir). The ideal of the Bursfelde Reform was to follow the Rule of St. Benedict as closely as possible. The monks saw the religious service and the daily meditation as their main tasks. This essentially contemplative approach resulted in a somewhat dismissive attitude to pastoral activities, university education, and to the fostering of expertise in the Bursfelde Congregation.

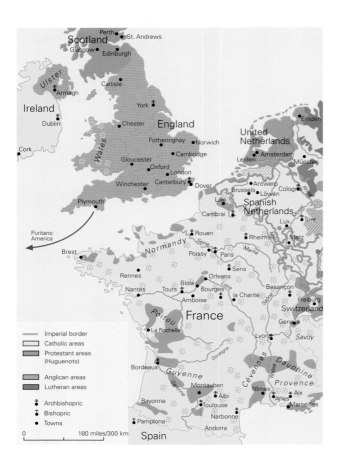

Regional denominational distribution following the Reformation in central and western Europe.

Iconoclasm, woodcut print, c. 1525–27. A Counter-Reformation denunciation of the destruction, from a pamphlet.

The Reformation

No other historical event changed the map of European monasticism more than the Reformation. In the countries it encompassed, the system of monasteries and religious houses that had grown up over the centuries was dissolved or violently destroyed within a few decades, in some cases within no more than a few years. The Reformation did not follow a steady, uniform course everywhere, but was a far more complex process, implemented differently in the various towns, countries, and territories.

The writings of the Wittenberg theology professor Luther (from 1517) and the sermons of the Zurich priest Zwingli (from 1519), in which grievances about the practice of the faith and the leadership of the Church were voiced, were intended as reform efforts within the existing Church. Yet the questioning of central tenets of the Catholic faith—the doctrine of justification by faith, the understanding of the Last Supper, the doctrine of the sacraments, the institutional Church with the Pope at its head—led to the development of an independent theological position recognizing only that laid down by the Bible or justifiable by it, but not, or only to a limited extent, the historical tradition on which the Church based itself. What began as a late medieval reform, like others before it, ultimately led to the changing of the religious service (granting of communion in both forms—bread and wine, use of the popular language instead of Latin, abandonment of Mass vestments) and the implementation of reform measures (such as abolition of relics, discontinuation of indulgences, feasts, pilgrimages, and processions) and to the division of the Church.

Like the poverty and piety movements of the High and Late Middle Ages, the Reformation was a spiritual rebellion, but one with a social background. Its supporters were primarily the educated urban middle and upper classes, even though its influence did not remain restricted to these circles, going on to involve some of the aristocracy and the rural population. The educated and economically successful urban population, which saw itself excluded from the numerous Church privileges, supplied the momentum for the Reformation. Most of the members of the lower and middle clergy who joined the Reformation also came from this milieu and were characterized by their experience of scarce career opportunities and ecclesiastical grievances. It is no coincidence, therefore, that the Reformation was successful in Germany, initially in the towns and especially in the independent imperial cities. In France many localities that had become ambitious country towns due to their dynamic economies and growing populations turned Protestant. The subsequent religious wars and ultimately the abolition of the Edict of Nantes (1685), causing the exodus of the French Protestants, meant the ruin of these late medieval towns and led to the centuries long stagnation of large parts of provincial France.

The theological positions of the three great reformers—Luther, Zwingli, and Calvin—differed not only from the conventional teaching of the Church but also from one another, such that varying forms of the Reformation took effect in different countries. The decisions regarding the introduction and

implementation of the Reformation usually lay with the landowner and/or the town authorities. In all of the Protestant territories from Switzerland to Scandinavia there was a move towards the dissolution of the monasteries, accompanied by the conversion or the demolition of the monastery buildings, sometimes also the church. The monastic possessions went to the landowner or the town. The handling of the artistic legacy of Catholic worship, however, differed according to denomination. Those under the influence of Zwingli's Reformation, which was opposed to imagery, opted for a "clean slate" when it came to the former church decoration; they inflicted a path of iconoclastic destruction on France's medieval architectural sculptures, which were attacked by Calvinist troops in the religious wars of the 16th century. In contrast, in the Lutheran areas the pre-Reformation ornamentation remained largely intact. Instead of parting company with Catholic "cult objects," older figures of the saints were even integrated into the new imagery and in some places the Late Gothic winged altarpieces were converted to Evangelical altar retables. Some of the time-honored nunneries in northern Germany continued to exist as aristocratic Evangelical convents; some of them are still in existence today (Wienhausen, Fischbeck).

The introduction of the Reformation in England by Henry VIII, on the other hand, served only the political interests of the King, who used it to elude papal influence. Following the dissociation from Rome, he formed the independent Anglican Church, of which he declared himself head in 1535. The violent dissolution of the monasteries (1536–39) initially led to the confiscation, and later to the sale, of monastic property and to the destruction of the churches and monastery complexes, the ruins of which still survive in many places today, sometimes integrated into landscaped gardens.

▲ **Luther in the Vineyard,** painting by Lucas Cranach the Younger, 1569. The left side of the vineyard, worked by the monks and clerics of the Catholic Church, is barren and stony, while the right side, cultivated by reformers under Luther, appears well ordered and will bear fruit. The well on the right side provides fresh water; the painting's message is that this part of the vineyard has God's blessing.

▼ **Saint-Gilles-du-Gard, detail of sculpture from the façade.** Although the monastery church at Saint-Gilles was burnt down by the Huguenots (the French Protestants) in the 16th century, the Romanesque sculptures of the façade survived, though damaged.

The Counter-Reformation and Catholic Reform

While, with the exception of the towns, the adoption of the Reformation lay in the hands of Protestant-minded landowners, in its aftermath the rulers and princes who remained true to the Catholic faith took the initiative against the spread of reforming ideas and the Protestant "heresy." In addition to supporting the internal reform of the Catholic Church, this often meant an aggressive doctrinal policy aimed at recatholicization that used bans, compulsory measures, and expulsion as its methods in the face of the equally uncompromising stance of its opponents. The lack of tolerance on both the Catholic and the Protestant sides, which, within German territory, was made all the more complicated politically by the contradictions between the Lutherans and the other Protestants, was directly responsible for a series of wars—from the Schmalkaldic War (1546/47) to the French religious wars (1562–98) and the struggle of the Protestant Netherlands to free themselves from Catholic Spain (1568–1648) through to the Thirty Years' War (1618–48).

The Council of Trent (*Tridentinum* in Latin), summoned by Pope Paul III in 1545, became the most important forum for the Catholic Reform; with interruptions, it sat until 1563. The Council affirmed the tenets of the Catholic faith—including the equal acknowledgement of the apostolic traditions in addition to the Holy Scriptures, the instrumentality of Man in his vindication before God through good works, the Seven Sacraments, the rejection of lay communion in both forms, the retention of Latin, of the veneration of the saints and of relics, of the fires of hell, and of the primacy of the pope. The reform measures passed—in particular the promotion to the office of bishop according to personal suitability, the tightening of the bishops' obligation of residence within their diocese, the central responsibility to provide spiritual guidance, the inspection obligation, as well as the establishment of seminaries for the training of priests—were implemented in different ways in the individual countries and with varying consequences. Nevertheless, the Tridentine decree on reform, together with the starting signal that came from the Council, gave the Catholic Church the inner strength and the stimulus which was necessary to withstand the crisis and to reinforce its own identity,

The Council of Trent, copy after Titian, c. 1565 (Paris, Musée du Louvre). In December 1545 Pope Paul III opened the 19th Ecumenical Council in Trent, which, with interruptions, lasted 20 years and formed the basis of the Counter-Reformation.

as well as to overcome institutional grievances and pursue a renewed, active religious policy.

In addition to the bishops, who were accorded a central role in the implementation of the Tridentine resolutions, a series of newer orders founded in the first half of the 16th century—parallel to the start of the Reformation—were entrusted with reform tasks, some of them developing specific areas of activity.

The Theatines, an order for secular clerics founded in 1524 and especially widespread in Italy, Spain, and southern Germany, campaigned for the revival of the Church through the reform of the clergy, based on the training of priests and a return to provision of spiritual guidance and performance of charitable works.

The Ursulines, established in Brescia in 1535 as an association of women who pledged to live a life of chastity in accordance with a common rule but outside convent walls, dedicated themselves to the education of young women. Supported by the bishop of Milan, Carlo Borromeo, one of the prominent advocates of the Tridentine Reform, Ursuline communities spread initially to northern Italy, then to France, where there were over 300 convents before the Revolution, and also to German-speaking regions from the 17th century. In France, in contrast to their original intentions, from 1612 the Ursulines were subjected to an enclosed convent system under the Rule of St. Augustine. Their communities were always connected with the establishment of girls' schools, including higher institutions of learning with boarding facilities, and paving the way for the modern concept of women's education.

The Capuchins—so called because of their habits with long, peaked cowls (from *cappuccio*, Italian for hood)—derived from a split in 1525 within the Franciscan Observants. The capuchins wanted to pursue a traveling life in strict poverty. With the rapid affiliation of additional highly educated Observants this branch of the order took on an intellectual focus, and the study of the scriptures became the basis of the sermons in which the Capuchins specialized. Their work as preachers had a strongly anti-Reformation focus in Germany and France, in particular. Initially wandering preachers proficient in the language of the people, as parish, monastery, cathedral, or court preachers in fixed employment, the Capuchins later developed a penchant for baroque rhetoric. Their expansion took place at a rapid pace, similar to that of the Franciscans 300 years earlier, encompassing both Europe and the New World and lasting until well into the 18th century. In 1619 they were formally released from subjugation to the Franciscan Conventuals and acknowledged by the pope as an independent order.

The Jesuits

The most important and most influential of these new orders and, at the same time, that with which a brand new, radical, modern form of monastic ideals took shape, was the Societas Jesu (Latin for Society of Jesus). It was the first order without monasteries, whose members placed themselves freely at the disposal of the pope, but who otherwise led a normal life as "respectable priests" in the secular world. The Jesuits were founded by a group of seven Parisian students who made their vows on August 15, 1534 (Assumption Day) at Montmartre in Paris, pledging themselves to poverty, chastity, and missionary work in the Holy Land. Since travel to Palestine was impossible, however, the group made themselves subject to the pope in 1538, and made preparations for deployment where they were most needed for the dissemination of the faith. The order's program submitted in 1539 received official acknowledgment in 1540.

The Jesuits' first Superior General and leading initiator of their foundation was a Spanish nobleman named Iñigo López de Oñaz y Loyola, who Latinized his name as Ignatius Loyola. Brought up in the knightly milieu of the court, he was badly wounded in battle and was converted during his convalescence, undergoing a spiritual crisis in the Catalan monastery at Montserrat, and withdrawing for year, which he spent practicing penitence. During this time his reading material included the *Imitatio Christi* (Latin for Imitation of Christ) and the *Devotio moderna*, by far the most important book on mediation and the most widespread text in the Late Middle Ages, after the Bible.

▲ **S. Pedro de Alcántara,** painted wooden figure, 1633, by Pedro de Mena (Valladolid, Museo Nacional de Escultura). The Spanish Franciscan reformer Pedro de Alcántara wrote a treatise on prayer and meditation, of which there were more than 300 editions in several languages.

▼ **Ignatius Loyola,** co-founder of the Jesuit order, canonized in 1622 by Pope Paul III. (Rome, Il Gesù).

► **Montserrat and its Benedictine monastery,** viewed from Mount S. Joan. Ignatius withdrew to Catalonia following his injury in battle against the French in 1521. He stayed there initially and then lived in a cave near Manresa for eight months; his mystic experience during this time determined the path of his future life.

►► **Salamanca, Jesuit college of La Clerecía,** begun in 1617, interior view of the church; and college courtyard. The college, which dominates the town, is situated in close proximity to the cathedral, university, and Dominican monastery, was constructed against the wishes of the Commune. Begun on the basis of plans by Gómez de Mora, the intimidating complex was completed only around the middle of the 18th C.

The *Spiritual Exercises*

The *Exercitia spiritualia* (Latin for Spiritual Exercises) are not a book on meditation but rather an introduction to meditation and prayer, with explanations and advice, as provided by a spiritual teacher to his pupil in the form of exercises. The intention was that, during a long period of withdrawal, originally lasting for four weeks, the initiate should consolidate his faith, ordering his life to focus on the will of God, through a process of self-examination and reflection. The main events in the life of Jesus served as a basis for meditation, bringing the student step by step to an examination of his own life, to his decision in favor of Christ's example, to the consolidation of this decision, and ultimately to his complete surrender to God.
Even though every Jesuit had to complete the *Spiritual Exercises,* these were not directed solely at the members of the order, but at all believers. The aspired goal was not an external one—it was neither the entry into the Society of Jesus nor the calling to another form of spirituality, but an inner realignment of one's life and a reversion to Christianity. For these reasons the *Spiritual Exercises* are still used today as a means of introduction to the quest for God. In recent times, an abbreviated and significantly modified version has been incorporated into the religious practice of other denominations.

Ignatius was probably also familiar with the *Ejercitatorio de la vida spiritual* (Exercises for the spiritual life) by the abbot of Montserrat, García Jiménez de Cisneros, which was also strongly influenced by the *Devotio moderna*. It was on the basis of this late medieval piety that Ignatius developed his own *Spiritual Exercises*, which continue to be a focal point of Jesuit spirituality today.

Nevertheless, Ignatius did not rely on the power of conversion alone. Instead, he saw the need for it to be backed up by knowledge, and therefore took up the study of philosophy and theology, in order to be equal to the task he felt he was called upon to perform. With this move towards the principle of scholarship and learning, he paved the way for the Jesuits' involvement in educational work, which began during his own lifetime with the foundation of colleges (schools) in numerous Italian and Spanish towns, as well as north of the Alps (Ingolstadt, Vienna).

The Jesuit constitution drawn up by Ignatius as Superior General of the order (1541–56) has a strongly centralist structure that clearly distinguishes it from typical constitutions of mendicant orders. Only the Superior General is elected for life, by the General Congregation, the order's highest and only legislative authority; all of the subordinate positions in the order were nominated by him. The principles of personal leadership and obedience applied to the order's hierarchy. Acceptance into the order took place in two stages: a straightforward vow after two years as a novice; the final vow only after ten years. There are priests and secular brothers (coadjutors). Only those brothers possessing educational skills, who are suited to apostolic missionary work, and are designated for official positions within the order take the vow, which is made to the pope. There is no choral prayer, no monastic customs, penitential practices, enclosure, or monks' habit, only "normal way of life" in the secular world and complete mobility, enabling the Jesuits to be wherever needed.

The expansion of the new order, which broke away from what had previously been the conventional lifestyle for members of religious orders, took place against the background of its modest beginnings but was rapid and sustained. By 1620, there were some 14,000 Jesuits, who stood at the head of Catholic Reform or, in France and Germany, were energetic champions of the Counter-Reformation. Their main area of activity was that of education, with some 500 colleges run by the Jesuits c. 1650 and a worldwide network of schools by the end of the 18th century. In addition they were active as preachers as well as confessors, in religious instruction as well as in the research of church history (*Acta sanctorum*: Lives of the saints), and in the natural sciences. In particular, however, the Jesuits were involved in missionary work. Their pedagogical methods, developed in their work as educators and father confessors were successfully implemented in the Christianization of the newly discovered lands outside Europe and they thus became the largest missionary order in America, India, China, and Japan.

Within their communities, instead of monasteries the Jesuits erected churches and colleges, which also had to provide school rooms, libraries, and study rooms, together with living quarters for teachers and pupils, as well as dining rooms and kitchen facilities. At first glance the extensive complexes grouped around one or several courtyards, with the church usually situated to the side, hardly differ from monastery buildings. Despite the rule of poverty that applied to the order as well as to its individual members, the college

▲ ▼ **Rome, Il Gesù,** Vignola and Giacopo della Porta, post-1568, interior view; and façade. The Jesuit order's mother church is also seen as the prototype of baroque architecture, its stylistic elements having made a major contribution to the Counter-Reformation's orchestration of the faith.

buildings often exhibited monumental tendencies and the churches were frequently large and elaborate in design. However, there was neither an architectural "Jesuit style" nor was there any other form of order style. The design of Jesuit churches corresponds to the diversity of designs in the contemporary architecture of the country in question and to their often resplendent, verging on the overwhelming, orientation towards the baroque style dominant at the time. Nevertheless, there are two prominent buildings that have had a decisive influence on the overall image of Jesuit churches and a limited function as models for other churches constructed by the order: the church at the Jesuit headquarters in Rome, Il Gesù, and St. Michael's Church in Munich. Both feature wide naves lined with chapels on both sides, but their individual interior and façade designs are very different. In contrast to these two prominent churches, the fronts of which are devoid of towers, numerous later Jesuit churches had distinctive twin tower façades.

As a result of internal church and political rivalries the Jesuits, as the extended arm of the pope, were banned in the majority of European countries in the second half of the 18th century. Dissolved in 1773, the order was re-established in 1814 during the course of the European Restoration and continues to exist today.

Vienna, University Church, vaulting with ceiling frescoes by Andrea Pozzo. A Jesuit lay brother, Pozzo was commissioned to undertake the painting of the Viennese Jesuit church in 1704. Despite the difficult architectural conditions (wide, protruding transverse arches between the vault spans), the painter was able to achieve the desired illusory effect of depth. He painted an illusory dome in the middle vault span with a view of heaven next to it—in line with the contemporary tendency towards dramatic staging.

◄ **Munich, St. Michael,** 1683–97, interior. The imposing hall-like nave of the Jesuit church in Munich is spanned by a 65 ft (20 m) wide half-vault resting on the mighty wall pillars and the transverse barrel vaults of the flanking chapels and arcades. The space gives by an overwhelming impression of breadth.

Solothurn, Jesuit church, from 1680, interior view to the west. The collegiate church was the basis for the success of the Vorarlberg school of architecture. Its design—a nave church with wall pillars and chapel recesses, arcades, a narrow, transept protruding only slightly, etc—was widespread throughout southern Germany and Switzerland c. 1700.

Rome, Sant' Ignazio, 1626–80, view of the apse (▼), ceiling fresco by Andrea Pozzo, 1691–94 (▶). Work on this church, dedicated to Ignatius Loyola, began four years after his canonization. As was usual for the Jesuits, it was primarily members of the order who were involved in the planning and construction work. Andrea Pozzo created the magnificent illusory ceiling fresco: an allegory of the Jesuits' missionary work. His artificial architecture on the crossing dome is a masterpiece of trompe-l'oeil painting.

XI

The Culmination of Benedictine Baroque

Monastery Life in the Baroque Era: the Benedictine Congregations and Scholarship

A comprehensive religious renaissance took hold in Catholic countries from the end of the 16th and especially in the 17th century. This led to an unparalleled revival of piety within both the population and the orders. The increased spiritual guidance and efforts in the field of youth education were bearing fruit. Unlike in the past, the Catholic Church this time tried to monitor the piety movement closely. The numerous brotherhoods and pious associations were closely watched by the local priests and their deputies, the curates and chaplains, and their rules were subject to episcopal control. The monasteries also experienced increased membership, which continued in the German-speaking territories until well into the 18th century. Apart from the new orders, which have already been mentioned, which developed in the aftermath of the Catholic Reform, the reform congregations of the older orders also benefited.

The congregations of the older Benedictine monasteries played a special role in the establishment of an independent monastic spiritual culture in the 17th and 18th centuries. This no longer involved the pursuit of theological studies only, but saw renewed interest in the treasures hidden away in the monasteries' own libraries: textual criticism and historical studies thus became one of the domains of the Benedictine scholars.

Associations of reform monasteries, such as the Spanish congregation of S. Benito de Valladolid, the Vallombrosans in Italy, and the Lorraine congregation of Saint-Vanne in Verdun, founded in 1608, based themselves on the statutes of S. Giustina in Padua. These abolished abbots' life tenure of office in favor of limited terms, and regular communication among the monastery hierarchy via the annual general chapter. The reason for these measures, which did away with deeply rooted, conventional monastery traditions, was

Dom Denys de Sainte Marthe, Superior General of the Benedictine congregation of Saint-Maur (Paris, Bibliothèque Nationale). His name is associated with the impressive communal work *Gallia Christiana*, a history of the French church in several volumes. His portrait is typical of those of Benedictine historians and scholars of the period.

Admont, abbey library. The rebuilding of monasteries during the baroque age (17th and 18th C.) saw the construction of many magnificent libraries. Belonging to the Benedictine abbey of St. Blasius in Admont, and built in 1776 according to plans by Josef Hueber, this is one of the finest.

the attempt to stem the widespread abuse of commendams—when an eccle-siastical benefice (living or property) was transferred in trust to a patron, who received the income but performed no duties. Since the Late Middle Ages most monasteries had been subject to their respective national rulers, while the pope accorded the confirmation of a newly elected abbot. Both sides viewed the monastery incomes with keen interest. During their exile in Avi-gnon the popes often kept the well remunerated abbots' positions for them-selves, in order to be able to allocate them to their supporters in "usufruct," i.e. exempted from official tasks. This practice was forbidden by the Councils of Basle and Trent, but the influence of the national rulers remained. With the local clergy under pressure to oppose the pope, a treaty thus accorded to the French King the right to nominate abbots, an arrangement lasting until the Revolution. The commendatory abbots installed for political purposes and with no regard to their personal suitability did not live in their monastery, did not generally concern themselves with monastery affairs, and used the income for nonmonastery purposes. Even though the statutes of S. Giustina were not able in every case to successfully counteract the commendams and the financial drain on the monasteries, the tighter clerical supervision did make a significant contribution to the improvement of internal conditions in the monasteries.

The Saint-Maur Congregation

Several French abbeys affiliated themselves to the congregation of Saint-Vanne after 1613. The affiliation of French monasteries to an organization that was based in German territory met with the disapproval of the French king, however. An independent French reform congregation was therefore formed in 1618, calling itself the Congrégation de Saint-Maur, after Maurus, Benedict of Nursia's Gallic pupil, according to legend. By 1670 the majority and also the most important French Benedictine monasteries belonged to this congregation, with Cluny one of the significant exceptions. In the 17th cen-tury the Cluniac monasteries, which still retained their own network, were

▲ ▼ **Cluny, postmedieval buildings.** Very little of the medieval abbey at Cluny remains today; the majority of the present day abbey structures date from the late 15th C. through the 18th C. The palace of Abbot Jacques d'Amboise (▼), displays a combination of Late Gothic decoration and Renaissance style and is used today as a town hall. The 18th century abbey buildings exhibit a strictly prosaic style; their eastern section, with its prominent side wings enclosing a garden area, (▲), is reminiscent of contemporary châteaux.

Paris, Val-de-Grâce. Façade of the former abbey church, based on plans by François Mansart, foundation stone laid in 1645, completed in 1667. A convent of Benedictine nuns was transferred here from Bièvres in 1621 by Queen Anne of Austria. The first buildings were constructed in 1624; in 1645 the Queen fulfilled her vow to build a church upon the birth of the heir to the throne (1638: later Louis XIV, the "Sun King"). The building of the abbey south of the church commenced in 1655; it was abolished in 1790.

deeply split between reformist and antireform monks. In some instances the division ran right through individual monasteries, between the representatives of the *étroite observance*, who practiced a strict interpretation of the rule, and those who represented the *ancienne observance*, who continued to adhere to the old practices. Despite repeated efforts, the politically desirable integration of the Cluniac monastery network into the congregation of Saint-Maur, which was also aspired to by the reformists, had still not materialized by the time of the Revolution.

The Maurist constitution, initially adopted from Saint-Vanne but then adapted to their own requirements by the Superior General Grégoire Tarisse (1630–48), provided for a general chapter that met every three years and that elected the Superior General, his two assistants, the provincial inspectors, and the priors of the individual monasteries. All of the office holders, with the exception of the Superior General, could be re-elected to the same function only once. The commendatory abbots appointed by the king were excluded from participation in congregation affairs. In each of the six provinces, there was at least one monastery that housed a novitiate, and one or even more that had institutions of learning attached to them. The monks could be transferred from one monastery to another but seldom changed provinces.

In addition to choral service and prayer, Tarisse prescribed spiritual activities for the Maurist monks according to the abilities of the individual. The initial requirement was the basic education of new entrants in the institutions of learning, where the novices received two years of instruction in philosophy and three years in theology. Talented monks could become teachers themselves after further study. The especially gifted also had the option of undertaking scholarly activities—particularly in the historical research that was encouraged by Tarisse and his successors, using the documents housed in the monastery archives. The Maurists brought together talented and well educated young monks from a variety of monasteries for the purposes of this research and they worked on the editing of texts or on other historical works in "project groups" under the guidance of experienced scholars. With its library which, before the Revolution, comprised some 50,000 printed volumes and over 7000 manuscripts, the congregation's headquarters, the abbey of Saint-Germain-des-Prés in Paris, became a center of scholarly activity.

The preoccupation with the past was not an end in itself. The study of the Church Fathers, of the lives of important Benedictine saints, and of the history of the order was intended to provide a secure basis, through historical awareness, for the monastic way of life, enabling it to defend itself against attacks by opponents of the faith. The old manuscripts from the monasteries' own libraries initially provided the basis for the publication of the writings of the medieval Church Fathers and theologians. The skills of critical editing, in which all kinds of texts in a variety of scripts were commentated, compared, and their reliability discussed, were also transferred to work with historical sources such as deeds and chronicles. This methodology thus gave rise to the first scholarly approach to history, replacing legendary depiction with serious investigation that was critical of its sources. This critical methodology was championed by Jean Mabillon (1632–1707), whose work *De re diplomatica* (Of diplomatics—i.e. the study of official documents), which appeared in 1681, established the fundamental terms of scholarly work with historical sources, thus founding modern diplomatics, which remains an essential feature of historical research today.

With a staff numbering about a dozen monks in Saint-Germain-des-Prés and smaller teams in other monasteries, the Maurists produced an astounding number of comprehensive publications within a period of only about 80 years (c. 1660–1740). These included text editions (compilations of the works of the Latin Church Fathers like St. Augustine, of famous medieval authors such as Bernard of Clairvaux, and of important Greek religious writers), works on the history of the order (a history of the Benedictine order by Mabillon, biographies of Benedictine saints by Mabillon and his staff, a compendium on French monasteries including contemporary engravings (*Monasticon Gallicanum*), a treatise on monastic liturgy by Edmond Martène, and numerous monastery histories), a history of the church in France (*Gallia christiana*), and collections of source material. The 18th century saw the appearance of important city and regional histories, such as the *Histoire de la ville de Paris* by Michel Félibien and the *Histoire du Languedoc* by de Vic and Vaissette. The series of French history books (*Recueil des historiens des Gaules et de la France*) was continued beyond the Revolution and the end of the congregation, as was the *Gallia christiana*. Both works became models for other

▲ **The Death of St. Scholastica,** Jean Restout, 1730 (Tours, Musée des Beaux-Arts). Baroque art features a great many paintings with vanitas symbolism—the skull, the abbess's staff lying on the floor. The combination of this style with a religious history painting is less common, however. In the Middle Ages, one or more angels would have been depicted in the place of the "mystic" light, up into which the soul (in the form of a dove) rises. Such divine messages had to take on a different form in the 18th C.

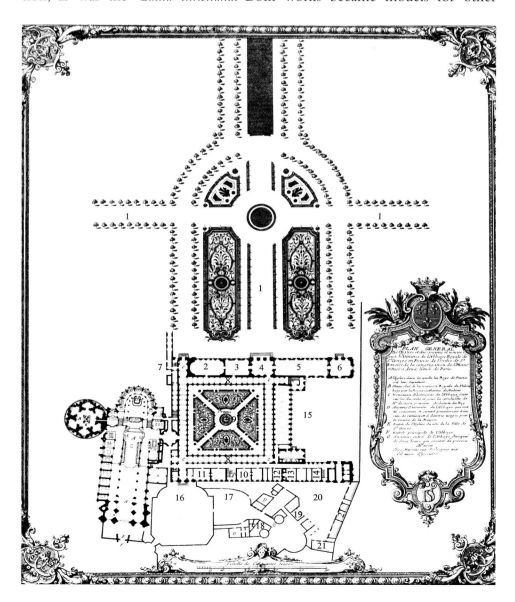

Former Maurist abbey of Saint-Denis-en-France, plan from *Architecture française* by Mariette, 1726. The plan shows the design by Robert Cotte for the reconstruction of the abbey; it was built after 1700 and prior to 1719, the year in which the Valois dynasty's great mausoleum rotunda next to the church was destroyed.
A Church with the tombs of the French kings
B Valois mausoleum, built by Catherine de Médicis
C New abbey buildings supervised by M. de Cotte
D Old abbey buildings
E City-side church entrance
F Main entrance to the abbey
G Old entrance to the abbey, flanked by two towers that served as a prison
1 Garden 2 Chapter house 3 Hall 4 Vestibule 5 Large hall
6 Parlor 7 Passageway (incomplete) to the infirmary
8 Cloister 9 Cloister courtyard 10 Reception 11 Apartments
12 Guests' reception 13 Bakery 14 Offices 15 Chicken run
16 Front courtyard 17 Old courtyard 18 Prison 19 Storerooms
20 Paddock 21 Stables

Montmajour, former Maurist abbey of Saint-Pierre, ruins of the north façade, in the background to the left the tower of the medieval keep. While the surviving remains of the medieval abbey include the keep, the Romanesque church, the cloister, and two chapels, only the ruined façade remains of the 17th and 18th C. abbey buildings. The Maurist facilities suffered particular devastation in the Revolution.

Melk, abbey church, high altar, 1725–35, Antonio Beduzzi, Lorenzo Mattielli, Peter Widerin. The foundation stone for the Benedictine abbey at Melk was laid in 1702 (see pp. 394-95). Melk developed into a center of scholarly activity during the 18th C.

national histories. Bernard de Montfaucon (1655–1741) was the first scholar to deal not only with Antiquity's material legacy (*Antiquité expliquée*, 1713/24), but also with French architecture and works of art (*Monuments de la monarchie française*, 1752–54). The diagrams, designs, and sectional drawings of buildings such as the rotunda at Saint-Bénigne in Dijon produced for regional and monastery histories are also testimony to a new awareness of medieval architecture as historical document.

Through their scholarly work the Maurists also had access to the following generations of texts and documents, which provided the basis for further research and which have had a lasting influence on our image of history—especially the French Middle Ages. Since the originals of many of the sources published by them were lost during the French Revolution, or due to other circumstances, many of their works are today considered to be historical sources themselves.

The Maurists' most important instrument needed for their scholarly work was an extensive and well organized library. Trained monks were dispatched to search all of the congregation's libraries and monastery archives for definitive manuscripts for the respective projects and to then send the manuscripts, or copies thereof, to Saint-Germain-des-Prés. There the greatly increased inventory was organized by Luc d'Achery (1609–1685) according to the needs of the Maurist scholars, thus building up a research library for historical and philological studies. Not only did scholars such as Mabillon, Montfaucon, and others carry out comprehensive correspondence about sources and archive inventories, they also undertook extensive research journeys to libraries in France, Italy, Germany, and Switzerland, in order to view documents and gather manuscripts. The descriptions of their travels—the best known of which is *Voyage littéraire de deux religieux bénédictins* by Martène and Durand—are important sources for our knowledge of the monastic world and monastery libraries of the 17th and 18th centuries.

Benedictine Scholarship outside France

Despite the Maurist scholars' far-reaching contacts and travels, only in isolated cases did their activities act as a model for monasteries of other congregations. At Melk in Austria, which experienced an internal revival at the start of the 18th century coinciding with the rebuilding of the abbey complex, the librarian Bernhard Pez (1682–1735) and his brother Hieronymus undertook activities comparable to those of the Maurists: visiting numerous archives and producing important source publications. The young Johann Baptist Kraus (1700–62) was sent from St. Emmeram in Regensburg to study at Saint-Germain-des-Prés (1721–23), working as a teacher within a circle of educated monk colleagues following his return and, as abbot, carrying out a reform of monastic study. A Bavarian Benedictine academy was established at St. Emmeram in 1684 under his successor. Unlike the Germans, the Spanish Benedictines had already begun historical studies prior to the Maurists. Antonio de Yepes, a monk from the Congregation of S. Benito de Valladolid, published the first history of the Benedictine order at the start of the 17th century (*Crónica general de la Orden de San Benito*). Although Yepes' work was still far removed from Mabillon's critical standards, it was successful in its own right in the 17th century and was translated into French, among other languages. Educated at Saint-Germain-des-Prés, Romuald Escalona (died 1801), from the former royal monastery of Sahagún, on the other hand, was schooled in Maurist scholarship and was active as a teacher within the Valladolid congregation, running a national Spanish editorial project commissioned by the monarchy. The sources published as an appendix to his history of the Sahagún monastery (1782) make it exemplary for its age. The direct influence of the Maurists was also reflected in the history of the Spanish church (*España sagrada*) by the Augustinian hermit Enrique Flórez, based on the example of the *Gallia christiana* and in the travel journals of the Dominican Jaime Villanueva (*Viaje literario a las iglesias de España*, 22 vols), who at the start of the 19th century visited the Spanish monasteries to study their archives and also described the churches he visited.

Historical Awareness and Baroque Building Mania

The preoccupation of the Maurists and other monks with the past was an activity based almost exclusively on text sources that took place primarily in libraries and archives. The scholars seldom paid any attention to the material evidence of the sacral and monastic history that determined their living environment. The older church decoration—altar retables, the figures of the saints, tapestries, reliquaries, and liturgical objects—were noted for their artistic or religious value but not because of their historical significance. Tombs were the only exceptions because their biographical information made possible a reference to the textual sources. Neither was architecture paid much more attention. The churches were often described but were not perceived as buildings with specific features and their own history, rather as stone monuments defining a historical location and providing the parameters for the material remains of the events documented by the text—such as relics or the tombs of saints or historical personalities. The architecture was seen as a container for the history that had taken place within it, but not as a historical source in its own right.

The consequence of this attitude was a widespread indifference to historical buildings. While written testimonies of every kind were items worth preserving, buildings of the same era were demolished without hesitation as required or once dilapidated, and replaced by more attractive and "worthier" new buildings—and this in the consciousness that the monastery's historical significance was being in no way comprised by such actions; on the contrary, the historical location was dignified by an appropriate aesthetic appearance. This applied to churches and even more so to monastic buildings. The monasteries' revival in the 17th and 18th centuries and the accompanying improvement in their economic situation led to the emergence of new

▲ **Füssen, library of the former Benedictine abbey of St. Mang.** The oval library is one of the loveliest of the largely baroque monastery buildings. It is decorated with frescoes by Francesco Bernardini.

▼ **Ettal, Benedictine abbey.** Founded in 1330 by Emperor Ludwig the Bavarian, it experienced its golden age in the 18th C. The late 15th-C. church is a Late Gothic centrally aligned building gaining its baroque style after a fire in 1744.

▲ **Neresheim, domes of the Benedictine church.** Founded in 1095 for the canons regular, Neresheim was settled soon thereafter by Benedictines from the Hirsau Reform. The abbey was part of the Melk Reform during the late Middle Ages, remained Catholic after the Reformation, and ran a secondary school until its abolition in 1806. It was re-established by Beuron monks in 1920.
The church (1747–77) is the work of Balthasar Neumann. Its elongated space is spanned by low domes, which are slightly horizontally oval in shape. The dome frescoes are by Martin Knoller.

▶ **Zwiefalten, interior of the former Benedictine church.** The abbey, founded in 1089, was settled by monks from Hirsau; the extensive library and important scriptorium were features of its golden age in the 12th C. Despite the introduction of the Reformation in the Duchy of Württemberg it was granted special status until secularization in 1802. The abbey buildings have housed a psychiatric clinic since 1812. The baroque church (1739–65) was begun by local builders and completed by Johann Michael Fischer. The nave, lined with oval chapels and galleries, is elaborately decorated with stucco work by Johann Michael Feichtmayr and with frescoes by Franz Joseph Spiegler.

buildings of gigantic proportions, to which fell victim the medieval monastery complexes, most of which were still in existence at that time, and many, also famous, church buildings from earlier centuries. The engravings in *Monasticon gallicanum* provide impressive evidence thereof. Hence Saint-Riquier, Saint-Rémi in Rheims, Saint-Germain d'Auxerre, Marmoutier, Bernay and Fécamp, along with many other old abbeys, received new monastic buildings prior to 1700. The medieval abbey complex at Cluny, much of which derived from the abbey's prosperous eras in the 11th and 12th centuries, was demolished only a few decades before the Revolution and replaced by new buildings characterized by classic severity. In Montecassino Abbot Desiderius' church, consecrated in 1071 and right up the eighteenth century constituting a model example for the whole of southern Italian sacral architecture, was replaced by a new building in 1725. Throughout southern Germany time-honored monasteries, together with their churches, some of which dated from the Early Middle Ages, were endowed with brand new buildings in the magnificent baroque style; examples were St. Gallen, Einsiedeln, St. Blasien, Weingarten, Zwiefalten, Obermarchtal, Neresheim, Fürstenfeld, Weltenburg, Göttweig, Melk, and others.

The reasons for erecting these new buildings were in part the same as they had been in the Late Middle Ages. The increased standards of living and the changed living conditions of the monks were no longer reconcilable with the medieval facilities. Instead of dormitories with the later addition of individual cells, larger and well-lit rooms were required that could be heated and also serve as studies. Refectories needed to be well heated in winter and pleasantly cool in summer, which is why separate summer and winter refectories were often constructed. Until the Late Middle Ages the majority of monasteries had not had their own libraries but these were now required to house the inventory of books and manuscripts and to provide work places.

However, it was primarily the prestige-related requirements that set the tone when it came to decisions on new buildings. The abbots of a series of German monasteries also exercised secular power over the territories belonging to their abbey. Endowed with sovereign rights over these areas by the emperor, they were counted among the imperial princes—which is why they are sometimes also referred to as "prince-abbots"—and as such were anxious to display an external appearance befitting their social standing, which included ostentatious buildings as much as the corresponding holding of

court. In addition, regular and commendatory abbots, who did not belong to the princely classes, also often aspired to express the importance and wealth of their monastery—and therefore of their position—by means of large scale new edifices. Many abbots therefore channeled their incomes into elaborate building projects and the construction of grand official residences. Many baroque monastery complexes were thus comparable to the residences and palaces of the age—with long façades featuring several levels, divided by pillar arrangements, and accentuated by pillared porches crowned with gables. The monastic buildings were consolidated into closed building entities that were grouped around one or more courtyards. The west wing in particular, which in baroque monastery complexes usually housed the abbot's apartments, also called the prelature (from the Latin praelatus = church official, high ranking church dignitary), and the guest quarters, was accorded the appropriate design both outside and inside; this status was also expressed in the designation of the rooms as "emperor's" or "prince's". This section might adjoin a three-winged complex comprising a *cour d'honneur* (court of honor, or courtyard used for reception purposes)—both adopted from contemporary palace architecture. Libraries, too, were no longer designed solely as functional rooms but rather tended towards ballroom architecture, with pillars superimposed on bookcases, a circular gallery for accessing the uppermost

Banz, interior of the former Benedictine church. Banz, too, was settled by monks from Hirsau in the 12th C. and experienced a volatile history with many highs and lows. The abbey's golden age was in the 18th C., coming to an abrupt end in 1803 as a result of secularization. Johann and Leonhard Dientzenhofer were responsible for the abbey's architectural design from 1698. The church, with its dynamic spatial structure, exhibits the influence of the Italian architect and theorist Guarino Guarini.

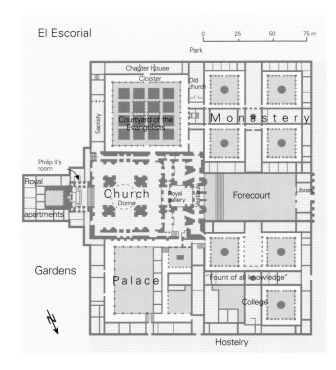

El Escorial

bookshelves, high ceilings, and cycles of frescoes. These libraries expressed the value of the old manuscripts and the newly acquired books as well as pride in their ownership, and are evidence of the fact that the library inventories, like the relics and liturgical objects made from precious metals, were seen as part of the monastery treasure. Extensive, strictly ordered baroque gardens were laid out beyond the monastery, and orangeries were built in order to house the nonhardy plants.

The most elaborate baroque monastery complexes were arranged symmetrically along a central axis, along which the church also lay. The model for this layout and also the most prominent example of the combination of princely residence and monastery complex is the Escorial (1563–84) near Madrid, a Hieronymite monastery founded by Philip II as the result of a vow. The presence of the King in the monastery is reflected in the design of the building. The interior of the rectangular complex, with closed outer façades emphasized by corner towers, is arranged according to strict, largely symmetrical courtyards. The towering church stands at the center, while the court accommodation is to the north, the monastery buildings to the south, and the royal apartments to the east behind the church and extending out of the rectangle. The design of the Escorial merges the representation of secular power and the spiritual way of life into a single entity.

S. Lorenzo el Real de El Escorial, ground plan and view of the whole complex. The edifice constructed in 1563–84 by Juan Bautista de Toledo and Juan de Herrera, which remained influential in Spanish architecture into the 20th C., is both the earliest and the most famous example of a so-called palace-monastery. This combination of princely residence and monastery was the object of impressive imitations by the "prince-abbots" of the baroque era in Austria, Bavaria, Swabia, and Switzerland.

▲ ▲ **S. Lorenzo el Real de El Escorial,** façade and library. Philip II was able to complete the construction of the Escorial with the library, finished in 1593/94, on the upper floor of the west entrance façade. He had purposely assigned the monastery to the Hieronymite order, which dedicated itself largely to study and a life of meditation. The manuscripts, books, and drawings compiled since 1565 encompass all areas of 16th C. scholarship.

Göttweig, Austria

The Benedictine monastery destroyed by fire in 1718 was rebuilt from 1719 according to plans by Johann Lukas von Hildebrandt that envisaged a symmetrical complex, with the church, lent extra height by a dome, in the centre, based on the example of the Escorial. The new building was incomplete, however, with only the east and west wings, and parts of the gatehouse and the south wing, being erected by the end of the 18th century. The church, a hall-like nave with a Late Gothic choir, was accorded a superimposed façade.

Klosterneuburg, Austria

Founded in the 12th C. beside the Danube close to Vienna, this canons regular priory underwent a revival from the 17th C. Following the baroque redecoration of the Romanesque church, work on a large palace-monastery according to plans by Donato Felice d'Allio was begun in 1730, commissioned by Emperor Charles VI. It was to have been grouped around five courtyards but only the northeast court was built, with grandiose baroque rooms, including the oval marble hall.

Mafra, Portugal

The construction of this Franciscan religious house in the form of a giant complex of buildings which, like the Escorial, combined the monastery and the palace, was largely completed, with gold from Brazil and the deployment of over 40,000 workers, between 1717 and 1730/35, while the decoration lasted until the second half of the 18th century. The work of architect João Frederico Ludovice was influenced by Roman models (Bernini, Borromini, Maderno, Fontana).

Göttweig, imperial staircase. The ceiling fresco is by Paul Troger, 1739.

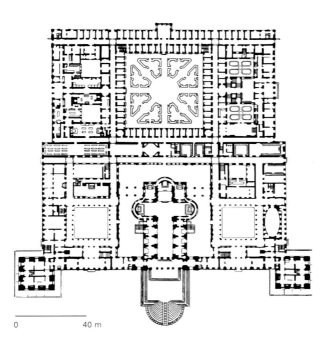

Mafra, church atrium and ground plan. The church is located in the middle of the palace complex; the monastery buildings are behind it, grouped around the central cloister.

0   40 m

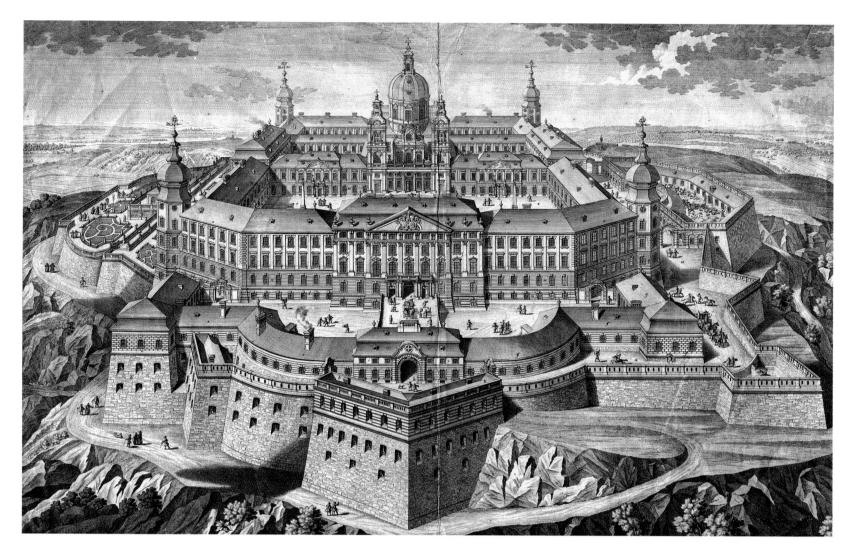

▲ **Göttweig.** Idealized view, from the west, of the whole monastery complex designed by Johann Lukas von Hildebrandt in 1719, based on an engraving by Salomon Kleiner, 1744.

▼ **Klosterneuburg.** Idealized view of the new baroque building planned in 1730, watercolor and ink drawing by Joseph Knapp, 1744.

▶ **Rohr, canons regular priory church,** *Assumption of the Virgin*, 1723, Egid Quirin Asam. The late baroque altar ensemble, Asam's famous masterpiece, forms an exceptionally dramatic combination between architecture and "floating" sculpture. The events are accompanied by the gesticulations of the disciples.

Klosterneuburg Priory, dome fresco in the imperial hall, Daniel Gran, 1749. The religious concept of the Cosmocrator, the ruler over heaven and earth, is applied here to Charles VI as Roman emperor and lord over war and peace, seated amidst the virtues, arts, and sciences.

Zwiefalten, Benedictine abbey church, *The Prophet Ezekiel*, 1752–56, J.J. Christian. This life size stucco figure expresses emotion in every respect: physical stance, walking pose, billowing robes, gesture, and facial expression. What is Ezekiel's message to the faithful? He tells of the horrors of Judgment Day and prophesies perdition for all those of unrepentant heart and who have no fear of the Word of God.

Orchestration of the Faith

In addition to status-related demands, in many cases the new monastery buildings were also simply intended to be "modern" constructions, built in the style of the age, in order to create a living environment in keeping with contemporary tastes. It was for the same reason that older monastery rooms were rebuilt and redecorated, the medieval decoration—often considered an aesthetic imposition—was removed from the old churches, in order to reinvent them in the baroque style: imposing pillars with rounded responds and rudimentary profiles were replaced by elegant, fluted pilaster strips and classical entablature; white walls with brightly colored frescoes and stucco work took the place of wall paintings darkened by soot; multicolored stained glass was replaced with clear window glass; dark vaulting gave way to ceiling frescoes that appeared to provide a glimpse of heaven.

The contemporary understanding of religion, wherein the orchestration of the faith through images pushed the sacred itself into second place, is reflected in these baroque ecclesiastical buildings, be they re- or newly built, and in their decorative regime. While the Middle Ages sought as much contact as possible with the sphere of the sacred—through proximity to the altar, nearness to relics (with the exhibition of relics secondary)—the display was now the focal point, meaning the dramatically coordinated spectacle of ostentatious images. The images evoked in the meditation exercises are "projected" onto the walls of God's house. The architectural system is assimilated by the paintings, which pursue it further with illusory effects, so that the boundaries between the constructed and the painted space become blurred. In the place of vaulting there is a view of light, colorful—almost heavenly—worlds of imagery. The church interior surrounds the faithful with depictions of the saints' lives and the history of salvation are no longer separated from one another thematically and iconographically, but woven into a single image unit and permeating each other. It becomes a monumental reification of religious concepts in the same way that the Jesuit Spiritual Exercises and other devotional techniques sought to evoke them: a vision in stone, stucco, and color. Architecture, sculpture, and painting combine to take emotional possession of the faithful, to inspire their religious sentiments and to guide them towards an inner acceptance of the divine truth and to an appropriately pious life. This concept of religious "catharsis" by means of emotional induction was in complete accordance with the principles of contemporary aesthetics and was in no way limited to the visual media. Church music, which already looked back on a long tradition, attained a productive peak in the 18th century, with cantatas, arias, religious musical plays, and Masses. While the church interiors became worlds of visual illusion overwhelming the eyes of the faithful, the religious music took possession of their aural faculties in order—so it was believed—to gain direct access to the soul.

Einsiedeln, Switzerland

In 934 an abbey was built, with the support of the Swabian ducal family, on the site of where the hermit Meinrad (died 861) had lived in the 9th century. The abbey soon also acquired royal protection and underwent a further revival in the 15th century as a result of an important pilgrimage in honor of the Virgin Mary. In deliberate contrast to Protestant Zurich, Einsiedeln (with a secondary school since 1848) established itself as a center of Catholic Switzerland. The choir of the abbey church was built anew in 1674–76. In 1702 the decision was taken to build an entirely new monastery. The construction was entrusted to the builder Caspar Moosbrugger, who had lived in the abbey as a lay brother. The decoration and painting program of the nave was carried out in 1724–27 by the brothers Cosmas Damian (frescoes) and Egid Quirin (stucco) Asam. The corresponding renewal of the choir followed in 1746–48, carried out by Fr. A. Kraus and J.A. Feichtmayr (stucco). The abbey complex comprises a rectangle with corner risalits (higher sections). The sweeping convex church façade rises above the west wing, flanked by two side towers. The west section of the choir interior, a three-aisled pilaster construction, houses an octagonal Chapel of Mercy dating from 1617 on the site of Meinrad's cell. Frescoes and stucco work by the Asam brothers illustrate the history of salvation with reference to key events in the abbey's history.

◄ **Western section of the abbey church,** beginning of the 18th C., with the Chapel of Mercy, 1617, designating the site of the hermit Meinrad's cell.

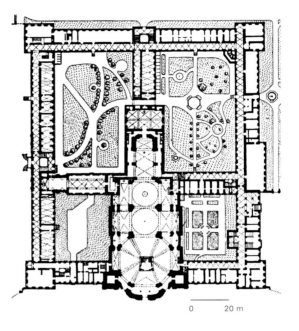

► **Nave of the abbey church** with elaborate rococo-style stucco decoration. The wrought iron grille with the perspective-style archways separates the lay area from that of the monks.

0   20 m

▼ **Western view of the abbey.** In the middle of the two towers is the sweeping church façade, the reaction to which is provided by the arcades on the abbey forecourt.

Ottobeuren, Germany

This Benedictine abbey, founded in 764 in the Allgau is one of the oldest south German monasteries still in existence. Reformed according to Hirsau by Abbot Rupert I (1102–45) it was an important regional abbey with an adjoining convent. Following a decline, the 16th-century abbots encouraged study and scholarly activity with the purchase of books, the setting up of a printing press, and the establishment of an academy. During the 17th century Ottobeuren monks taught in Salzburg, Freising, Fulda, and Rottweil. With secularization in 1802 the landed property went to the state of Bavaria but the abbey itself was resettled as early as 1834.

The rebuilding of the entire complex took place under Abbot Rupert II Ness in 1711–31. The four story abbey buildings with uniform rows of windows and corner risalits (higher sections) stand on a rectangular ground plan. The east section houses the monks' quarters, the west wing the school, administration, and reception rooms, with the abbot residing in the middle wing. The church, framed by the towers, is positioned symmetrically in the monastery square on the northern extension of the middle wing. It was completed in 1766 by J.M. Fischer on the basis of an already established ground plan as a wide, cruciform, domed hall with side chapels and semicircular, closed transept arms. Fischer designed the interior together with J.M. Feichtmayr as an "integrated work of art" comprising decoration in painting and sculpture.

◀ **View of the main altar,** completed in 1766. Architecture (J.M. Fischer), frescoes (F.A. and J.J. Zeiller), and sculpture (J.J. Christian) are blended into one entity by the stucco work (J.M. Feichtmayr).

▼ **Church and abbey complex** from the northeast.

▲ **The "Imperial Hall" in the west wing,** 1723–26. There are 16 eponymous statues of the Habsburg emperors in front of the double columns supporting the circular cornice. Stucco by Maini, Feretti et al., painted ceiling by J.C. Stauder, statues by A. Sturm.

Weltenburg, Germany

This picturesque Benedictine abbey located on a bend in the Danube (and therefore threatened by flood waters) was founded at the start of the 7th century by a pupil of Columban from Luxeuil and richly endowed by Duke Tassilo III of Bavaria in the 8th century. It underwent the Hirsau Reform in the 12th and the Kastl Reform in the 15th century. Despite financial difficulties, with the support of the Bavarian electors the abbey undertook the building of a new church and monastic buildings at the start of the 18th century. Secularized in 1803, the abbey was re-established as a priory in 1842 and has been an abbey again since 1913.

The church at Weltenburg—begun in 1716, consecrated in 1721—is the first building planned by Cosmas Damian Asam as architect. Despite the limited financial resources, he achieved the design and implementation of an "integrated" work of baroque art in which space, structure, sculptural decoration, frescoes, and altar images combine to form a single unit. Long and oval shaped, the main body of the church includes four side chapels. To the east and west are the sanctuary and the entrance hall, above which the monks' choir is situated in order to keep the nave freely accessible.

▲ **High altar** with the mounted figure of St. George. In sharp contrast to the bright fresco on the apse wall, the dark silhouette of the saint, set in the tall arcade opening of the high altar, rises up towards the brightly lit apse space.

▼ **Abbey church and buildings** from the east. The construction of the abbey was begun according to a design by Franciscan Philipp Plank near to the front of the church. Only the lower floors of the choir tower derive from the previous 12th-C. building.

▶ **Dome and ceiling fresco of the main body of the church.** Here, too, Cosmas Damian Asam augmented the effect of the fresco by giving the dome a wide opening into the tambour above it, which is lit by 12 windows. This skylight gives the painting on the flat tambour ceiling an otherwise unattainable sense of space and bathes it in "heavenly" light.

Melk, Austria

After 976, the ancient cliffs alongside the Danube, inhabited since the dawn of time, became the site of the Babenberg family's headquarters as well as their burial place. Leopold II founded an abbey there in 1089 (with Benedictines from the Hirsau Reform monastery of Lambach in Upper Austria), which soon developed into a cultural center with an important scriptorium. Abbot Nikolaus Seyringer introduced the *Consuetudines* from Subiaco to Melk at the start of the 15th century, thus making the abbey the source of the successful Melk Reform in Austria and southern Germany in particular. Following the Reformation Melk enjoyed a spiritual and scholarly revival in the 17th century due to the activities of its librarians Bernard and Hieronymus Pez. This was evidenced by the rebuilding of the church and the abbey complex from the start of the 18th century. The abbey, which escaped secularization, exists to this day, as does the renowned secondary school it has maintained since 1160.

The Melk abbey complex, begun in 1702 by Jakob Prandtauer, is one of the largest of baroque monasteries and, with its location on the cliffs high above the Danube, is undoubtedly one of the most scenic. Its 800 ft (250 m) long south front rises like an immense palace façade over the town. The rebuilding

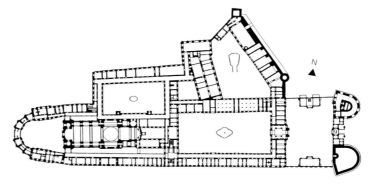

◀ **Abbey church.** With its harmonic interaction between architecture, painting, and sculpture the Melk church is a characteristic example of an "integrated" work of baroque art.

▲ **Abbey complex.** Prandtauer had an effective solution for closing the long south wing, the core of which had already been constructed in the 17th C.: with the western "display side" and the eastern reception wing.

began with the abbey church, a cruciform galleried hall with a high crossing dome under a well lit tambour. The church's twin tower front faces the Danube. In addition to Prandtauer, according to whose plans the monastic buildings were completed by his nephew Joseph Munggenast in 1736, the painters Johann Michael Rottmayr and Paul Troger, the stucco artist Johann Pöckh, and the interior designer Antonio Beduzzi were also involved. A disastrous fire in 1738 necessitated extensive renovations lasting until the middle of the 18th century.

St. Florian, Austria

▲▲ **Abbey gate in the west wing,** completed in 1713, with elaborate figural decoration by L. Sattler.

▲ **Library** by Johann Gotthard Hayberger, with painted ceiling by Bartholomeo Altomonte and Antonio Tassi, built after 1745 as one of the last sections. The perfect baroque room, its design, both elaborate and intimate, evokes a studious atmosphere.

Evidence of a canons regular monastery having existed at the burial site of the martyr Florian (died 304), southeast of Linz, built on top of Roman ruins, goes back to the 9th century and perhaps as far as Late Antiquity. In 1071 Bishop Altmann of Passau settled canons regular living according to the Rule of St. Augustine there, thus initiating a period of sustained prosperity that lasted into the 14th century. In c. 1300 St. Florian possessed a scriptorium with an important school of book illumination. A comprehensive rebuilding of the complex was begun at the end of the 17th century, which was only completed in the middle of the 18th century. The abbey outlived secularization and developed its position further in the 19th century with teaching activities. Dispossessed under the Nazis, it was re-established after the war.

▲▲ **The long front of the west wing** from the south, showing the abbey gate, the gate tower, and the twin tower façade of the church, demarcated by colossal pilaster strips extending over all three stories.

▲ **Marble hall,** built by Jakob Prandtauer 1717–24, with painted ceiling by Bartholomeo Altomonte. Illuminated on both sides, this is a domed ballroom with pilasters of red stucco marble on high pedestals and double columns of white stucco marble on the center axis.

Despite the long construction period and a change of builder, this baroque complex represents an artistically complete ensemble and is one of the most attractive monastery complexes in Austria. It extends around one large and two smaller court-yards south of the church, a four-span hall building based on Il Gesù with side chapels and galleries, a domed crossing, and choir. Begun in 1686 by C.A. Carlone, who completed the church, the buildings were continued by Jakob Prandtauer 1708–26 following Carlone's death. A long west wing adjoins the high twin tower façade of the church through the opening of the abbey gate with its dominant gate tower. The imperial hall and the staircase lie to the west on the large courtyard, with the marble hall in the middle risalit (higher section) of the south side. Gotthard Hayberger's library (1745–51) is located in the east wing.

Staircase in the middle pavilion of the west wing, 1706–14 by Jakob Prandtauer, one of the most magnificent baroque staircases in southern Germany and Austria. The symmetrically arranged, single flight pair of stairs open onto the courtyard on both floors through arcades with columns to the side rising with the height of the stairs.

XII

Monasticism and Life in Religious Orders in the 19th and 20th Centuries

Emperor Joseph II, 1741–90. Following the death of his father Franz I Stephan, Joseph II initially ruled together with his mother Maria Theresa, until her death in 1780. Thereafter, the concept of imperial power by divine right no longer formed the basis of his rule and he saw himself as the "first servant" of the state. Joseph II abolished a number of older aristocratic privileges and forbade the pomp characteristic of funerals within this social class. His reserved stance towards the Catholic Church led to the dissolution of many monasteries during a radical wave of secularization.

▶ **Vienna, Franziskanerplatz,** with the Well of Moses dating from 1798. The positioning of Johann Martin Fischer's neoclassical fountain in front of the façades of the Franciscan church (1603–13) and the adjoining monastic buildings, which, despite the decorative Renaissance elements, exude a rather sober air, seems very appropriate. Whole new districts arose in the inner city of Vienna on the sites of abandoned monasteries; the Franciscan church survived this phase of city secularization well.

Secularization and its Consequences

The lengthy golden age of the monasteries deriving from the Catholic revival of the 16th and 17th centuries came to an end with the French Revolution. The political upheavals and wars that resulted from the Revolution led to the nationalization of church property and the closing of religious houses in France and other countries. This course of action on the part of the secular authorities against their spiritual counterparts, referred to as "secularization," brought the second set of lasting changes to the monastic map of Europe (the first being the Reformation). The monasteries were dissolved in almost all Catholic countries, at least for a time, the monks were expelled, the monastic land was taken over by the state, while the monastic buildings and churches were sold, and often demolished thereafter. In France the Revolution took possession of monastery lands in 1789 and dissolved religious houses and orders in 1790. Church and monastic property was confiscated in Germany in 1803 in order to compensate the regional princes affected by the French annexation of the imperial territories west of the Rhine. Secularization took place in Spain in 1809 as a result of the Napoleonic occupation and the monasteries were dissolved in 1836. The major monasteries of Italy were dissolved in 1811. Secularization was also frequently accompanied by vandalism and destruction. Most of the valuable art works and cultural assets in the possession of the monasteries?paintings, manuscript collections, important historical source documents—were secured by the state.

The way for these developments had been paved by the Enlightenment with its emphasis on the principle of reason, which aided and abetted ostensibly utilitarian thinking and could see no value in a contemplative way of life. It is no coincidence that the first wave of secularization had already taken place in Austria in 1782 under an enlightened monarch. Emperor Joseph II had dissolved the settlements of "idle" orders such as the Benedictines, Cistercians, and Carthusians, whom he saw as being of no use to society, and used

the confiscated properties for the establishment of parishes and priests' seminaries. Instead of retreating behind monastery walls, religion was to be brought closer to the people.

Even more dramatic than the material losses was the fundamental change that secularization effected in the relationship between the Church and the state. With the spread and implementation of enlightened ideas, the concept of a divinely ordained ruler was overshadowed by the principle of rational state action that no longer required divine legitimation. The state had emancipated itself from the Church, which no longer stood at the center of national politics or represented national order.

As a result of the separation of Church and state, which began with secularization but, in most cases, was only formally implemented at a much later stage, religion became a personal matter. It is no coincidence that the emancipation of the Jews—the granting of civil rights for Jewish residents—took place directly after secularization. The "free man = citizen = Christ" equation had lost its validity for the first time since the collapse of the Roman Empire and the emergence of the Christian kingdoms at the end of Late Antiquity. The state was no longer a Christian state and, as a result, its citizens could belong to different faiths as well as to different Christian denominations.

For the monks, who had always seen themselves as a Christian elite in a Christian society, this new situation meant a fundamental alteration in their social standing and their self-image. Since the Early Middle Ages they had constantly been cheek by jowl with the wielders of power and had always played an active role in national politics, be it in land development and missionary work, as scholarly advisors, spiritual counselors, royal pastors, or in Counter-Reformation propaganda. They now found themselves abruptly shoved to the periphery of society and, at that, one which no longer defined itself as predominantly Christian.

Following their reauthorization the majority of the orders therefore undertook a radical reorientation. Instead of a life of withdrawal from the world in a monastery, the majority of the orders' members took up a life in service of society's ailing and needy. The apostolic example was understood in the sense of Jesus' championing the poor and the suffering. With this focus on charitable works, which was in no way new to some of the orders but which was now generally and resolutely adopted, the monks acted on the Enlightenment's criticism of their way of life. In order to evade the verdict of idleness

Napoleon's Coronation as Emperor, painting by Jacques-Louis David, 1805–07 (Paris, Musée du Louvre). Napoleon crowned himself—in the presence of the Pope—"Emperor of the French People" on December 2, 1804 after a referendum had produced 3.5 million yes and only 2580 no votes. Wholly secular in his thinking, Napoleon was a political pragmatist, however, and understood religion to be the "secret behind social order" (Bergeron), because it taught the people to tolerate inequality and yet still be satisfied. This view led him initially to a policy of appeasement with the Pope (Concordat of 1801), which he then abandoned in the years that followed, replacing it with an outright "ecclesiastical terror".

Mother Teresa, born in Skopje (Macedonia) in 1910; she decided early on in favor of life as a nun. At the age of 18 she asked to be accepted into the Loreto Order and took her first vows in Calcutta, where she was initially active as teacher and head of St. Mary's School for 17 years. In 1946 she answered her "divine calling" to help the poor in the city's slums, dedicating herself thereafter to orphans, the sick, especially lepers, and the dying. In 1950 she founded the order of the "Missionaries of Charity," to which over 3000 sisters worldwide belong today. Mother Teresa died in 1997 and was beatified in 2003.

and lack of use to society, the seclusion of the cloister was exchanged for social work in those areas of society neglected by the state, and the tranquility of the monastic study for work in the schooling of the disadvantaged and of youth in general. A new form of social missionary work in non-church circles went hand in hand with relief for the poor and with education. In addition to the monks and nuns active in social work, there were also those who still sought a contemplative lifestyle, despite society's changing attitudes, but they remained the minority.

The missionary work that had been carried out in the non-Christian world outside Europe since the discoveries of the 16th century was taken up again in the 19th century and continued with renewed vigor. Such forms of missionary outreach were almost always coupled with charity work or with the running of a school. While such endeavors initially remained restricted to the colonies of the orders' European home countries, since the end of the Second World War they have been supplemented by numerous development aid projects that have multiplied the activities of almost all of the orders in the "Third World." These efforts primarily include relief for the poor, the running of schools for the education and training of children, adolescents, and adults, as well as medical care through the maintenance of hospitals and social services. Active missionary work has tended to take a back seat in many orders today due to the changed relationships between cultures and the greater respect for other religions, especially as it is discouraged and even forbidden in many countries, particularly—but not only—in Islamic countries. Instead, it is the fulfillment of self-defined social functions in service of the poor, following Christ's example, which plays the leading role. Due to the degree of need around the world and the vast choice of options where help of this nature is required, today all of the orders are active outside Europe and North America, some of them primarily so. One example of an order focused solely on the "Third World" is the "Missionaries of Charity," founded by Mother Teresa for the care of the sick and the dying in Calcutta.

As donations and endowments for the financing of religious houses no longer flow as freely today as they did in the Middle Ages, and the former landholdings were lost due to secularization, the monasteries have to earn their living themselves as far as is possible. A variety of activities have therefore been developed to this end, extending from gastronomy in the many monastic catering establishments to the production of foodstuffs (cheese and other milk products at Andechs Abbey in Germany, beer in the Belgian Trappist houses, monastery schnapps from a variety of locations), the opening of

Armand-Jean Le Bouthiller de Rancé (1626–1700), founder of the Trappists, a radically ascetic reform branch of the Cistercians that was granted order status in 1892. The Trappist monks and nuns—their exact designation is "Cistercians of the Strict Observance"—lead a stringent life of withdrawal according to the contemplative tradition.
▶ **La Trappe,** the order's mother house in Normandy, over which abbot de Rancé once presided.

book and souvenir shops, and the running of publishing businesses (Éditions Zodiaque in La Pierre qui Vire). Many monasteries, especially those in country areas, have opened themselves up to a controlled degree of tourism, enabling paying guests to gain an insight into monastery life, as well as offering seminars, workshops, and leisure activities in the surrounding countryside (e.g. Camaldoli and many others).

Examples of some of the different characteristics of monastic life over the last two centuries are given in the following pages.

The Trappists

The Trappists derived from a radically ascetic division of the Cistercians of the Strict Observance. Having undergone a spiritual crisis, the courtier and commendatory abbot of La Trappe in Normandy, Armand-Jean Le Bouthillier de Rancé (1626–1700), became a monk in 1664 and subsequently a regular abbot. He imposed a return to the order's original ideals in his abbey and enforced a rule of absolute silence, strenuous manual labor, and the strictest degree of asceticism. Neither meat nor fish, eggs, cheese, or butter were to be eaten at La Trappe. Rancé's rejection of study on the grounds that it compromised the monks' humility provoked a strong reaction from Mabillon (*Traité des études monastiques*). In 1791 the monks expelled from La Trappe during the Revolution settled in the former Carthusian La Valsainte in Switzerland, where they practiced an even harsher form of asceticism than before. Following the resettlement of La Trappe there were therefore two different types of Trappists; they were united in 1892, however, and are today called the "Order of Cistercians of the Strict Observance."

Despite their extreme lifestyle, the Trappists were able to found daughter houses in Western Europe and North America, and more recently in Asia, Africa, and Latin America. Since the Second Vatican Council, they have observed a comparatively milder form of asceticism, one that now allows study but still demands the rule of silence and abstinence from meat. Given the contemplative nature of the order and its deliberate return to the ideals of the early Cistercians, the Trappists have adopted a profoundly traditional position that gives absolute precedence to the *Opus Dei* and rejects both charitable and pastoral work. Their stringency and lack of ambiguity does, however, lend them an appeal that is not to be underestimated, one that has since enabled them to outperform the Cistercians with regard to the number of

◀ ▲ **Acey, abbey of Notre-Dame-d'Acey,** monastery complex, and side aisle of the church. Of the 13 abbeys in Franche-Comté, only Acey (Trappist monks) and the nearby La-Grâce-Dieu (Trappist nuns), both founded in the 12th century, are still inhabited. In accordance with established Cistercian tradition, a ridge turret instead of a bell tower rises above the crossing of the abbey church. The church is one of the finest Gothic buildings in the region.

Heimbach, Mariawald Abbey. The only Trappist abbey in Germany, founded by the Cistercians at the end of the 15th century, is situated in a scenic location in the northern Eifel region. As a result of political circumstances, over the last 200 years the monks have been forced to leave the abbey on several occasions, the last time in 1941. In 1945 the Trappists began rebuilding the abbey, destroyed at the end of the Second World War. Today it is surrounded by agricultural buildings.

monasteries and members. The mother house at Cîteaux was resettled by Trappists in 1898.

The Salesians of Don Bosco

While the Trappists endeavor to maintain their way of life based on the strict observation of the Rule of St. Benedict, despite the changes in social circumstances, the Salesians of Don Bosco have chosen the opposite path. Consciously embracing modern problems, they dedicate themselves to the education and Christian upbringing of disadvantaged young people in both the wealthy industrial nations and the many poor countries of the world.

Ordained as a priest in 1841, their founder, Giovanni Bosco (1815–88), who himself came from a poor background and received a school education only later in life, began teaching young people from the Turin industrial working class who had not been attending school. Initially without fixed lodgings, the young people were attracted by their teacher's cheerfulness and the prospect of a meal, and so followed Don Bosco wherever he went. Despite hostility and mistrust due to the growing number of young boys who came to him, he established his first youth center in the Valdocco area of Turin in 1846, which was soon followed by two more. In addition to the school rooms for elementary instruction and evening classes, the youth center included accommodation for adolescents as well as training workshops and a church. A secondary school and a printing office were added later. Don Bosco's educational concept was a "Pedagogy of Care,": countering neglect and negative influences with love, familial affection, and sustained care, avoiding threats and punishment in as far as was possible, thus enabling him to win

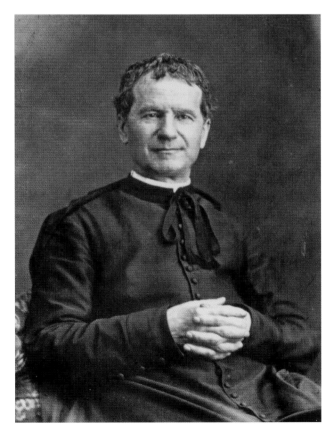

Heimbach, Mariawald Abbey. The single-aisle, Gothic style abbey church, the only building open to visitors, has a screen separating the monks' section from that open to the general public. The 16th-century porch is all that remains of the original abbey, which was destroyed on several occasions.

the trust of even the more difficult youngsters. In order to safeguard his youth work he founded an order community in 1859, to whom he assigned the running and maintenance of the schools and homes he had established. He gave them their own rule and placed them under the protection of St. François de Sales (1567–1622), who, coming from Savoy like Don Bosco, had founded the Order of the Visitation for the care of the poor and the sick. In 1872 he went on to found a female branch, the "Don Bosco Sisters", for performing practical tasks in the youth center as well as giving lessons to girls, and in 1876 he formed the "Pious Union of Salesian Cooperators", who provided material and spiritual support for the youth efforts. Missionary activity also played a role, in addition to the Christian youth work in Europe, during Don Bosco's lifetime.

Today the Salesians run institutions known as oratories: youth homes, orphanages, hostels, and teaching establishments, as well as training workshops and vocational schools, secondary schools for mature students, technical colleges for social pedagogy, disabled schools, meeting places, and voluntary youth programs. They also undertake parish work and many of them are also bishops. Outside Europe the Salesians are especially active in South America and they maintain missions in the Middle and Far East, in India and, particularly, in Africa.

John (Don) Bosco (1815–88). The priest and founder of the order was canonized in 1934 in recognition of his life's work.

Vincent de Paul
(1581–1660), priest and order founder. Coming from a poor family, Vincent de Paul was ordained as a priest at the age of 19 and became a Doctor of Theology in 1604. He was responsible for the foundation of several religious houses for the poor and for rural populations. The first "charitable work" was established in 1617, the lay sisters of which called themselves the "servants of the poor" (later the Merciful Sisters). Vincent founded the *Congregatio Missionis* for the purposes of rural missionary work; it was also involved in work with prisoners. His third order (Sisters of Charity) was founded with the support of his spiritual daughter **Louise de Marillac** (1591–1660). Louise took a number of young farm girls into her home in 1633, thus laying the foundations for the Company of the Daughters of Charity, also called the Sisters of St. Vincent.

Solesmes, Saint-Pierre Abbey. This abbey, located on the banks of the Sarthe river, looks like an imposing fortress. As archabbey and seat of the most important Benedictine congregation in France, Solesmes has taken on the Benedictine legacy of Cluny and the Congregation of Saint-Maur, which had once characterized the monastic tradition in France and in Europe as a whole. Both the liturgy and the Gregorian chants are accorded great importance in the monasteries of the Congregation of Solesmes.

The Sisters of St. Vincent (Sisters of Charity of St. Vincent de Paul)

Social work involving the care of the sick and other charitable activities continues to form the basis of the Catholic order with the largest number of members worldwide: the Sisters of Charity of St. Vincent. Founded in 1633 by the cosmopolitan priest Vincent de Paul and Louise de Marillac, in the 17th century the order brought together a large number of associations for religiously motivated women, those who wished to work in the care of the sick or in education but who did not want to live behind convent walls. In order to bypass the system of orders and the requirement for enclosure the women initially made private vows only. Their training as nurses took the place of choral prayer and their work ultimately earned them recognition both from the church and from society. Following their dissolution during the Revolution the Sisters of Charity of St. Vincent were readmitted as early as 1807 and during the 19th century spread from North Africa to the Middle East, and as far as China, Mexico, and the USA.

Solesmes and Beuron

The 19th-century revival of Benedictine monasticism was driven from two centers, both of which became significant well beyond the monastic world for the renewal of the liturgy and the religious service. Solesmes Abbey near Le Mans was resettled in 1833 on the initiative of Prosper Guéranger, who also became the first abbot. Guéranger initiated a quest for the "true," i.e. the historically grounded, tradition of the church. The liturgical and music history studies carried out in the abbey led, amongst other things, to the reinstatement of the Gregorian choral melodies that are now solely used in the monastic Mass and officium. The influence of the liturgical revival in Solesmes, the focus of which was the Roman liturgy as a guarantee of church unity, was felt throughout France and beyond. The role model provided by Solesmes also had a determining influence on the former canons regular abbey in Beuron in the upper Danube valley, which was refounded in 1863 as a Benedictine abbey under the brothers Maurus and Placidus Wolter. Threatened with dissolution during the cultural conflict between the state of Prussia and the Catholic Church (1875–87), one of the places the monks moved to was Maredsous in Belgium, the first daughter house, which was followed by others in England, Austria, and Germany. Since 1885, Beuron has stood as archabbey at the head of a congregation comprising a series of resettled, older abbeys, including Maria Laach, Neresheim, Weingarten, and St. Matthias in

Beuron, archabbey of St. Martin, refounded in 1863 as a Benedictine monastery and promoted to abbey in 1868; view of the entire complex (▲), St. Maurus Chapel (▶). The monks had to vacate Beuron between 1775 and 1887 due to the cultural conflict between the state of Prussia and the Catholic Church, leading to the founding of new monasteries both within Germany and abroad. The Beuron congregation grew out of the later union of these daughter houses. St. Maurus Chapel, a "temple" of the Beuron art school, is situated a little apart from the abbey and is easily reached after a walk through the forest.

Trier. As in Solesmes, Beuron initially dedicated itself to the research of liturgical history, resulting in 1882 in the publication of the *German-Latin Missal* by Anselm Schott, which remained valid until the reforms of the Second Vatican Council.

Due to a group of artists centered around the sculptor Peter Lenz, the abbey also became a focus of intensified efforts towards a new style of language appropriate to the religious content. The quest for a common form of expression took Lenz away from his naturalistic forms towards symbolism and stylization through the emphasis on contours and the tendency towards geometric shapes. It was the religious conservative tenor that paved the way for modern abstraction, which found the most comprehensive expression of its artistic synthesis in the architecture and imagery of the Beuron St. Maurus Chapel. However, Lenz's principles were not able to maintain their influence within the Beuron art school in the long term. They were replaced by idealized depictions in the style of late Nazarene art, which continued to characterize the (mass) production of religious art (particularly images of Christ, the Madonna, and the saints) until well into the postwar era.

Beuron Art School

With the exception of the English Pre-Raphaelites, very few of the significant artists of the second half of the 19th century still concerned themselves with religious subjects. Peter Cornelius (died 1867), once the "Nazarene" of the Romantic era, in 1859 enjoyed renewed success with exhibitions in Berlin and Brussels of his fresco designs for the Campo Santo (royal mausoleum) commissioned (but not realized) by the Prussian king. His cartoons, measuring over 6 x 16 ft (2 x 5 m) and bearing titles such as "Seven Angels with the Vial of Wrath" and "The Downfall of Satan," remained as drafts. Thereafter it was salon art, impressionism, pointillism, and other artistic directions that predominated. Serious religious art lived a shadow existence; Christian didactic imagery, with its mawkish naturalism, was insignificant as an art form. Maurus (Rudolf) Wolter, Beuron's founding abbot, who determined the abbey's fate until 1890, had a sense of the problems facing Christian art in his time and sought to open up new avenues. This was indeed achieved during the time of architect and sculptor Peter Lenz's sojourn in Beuron in 1868. Princess Katharina von Hohenzollern commissioned him with the construction and decoration of the chapel in honor of the abbot St. Maurus. Lenz secured the services of two painter friends

◀ ▲ **Beuron, Chapel of Mercy.**
▶ **Beuron, St. Maurus Chapel.**

from his academy days to help with the commission: Jakob Würger and his pupil Fridolin Steiner. The three artists entered the monastery and formed a working group whose activities did not remain restricted to Beuron. The St. Maurus Chapel is seen as their masterpiece because it is only here, in this initial phase, that Lenz's artistic principles, which he himself compiled in a small volume of work entitled *Towards the Aesthetics of the Beuron School* (1898), were implemented on their own and without external influence. Lenz's new "holy art" was based on "aesthetic geometry," in which the "numerical proportions of the Egyptians" played a role. Overall it appeared somewhat contrived but the result was impressive and comparable with some of the works of the Viennese art nouveau stylists. The works of the Beuron art school also earned significant recognition in Vienna, where they were displayed in the 1905 autumn exhibition of the Vienna Secession. The Beuron art works did change later: "The stringency was softened in favor of popularity; the dimensions ossified becoming a formula." (H. Krins). The Beuron Chapel of Mercy exhibits Byzantine and art nouveau influences, and the interior does not match the quality of that of St. Maurus Chapel.

La Tourette: Modern Architecture as an Expression of Monastic Spirituality

The construction of the Dominican monastery of La Tourette in Eveux-sur-Arbresle near Lyons by the architect Le Corbusier represented a different, and this time successful, combination of modern art and monastery culture. The commission was deliberately awarded to Le Corbusier as the declared representative of a modern style, in order to "show that prayer and a spiritual lifestyle are not bound to a conventional style but that the most modern of architecture can produce a rapport between them" (Brother Belaud OP).

The Dominicans, re-established in France since the 1840s by the priest Henri-Dominique Lacordaire, remained faithful, even in the modern age, to their traditional areas of activity: preaching, religious services, study, research, and teaching, supplemented by an increasing involvement in the print media, radio, and television, in keeping with the times. The monastery at La Tourette also included a college with meeting rooms. The exposed concrete complex constructed on a slope is grouped as a rectangle around a courtyard divided by gangways. One edge comprises the church, while the other three sides are made up of the monastic quarters on three levels. The church, an elongated, narrow, and high rectangular space with a lower extension to the side for the side altars is divided into the choir area with the stalls and the elevated sanctuary with the main altar opposite. The sophisticated lighting highlights the main and side altars, and places the rest of the room in a half-light conducive to meditation. The rectangular building does not constitute a closed complex, in contrast to conventional monasteries. Instead, the church is free standing and the monastic buildings are raised upon the typically Le Corbusier columns (pilotis), the space underneath them being both visible and accessible. The landscape is integrated by means of the large refectory window looking out over the valley: the monastery opening itself to the world.

▼ **Vaals, St. Benediktusberg, crypt.** The Benedictine monk Hans van der Laan was commissioned with the building of the monastery church in Vaals, Netherlands, in the 1950s. It was intended as an extension of the monastic buildings designed by Dominikus Böhm in 1922. The crypt, completed in 1962, is dominated by square and rectangular shapes and has a minimalist décor.

Eveux-sur-Arbresle, the Dominican monastery at La Tourette, exterior view of the monastery church (◄), overview of the monastery complex (▲), courtyard from the east (▼),

1953–57. La Tourette is Le Corbusier's last major work in Europe. The complex also comprises 100 individual cells in addition to the church, cloister, library, studies, and refectory.

◀ **Taizé,** ecumenical community. In addition to the celebration of Mass and prayer, the spiritual life of this ecumenical community also includes devotions with music and meditation. Young people in particular are drawn to Taizé from all over the world.

▼ Roger Schutz (1915–2005), founder and spiritual leader of the community. Following his death the leadership was transferred to the German Brother Alois, whom Schutz had already named as his successor during his lifetime.

Taizé

The ecumenical community of Taizé was founded in 1949 by the Protestant theologian Roger Schutz (1915–2005) and seven brothers, who took the classic religious order vow of celibacy, community of property, and obedience. Originally from Switzerland, Schutz had been living in a small Burgundian village near Cluny since 1940 where, contrary to the spirit of the age, he had provided help to those in need. Together with his sister and friends of his, he gave refuge to Jews and other individuals being persecuted by the Nazis during the German occupation. After the liberation he cared for local orphans and German prisoners of war.

This level of engagement reflects the nature of the Taizé community: prayer and contemplation to consolidate a way of life based on the reconciliation of the Christian faith and the battle against poverty and injustice. Today the community numbers over 100 members from numerous countries and a variety of Christian churches. Some of these members continue this fight in the world's social problem areas such as India, for example, where Schutz worked together with Mother Teresa. The community also received acknowledgment from the Catholic Church at an early age, with Schutz invited to attend the Second Vatican Council as an observer.

Taizé's particular significance, however, lies in its role as a place of community for young Christians from all over the world. Due to the constant stream of youthful visitors who come to the weekly gathering and to the regular international youth meetings, the community has developed a degree of prominence in direct contrast to its size. The important factor for this success among young people is the free form of participation in the spiritual life at Taizé, in which music and meditation play an important role during the daily devotions in the church. For many of the young in largely a religious modern Western society, Taizé has become a place of initiation into the life and practice of the Christian faith. Whether this is likely to change following the death of the charismatic Schutz, who was stabbed by a mentally disturbed woman during a service in the church in August 2005, or whether the community will enjoy sustained monastic success, as the neighboring Cluny once did, remains to be seen.

◀ ▲ **Saint-Wandrille,** Normandy, Benedictine abbey of the Solesmes congregation. Interior of the abbey church, which was erected in a converted 16th-century barn in 1968; a monk in the Gothic cloister, one of the few surviving older sections of the abbey.

Freddy Derwahl
Hermits—The Great Solitude

Hermits Today: The Rediscovery of an Ancient Way of Life

The village of C lies in a narrow, tributary valley in Ticino, Switzerland. An atmosphere evocative of fine living predominates initially but the valley is a dead end; the deeper you go into it, the more remote and gloomy it becomes. The jagged cliffs are reminiscent of old peoples' teeth; in fact, the elderly will soon be in the majority here, and the guesthouse has already had to close. A blue lake glitters in the distance: Hermann Hesse lived and wrote on its shores—not irrelevant to our story, which tells of seekers and hermits. Behind the village church a stony path winds through the chestnut forest. The holiday homes of the city dwellers, the tourists, and those in retirement continue to encroach upon the ancient trees. The people here want to be at a distance; some of them want to be entirely alone. If you climb a little higher, at the edge of a small clearing you will see what used to be three stalls once serving as animal shelters. They have since been renovated and converted into weatherproof houses. *Eremo Santa Croce* is written on the gate. When you pull the bell it echoes through the forest but access is strictly controlled: there are no visiting times here, at best prayer and spiritual advice. The "Hermitage of the Holy Cross" is a hidden place but it is not one that is detached from the world. There are not many such locations in Europe but they have undergone a revival in recent years. Perhaps it is more appropriate to talk in terms of "yearning": for silence, solitude, and proximity to God, similar to the idyllic aspirations of secular individuals.

Apart from All, Connected with All

Up here in the chestnut forest, hermit A smiles poignantly, devoid of illusions. He has been living in this remote outpost for a quarter of a century. Of the young refugees from the world who have wanted to join him over the years, only one remained: brother B, an ordinary farmer's son from the neighboring valley, who came into his own in the solitude. He died recently, however, a lengthy and courageous end; perhaps everything had simply been too much; he had put up a fight, but in vain.

Father A is completely alone again. In his mid-sixties he feels the burden of the years but looks back over a life that could not have been more adventurous, even in a world of wars and drugs. He comes from a

wealthy family in Cologne; his father was Protestant. The talented young man had the world as his oyster. Instead he chose early on to enter the Benedictine abbey at Meschede. Fascinated by the Christian East he moved while still a novitiate to the ecumenical monastery at Chevetogne in the Ardennes, Belgium. He earned a doctorate and was appointed librarian. Books had always been his focus but his scholarly

interests were not enough to keep him. Against the will of his abbot he chose the path of solitude. With his unpracticed hands, which until now had been spared from manual labor, he began a new life in a

A Coptic hermit monk in front of the ruins of the desert monastery of St. John Kolobos.

former cow shed. He adopted the motto of his role model, the Desert Father Evagrius

▲ Pater Gabriel Bunge, Benedictine, author, and hermit.

◄ The hermit Fra Rafael and the hermits' abbot, Pater Martin (right).

of Pontus (second half of the 4th century): "That is the monk, apart from all, connected with all." During the course of a long struggle he has learnt that such a regime takes a lifetime.

The Radicalism of the Desert Fathers

The ancient tradition of the Egyptian Desert Fathers, founded in the middle of the 3rd century by St. Anthony the Great (also called the Hermit) and St. Paul of Thebes in the wilderness of Mount Colzim, has lost none of its appeal over time. Its essence lies in its radicalism: he

who seeks anything else fails. "We hold the awful nakedness of this solitude up to the pleasures of the world, the infinite sadness of the sand," is how Abba Abraham explained the basis of the hermit's life to his Latin pupil Cassian (365–435), a lifestyle that, based on the example of the Desert Father Anthony, led to an 'escape from the world' movement in Egypt, Syria, and Palestine, the historical and sociological bases of which remain a matter of dispute today. "Like lemmings," was how princes, criminals, adulterers, child abusers, outsiders, heathens, farmers, laborers, scholars, the young, and the old flocked into the hermitages and hermit colonies in the deserts of Kellia, Sketis, and Nitria, as well as to the Red and White Monasteries of Upper Egypt. The phenomenon was too widespread for it to be reduced to pious ideals and fears of the apocalypse on the part of the escapees. Some experts have seen it as the deep need of a devout population to perpetuate the martyr-like experiences of the Christian persecutions under Diocletian (284–305) using other means of extermination. The lives of the desert hermits reached the limits of what can be borne by human beings. They lived in tombs and ruins, surrounded by snakes and wild animals; they complied with the strictest requirements of fasting and silence; they subjected themselves to night vigils that lasted for hours; they worked hard, and were exposed to extremes of heat and cold, and to sandstorms.

Another interpretation of this extreme lifestyle is as a comprehensive protest movement against secular vanity: an ancient Christian tendency towards being "in the world but not of the world." It was a form of existence that literally turned upside down all of man's aspirations of happiness, satisfaction, security, and diversion, as a reaction against wealth and the debauched lifestyles that go with it, as was the case in the harbor city of Alexandria, for example. The protest by the great monk and hermit personalities took on heroic dimensions. It was not only a signal for conversion, penitence, and emulation; it was also an ongoing political provocation. Anthony the Great's biographer, St. Athanasius, reports on how the hermits had become national heroes during their own lifetimes, acknowledged and respected as authorities by both friend and foe.

Today's strong revival in interest in the Desert Fathers' way of life, however, is not explained by historical or sociological reasons of any great significance, but rather by a perspective developed by Uta Ranke-Heinemann in her theological dissertation "Early Monasticism" in 1964. Here she states that the monks and hermits in the Egyptian desert were concerned with a causal "freedom from the world." Their hard fight for survival was

The German hermit monk Pater Winfried on his way to the hermitage of the Blessed Paul Guistiniani in the Camaldulensian S. Girolamo hermitage.

Basement vaults in the Camuldensian hermit monastery of S. Girolamo.

direct confrontation with the "powers of compromise" and the "snares of the opponent." The struggle with demons, the temptations, deceptions, and attacks they experienced, are comparable to close combat fought with bare knives. Highly dramatic and therefore with a sustained impact and fascination that remains to this day. The words of Evagrius already cited above are echoed when Ranke-Heinemann writes that desert monasticism is a

"task for the world and not a giving up of the world." Laotse expressed a similar concept with "The holy man is alone in the world, but his heart has room for all." This relates to the very current debate about the relationship between "action and contemplation," an issue that had also greatly concerned the late prior of the Taizé monastic community, Frère Roger Schutz.

The "Abba" as the Focal Point

This humble struggle for salvation and overcoming the world is also related to the hermits' means of communication. In a life adapted to the emptiness of the sand and the rocks, they reduce their speech and imagery to elementary signs. The plain crosses on the walls of their cells correspond to the simple clay buildings, the utensils, and their garments. This *arte povera* architecture does not house any libraries. The Bible is usually the only book read, the Psalms and the Old Testaments not only being used in prayer day in and day out, but also learnt by heart through constant practice. The focus itself is provided by the "Abba," the good, wise father who has gathered a group of young aspirants around him in a colony; they pray together with him during the weekly communal celebration of the Eucharist and listen to his instructions. These teachings are characterized by a striking simplicity and draw on the experience and challenges of an entire lifetime. They offer rather than instruct and the answer is often disguised as another question. Their educational fascination lies in the element of surprise and in the bizarre. They always react to the needs and problems of their pupils with mercy and with solidarity:

"Father Anthony spoke to Father Poimen: 'It is man's greatest work that he holds up his sins to God and that he reckons with temptation until he draws his last breath.'"

It was only a matter of time before the fascination of the deserts reached the West. The travel reports by Pelagius and the personal hermit experiences of Cassian (365–435) meant that translations of a compilation of the Fathers' dicta soon became known and sought after in the West as well. In the Latin world they were circulated as the *Apophtegmata patrum*, in Greek as the *Alphabetikon*. The consistent emulation of Christ that they required had a significant influence on the Rule of St. Benedict of Nursia. The liberation sought in the desert through the living, holy word was summarized by the Western Father of the monks as *discretio*. When St. Bernard of Clairvaux reverted to the original purity of the rule in the 12th

A Coptic cross stands above a hermitage in Wadi Natrun, the heartland of the hermits and the Desert Fathers.

century, he loved the dicta from the desert for the wisdom they contained. There was no medieval library that did not draw on these sources; the *Apophtegmata* or the writings of Isaac the Syrian were the best-sellers of the age. Their impact was felt during the Reformation as well: Luther and Calvin were deeply influenced by the Desert Fathers' resistance to secularization. When one looks into the revival of hermitism in the West since the middle of the 20th century, the experiences of death and terror in two world wars, as well as the affluence and trivial emptiness of the postmodern era, are important catalysts. These are factors to which neither church decrees, theological dialogue, conference fervor, nor esoteric-mystic compensation have been able to provide a helpful answer. The Desert Fathers' alternative, which is both simple and strict, is one of a consistently Christian life and has been proven over centuries. With their particular sensitivity, artists and poets recognized and depicted these strengths at an early stage. Their works provide effective encouragement for the present day spiritual quest for the 'desert experience' in contrast to contemporary superficiality and contempt.

Artists and Philosophers as Interpreters of Spiritual Yearning
The "cell," the "shelter," the "Thebaid," or the "forest" have been a source of inspiration for classic works by masters of the visual arts such as Bosch and Brueghel through to Beckmann, Dalí, Ensor, and Max Ernst. Goethe, Flaubert, Schopenhauer, Heidegger, and Handke are just some of the examples from literature and the humanities. The reconnaissance pilot Antoine de Saint-Exupéry, who crash landed in the Egyptian desert near Wadi Natrun in 1936, was discovered by a

The hermitage of Abuna Makarios in a sandstorm, on the Dead Sea.

Bedouin several days later and taken to the Coptic monastery of Dier el-Baramus. In danger of losing his life, the author of *The Little Prince* wrote in his diary: "… we are at the mercy of God's discretion," thus reaching the interface between poetry and proximity to God. In accordance with the observations of the orthodox theologian Olivier Clément, the hermits experienced this *point vierge* (zero point) not as a "form of divine terror, but as a healing awakening … as a metaphysical shock extending beyond this world." The Marxist philosopher Ernst Bloch described the background to this yearning in similar way: "Too much is full of something which is missing. There is something growing inside us, it wants to go further, it cannot abide us, it wants to get out of itself." In his famous interview with the German magazine Spiegel, Martin Heidegger said to Rudolf Augstein, editor of the magazine: "What we are lacking is a God." This yearning on the part of individuals weary of the world for the hermits' path into the desert is bound up in a concrete, existential loneliness that can also exist in the hustle and bustle of the city. The late bishop of Aachen and

spiritual writer Klaus Hemmerle spoke of a world of "synchronized loneliness." The Egyptian desert of the 4th century was the ideal place in which to revitalize this instead of merely enduring it, and that remains the case today. Solitude, in all of its harrowing exclusivity, is presenting to God the only relevant question. The Prophet Elias saw the answer in neither an earthquake nor in a storm, but in the "whispering of the wind." The Prophet Hosea fought for the love of his unfaithful wife with the words: "I want to take her into the desert and try to win her back." The last of the prophets, John the Baptist, proclaimed the proximity of the Savior in the desert. Jesus went into the desert, against the will of the Father, and resisted its temptations.

Female Hermits
The fact that more and more women are opting for such a way of life is not only a sign of the times and of their feminist emancipation. There had been "Desert Mothers" at the time of the Desert Fathers but they were the exception and were in fact also regarded as a "danger" by the suspicious hermits. It was not uncommon, however, for these women to take their isolation so far that they lived their lives dressed as men: it was only after their deaths, during the ritual washing, that it was realized that they were women. The "Ammas" are specifically mentioned in the context of wise dicta in the *Apophtegmata* under the names Synkletika or Theodora. As a sinner and former prostitute St. Mary of Egypt played a dominant role among the desert women. Her conversion had a sustained influence on writers such as Goethe, Brentano, Rilke, and

Father Makarios greets the Belgian author Freddy Derwahl in front of his hermitage in the "inland desert" at Wadi Natrun, Egypt.

Dostoevsky. This trail led from the desert via Scholastica, Hildegard of Bingen, Teresa of Ávila, Thérèse of Lisieux, through to Edith Stein, whose spirituality today constitutes a strong model for all of those women living near her abbeys or in a life of complete withdrawal in the forests or mountains, having pledged themselves to solitude with God. In this context the life of Nazarena, the former American sportswoman and bank secretary in Rome, does indeed make a spectacular exception, the details of which were only made public after her death. A recluse for decades, practically enclosed in a secluded cell in the Camaldulian nuns' convent on the Aventine Hill in Rome, she lived a life of absolute austerity and solitude. While she was certainly a borderline case psychologically, this did not prevent Popes Paul VI and John Paul II from appearing in front of the grille of her cell and listening to her voice.

Dwindling Fatherhood
In contrast to their predecessors in the Egyptian desert, the hermits of today are confronted with a serious problem, indicative of the extent of the religious crisis in the western world: there are not enough Fathers; they are threatened with extinction. There are hardly any of them left to provide advice, support, and a role model for those seeking God in solitude. The point in time will come when the flame can no longer be passed on. The situation is so grave that Godefroid Dayez, former Benedictine abbot at Maredsous in Belgium, claims that such forms of Fatherhood will only reappear "again in a hundred years." This reveals much of the homelessness of the lost and lonely children of the affluent society: they have

everything but possess nothing. And it says even more about the crisis in the Church, whose "word of life" is broadcast only faintly and heard, at best, by a minority. The real problem is not one of trends or structures; it is about the extent of the estrangement from God. The tentative awakening of hermitism is taking place in a very different "desert." There may be no sand but there is emptiness, barrenness, abandonment to impulse, excess, and a lack of faith. The search for the lost God in the place to where he has withdrawn, in solitude, seems like an attempt at a new start on the part of determined men and women. There are sound reasons why it is linked with the place that saw the flowering of Christian monasticism. Contemporary experts familiar with the Eastern Church and Monks' Fathers do not doubt the quality of these sources. Henri Brémond underlines the significant and enduring influence of the Desert Fathers on Christendom. The hermit Gabriel Bunge, in his many books, makes reference to their "orienting help.".

Edith Stein and Charles de Foucauld
From among the spiritual dignities bestowed by the Catholic Church in recent years there are two names that come to mind as indicative of a special direction: the Carmelite nun Edith Stein (canonized) and the desert monk Charles de Foucauld (beatified) have gone from being unknown outsiders to attracting significant attention from well beyond the boundaries of the Church. Further, the paths of their lives, their solitude, their failure, and their violent deaths communicate a sudden proximity of truth and purity. Edith Stein—converted Jew, assistant to the philosopher Edmund Husserl,

and nun—murdered in Auschwitz, as well as Charles de Foucauld—former bon vivant, ladies' man, legionary, adventurer, Trappist monk, and Sahara pastor—were primarily advocates of prayer. Nothing in their lives or their deaths happened without solitary, devout worship that lasted for hours at a time. To this end Edith Stein had undergone a painful conflict with her Jewish mother, had foregone a promising academic career, and had sought out the dark solitude of a contemplative convent. When the Gestapo arrested her and her sister for deportation to the concentration camp, she said: "Come, let's go, for the sake of our people."
Charles de Foucauld left his mistress, his officer's career, and his life as a successful explorer to enter the silent monastery of

Fra Gerlach (died 1994), a Dutch hermit in Italy.

Notre-Dame-des-Neiges. There he was dissatisfied with the degree of poverty, seeing people in Akbès in Syria whom he considered to be even poorer than he was. In Jerusalem he lived like a tramp in the garden shed belonging to a convent of nuns. Ultimately he was drawn to the expanses of the North African desert, where he learnt the language of the nomads, established a hermitage in the Hoggar Mountains and as a "marabout" fell victim to an attack by a fanatic. Both of these solitary lives and deaths symbolize a different Christian consciousness, providing not only an alternative to the normality of contemporary society, but which also extended, shook, and galvanized the conventional boundaries within the Church. The point of holiness is not far removed from the borders of insanity. Yet it is the holy itself that constitutes the ongoing scandal of faith. The place of absolute rejection can only be reached through total abandonment. Which is why the advocates of prayer experience brand new horizons in our world. The life of the American Trappist monk, writer, and hermit Thomas Merton (1915–68) provides a fascinating example of this.

Thomas Merton

Born in southwest France the son of an artist couple, Merton lost his parents at an early age and went on to live a life of excess. He became the father of an illegitimate child, who was killed together with the mother during one of the first air bombardments of London. Following a brief Communist phase, he became affiliated to a group of artists at the Columbia University in New York that included Robert Lax and Ed Reinhard. Influenced by the poetry of William Blake, Etienne Gilson's "Mystic Theology," and a journey to Italy, he converted to Catholicism. He entered the Trappist order at Gethsemane (Kentucky) on December 13, 1941, to which he belonged for 27 years until his death, going by the monastic name of Louis. His superiors immediately encouraged him to write and at first he published poems, followed by his life story, which made him famous overnight. Numerous other books followed: diaries, the lives of saints, spiritual and literary essays, as well as controversial political and church commentaries. Ordained as a priest, for many years Merton was responsible for the training of novices and also corresponded regularly with friends and readers throughout the world. A decisive step taken during this busy time in his life was the desire to move to a stricter, more solitary monastery. He was passionately interested in the hermit orders of the Carthusians and the Camaldulians.

The restless monk's enthusiasm was met with energetic resistance by his abbot, however, partly because the order was anxious not to lose the prominent writer. A lengthy period of conflict followed between the abbot and his monk, one that was trying for both parties, with Merton nevertheless adhering to his vow of consistency. He was finally permitted to live for a period in a forester's hut near the abbey. This soon became his permanent residence, which he left only to attend the

The Trappist monk and hermit Thomas Merton.

nightly officium together with the community of monks.

His time as a hermit was to be the happiest and also the most unsettling period of his life. More than ever before, he became involved in day-to-day politics and was a member of a protest movement against the racial and atomic policies of the US government. His circle of friends included Joan Baez and Bob Dylan. There was no stopping the stream of visitors over the monastery walls at Gethsemane. A love affair with a nurse from neighboring Louisville resulted, a love which undoubtedly tore him apart. The writer and politically active hermit increasingly turned to the mysticism of the Far East and even toyed with the idea of retreating to the solitude of Alaska.

The changes brought about by the Second Vatican Council had also resulted in a reform of the statutes of the Cistercians of the Strict Observance (Trappists). The option of life as a hermit was expressly included therein and Merton's former abbot also settled in a hermitage. The world-renowned author traveled to Bangkok to attend a congress of western and eastern monks, where he met the most prominent masters of oriental mysticism. It was here that he died, on December 10, 1968 as the result of suffering an electric shock.

When the six volumes of Merton's private diaries appeared in New York in 1997, following the usual period of grace, they were heralded by the press as a "brilliant commentary on contemporary history" (*New York Times Book Review*) and as the "American version of the 'Confessions' of Saint Augustine." People were deeply touched by the exciting life led by the monk and hermit. Its honest approach corresponded to their hidden, shaken yearning for God, no longer fulfilled by

the church's traditional way of life. "The monastic church is the church of the wilderness," wrote Merton. It was an affirmation of the solitude of the desert, the call of which has not lost its divine fascination with the nearness of God, even in the commotion of the world.

Coptic Hermits in Egypt

As the successors of the Desert Fathers, the Coptic monks and hermits in the monasteries of St. Anthony the Great and St. Paul of Thebes on the Red Sea, as well as those in the four great monasteries at Wadi Natrun in the desert between Cairo and Alexandria, for a number of decades now have been experiencing a very fruitful period. All of these monastic communities, often numbering hundreds of members, in the proximity of their extensive complexes have hermitages, located in the mountains or in the remote "inland desert." The hermits, who live in dwellings fortified against the sandstorms, or in caves, lead a strict life of prayer and

Coptic hermits from Wadi Natrun.

comprise men of all ages. The flourishing Coptic Church has recently experienced a veritable onslaught of young intellectuals opting for monastic life. Many of them have settled in hermitages. The Coptic Pope, Shenuda III, a former journalist, was himself a hermit and still has a hermitage on the property of the Bishoi monastery, to which he withdraws on a regular basis. A particular challenge facing this community is the difficult relationship with the Muslim minority. The Christian revival, with the spread of settlements, pioneering agriculture, and ecumenical contacts are a thorn in the side of many of them.

Father Seraphim of the Hagi Anna hermit community on the west coast of the holy Mount Athos.

Robert Lax, for example, one of Thomas Merton's close friends, who initially worked as a travel journalist and as a member of a traveling circus. The son of Jewish immigrants, he had converted to Catholicism and, in middle age, decided to lead a hermit's life on the Greek island of Kalymnos and then on Patmos. His existence was not subject to any monastic observance but nevertheless drew on the great mystic traditions of both the East and the West. His books are full of a spontaneity and freedom that enable the renewal of a deep faith outside the traditional structures. When he died in 2001 an American newspaper wrote that the gates of paradise had "opened for a saint."

Hermits in the Orthodox Church

Hermitism also continues to be accorded esteem in the Orthodox Churches in Greece, Russia, Romania, Serbia, and Bulgaria. Mount Athos in northern Greece, a 1000-year-old monastic republic, is its spiritual center, currently with around 2000 members, spread between the 20 large monasteries, as well as the many monks' villages, communes, and hermitages. Athos experienced a new expansion during the 1970s, resulting in particular in the remote hermitages on Cape Athos, near Katounakia, developing into prominent spiritual locations. Their Fathers have also attracted numerous monks and hermits from western countries and from the USA. The monasteries of the Russian Church, which lay disused during the Communist era, have also been resettled since Perestroika. At their center is the monastery of St. Panteleimon on the west coast of Athos, the monk Siluan having lived as a hermit in the mill there for the first half of the last century. He is now honored as a saint in all of the Orthodox religions. A further prominent

spiritual figure on Athos is Joseph the Elder (died 1959), from the monastery of Vatopedi, who practiced the hesychast (quietist) tradition of prayer and who revived a number of larger monasteries with his small community. What is particularly striking is the radicalism of his asceticism, with which he knew how to inspire younger people.

Important spiritual rituals, such as the use of icons or the practice of the Jesus prayer, have also found many followers in the Western Church. Here, as there, the hermit is seen as an outstanding spiritual personality and a saintly Father, who retreats into solitude only after years of probation within the monastery community and who often builds up a group of young pupils around him. For the first time in the long history of Athos, a few years ago the Simonos Petras monastery founded a *metochia* (settlement) in France, outside the Eastern Orthodox Church, which is headed by the former Trappist monk Placide Deseille. Here, too, the example of the Christian East and the new yearning for a solitary quest for God in Western industrial society has brought about a revival of hermitism. Often it was their weak institutional structures that meant it took longer for remote hermitages to deal with Napoleon's systematic oppression than was the case in the monasteries. Today hermit life in more densely populated countries usually develops in the proximity of abbeys and monastic communities, from where the candidates are recruited. Around 1000 hermits, male and female, currently live in Italy and also in France: it is a growing trend.

Yet this impressive way of life based on ancient spiritual traditions also has its exceptions, such as the American poet

Robert Lax, the 87-year-old writer and hermit from Patmos.

The Coptic Pope, Shenuda III, a former journalist and hermit.

The Most Important Catholic Orders

With their Latin names and abbreviations

I. Monastic Orders

Rule of St. Benedict
Benedictine monks/nuns (6th C., confederation 1893), *Ordo Sancti Benedicti*, OSB
Camaldulians (c. 1000/12), *Ordo Sancti Benedicti, Eremitarum Camaldulensium*, OSBCam
Cistercian monks ("White Monks")/nuns (monastery foundation 1098), *Ordo Cisterciensis*, OCist (formerly: *Sacer Ordo Cisterciensis*, SOCist)
General observance:
Feuillants (reform 1577, independent order 1596)
Trappists (reform 1605, order 1892)

Own Rule
Carthusian monks/nuns (monastery foundation 1084, order 1140), *Ordo Cartusiensis*, OCart

II. Canons/Canonesses (Rule of St. Augustine)

Augustinian canons/canonesses (canons/canonesses regular, 11th C.), *Canonici/ Canonissae Regulares Sancti Augustini*, CRSA, CSA
Premonstratensian monks/nuns (Norbertines, first settlement 1120, nuns 12th C.), *Ordo Praemonstratensis*, OPraem

III. Hospitaller Orders

Antonites (c. 1095–1774/75), *Canonici monasterii Sancti Antonii Viennensis*
Order of the Holy Ghost (c. 1200), *Ordo Hospitalerius de Sancti Spiritus*
Hospitaller Brothers of St. John of God (founded 1540, order 1572), *Ordo Hospitalarius Sancti Joannis de Deo*, OSJdD, OH

IV. Military Religious Orders

Knights Hospitaller, Order of St. John of Jerusalem, Knights of Malta (c. 1080), *Sacra Domus Hospitalis Sancti Johannis Jherosolimitani, Ordo Melitensis*, OMel
Knights Templar (1119–1312), *Fratres militiae templi, Sacra Domus Militiae Templi Hierosolimitani*

Teutonic Knights (Teutonic Order, 1190), *Ordo Hospitalis Sanctae Mariae Theutonicorum in Jherusalem*, OT, OTeut

V. Mendicant Orders

1. Franciscans (Friars Minor, 1209), *Ordo Fratrum Minorum*, OFM
First Order:
  Conventual Franciscans (Friars Minor, "Black Franciscans," independent order 1517), *Ordo Fratrum Minorum Conventualium*, OFMConv
  Observant Franciscans ("Brown Franciscans,", 14th C., union 1897), *Ordo Fratrum Minorum (Regularis) Observantiae (de Observantia)*, OFMObs, OMRegObs
  Reformed Franciscans (1532–1897), *Ordo Fratrum Minorum (Strictioris Observantiae) Reformatorum*, OFMRef
  Discalced Franciscans (Alcantarines, 1542–1897), *Ordo Fratrum Minorum Discalceatorum (Exalceatorum, Alcantarinorum)*, OFMDisc, OFMAlc
  Recollect Franciscans (16th C.–1897), *Ordo Fratrum Minorum (Strictioris Observantiae) Recollectorum*, OFMRec
  Capuchins (papal recognition 1528), *Ordo Fratrum Minorum Capuccinorum*, OFMCap
Second Order:
  Poor Clares (Vesting of St. Clare 1212), *Ordo Sanctae Clarae*, OSCl
Third Order:
  Franciscan Tertiaries (Third Order Secular, begun c. 1221), *Tertius Ordo Franciscanus*, TOF; also: *Ordo Franciscanus Saecularis*, OFS
  Franciscan nuns (Third Order Regular, first rule 1289), *Tertius Ordo Regularis*, TOR
  Capuchin Poor Clares, *Ordo Sanctae Clarae Capuccinarum*, OSClCap

2. Dominicans (Order of Preachers 1215), *Ordo Praedicatorum*, OP
Second Order:
  Dominican nuns (1207)
  Third Order of Penance of St. Dominic (first rule 1285)

3. Carmelites (12th C, first rule 1206/14), *Ordo Fratrum Beatae Mariae Virginis de Monte Carmelo; Ordo Carmelitarum*, OCarm
First Order:
  Carmelites of the Old Observance
  Teresian Carmelites (Discalced Carmelites, reform monastery 1568, order 1593), *Ordo Fratum Discalceatorum*, OCD; also: *Sororum Discalceatorum Beatae Mariae Virginis de Monte Carmelo*
Second Order:
  Carmelite nuns (1452), discalced (reform monastery 1562, order 1593)
  Third Order: (c. 1400, papal recognition 1452)

4. Augustinian Hermits (papal recognition 1256), *Ordo Fratrum Eremitarum Sancti Augustini*, OESA; since 1969: Augustinians/Augustinian nuns, *Ordo Fratum Sancti Augustini*, OSA
Recollect Augustinians (congregation 1621, order 1912), *Ordo Augustinianorum Recollectorum*, OAR; also: *Ordo Recollectorum Sancti Augustini*, ORSA, OERSA
Discalced Augustinians (congregation 1596, order 1931), *Ordo Fratrum Eremitarum Discalceatorum Sancti Augustini*, OFEDSA, OSAD

VI Jesuits (Society of Jesus, papal recognition 1540), *Societas Jesu*, SJ

Other Religious Orders or "Institutes of Consecrated Life"

(An alphabetical selection)

Alexians, named after St. Alexius (5th C.), founded in 14th C. as a congregation of lay brothers for the care of the sick, in particular the mentally ill, and for the burial of the dead; as of 1472 officially under the Rule of St. Augustine (therefore also named Augustinians); still in existence today.

Annunciates, order in honor of the Annunciation of the Virgin Mary, a strictly contemplative women's order: Lombard Annunciates, founded 1408; French Annunciates 1501; Italian Annunciates 1604; only a few convents remaining today.

Barnabites, named after the St. Barnabas mother house in Milan, Order of Canons Regular of St. Paul (also called Paulists), founded c. 1530 by Antonius Maria Zaccaria; original mission: exemplary way of life and mission work, still in existence today (approx. 380 members).

Bartholomites, named after their founder Bartholomäus Holzhauser (died 1658), founded 1640 as international association of priests, (through an oath of allegiance, without vows); dissolved through secularization at the beginning of the 19th C.

Beghards (also called Lollards or Cellites), arising in the course of the poverty movement in the early 13th century in the Netherlands (then to the Upper Rhine): semireligious male communities, often suspected of heresy, disbanded in the Late Middle Ages or converted to new communities (often Franciscan Tertiaries).

Beguines (see p. 264)

Brigittines (Order of the Most Holy Savior), name, concept, and rule were originated by the mystic Bridget of Sweden (see pp. 270–71), c. 1374; building and extension of Vadstena Abbey by Bridget's daughter Catherine, who combined her mother's *Regula Salvatoris* with the Rule of St. Augustine; initially both women's and men's communities; today—along with an old branch—only a few nuns are left from a congregation revived in 1911 with about 500 members.

Brethren of the Common Life, founded at the suggestion of Geert Groote by Florens Radewijns 1380/81 in Deventer, Netherlands; community of lay brothers and priests; aim is to live a spiritual life in the sense of the *Devotio moderna*, different from the traditional orders; very widespread in the Netherlands, and central and northern Germany, until the Reformation.

Caracciolos, also called Marians (Minor Clerks Regular), founded in 1588 in Naples by the priest Francesco Caracciola with two companions; main mission: care of the poor and of convicts; papal confirmation of the rule 1588 and 1605; still in existence today (1990: 73 members).

Claretians (Congregation of the Missionary Sons of the Immaculate Heart of Mary), founded in 1849 in Vich, Spain, by Antonio Maria Claret y Clará; mission: domestic and foreign missionary work, active worldwide—Claretian nuns founded in 1855 by A.M. Claret in Cuba for the upbringing and education of young women; merged with a congregation

since 1920; over 500 members today.

Clemens Sisters (Sisters of Mercy Dedicated to the Immaculate Heart of the Blessed Virgin Mary), name from their first workplace, the Clemens Hospital in Munster; order founded 1808 by August von Droste of Vischering (Vicar-General); care of the sick and other charitable activities, particularly widespread in northwestern Germany.

Colettines (Poor Clares), reform order of the Poor Clares, named after founder St. Coletta of Corbie (died 1447); still in existence today (2003: 750 nuns in the Spanish-speaking world).

Congregation of Jesus (previously Sisters of Mary Ward), in Rome, at the time of their founding, called "Jesuitesses," also known as "English Ladies"; founded 1609/10 by Englishwoman Maria Ward in Saint-Omer; institute for education of young women based on the Jesuit model (no enclosure or habit, only a simple vow); initially active primarily in Bavaria, worldwide since the 19th C.; full papal approbation only in 1877; today an alliance of 21 provinces in Europe and abroad with over 2100 members.

Congregation of the Blessed Sacrament, founded 1856 in Paris by the priest Pierre-Julien Eymard (1858 female branch), 1863 recognized as congregation; mission: veneration of the Most Holy Sacrament, promotion of frequent communion in their spiritual guidance; still in existence today (male branch, 2000: some 1000 members).

Felicians, founded 1834 in Warsaw, initially active

in Poland, due to emigration also provide education and charitable services abroad; the major association, linked to the Capuchins (12 provinces), has around 2200 sisters.

Grandmontines (Order of Grandmont), founded by students of the hermit Stephen of Muret (died 1124) in Grandmont; life of strict poverty, their livelihood the responsibility of lay brothers; spread quickly, their focal point in southern France. In 14th C. Grandmont elevated to an abbey, all other monasteries dependent priories; oppression and demise in 18th C.

Sacred Heart of Jesus, Sacred Heart of Mary, Sacred Heart Orders, a total of 449 foundations with this nomenclature, Sacred Heart of Jesus most frequent (244 female, 44 male); already widespread in Middle Ages, reaching high point in German mysticism of 13/14th C., most foundations 17–20th C.; mission: largely missionary, educational and social/charitable activities.

Jesuates (*Pauperes Christi*, Apostolic Clerics of St. Jerome), founded c. 1360 in Siena by patrician Giovanni Colombini; community of lay brothers following the Benedictine, later the Augustinian rule; mission: penitential preaching and care of the poor, sick, and dead; initially itinerant, then based in monasteries, as of the 17th C. each with one or two priests; treated with hostility by mendicant orders because regarded as (heretical) Fraticelli; dissolved 1668 by Pope Clement IX. – Female branch of the Jesuates founded by Caterina Colombini (died 1387), dissolved in 19th C.

Camillians (clerks regular—order in the service of the sick), founded 1582 by St. Camillus of Lellis, confirmed by the pope in 1591, Rule of St. Augustine, care of the sick and dying, widespread in Europe and Latin America; almost discontinued c. 1800, 1842 new beginning and new organization; focus: spiritual guidance in hospitals, sanatoria, and old age homes; 2000: approx. 1000 members.

Catherines (Sisters of St. Catherine, virgin martyr), congregation in papal law, founded 1571 in Braunsberg (today Braniewo, Ermland, Poland) by Regina Protmann; Rule of St. Augustine; mission: care of the sick and education; c. 2000: some 800 sisters.

Little Brothers/Little Sisters of Jesus, founded 1964 and 1968; both inspired by the spirituality and lifestyle of Charles de Foucauld (1858–1916), one of the greatest spiritual figures of the 20th C.: living in poverty and in the service of the poor, precedence of the witness to life over the witness to the Word, silent prayer times; active throughout the world, living in small communities (2002: 266 brothers and 1258 sisters).

Lazarists (Vincentians), named after Lazarus of Bethany, whom Jesus woke from the dead (John 11, 1-4), are various religious communities for the care of the sick.

Marianists (*Societas Mariae*), also called Marianist Brothers, congregation of largely equal priests and laymen, founded 1817 in Bordeaux by Guillaume-Joseph Chaminade, confirmed by Pius IX 1869; mainly active in education and teaching in schools, daily consecration to Mary; active worldwide (2000: over 1500 members).—Marianist Sisters (1816), congregation also founded by Chaminade, comprise some 400 members.

Mariannhill Missionaries, derived from the Trappist abbey Mariannhill in Natal, South Africa, founded in 1882 by Franz Pfanner (died 1909); after Pfanner's death converted to the Mariannhill Missionaries Congregation, the most successful mission station in South Africa, with branches also in Europe and elsewhere.—Congregation of the Missionary Sisters of the Precious Blood, founded by Pfanner in 1885, comprises about 950 sisters worldwide.

Marists (*Societas Mariae*), founded 1824 by French priest Jean-Claude-Marie Colin (died 1873) in Lyons, papal recognition 1836; mainly active in education of young people, spiritual guidance, and missionary work worldwide (2002: about 1250 members).—Congregation of the Marist Sisters, founded by

Colin in 1817 (papal recognition 1884), is dedicated to the education of young women and to social work (about 600 sisters).

Marist School Brothers, lay congregation for the education and tuition of young men, founded 1817 by Marcellin-Joseph-Benoît Champagnat (died 1840), papal recognition 1863; active worldwide (2002: about 5000 members).

Mechitharists, an Armenian order in union with the Catholic Church, founded 1701 in Istanbul by Abbot Mechithar of Sebaste, Rule of St. Benedict, papal recognition 1711, settlement in Venice 1717; following founder's death (1773) division into two congregations: Mechitharists of Venice and Mechitharists of Vienna; common objective: maintenance and fostering of Armenian culture, valuable libraries in both headquarters; reunited since 2000 (c. 2002: about 40 members).

Mercedarians (from medieval Latin merces, grace, mercy), founded 1218 by Petrus Nolascus (died 1247) as military order for laymen and clerics to pay ransom for Christian prisoners held by the Muslims, papal recognition 1235, Rule of St. Augustine; in 14th C. alignment with mendicant orders; in addition to Spain, also widespread in southern Italy, as well as, in modern times, in South America. Revival following secularization: youth education and missionary work (2002: 730 members).—Mercedarian Sisters, founded 1265, name later adopted by a variety of female communities in the Catholic Church who today carry out missionary work, education, and care of the sick worldwide (3500 sisters).

Missionaries of Charity, founded by Mother Teresa (see p. 402).

Niederbronn Sisters, founded 1849 by Elisabeth Eppinger (died 1867) in Niederbronn, Alsace, as "Daughters of the Divine Redeemer," 1866 papal confirmation as congregation; original mission: hospice care and care of the poor, today various charitable works, widespread in Germany and neighboring countries (1998: about 2000 sisters).

Oblates, name adopted by the members of several Catholic religious communities in the 19th and 20th centuries, usually with simple vows: the Oblates of St. Francis de Sales (founded 1871), the Oblates of the Blessed Virgin Mary (founded 1815), the Congregation of the Missionary Oblates of Mary Immaculate (founded 1816)—active in education, spiritual guidance, and (partly) missionary work.—Even more numerous are the various female oblate orders, including the Lioba Sisters, the Missionary Benedictine Sisters of Tutzing, the Oblate Sisters of the Assumption, and many others.

Olivetans, Benedictine order congregation, started by a small group of hermits on Monte Oliveto near Siena in 1313, papal confirmation 1344; more than 150 monastic foundations in 14/15th C. Of major significance in Italy, almost dissolved in 19th C.; since 1960 attached to a small Benedictine congregation (2000: about 250 monks).—Olivetan Sisters, founded in Belgium in 1926, are an independent association.

Opus Dei (*Praelatura personalis Sanctae Crucis et Operis Dei*, Personal Prelature of the Holy Cross and Opus Dei), founded 1928 by the Spanish priest Jose Maria Escrivá de Balaguer y Albas (died 1975) as a lay community, 1930 female branch, 1943 foundation of Priestly Society of the Holy Cross, adopted by Pope John Paul II in 1982 as personal prelature (clerical association, international in nature, for the fulfillment of specific apostolic tasks); Opus Dei is active worldwide (2000: about 80,000 members, 98% laypeople).

Oratorians, members of an international Catholic priests' association with its origins in the meetings of priests serving worldwide in the oratorium (prayer room) in the priest's house of founder St. Philip Neri (1515–95) in Rome; communal prayer and intensive spiritual guidance; no vow, love as the only bond of solidarity; numerous branches in and outside Italy; 1943 loose association of the Oratorians with a confederation; members are subordinate to the relevant diocesan bishop.

Ottiliens, members of the Congregation of Missionary Benedictines of St. Ottilien (first mission station 1887); revival of missionary activities in the Benedictine orders by the Beuron monk Andreas Amrhein (died 1927), 1896 confirmed by Rome; St. Ottilien elevated to abbey 1902, as archabbey soon mother house for several monasteries both at home and abroad (2002: more than 1000 members).—Female branch since 1885, co-founded by P. Amrhein: Missionary Benedictine Sisters of Tutzing (named after the location of their mother house as of 1904).

Pallottines, Society of Apostolic Life, founded 1835 as priests' and laymen's community by Vincent Pallotti (died 1850) in Rome, instead of a vow, commitment to a life according to the evangelical counsels (voluntary adoption of poverty, chastity, obedience), papal recognition 1903; mission: missionary work and various apostolic activities; active worldwide (2000: about 2300 members).—1838 female branch, for carrying out charitable and teaching activities; German branch from 1891: Missionary Sisters of the Catholic Apostolate (2002: over 600 sisters).

Passionists, clerical congregation committed to the veneration of Christ's Passion (in addition to the other three vows), founded 1720 by Paul of the Cross (died 1775); the initial excessively strict rules were amended several times and a milder version granted papal recognition in 1741; originally strongly contemplative, in 19th C. focus was on the apostolate, active worldwide (2002: about 2300 members).—Female branch is strongly contemplative, also founded by Paul of the Cross.

Minims, or Order of the Hermits of St. Francis, founded 1445 by Francis of Paola (died 1507) in Calabria, papal recognition 1474; very strict rules with penitence and "eternal fasting" as special vow; spread rapidly before strong decline due to secularization, also for the female second order (Minim Sisters) founded in Spain in 1495; c. 2000: some 200 male members, about 100 in the female orders.

Paulines, Order of St. Paul (of Thebes, the "First Hermit"); founded c. 1250 in Hungary as a hermit congregation, dissolved in 1786 by Joseph II, still in existence today in Poland (1990: 380 members).

Piarists, founded 1597 by Joseph of Calasanz (died 1648) in Rome as an association of pious men for the education of poor children, papal recognition 1617; following crises, from 1669 spread in Catholic countries as a teaching order, considerable losses due to secularization; today some 1500 members.

Redemptorists, founded 1732 by Alfons Maria di Liguori (died 1787) in Scala near Amalfi (southern Italy) as community of Catholic clerics; mission: religious activation of the rural population; papal confirmation of the rule devised by the founder only in 1749; 1784 Redemptorists spread in northern Europe due to Clemens Maria Hofbauer (died 1820); from Vienna development of even greater effectiveness; most widespread in the 20th C. (2000: 5700 members).—Redemptorist Sisters, founded 1731 by di Liguori, second founding 1831, contemplative order with strict enclosure; 2002: about 400 nuns.

Salesians of Don Bosco, founded 1859 by Giovanni Bosco (see pp. 404–05).

Salvatorians, founded 1881 by John Baptist Jordan (died 1918), initially as an "apostolic teaching society," 1894 shift towards spiritual objectives, 1905 first, 1922 final papal recognition; mission: domestic and foreign missionary work; currently about 1200 members.—Female branch, the Salvatorian Sisters, founded by Jordan and Therese von Wüllenweber (died 1907); common objectives, but independent; active worldwide (2000: about 1300 sisters).

Servites (Order of the Servants of Mary), deriving from one of seven fraternities of Mary founded by Florentine patricians 1233, Rule of St. Augustine, statutes and objectives based on the mendicant orders, final papal confirmation 1304; widespread throughout Europe, significant losses due to the Reformation and secularization, revival in the 19th

C., foundations outside Europe, currently about 900 members.—c. mid-13th C., foundation of a female second order: Servite Sisters, originally enclosed and contemplative; in 14th C. foundation of a third order by Juliana Falconieri, similarly Servite Sisters (also called Mantellates); today both female communities work in the social/charitable field.

Silvestrines, originated 1231 at Montefano Monastery, Marches, founded by Silvestrino Guzzolini (died 1267), originally comprising largely laymen, a community characterized by the contemporary poverty movement, based on the Rule of St. Benedict, papal recognition 1248; increasing clericalization and urban orientation in Late Middle Ages; initially only in Italy, from 18th C. also in other countries on an isolated basis; since 1973 own congregation within the Benedictine order, currently about 200 members.—1233 foundation of female branch: Silvestrine Sisters, 1822 dissolution of last convent.

Somaschi, order of clerks regular, founded 1534 by Hieronymus Aemiliani (died 1537), Rule of St. Augustine, papal recognition 1540; main mission: running of orphanages and poorhouses, youth education and parish-based spiritual guidance; currently about 500 members.—Two female branches: first founded 1680 in Genoa, second 1975 in Central America (due to split from Genoa); the latter in 2000: over 160 members.

Spiritans (Congregation of the Holy Ghost/Holy Ghost Fathers), founded 1703 in Paris by Claude-François Poullart-des-Places (died 1709); mission: training of priests and missionary work, refounded 1806 and 1819, papal recognition 1824, 1841 unification with the Congregation of the Immaculate Heart of Mary, active worldwide (2000: over 3000 members).

Steyler Missionaries and Missionary Sisters, name in the German speaking world for the members of the "Society of the Divine Word," 1875 opening of the St. Michael mission station in Steyl, Netherlands, by Arnold Janssen; a community of priests and brothers with simple vows developed from the missionary training center, papal recognition 1901 and 1910, from 1928 order managed from Rome; missionary work worldwide, also teaching activities and encouragement of the sciences; currently over 6000 members.—Holy Spirit Missionary Sisters (founded 1887 by Janssen) number about 3700 and are also active worldwide.

Sulpicians, international community of priests (no vow), founded 1642 by Jean-Jacques Olier, priest at St. Sulpice in Paris; mission: training and spiritual development of the diocesan clergy; inspired by the Oratorians; widespread in France and in francophone countries; currently 350 priests.

Theatines, order of clerks regular, founded 1524 in Rome for religious revival of the clergy by Cajetan of Thiene, Bishop of Chieti (Latin Theatinus), and Giampietro Caraffa, later Pope Paul IV; particularly widespread in Italy, elsewhere isolated (in 17th C. very grand monasteries in Munich, Prague, Salzburg, Vienna); almost eliminated by secularization, revival from beginning of 20th C.; currently about 200 members in Italy and the USA.—1875 founding of the Theatine Sisters (successor of an order founded in the 17th C.) with branches in Italy, Spain and the USA, education of young women, currently over 200 sisters.

Trinitarians (Order of the Holy Trinity for the Ransom of Captives), founded end of the 12th C. by John of Matha (1213) near Soissons; mission: prisoner exchange and ransom between Christians and Muslims during the era of the Crusades, associated with hospice services; particular veneration of the Trinity; papal recognition 1198; 13th C.: foundation of a second (Trinitarian Sisters) and third order (secular, Tertiaries); since 1609 Trinitarians have belonged to the mendicant orders; activities today are missionary work, spiritual guidance among prisoners, parish-based spiritual guidance; currently about 550 male, 220 female members.

Ursulines (Order of St. Ursula), founded 1535 in Brescia by Angela Merici (died 1540), female community committed to the evangelical counsels (no vow) with regulated life based on the example of St. Ursula; mission: catechesis for young girls, papal recognition 1544; widespread in many Italian cities, in France at end of 16th C., then also in German-speaking countries; no unified order, association with affiliated convents; revival of order in 19/20th C., active worldwide in the field of education; 2002: around 10 000 members.

Glossary

Abbey, since the 11th C., term for a house of monks, canons regular, nuns, or canonesses under the leadership of an abbot (abbess) with financial and administrative powers.

Abbot/Abbess, leader of a community of monks/nuns.

Anchorite, see box p. 17.

Asceticism, collective term for practices such as fasting, abstinence, silence, celibacy, sleep deprivation, isolation, itineracy, physical castigation, as well as spiritual attitudes such as humility and abasement, among others; key requirement is that the asceticism be voluntary and performed for the sake of a higher cause.

Canons/Canonesses, regular or secular members of order committed to communal choral prayer (canons regular, see pp. 159 f.).

Cellarar (Latin *cellerarius*, relating to the pantry/cellar, head cook), administrator of the monastery's housekeeping.

Clerics, see box p. 20.

Consuetudines, (Latin for customs), supplementary, precise or specific conditions relating to an order's statutes.

Convent (or nunnery), community of nuns or sisters.

Dispens (Latin for repeal, exemption), in the context of an order's statutes means exemption from specific regulations.

Donati see Oblates.

Dormitorium, communal sleeping area in a monastery/convent.

Evangelical counsels, the three vows: chastity (celibacy), poverty, and obedience, the voluntary adoption of which is the prerequisite for life in an order.

Filiation (from Latin *filia*, daughter), the relationship of newly founded religious houses (*filiae*) to the founding mother house); monastic network system according to the filiation principle was introduced by the Cistercians.

Frater (Latin for brother), originally mutual term of address among monks; following the division of the communities into priests and lay brothers, the term was restricted to the latter.

Grange, (medieval Latin *grangia*, granary, large barn), with the Cistercians of the Middle Ages, a monastery/convent's farmstead run by lay brothers. Habit, robes of an order, usually those of monks.

Hermit, see box p. 17.

Horae (Latin for hours), individual prayer times in the Liturgy of the Hours.

Icon(oclastic) Controversy, the dispute regarding the display and veneration of images, which shook the Byzantine Empire in the 8/9th C. (see p. 332–35).

Imperial monasteries, see box p. 44.

Incluse/recluse, practitioner of specific form of hermitism: man or woman who locked themselves in a cell or who had themselves enclosed within walls (immured) for a lengthy period of time or for life.

Infirmarius (Latin *infirmus*, meaning sick) in monasteries the monk in charge of the sick; the separate part of the monastery/convent reserved for the sick is the infirmarium.

Laura (or lavra), monastery type in Eastern monasticism: hermits' place of residence in an enclosed area with communal church and other monastic spaces; since the Middle Ages a term for large monasteries (e.g. on Mount Athos).

Lay brothers/lay sisters, members of order, not full monks or nuns, who carried out the necessary practical work; monks also called *fratres barbati* (Latin for bearded brothers).

Laypeople, see box p. 20.

Liturgy of the Hours, see box p. 24 and pp. 198–99.

Mass, see box p. 24.

Monastery (Greek *monasterion*, hermit's cell), the communal place of residence for a group of religious persons; (secluded) complex of monastic buildings/monastic community.

Monk, see boxes pp. 17, 20.

Novice, term for a person wanting to enter a monastery, convent, and/or order and therefore undertaking the required period of probation.

Oblate (from the Latin *oblatus*, sacrificed), boy or girl presented by parents and/or guardians to a monastery or convent, a practice continuing well into the Middle Ages.

Officium, see box p. 24.

Opus Dei, key concept in the Rule of St. Benedict: religious service, in traditional terms identical with liturgical service, later also denoting "daily work" itself.

Oratorium, prayer room (chapel) in a religious community.

Parlatorium, room in monastery/convent where conversation is permitted.

Peregrinatio (from the Latin *peregrinare*, travel about), wandering and exile as an ancient monastic ideal (especially predominant in Irish monasticism).

Priest, see box p. 20.

Prior/Prioress, in Catholic orders: 1. of second rank in abbey and abbot/abbess's deputy, 2. head of an independent monastery/convent that is not an abbey (e.g. priory), 3. head of a monastery/convent or other settlement of orders that do not use the title abbot (e.g. the Carthusians).

Profession, in Catholic orders: public taking of the vow.

Refectory, dining hall for communal meals in a monastery or convent.

Religious, member of an order.

Scriptorium, writing room in medieval monasteries.

Stabilitas (Latin for resolution, stability), a monk remaining in the community that he entered as a novice and in which he took his vows.

Tonsure, monastic shaving of the head in a variety of forms.

Vesting, handover and clothing with the order's robes during a liturgical celebration, start of the novitiate.

Visitation, visit by the order superior to inspect adherence to rules and customs.

Vow, a promise to God in which the vower undertakes a commitment relating to Christian life in an order: obedience, poverty and chastity, sometimes also supplemented with additional practices; celebratory vows are taken in the orders, simple vows in the communities.

Biographies

Abaelard, monk and scholar, 1079–1142, early conflicts with his teachers; love for his pupil Heloise, niece of a Canon Fulbert, by whom Abelard was captured and castrated. Heloise became a nun, Abelard a monk: they remain in contact by correspondence. Return to intellectual life in Paris c. 1135; Abelard's theological writings were a source of dispute from Bernhard of Clairvaux, amongst others; Abelard was sentenced to silence by the Pope. Mediation in Cluny by Abbot Peter the Venerable. Widespread circulation of his writings; his scholarly methods contributed to the development of scholasticism.

Adalbero of Rheims, archbishop and monastery reformer, c. 920/30–89, brought up at Gorze Abbey, became capitular of the church at Metz and Odalrich's successor as archbishop of Rheims; outstanding role as provider of spiritual guidance; reformed the Mouzon and Saint-Thierry abbeys, strove for the unification of monastic customs in the province of Rheims, prescribed the communal way of life for his chapter.

Aegidius (St. Gilles), hermit, died c. 720, founder abbot of the Benedictine monastery named after him, Saint-Gilles, in Provence. The cultivation of legends at the beginning of the 8th C. attracted a large Aegidius cult including pilgrimages.

St. Aegidius (detail), Hans Memling, 15th C.

Aelred of Rievaulx (St.), Cistercian abbot and theologian c. 1100–67. Monk from 1134, abbot of Rievaulx from 1147. Under him the abbey had one of its most successful periods (140 monks, 500 lay brothers). Important exponent of monastic theology.

Aethelwold, bishop of Winchester, born c. 910, early education partly at the royal court; following consecration in 935 he entered the abbey at Glastonbury, led a strict monastic life; 963–84 bishop of Winchester, replaced the secular clergy in the cathedral with monks, completed an English translation of the *Regula Benedicti*; played an important role in the reformation of monasticism in England (co-author of the *Regularis Concordia*).

Albertus Magnus (St. Albert the Great), universal scholar, c. 1200–80. Joined the Dominicans 1223, teaching activities at a number of order schools, continued his studies in Paris: doctoral degree, Magister (teacher) in theology faculty. Bishop of Regensburg for one year, 1260; from 1271 mainly in Cologne, where he died. Extensive writings. Honorary title Doctor Universalis awarded posthumously.

Alcuin, Anglo-Saxon scholar, c. 730–804. Trained at the cathedral school in York, teacher and head of the school. 781 appointed head of Charlemagne's court school, influential advisor to Charlemagne in all matters of the church. From 796 abbot of the Saint-Martin abbey in Tours, where he died. Although not a monk himself, Alcuin was a strong advocate of monasticism, particularly with regard to discipline and education.

Ambrose (St.), bishop, important church politician, c. 339–97. Educated in Rome for a political career, 370 consul of Aemilia-Liguria province. While still a baptism candidate Ambrose was elected bishop of Milan in 374; he founded a monastery there. His writings include important texts on female monasticism (about virginity).

Anselm of Canterbury, archbishop and scholar, 1033–1109. 1060 entered the Benedictine order, in Lanfranc's abbey school at Bec, became prior in 1063, later abbot and head of this famous school. As archbishop of Canterbury (from 1093) was head of the English Church. Conflict with the English Kings William II and Henry I (English investiture controversy). Numerous writings on theological and philosophical problems: significant influence (due to his *Proof of the Existence of God*, amongst other works).

Anthony (St.), the Great, the Hermit, or Abbot, hermit and important Father of Monks in Egypt, 251–356 (see p. 18).

Anthony of Padua (St.), monk, theologian, and preacher, 1195–231. Born into a noble family in Lisbon, Anthony entered the Augustinian Canons at 15; studied in Coimbra, 1220 conversion to the Franciscan order, from 1222 preacher against the Cathars in northern Italy and southern France; theology lecturer in Bologna, Montpellier, and Toulouse.

Athanasius the Great, Doctor of the Church and bishop of Alexandria, c. 295–373, early contacts with the ascetics of the Thebaid. Elected deacon in 318, participated in the Council of Nicaea 325. Lifelong campaign against Arianism, which several times resulted in exile (for 17 years). Strong advocate of monasticism, especially through his *Vita Antonii*.

Augustine (Aurelius Augustine, St.), bishop and Doctor of the Church, Latin Church Father, 354–430 (see p. 20).

Basil the Great (St), monk, bishop, great teacher of Eastern monasticism, 329–79. Born in Caesarea (Cappadocia), studied at various schools of rhetoric; baptized 356, became a monk, lived with ascetics for some years. 357/58 founded monastery with like-minded monks in Pontus; worked together with Gregory of Nazianzus, compiled the "Monks' Rules". 364 emigrated to Caesarea, where he became bishop and died in 379.

Bede, the Venerable, monk and scholar, 673/74–735, entered monastery at Jarrow as oblate where, with the exception of two short journeys to Lindisfarne and York, he then spent his life "learning, teaching and writing"; became a priest at 30. His extensive writings, which focus on education and ethical teaching, have had a significant influence.

Benedict of Aniane, monastery founder and promoter of Benedictine monasticism, c. 750–821 (see p. 47–48).

Benedict of Nursia (St.), father of Western monasticism, c. 480–560 (see pp. 23–25).

Bernard of Clairvaux (St.), Cistercian abbot, most important exponent of monastic theology, 1090–1153 (see p. 172).

Bernardine of Siena (St.), Franciscan monk and preacher, 1380–1444. 1402 entered the Order of the Friars Minor, ordained priest, from 1405 first sermons in central and northern Italy, from 1407 regular traveling preacher. 1438 Vicar-General of the Observants (Third Order of the Franciscans); Bernardine held the view that ignorance and poverty are equally hazardous for monks.

Bonaventure (St.), Franciscan theologian, Doctor of the Church, cardinal, 1217–74; studied theology in Paris, 1243 entered the Franciscan order, defended the poverty theology of the mendicant orders, drew up the General Statutes that updated the Rule of St. Francis, arbitrated in disputes within the order over the real successor to St. Francis. 1273 Bonaventure became cardinal bishop of Albano; numerous writings with significant influence.

Boniface, Winfrid (St.), missionary and archbishop, 672/75–754 (see p. 42).

St. Bonaventure (detail), Francisco de Zurbarán, 1629.

Bridget of Sweden (St.), mystic and order founder, 1303–73 (see p. 270).

Bruno of Cologne, founder of the Carthusians, c. 1030–1101 (see p. 148).

Caesarius (St.), bishop of Arles, 470–542. 491 monk in Lérins, 499 ordained priest, 502 bishop of Arles, active church politician, provider of spiritual guidance, preacher, concerned about monastic discipline. Wrote a short rule for monks in 534 and more extensive one for the nunnery founded by him and run by his sister: the oldest rule for nuns in the West.

Cassiodorus (Flavius Magnus Aurelius), c. 485–after 580, over 30 years in civil service, lengthy sojourns in Ravenna and Byzantium. Founded the Vivarium monastery on his estate in Calabria c. 554. Little is known about life in this monastery: central role of the library and cultural life; monks committed to study, copying work, etc. Cassiodorus, last philologist of classical antiquity, is a significant figure in intellectual history.

Catherine of Siena (St.), mystic and popes' advisor, 1347–80. Characterized by a deep religiosity from an early age, she rejected marriage, withdrew into meditative solitude at home; 1364/65 joined the Dominican Tertiary Sisters, dedicated herself to charitable works. Her spirituality deepened under the guidance of her Dominican confessors; a circle of advice seekers built up around her. The Dominican scholar Raymond of Capua became her spiritual guide. Was interested in problems of church politics, made contact with leading personalities, including Pope Gregory XI, began to dictate letters: exhortation for the transfer of the Curia of Avignon back to Rome, appeal for church reform, appeal for tolerance, etc. Performance of miracles increased the renown of her short, but influential, life.

Chrodegang (St.), bishop of Metz, c. 712/13–66, member of Franconian nobility, 742 (?) bishop of Metz, 754 archbishop by the Pope. Fostered monasticism: founded the "model monastery" at Gorze, established a monastery network. Chrodegang also committed the cathedral clergy to *Vita communis*; his canonical rule of 755 later served as the basis for other rules of the *Vita canonica*.

Clare of Assisi (St.), abbess, 1193/94–1253. Following repeated encounters with Francis of Assisi she left her parents' aristocratic home to become one of his followers; she had her hair cropped, received a veil and was housed in S. Damiano, where a community built up around her. 1215/16 granted the right by Innocent III to live without possessions or income; one of the rules she compiled corresponding to the Franciscan way of life was approbated by the Pope only shortly before her death. The Order of the Poor Clares only became a subject for discussion ten years after her death.

St. Bernardine of Siena (detail), Vincenzo Foppa, c. 1514.

Columba of Iona (St.), great Irish cleric and monk, 520/21–97. Founded several monasteries in Ireland, 563/65 moved to Scotland, founded further monasteries there, with Iona (Hebrides) at the head. Strong influence on Irish and British monasticism.

Columban(us) (St.), monk and monastery founder, c. 543–616 (see p. 40).

Dominic (St.), founder of the Dominican order, c. 1170–1221 (see p. 294).

Dunstan (St.), one of the great figures of the English church, c. 909–88. 934 monk, c. 940 abbot of Glastonbury, 957 archbishop of Canterbury. Decisive role in the reform of Anglo-Saxon monasticism in the 10th C. (commitment to the Rule of St. Benedict).

Eusebius, bishop of Vercelli, c. 283–370, first western bishop to implement communal life for his clergy.

Eustathius of Sebaste, bishop and initiator of monasticism in Asia Minor, before 300–after 377; initially a follower of rigorous asceticism, sharp critic of the Church; sentenced by several synods; c. 365 bishop, strove for integration of ascetic monasticism in Church; his most important pupil was Basil of Caesarea.

Euthymius the Great (St.), important figure in Palestinian monasticism, c. 377–437; went to Jerusalem with his friend Theoktistos 405, the two of them founded a monastic community in 411 in the Judean Desert with Theoktistos as abbot. Due to large influx of pupils founded their own laura (monastic settlement); with his emphasis on humility, love, and hospitality he was a powerful model for monastic virtues.

St. Gregory the Great as scribe (relief detail), 10th C.

Fra Angelico, Dominican monk and painter, c. 1400–55, as Fra Giovanni in the S. Domenico monastery in Fiesole. "Angelico" was an honorary title granted at an early stage. Numerous strict meditational works for the affiliated S. Marco monastery in Florence (today a museum).

Frances of Rome (St.), 1384–1440, was married at 12 against her will, dedicated herself to the care of the sick, practiced asceticism; in 1425, together with other women, she founded a community dedicated to prayer and charitable work, which she entered following her husband's death in 1436. Had the reputation of a saint even during her lifetime (miracle healings).

Francis of Assisi (St.), major figure in Christian spirituality, founder of the Franciscan order, 1181–1226 (see p. 286).

Fructuosus of Braga (St.), metropolitan bishop and monastery founder, c. 600–75; related to the Visigoth royal dynasty, founded several monasteries around León and in Galicia. Compiled a rule for the Compludo convent, which expelled him as an ascetic with hermitic tendencies; from 656 metropolitan bishop of Braga.

Gertrude the Great (St.), nun and mystic, 1256–1301/02, was given as an oblate at the age of five to the Helfta nunnery near Eisleben, where she received a good education. From 1281 she had mystic visions, hallucinations, voices, which she reported to her fellow sisters, who then recorded them. At times she herself wrote: main work the revelatory text *Legatus divinae pietatis*. Also took part in the recording of the revelations of her fellow sisters Mechtild of Magdeburg and Mechthild of Hackeborn. Important motifs in her spiritual life were: Christ's love, devotion to Mary and the saints, the Eucharist, the poor souls, amongst others.

Gregory the Great (St.), monastery founder, monk and Pope, 540–604. From a wealthy Roman senator family, founded seven monasteries, some in Sicily, and St. Andrew's Monastery in Rome, which he entered himself as a monk, and in 585/86 he became abbot there; 590 became first monk to be Pope. Advocate of monasticism, wrote the famous life of Benedict of Nursia.

Groote, Geert, originator of the *Devotio moderna*, 1340–84. Studied in Paris and at other universities, canon in Aachen and Utrecht. 1374 encounter with Heinrich Eger of Kalkar, who directed him to the spiritual life. Gave up his benefices, left his parents' house in Deventer to a community of God-seeking women (the original cell of the Sisters of the Common Life), lived as a hermit, then as a traveling and penitential preacher; was charged with heresy.

St. Jerome as hermit (detail), Zanetto Bugatto, 15th C.

Hildegard of Bingen, convent founder, abbess, visionary theologian, 1098–1179 (see p. 270).

Honoratus, bishop of Arles, outstanding figure of Gallic monasticism, died 429/30 (see pp. 20–21).

Hugh of Semur (St.), 6th abbot of Cluny, 1024–1109. After attending the cathedral school in Auxerre, entered the abbey of Cluny as a monk at the age of 15 against the will of his father, 1047–49 prior, from 1049 abbot (Odilo's successor). The *Ecclesia Cluniacensis* achieved its most extensive expansion during his 60 year term of office; more so than his predecessor, he combined the adoption of reforms with legal binding to Cluny, which also increased in economic importance under his leadership. Good relationships with both Emperor Henry IV, whose godfather he was, and Pope Gregory VII, enabled him to act as intermediary at the height of the investiture controversy in Canossa (1077).

Hugh of St. Victor, theologian and philosopher, died 1141. Brought up in the regular canons' priory at Hamersleben, he entered the abbey of Saint-Victoire in Paris (Augustinian canons), founded by Louis VI at a young age, where he developed into a highly influential teacher. Exegetical works form the main focus of his writings because he considered a true understanding of texts to be the highest value of all study. His spiritual works had a significant influence up to the Reformation.

Ignatius Loyola, founder of the Jesuit order, 1491–1556 (see pp. 363–66).

Isidore of Seville, bishop and important early medieval writer, c. 560–636. Following his parents' early death was brought up by his brother Leander, initiator of the conversion of the Visigoths to Catholicism; 599/600 became the latter's successor as bishop of Seville. Extensive writings with significant influence. His *Regula monachorum* (also called the Rule of Isidore), a summary of monastic tradition, was written for the monasteries he founded.

Jerome (Sophronius Eusebius Hieronymus, St.), priest, theologian, Doctor of the Church, c. 347–420. Studied in Rome, 368 affiliation with a group of hermits, 370 to Syria in the Egyptian desert, ordained priest in Antioch. 382 "secretary" to the Pope in Rome, 386 to Bethlehem, where he settled permanently and founded a nunnery. Highly educated and talented at languages, extensive writings: Vulgate (Latin Bible translation), Bible commentaries and other exegetical works; his monastic works (monks' lives, translation of the Rule of Pachomius) are testimony to his strong interest in a monastic-ascetic way of life.

Joachim of Fiore, abbot and important monastic theologian of the 12th C., c. 1135–1202/05. Brought up at the royal court of Palermo, abandoned his studies and turned to religious life; undertook pilgrimage to the Holy Land, following his return led an itinerant life between the various monasteries in Calabria. Became affiliated to the Cistercians and founded the S. Giovanni abbey in Fiore (Calabria) in 1192/93, over which he presided as abbot until his death. Works significant primarily with regard to his historical theology and his exegetical methods (allegorical structure of his writings).

John Cassian, monastery founder, important figure in southern Gallic monasticism, c. 360–430/35. Ten years' experience of Egyptian monasticism (see p. 20).

John Chrysostom, bishop of Constantinople, preacher, Doctor of the Church, 349/350–407. Received a sound education in his home town of Antioch, following baptism in 372 an ascetic life among monks near Antioch, then two years as anchorite; 381 deacon, 386 priest, made a name for himself as a great preacher. 397 Emperor Theodosius made him bishop of Constantinople. Met resistance as a reform bishop (especially in court circles), exiled in 404. Advocate of monasticism through practice and writings; extensive works.

John Gualbertus, founder of the Vallombrosan monks, early 11th C.–1073 (see p. 146).

John of the Cross (Juan de la Cruz, St.), founder of the Discalced Carmelites, mystic, 1542–91. 1560 became a Carmelite but dissatisfied with the state of the order; found support in Teresa of Ávila; from 1568 start of reform work, leading to foundation of the branch of the Discalced Carmelites. Encountered hostility from reform opponents, was slandered, incarcerated, and tortured; following his escape from prison, active in a number of offices within the order. His life of suffering lent even more charisma to his mystical writings.

St. Catherine of Siena (detail), Ambrogio da Fossano, 16th C.

Lioba (Leobgytha, St.), abbess, died c. 782. Relative of Boniface from an eminent Anglo-Saxon family, educated in the double monastery at Thanet under Abbess Eadburg. 732/35 heeded Boniface's call to Germania, where she became abbess of Tauberbischofsheim: ran the abbey in the spirit of the Rule of St. Benedict, evangelized through the teaching of young women. In her old age she retired to an estate in Schornsheim left to her by Charlemagne for her private use.

Maiolus (St.), 4th abbot of Cluny, 909–94. Entered Cluny in 943, where he was given responsibility for the library and the treasury. 954 coadjutor and successor to the ailing Abbot Aymard. Size of Cluny during his abbacy: approx. 100 monks. Cultivated contacts with the prominent figures of his era in the Church and internationally, including Emperor Otto I, Empress Adelheid, and Emperor Otto II. Declined offer from Otto II to become successor to Pope Benedict VI. His biographers emphasize his piety, humility, and quest for solitude.

Martin of Tours (St.), hermit and bishop, 316–97 (see p. 20).

Mother Teresa, order founder, 1910–97 (see p. 402).

Norbert of Kanten (St.), founder of the Premonstratensians, bishop of Magdeburg, 1080/85–1134 (see p. 230).

Odilo (St.), 5th abbot of Cluny, 961/62–1049 (see pp. 79–81).

Odo (St.), 2nd abbot of Cluny, 878/79–942 (see pp. 76–77).

Pachomius, monastery founder, c. 292–346 (see pp. 16–17).

Paulinus of Nola (St.), monk and bishop, 353/55–431. Following his training in Bordeaux became governor in Campania; retired from public life, married the Spanish woman Therasia, 389 baptism in Bordeaux. The couple sold their possessions and joined the new monastic movement (first wave of Western monasticism). 394 ordained as priest in Barcelona. Settled with his wife in Nola, where he was bishop 404-413. Exchange of letters with ascetic Christians, including Augustine and Jerome.

Peter Damian (St.), hermit, Doctor of the Church, 1007–72. Studied in Ravenna, Faenza, and Parma, led a hermitic life with Romuald, after 1035/36 entered the hermitage of Fonte Avellana, where, as prior, he realigned hermitic life. Consecration as priest c. 1041, begins work on the *Vita beati Romualdi* at the abbey of S. Vincenzo in Pietra Pertusa, about 15 years after Romuald's death. Strong commitment to the reform movement within the Church; condemned simony, marriage for priests, homosexuality; (probably cardinal of Ostia 1057–67) Extensive writings included *De ordine eremitorum et facultatibus eremi*, in which he assimilated his hermitic experiences. Advocate of strict asceticism.

Peter, the Venerable, 9th abbot of Cluny, c. 1094–1156. From an aristocratic family, entered Cluny in 1109; brief priorate in Vézelay, then in Domène; in 1122, following an ambivalent vote, became abbot of Cluny, which was facing significant problems after its 200-plus year history, due to criticism and the pressure of competition from monastic newcomers (esp. the Cistercians). Peter faced up to these challenges, compiled new, stricter rule in 76 statutes in order to restore failing discipline. Concerned with balance and tolerance both in his work and in his writings.

Pirmin (St.), monastery founder, died 755. Roman origin, called to Alemania, received a letter of protection from Charles Martel for the establishment of the abbey at Reichenau. Founded abbeys Murbach and Hornbach. Exponent of mixed rule monasticism, advocated the idea of *peregrinatio*; therefore his abbeys did not form a network.

St. Clare of Assisi (detail), retable of her life, 1284.

Poppo, abbot, monastery reformer, 978–1048 (see p. 79).

Ralph Glaber (Radulfus Glaber), monk and historian, died 1047. At age of 12 given to a monastery, which he then had to leave due to discipline problems; various sojourns in different Burgundian monasteries; traveled to Italy with Wilhelm of Volpiano, abbot of Saint-Bénigne, upon whose wish he worked on the *Historiae*, a portrayal of events since the early 10th C. Dedicated himself to this in the years c. 1000 and c. 1033 in particular (references to the divine laws of history); strong interest in unusual and frightening events, emphasized the moral decay of his epoch seen as anticipating the end of the world, conservative disposition. His work is significant from a cultural history perspective.

Richard of St. Vanne, abbot, monastery reformer, 970–1046 (see p. 79).

Richard of St. Victor, theologian and philosopher, died 1173. Of Anglo-Saxon origin, entered Saint-Victoire during Hugh's lifetime (died 1141), novice master, subprior, from 1162 prior. Following Hugh's example he had a strong influence on the tradition of the monastic school: unity of theological thinking and religious way of life; scholastic insight and spiritual experience are the maxims of both monastic theologians.

Robert of Molesmes (St.), abbot, c. 1028–1111 (see p. 164).

Romuald (St.), hermit, founder of Camaldoli, mid-10th C.–1027 (see pp. 144–45).

Rupert of Deutz, abbot, 1075/80–1129/30. Benedictine in Liège, 1116 in Siegburg, 1120 abbot of St. Heribert in Deutz, follower of the (late Cluniac) Siegburg Reform, main exponent of monastic theology in Germany.

Saba (St.), 439–532. Entered monastery at an early age, traveled to Palestine at 18, pupil of Euthymius the Great and Theokthistos; lived as a hermit at the Dead Sea, founded, amongst others, the "Great Laura" of Mar Saba in the Kidron Valley near Jerusalem, the oldest monastery in Palestine. As monastic teacher required anchorites to complete preparatory probation in monastic communal life. An important source of inspiration for Western monasticism.

Saba(s) the Younger (St), important representative of the Italo-Greek itinerant monasticism of the 10th C., died 990/91. From a wealthy Sicilian family,

entered the monastery of S. Filippo on the southern slopes of Mount Etna together with his parents and his brother, fled from the Saracens to Calabria, founding several monastic cells there. In the last years of his life retreated with his companions from the Saracens into the hinterland of Salerno. Visited Otto II and Empress Theophanu twice in Rome.

Schenute of Atripe, undertook 5th C. revival of Pachomian monasticism, c. 333/34–451/52 (or 465). From c. 388 2nd abbot of the "White Monastery" in Atripe (Upper Egypt), which he extended and which flourished under him. Presided over this large Coptic monastery with monk and nun communities according to a modified Pachomian Rule, intensified by his own monastery rules (not preserved). Extensive writings.

Scholastica (St.), sister of St. Benedict of Nursia, c. 480–c. 547. According to Gregory the Great in his life of Benedict she lived an ascetic lifestyle as a consecrated virgin near Montecassino (not as a nun). Brother and sister are said to have met annually for spiritual discussions. Very little is known about her life.

Simeon Stylites (the Elder), best known and greatly revered pillar-saint, c. 390–459. A monk initially, but had to leave the monastery due to very extreme asceticism; lived as hermit near Aleppo. In order to retreat from the many pilgrims he climbed up a pillar (which became higher and higher in consecutive years), where he spent over 30 years. Following his death his grave became a popular place of pilgrimage.

Stephen Harding, 3rd abbot of Cîteaux, c. 1060–1134 (see pp. 165–66).

Suger, abbot of Saint-Denis, 1081–1151. Came from a wealthy farming family, handed over to abbey of Saint-Denis as oblate at age of ten, receives lessons at nearby monastery school in L'Estrée; professor at 20, further training in Fleury-Saint-Benoît; showed administrative abilities as provost. Following a journey to Rome on behalf of Abbot Adam (died 1122) became the latter's successor at Saint-Denis. Became an ever closer confidant of the royal family, advisor to Louis VI on church issues. 1127 implemented a reformation of his abbey; following the death of Louis VI in 1137 was assigned national government duties for the first time, 1147 designated regent—representing Louis VII, who was taking part in a crusade. Following the latter's return, continued to play a dominant role in church matters, esp. the selection of bishops and the reformation of the abbeys; ensured that Saint-Denis, as royal burial place, became the symbolic center of the kingdom. His last decade was characterized by his work as a writer, builder (patron of the Early Gothic style), and regent.

Teresa of Ávila (St), convent founder and mystic, 1515–82. 1535 entered the Carmelite monastery in Ávila; years of spiritual crisis ended in a radical conversion in 1554; from then on stringent monastic life that led in 1562 to the founding of a monastery according to one of her concepts; a further 15 monasteries founded up to her death. From 1568 she supported John of the Cross in the foundation of reformed Carmelite convents (in 1593 these formed the Order of Discalced Carmelites). In addition to her energy, her extraordinary mystic grace set her apart (see p. 271), as did her extensive, influential writings.

Theodoretus, bishop of Kyros, important theologian, c. 393–460. 416 monk, 423 bishop of Kyros, played a decisive role in christological controversy; extensive theological writings including the

Historia religiosa, an important document in the history of Syrian monasticism, as well as a history of heresies.

Theodoros Studites, theologian, abbot, reformer of Byzantine monastic life, 759–826 (see pp. 332–37).

Thomas Aquinas (St.), most important theologian and philosopher of high scholasticism, Doctor of the Church, 1225–74. Handed over to the Benedictines of Montecassino as a boy, c. 1239 studied at University of Naples, 1244 entered Dominican order, 1245–48 studied in Paris, followed Albert Magnus, his most important teacher, to Cologne. 1252 returned to Paris, began his work as teacher, 1256 promotion to magister. 1261–65 taught at the order's school in Orvieto, from 1266 trained his fellow brothers in Rome, from autumn 1268 in Paris for a further three years as magister, then returned to Italy until his death. Very extensive writings, including his main work, *Summa theologiae*, a major influence on the Thomism of the Late Middle Ages and the modern age.

Thomas à Kempis, important representative of the *Devotio moderna*, c. 1379/80–1471. To Deventer at the age of 13 and entered the school of Johannes Boom, where he came into contact with the Brethren of the Common Life, from 1398 lived with 20 friars in the house of Florentius Radewijn, 1399 entered the St. Agnes priory of Augustinian canons near Zwolle; 1414 consecration as priest, 1425 prior. Provider of spiritual guidance, preacher, and author of numerous texts; also a diligent copier, "scriptor" (not author) of the didactic *Imitatio Christi*, which is one of the most widely read books in the Christian world after the Bible.

Ulrich of Zell (St.), monk, monastery founder, c. 1029–1093. Godson of Emperor Henry III, training in St. Emmeram in Regensburg; following a journey to the Holy Land and the failed foundation of a monastery, in 1061/63 entered Cluny as a monk, where he was the monks' confessor and advisor to Abbot Hugh of Semur; short spell as prior of Payerne, founded Zell (St. Ulrich) in the Black Forest and a convent at Bollschweil. 1079–1086, with Hugh's support, recorded the *Consuetudines* of Cluny for Abbot William of Hirsau: the most extensive surviving compilation of the practices there, which served as the basis for the Hirsau monastic reforms.

St. Thomas Aquinas (detail), Andrea da Firenze, c. 1367.

William of Hirsau, abbot, monastic reformer, died 1091. Handed over to St. Emmeram in Regensburg as a boy and educated there largely by Otloh, head of the monastery school; 1069 appointed abbot of Hirsau. In the investiture controversy took the side of Gregory VII, whom he visited in Rome in 1075. His monastic reforms were initially influenced by St. Emmeram, from 1079 by Cluny. Received a version of the *Consuetudines* of Cluny from Ulrich of Zell, which served as the basis of his reforms.

William of St. Thierry, abbot, important exponent of monastic theology, c. 1080–1148. From aristocratic family in Liège, studied in Liège, Rheims, and Lyons; 1113 became a Benedictine monk in Saint-Nicais in Rheims, 1119 abbot in Saint-Thierry; he supported the reforms within his order, which he then left in 1135. Friend and admirer of Bernard of Clairvaux, joined the Cistercians in Signy, Ardennes, as a simple monk. Extensive theological works, the most influential being his mystic writings, including *On the Nature and Dignity of Divine Love* and the *Meditations*. Divine love forms the focus of his teachings.

Bibliography

Reference works

Lexikon des Mittelalters, Munich 1980–1999

Dictionnaire d'histoire et de géographie ecclésias-tiques, Paris 1912 (Letters A–K)

Lexikon für Theologie und Kirche, Freiburg im Breisgau, 3rd Ed. 1993–2001; 2nd Ed. 1957–1968

Religion in Geschichte und Gegenwart. Handwörterbuch für Theologie und Religionswissenschaft, Tübingen 1998–2005

Catholicisme: hier, aujourd'hui, demain, Paris 1948–2004

Lexikon der Kunst, Harald Olbrich (Ed.), Leipzig 1987–1994

The Dictionary of Art, Jane Turner (Ed.), New York/London 1996

Glossaire de termes techniques (Introduction à La Nuit des Temps), La Pierre-qui-Vire 1983 (3rd Ed., Raymond Oursel, Rev.)

Bildwörterbuch der Architektur, H. Köpf, G. Binding (Eds), Stuttgart, 4th Ed. 2005

Overviews of Western Monasticism, Orders, Monasteries and Monastic Architecture (esp. Middle Ages)

Hans Urs von Balthasar, *Die großen Ordensregeln,* Einsiedeln, 7th Ed. 1994

Günther Binding, Matthias Untermann, *Kleine Kunstgeschichte der Mittelalterlichen Ordensbaukunst in Deutschland,* Darmstadt, 3rd Ed. 2001

Christopher Brooke, *Die Klöster. Geist, Kultur, Geschichte,* Freiburg 2001

Peter Dinzelbacher, James Lester Hoog (Eds), *Kulturgeschichte der christlichen Orden,* Stuttgart 1977

Isnard W. Frank OP, *Lexikon des Mönchtums und der Orden,* Stuttgart 2005

Karl Suso Frank, *Geschichte des christlichen Mönchtums,* Darmstadt 1996

Gudrun Gleba, *Klöster und Orden im Mittelalter* (short history), Darmstadt 2002

Max Heimbucher, *Die Orden und Kongregationen der katholischen Kirche,* Paderborn 1933 (Repr. 1965)

Peter K. Klein (Ed.), *Der mittelalterliche Kreuzgang: Architektur, Funktion, Programm,* Regensburg 2004

Juan Maria Laboa, *Mönchtum in Ost und West. Historischer Atlas,* Regensburg 2003

Cesare Romanò, *Abteien und Klöster in Europa. Illustrierter Führer zu 480 Zentren monastischen Lebens,* Augsburg 1997

Georg Schwaiger (Ed.), *Mönchtum, Orden, Klöster. Von den Anfängen bis zur Gegenwart,* Munich (Beck), 2nd Ed. 1994

Hanns Rudolf Sennhauser (Ed.), *Wohn- und Wirtschaftsbauten mittelalterlicher Klöster.* International Symposium, 26.9.–1.10.1995 in Zurzach and Müstair, Zurich 1996

Heidrun Stein-Kecks, *Der Kapitelsaal in der mittelalterlichen Klosterbaukunst: Studien zu den Bildprogrammen,* Munich 2004

Gerd Zimmermann, *Ordensleben und Lebensstandard. Die Cura Corporis in den Ordensvorschriften des abendländischen Hochmittelalters,* Munster 1973

Early Christendom

Peter Brown, *Die Keuschheit der Engel. Sexuelle Entsagung, Askese und Körperlichkeit am Anfang des Christentums,* Munich 1991

Peter Lampe, *Die Stadtrömischen Christen in den ersten beiden Jahrhunderten. Eine sozialgeschichtliche Untersuchung,* Tübingen 1987

Eckhard Plümacher, *Identitätsverlust und Identitätsgewinn. Studien zum Verhältnis von kaiserzeitlicher Stadt und frühem Christentum,* Neukirchen-Vluyn 1987

Wolfgang Reinbold, *Propaganda und Mission im ältesten Christentum. Eine Untersuchung zu den Modalitäten der Ausbreitung der frühen Kirche,* Göttingen 2000

Egypt

Peter Grossmann, *Die christliche Architektur in Ägypten* (Handbuchder Orientalistik 62), Leiden/Boston/Cologne 2002

Georges Descoeudres, "Privatoratorien in der Frühzeit des Mönchtums," in: *Art, Cérémonial et Liturgie au Moyen Âge,* Actes du colloque de 3e Cycle Romand de Lettres, Lausanne–Fribourg, 2000, N. Bock, P. Kurmann, S. Romano, J.-M. Spieser (Eds), Rome 2002, pp. 481–502

Early Western Monasticism

Friedrich Prinz, *Askese und Kultur. Vor- und frühbenediktinisches Mönchtum an der Wiege Europas,* Munich 1980

Karl Suso Frank, *Frühes Mönchtum im Abendland,* 2 Vols, Zurich 1975

Source texts:

B. Steidle, *Die Regel St. Benedikts (Latin-German)* , Beuron 1992

Karl Suso Frank, *Die Magisterregel,* St. Ottilien 1989

Adalbert de Vogüé, *Grégoire le Grand, Dialogues* (Scriptores christiani 251, 260, 265), Paris 1978–1980

Early Middle Ages

Arnold Angenendt, *Das Frühmittelalter. Die abendländische Christenheit von 400 bis 900,* Stuttgart, 2nd Ed. 1995

Achim Arbeiter, "Kunst der christlichen Spätantike und der westgotischen Zeit," in: S. Hänsel, H. Karge (Eds), *Spanische Kunstgeschichte. Eine Einführung,* Berlin 1992, pp. 9–30

Alexander Demandt, "Die Germanen im Römischen Reich," in: *Mit Fremden leben. Eine Kulturgeschichte von der Antike bis zur Gegenwart,* A. Demandt et al. (Eds), Munich 1995, pp. 68–80

Die Franken—Wegbereiter Europas. 5.–8. Jahrhundert (exhibition catalogue Mannheim/Paris/Berlin 1996/1997), 2 Vols, Mainz, 2nd Ed. 1997

Michael Grant (Ursula Vones-Liebenstein, Rev.), *Die Welt des Frühmittelalters,* Ostfildern 2003

Peter Harbison, "Early Irish Churches," in: *Die Iren und Europa im frühen Mittelalter,* Stuttgart 1982, pp. 618–629

Peter Harbison, *Die Kunst des Mittelalters in Irland,* Würzburg 1999

Konrad Hecht, *Der St. Galler Klosterplan,* Wiesbaden (no date)

Michael Herity, "The Layout of Irish early Christian Monasteries," in: *Irland und Europa. Die Kirche im Frühmittelalter,* P. Ni Chatain, M. Richter (Eds), Stuttgart 1984, pp. 105–116

Richard Hodges, *Light in the Dark Ages. The Rise and Fall of San Vincenzo al Volturno,* London 1997

Richard Hodges, Brian Hobley (Eds), *The Rebirth of Towns in the West AD 700–1050* (Council for British Archaeology, Research Report 68), Oxford 1988

H. Schlunk, Th. Hauschild, *Hispania Antiqua: Denkmäler der frühchristlichen und westgotischen Zeit,* Mainz 1978

Kunst und Kultur der Karolingerzeit. Karl der Große und Papst Leo III. in Paderborn (exhibition catalogue Paderborn 1999), 3 Vols, Mainz 1999

Hans Rudolf Sennhauser (Ed.), *Wohn- und Wirtschaftsbauten frühmittelalterlicher Klöster* (Institut für Denkmalpflege, ETH Zurich 17), Zurich 1996

Matthias Untermann, *Architektur im frühen Mittelalter,* Darmstadt 2006

Matthias Untermann, "Die archäologische Erforschung der Insel Reichenau," in: *Klosterinsel Reichenau im Bodensee. UNESCO Weltkulturerbe* (Landesdenkmalamt Baden-Württemberg, Workbook 8), Stuttgart 2001

D.M. Wilson (Ed.), *The Archaeology of Anglo-Saxon England,* London 1976

Alfons Zettler, *Die frühen Klosterbauten der Reichenau. Ausgrabungen—Schriftquellen—St. Galler Klosterplan,* Sigmaringen 1988

Source texts:

"Regula sancti Benedicti abbatis Anianensis sive collectio capitularis," in: Kassius Hallinger (Ed.), *Corpus Consuetudinum Monasticarum,* Vol. I, Siegburg 1963, pp. 515–536

"Institutiones Aquisgranenses," MGH Conc. II/1, 312–421; 422–456

"Institutio sancti Angilberti abbatis de diuersitate officiorum," in: Kassius Hallinger (Ed.), *Corpus Consuetudinum Monasticarum,* Vol. I, Siegburg 1963, pp. 283–303

Benedictine Monasticism in the 10th to 12th Centuries

Achim Arbeiter, Sabine Noack-Haley, *Hispania Antiqua: Christliche Denkmäler des frühen Mittelalters vom 8. bis ins 11. Jahrhundert,* Mainz 1999

Giles Constable, "Commemoration and Confraternity at Cluny during the Abbacy of Peter the Venerable," in: G. Constable, G. Melville, J. Oberste, *Die Cluniazenser in ihrem politischsozialen Umfeld* (Vita regularis 7), Munster 1998, pp. 253–278

Lin Donnat, "Les coutumes monastiques autour de l'an mil," in: *Religion et culture autour de l'an Mil.* Actes du colloque international "Hugues Capet 987–1987" (Auxerre, 26–27 June 1987 and Metz, 11–12 Sept. 1987), Dominique Iogna-Prat, Jean-Charles Picard (Es), Paris 1990, pp 17–24

Rudolf Hiestand, "Einige Überlegungen zu den Anfängen von Cluny," in: *Mönchtum, Kirche, Herrschaft 750–1000,* D.R. Bauer, R. Hiestand et al. (Eds), Sigmaringen 1998, pp. 287–309

Dominique Iogna-Prat, "Les morts dans la comptabilité céleste des Cluniens de l'an Mil," in: *Religion et culture autour de l'an Mil.* Actes du colloque international "Hugues Capet 987–1987" (Auxerre, 26–27 June 1987 and Metz, 11–12 Sept. 1987), Dominique Iogna-Prat, Jean-Charles Picard (Eds), Paris 1990, pp. 55–69

Dominique Iogna-Prat, *Agni immaculati. Recherches sur les sources hagiographiques relatives à saint Maieul de Cluny (954–994)* , Paris 1988

Dominique Iogna-Prat, "Romainmôtier et l'Eglise clunisienne des origins," in: *Romainmôtier. Histoire de l'abbaye,* Jean-Daniel Morerod (Ed.), Bibliothèque historique vaudoise 120, Lausanne 2001, pp. 85–95

Armin Kohnle, *Abt Hugo von Cluny (1049–1109)* , supplements to Francia 32, Sigmaringen 1993

R. Kottje, H. Maurer (Ed.), *Monastische Reform im 9. und 10. Jahrhundert,* Sigmaringen 1989

Kristina Krüger, *Die Romanischen Westbauten in Burgund und Cluny,* Berlin 2003

Jacques Leclercq, "L'idéal monastique de saint Odon," in: *A Cluny. Congrès scientifique en l'honneur des saints abbés Odon et Odilon, 9-11 July 1949,* Dijon 1950, pp. 227–232

Eliana Magnani Soares-Christen, "Saint-Victor de Marseille, Cluny et la politique de Grégoire VII au nord-ouest de la Méditerrannée," in: *Die Cluniazenser in ihrem politisch-sozialen Umfeld,* Giles Constable, Gert Melville, Jörg Oberste (Eds), Vita regularis 7, Munster 1998, pp. 321–347

Peter Segl, *Königtum und Klosterreform in Spanien. Untersuchungen über die Cluniazenserklöster in Kastilien-León vom Beginn des 11. bis zur Mitte des 12. Jahrhunderts,* Kallmünz 1974

Joachim Wollasch, "Les moines et la mémoire des morts," in: *Religion et culture autour de l'an Mil. Actes du colloque international "Hugues Capet 987–1987,"* Dominique Iogna-Prat, Jean-Charles Picard (Eds), Paris 1990, pp. 47–54

Joachim Wollasch, *Cluny—Licht der Welt,* Düsseldorf/Zurich 1996

Source texts:

Regularis concordia Anglicae nationis monachorum sanctimonialiumque, Patrologiae cursus completus, Series latina, Jacques-Paul Migne (Ed.), Vol. 137

Consuetudines Floriacenses antiquiores (Libelli duo de consuetudinibus et statutis monasterii Floriacensis) , Anselme Davril (Ed.), Corpus Consuetudinorum Monasticarum, Vol. VII/3, Siegburg 1984

Liber tramitis aeui Odilonis abbatis, Peter Dinter (Ed.), Corpus Consuetudinorum Monasticarum, Vol. X, Siegburg 1980

"Antiquiores consuetudines Cluniacensis monasterii O. B. collectore S. Udalrico monacho benediction," in: Luc d'Achery (Ed.), *Spicilegium*, Vol. IV, Paris 1661 (also: *Patrologiae cursus completus*, Series latina, Jacques-Paul Migne (Ed.), Vol.149)

"Ordo Cluniacensis per Bernardum Saeculi XI. Scriptorem," in: Marquard Herrgott (Ed.), *Vetus disciplina monastica, seu collectio auctorum Ordinis S. Benedicti maximam partem ineditorum*, Paris 1726, pp. 133–364 (Repr. Siegburg 1999)

Hermits and Carthusians, Canons Regular and Premonstratensians

James Hogg, *Die ältesten Consuetudines der Kartäuser*, Berlin 1970

La vita commune del clero nei secoli XI e XII. Atti della Settimana di Studi, Mendola, Sept. 1959, Milan 1962

Dominique Iogra-Prat, "Cluny comme 'système ecclésial' ", in: G. Constable, G. Melville, J. Oberste, *Die Cluniazenser in ihrem politisch-sozialen Umfeld* (Vita regularis 7), Munster 1998, pp. 13–93

Matthias Untermann, *Kirchenbauten der Prämonstratenser. Untersuchungen zum Problem einer Ordensbaukunst im 12. Jahrhundert*, Cologne (Archaeology Department, KHI, University of Cologne 29) 1984

Stefan Weinfurter, *Neuere Forschungen zu den Regularkanonikern im deutschen Reich des 11. und 12. Jahrhunderts*, Historische Zeitschrift 1977, pp. 379–439

Source texts:

Charles Le Couteulx, *Annales ordinis Cartusiensis, ab anno 1084 ad annum 1429*, Vol. I, Montreux 1887

Luc Jocqué, Louis Milis, *Liber ordinis Sancti Victoris Parisiensis* (Corpus Christianorum, Continuatio mediaevalis 61), Turnhout 1984

Josef Siegwart, *Die Consuetudines des Augustiner-Chorherrenstiftes Marbach im Elsaß (12. Jahrhundert)* (Spicilegium Friburgense 10), Fribourg 1965

Stefan Weinfurter, *Consuetudines canonicorum regularium Springirsbacenses-Rodenses* (Corpus Christianorum, Continuatio mediaevalis 48), Turnhout 1978

Cistercians

M.-Anselme Dimier, Jean Porcher, *Die Kunst der Zisterzienser in Frankreich*, Würzburg 1986

Immo Eberl, *Die Zisterzienser: Geschichte eines europäischen Ordens*, Stuttgart 2002

Terryl N. Kinder, *Die Welt der Zisterzienser*, Würzburg 1997

Jean-Francois Leroux-Dhuys, *Die Zisterzienser. Geschichte und Architektur*, Cologne 1998

Jürgen Michler, *Die Elisabethkirche zu Marburg in ihrer ursprünglichen Farbigkeit*, Marburg 1984

Matthias Untermann, *Forma Ordinis. Die mittelalterliche Baukunst der Zisterzienser*, Munich/Berlin 2001

Source texts:

J.-M. Canivez, *Statuta capitulorum generalium ordinis Cisterciensis ab anno 1116 ad annum 1786*, 8 Vols. Louvain 193341

"*Ecclesiastica officia,*" Gebräuchebuch der Zisterzienser aus dem 12. Jahrhundert (Latin-German; based on the Choisselet/Vernet Ed.), H.M. Herzog, J. Müller (Transl., Rev., Ed.), Quellen und Studien zur Zisterzienserliteratur 7, Langwaden 2003

Les "Ecclesiastica officia" cisterciens du XIIe siècle, Danièle Choisselet, Placide Vernet (Eds), Reiningue 1989

Military Orders

Malcolm Barber, *The New Knighthood. A History of the Order of the Temple*, Cambridge University Press 1994

G. Binding, M. Untermann, *Kleine Kunstgeschichte der mittelalterlichen Ordensbaukunst in Deutschland*, Darmstadt, 3rd Ed. 2001

Dan Bahat, *Carta's Historical Atlas of Jerusalem. An Illustrated Survey*, Jerusalem 1986

Hartmut Boockmann, *Der Deutsche Orden. Zwölf Kapitel aus seiner Geschichte*, Munich 1981

Marie-Luise Bulst-Thiele, *Sacrae Domus Militiae Templi Hierosolymitani Magistri: Untersuchungen zur Geschichte des Templerordens 1118/19–1314*, Göttingen 1974

Alain Demurger, *Die Templer. Aufstieg und Untergang*, Munich 1991

Alain Demurger, *Die Ritter des Herrn. Geschichte der geistlichen Ritterorden*, Munich 2003

Der Deutsche Orden in Europa, Gesellschaft für staufische Geschichte e. V. (Ed.), Göppingen 2004

Die Kreuzzüge, exhibition catalogue Mainz 2004, Hans-Jürgen Kotzur (Ed.), Mainz 2004

Die Ritterorden im Mittelalter—Les ordres militaries au Moyen Age (Greifswalder Beiträge zum Mittelalter), Danielle Buschinger, Wolfgang Spiewok (Eds), Greifswald 1996

Marie-Luise Favreau, *Studien zur Frühgeschichte des Deutschen Ordens*, Stuttgart (no date—after 1972)

Niels von Holst, *Der deutsche Ritterorden und seine Bauten*, Berlin 1981

Nikolas Jasbert, *Die Kreuzzüge* (short history), Darmstadt 2003

Bernd Schwenk, *Calatrava: Entstehung und Frühgeschichte eines spanischen Ritterordens zisterziensischer Observanz* (Spanische Forschungen d. Görres-Gesellschaft), Munster 1992

Berthold Waldstein-Wallenberg, *Die Vasallen Christi. Kulturgeschichte des Johanniterordens im Mittelalter*, Vienna/Cologne/Graz 1988

Female Orders

Irmingard Achter, *Querschiffemporen in mittelalterlichen Damenstiften*, Jahrbuch der Rheinischen Denkmalpflege 30/31 (1985), pp. 39–54

Hilde Claussen, Uwe Lobbedey, *Die karolingische Stiftskirche in Meschede. Kurzer Bericht über die Bauforschung 1965–1981*, Westfalen 67 (1989), pp. 116–126 (with note on transept galleries by H. Claussen, pp 125–126)

Doppelklöster und andere Formen der Symbiose männlicher und weiblicher Religiosen im Mittelalter (Berliner Historische Studien Vol. 18; Ordensstudien Vol. 8), Kaspar Elm, Michel Parisse (Eds), Berlin 1992

Carola Jäggi, *Frauenklöster im Spätmittelalter. Die Kirchen der Klarissen und Dominikanerinnen im 13. und 14. Jahrhundert*, Petersberg 2006

Clemens Kosch, "Organisation spatiale des monastères de Cisterciennes et de Prémontrées en Allemagne et dans les pays germanophones au Moyen Âge," in: Bernadette Barrière, Marie-Élisabeth Henneau, *Cîteaux et les femmes*, Paris 2001

Krone und Schleier. Kunst aus mittelalterlichen Frauenklöstern, exhibition catalogue, Art and Exhibition Hall of the Federal Republic of Germany, Bonn and the Ruhrlandmuseums Essen, Munich 2005

Michel Parisse, "Fontevraud, monastère double,"

in: Elm, Parisse (Eds), *Doppelklöster und andere Formen der Symbiose männlicher und weiblicher Religiosen im Mittelalter*, Berlin 1992, pp. 135–148

Mendicant Orders

Thomas Coomans, *L'architecture des ordres mendiants (Franciscains, Dominicains, Carmes et Augustins) en Belgique et aux Pays Bas*, Revue belge d'archéologie et d'histore de l'art, 70, 2001, pp. 3–111

Kaspar Elm, *Stellung und Wirksamkeit der Bettelorden in der städtischen Gesellschaft* (Berliner Historische Studien 3; Ordensstudien 2), Berlin 1981

I.W. Frank, *Bettelordenskirchen als multifunktionale Kulträume*, Wissenschaft und Weisheit, 59, 1996, pp. 93–112

Richard Krautheimer, *Die Kirchen der Bettelorden in Deutschland*, Cologne 1925; new ed. with epilogue by Matthias Untermann, Berlin 2000

Klaus Krüger, *Der frühe Bildkult des Franziskus in Italien*, Berlin 1992

C.H. Lawrence, *The Friars. The Impact of the Early Mendicant Movement on Western Society*, London/New York 1994

Wolfgang Schenkluhn, *Architektur der Bettelorden. Die Baukunst der Dominikaner und Franziskaner in Europa*, Darmstadt 2000

Wolfgang Schenkluhn, *Ordines Studentes. Aspekte zur Kirchenarchitektur der Dominikaner und Franziskaner im 13. Jahrhundert*, Berlin 1985

Byzantine Monasticism

Gilbert Dagron, "Christliche Ökonomie und christliche Gesellschaft (8.–10. Jh.)," in: Gilbert Dagron, Pierre Riché, André Vauchez (Eds), *Bischöfe, Mönche, Kaiser (642–1054), Die Geschichte des Christentums*, Vol. IV, Freiburg 1994, pp. 256–313

Athanasios D. Komines (Ed.), *Patmos. Die Schätze des Klosters*, Athens 1988

Konstantinos A. Manafis (Ed.), *Sinai. Treasures of the Monastery of Saint Catherine*, Athens 1990

John Rupert Martin, *The Illustration of the Heavenly Ladder of John Climacus* (Studies in Manuscript Illumination 5), Princeton 1954

Andreas E. Müller, *Berg Athos: Geschichte einer Mönchsrepublik*, Munich 2005

Paul M. Mylonas, *Bildlexikon des Heiligen Berges Athos*, Tübingen 2000

Anastasios K. Orlandos, *Monasteriake architektonike*, Athens 1958

Bissera V. Pentcheva, *Icons and Power. The Mother of God in Byzantium*, University Park, Pa. 2006

John Thomas, Angela Constantinides Hero (Eds), *Byzantine Monastic Foundation Documents. A Complete Translation of the Surviving Founder's Typika and Testaments*, 5 Vols (Dumbarton Oaks Studies 35), Washington, D.C. 2000

Treasures of Mount Athos. Exhibition catalogue, Thessaloniki 1997

Late Middle Ages, Reformation, and Counter-Reformation

Kaspar Elm (Ed.), *Reformbemühungen und Observanzbestrebungen im spätmittelalterlichen Ordenswesen* (Berliner Historische Studien 14; Ordensstudien 6), Berlin 1989 (esp. Introduction, pp. 3–19)

Klösterliche Sachkultur des Spätmittelalters (Internationaler Kongress Krems an der Donau, 18–21/9/1978), Institut für mittelalterliche Realienkunde Österreichs, No. 3, Vienna 1980

Erwin Iserloh, *Geschichte und Theologie der Reformation im Grundriß*, Paderborn 1980

The Jesuits. Cultures, Sciences, and the Arts 1540–1773, John W. O'Malley S.J. et al. (Eds), Toronto/Buffalo/London 1999

Marion Sauter, *Die oberdeutschen Jesuitenkirchen (1550–1650). Bauten, Kontext und Bautypologie*, Petersberg 2004

Marc Venard (Ed.), *Die Zeit der Konfessionen*

(1530–1620/30) (Die Geschichte des Christentums, Vol. 8), Freiburg/Basle/Vienna 1998

The Peak of Benedictine Baroque

Germain Bazin, *Paläste des Glaubens. Die Geschichte der Klöster vom 15. bis zum Ende des 18. Jahrhunderts*, Vol. II, Munich 1980

Yves Chaussy, *Les bénédictins de Saint-Maur, I: Aperçu historique sur la Congrégation*, Paris 1989

J. Daoust, "Mauristes," in: *Catholicisme*, Vol. 8, Paris 1979, col. 966–980

Pierre Gasnault, "Portrait du mauriste erudite", in: *Les mauristes à Saint-Germain-des-Prés*, Actes du colloque Paris, 2 Dec. 1999, Paris (Institut d'Études Augustiniennes) 2001

P. Gall Heer, *Johannes Mabillon und die Schweizer Benediktiner. Ein Beitrag zur Geschichte der historischen Quellenforschung im 17. und 18. Jahrhundert*, St. Gallen 1938

Max Heimbucher, *Die Orden und Kongregationen der katholischen Kirche*, Paderborn 1933 (Repr. 1965), Vol. 1, pp. 233–241

Edgar Lehmann, *Die Bibliotheksräume der deutschen Klöster in der Zeit des Barock*, 2 Vols, Berlin 1996

David Lunn, "Mauriner," in: *Theologische Real-enzyklopädie*, Vol. 22, Berlin/New York 1992, pp. 281–283

Michael Mette, *Studien zu den barocken Kloster-anlagen in Westfalen* (Denkmalpflege und Forschung in Westfalen 25), Bonn 1993

Marc Venard, "Spiegel und Rückhalt der Reform: die Welt der Ordensleute" and "Die Rolle der Laien," in: Marc Venard (Ed.), *Das Zeitalter der Vernunft (1620/30–1750)* (Die Geschichte des Christentums, Vol. 9), Freiburg/Basle/Vienna 1998, pp. 281–305

Monastic Life in the 19th and 20th Centuries

Kulturgeschichte der christlichen Orden in Einzeldarstellungen, Peter Dinzelbacher, James Lester Hogg (Eds), Stuttgart 1997

Terryl N. Kinder, *Die Welt der Zisterzienser*, Würzburg 1997, pp. 49–52

Max Heimbucher, *Die Orden und Kongregationen der katholischen Kirche*, Paderborn 1933 (Repr. 1965), Vol. 2, pp. 392–399

Georg Schwaiger (Ed.), *Mönchtum, Orden, Klöster. Von den Anfängen bis zur Gegenwart*, Munich 1994, passim

Beuron 1863–1963. Festschrift zum hundertjährigen Bestehen der Erzabtei St. Martin, Beuron 1963

Harald Siebenmorgen, *Die Anfänge der »Beuroner Kunstschule«: Peter Lenz und Jakob Wüger 1850–1875. Ein Beitrag zur Genese der Formabstraktion in der Moderne*, Sigmaringen 1983

Sergio Ferro et al., *Le Corbusier. Le couvent de La Tourette*, Marseilles 1987

Literature on Specific Topics through the Ages

Freddy Derwahl, *Eremiten. Die Abenteuer der Einsamkeit*, Munich 2000

Peter Dinzelbacher, *Christliche Mystik im Abendland*, Paderborn 1994

Peter Dinzelbacher, *Himmel, Hölle, Heilige. Visionen und Kunst im Mittelalter*, Darmstadt 2002

Stephanie Hauschild, *Die sinnlichen Gärten des Albertus Magnus*, Ostfildern 2005

Dieter Hennebo, *Gärten des Mittelalters*, Munich, Zurich 1987

Rolf Legler, *Tempel des Wassers. Brunnen und Brunnenhäuser in den Klöstern Europas*, Stuttgart 2005

Claudia List, *Wilhelm Blum, Buchkunst des Mittelalters*, Stuttgart, Zurich 1994

Otto Pächt, *Buchmalerei des Mittelalters*, Munich 1984

Gabriele Uerscheln, *Meisterwerke der Gartenkunst*, Stuttgart 2006

Ingo F. Walther, Norbert Wolf, *Die schönsten illuminierten Handschriften der Welt*, Cologne 2001

Index of Persons

Italics refer to illustrations

Index of Place Names

Image Credits

Most of the illustrations not listed below are either new images taken on behalf of the publisher by the Cologne photographer Achim Bednorz or come from the editor's archive. The publisher and the editor wish to thank the museums, archives and photographers for the provision of further master illustrations and for the granting of reproduction permission. Special mention is made of the following institutions in addition to those already named in the image captions:

t. = top b. = bottom l. = left r. = right

© akg images, Berlin (51 a., 53, 242 b., 245, 281 a., 340 a.l., 361 a., 385 b.; British Library Board, London 37 l., 242 a.l.; Hervé Champollion 352 a.; Erich Lessing 15, 51 b., 271 r., 321, 329 b., 352 b., 400 a., 401; Gilles Mermet 351; Jean-Louis Nou 333; Pirozzi 19 a.; Rabatti & Domingie 288 b., 289, 294 a., 305; Gerhard Ruf 293 a., 293 b.; Jürgen Sorges 353), © The Art Archive/Dagli Orti (332 a.), © Ateliers et Presse de Taizé (413 a.r.), © Badische Landesbibliothek, Karlsruhe (286 a.), © BAMSPhotoRodella (152 b.), © Bayerische Staatsbibliothek, Munich (69 a.), © bpk (42 a., 230 a.; Stefan Diller 287; Ann Münchow 76; Hilmar Pabel 402 a.; Jochen Remmer 14 b.), © Raffaello Bencini, Firenze (284, 285, 288 a., 296, 297, 315), © Biblioteca Apostolica Vaticana (332, 350 a.), © Bibliothèque Nationale de France, Paris (374 b.l.) , © Bildarchiv Monheim, Krefeld: (254/255), © Bischöfliches Dom- and Diözesanmuseum Mainz (248 b.), © Markus Bollen, Bergisch-Gladbach (12, 14, 247), © The Bridgeman Art Library (Bibliothèque Municipale, Dijon 170 a.; Bibliothèque Municipale, Dijon/Giraudon 199 b.l.; Bibliothèque Nationale de France, Paris 80 b.; Bibliothèque Nationale de France, Paris/Topham Picture Point 279; British Library Board [all rights reserved] 37 b.r., 77 b.; Kunsthistorisches Museum, Wien 1; Mission des Lazaristes, Paris/Archives Charmet 406 a.l.; Musée du Louvre, Paris/Lauros/Giraudon 362; Museo Catedralicio, Burgos 249 b.; Museo de Bellas Artes, Sevilla/Giraudon 148 a.; Museo di San Marco dell'Angelico, Florence 320 b.; Österreichische Nationalbibliothek, Wien/Alinari 280 a.l.; Prado, Madrid/Index 295 b.r.; San Francesco, Oberkirche, Assisi/Giraudon 285 b.l., 285 b.r., 286 b., 314; Templerkapelle, Cressac-Saint-Genis/Lauros/Giraudon 245 b.; Trinity College, Cambridge 68 a.r., 280 b.; The Board of Trinity College, Dublin 39; Victoria & Albert Museum, London 46), © The British Library Board [all rights reserved] (258 b.), © Stefan Diller/www.assisi.de (287 a.l.), © Europa-Farbbildarchiv Waltraud Klammet (200/201), © nach der Faksimile-Edition des Faksimile Verlags, Luzern/www.faksimile.ch [Kreuzritterbibel Folio 23v] (5, 240/241), © Foto Patrick Boyer/Musée des Beaux-Arts, Tours (377 a.), © Foto Edgar Knaack, ZBW Donauuni Krems (385 a.), © Foto Sabine Leutenegger (413 a.l.), © Fotostudio Rapuzzi/Museo Civico dell'Età Cristiana, Brescia (20), © Germanisches Nationalmuseum Nuremberg, Inv. No. Gm 576 (6, 72 a., 72 b., 256), © Joseph Martin, Madrid (250 a.l.), © Det Kongelige Bibliotek, Copenhagen (68 a.l., b.li, b.r.), © Koninklijke Bibliotheek, The Hague (244 b.l.), © MASC Foto Philippe Bridel (18 b.), © Museo e Tesoro del Duomo di Monza (31), © Photo Henri Gaud/Editions Gaud (22), © Photo Scala, Florenz (4, 6, 10/11, 16/17, 199 a.r., 270 b., 270 l., 282/283, 292, 302 b., 310 a., 335, 363 b.), © Pressestelle Don Bosco (405 b.), © Staatliche Graphische Sammlung, Munich (356), © Zev Radovan/www.biblelandpictures.com (330 b.), © Rosgartenmuseum, Constance (270), © Nicole Thierry (334 a.l.)

The pictures for this book have been chosen by the editor Rolf Toman. He also composed most of the captions and short texts on pages 38, 68/69,112/113, 216/217, 252, 270/271 and 408.

The editor and publisher have made every effort during the production of the book to identify the owners of all image rights. However, should further claims exist, the persons or institutions concerned are asked to please contact the publisher.

Illustration page 1:
St. Gregory with scribes, Meister der Wiener Gregorplatte, Carolingian, 9th C, Kunsthistorisches Museum, Vienna.

Illustration page 2:
Certosa di Pavia, cloister and south aspect of the church with crossing tower, 15th C.

© 2007 Tandem Verlag GmbH
h.f.ullmann is an imprint of Tandem Verlag GmbH

Original title: *Orden und Klöster—2000 Jahre christliche Kunst und Kultur*
ISBN 978-3-8331-4069-3
Compilation and production: Rolf Toman, Thomas Paffen
Photography: Achim Bednorz
Maps and images: Rolli Arts
Image sourcing: Barbara Linz, Helga Stoverock
Project coordination: Lucas Lüdemann

© 2008 for the English edition: Tandem Verlag GmbH
h.f.ullmann is an imprint of Tandem Verlag GmbH

Translated by Katherine Taylor in association with First Edition Translations Ltd, Cambridge, UK
Edited by Kay Hyman in association with First Edition Translations Ltd, Cambridge, UK
Typeset by The Write Idea in association with First Edition Translations Ltd, Cambridge, UK
Project managment by Sheila Waller in association with First Edition Translations Ltd, Cambridge, UK
Project coordination of this English edition by Christina Stock

Printed in China

ISBN 978-3-8331-4070-9

10 9 8 7 6 5 4 3 2 1
X IX VIII VII VI V IV III II I

www.ullmann-publishing.com

Iñs fili Dirac

Adeptus est gloziam in con
uerlatione gentus. exi · l. ·

ydolū

Di gha fecerut preste ab erroze bie
caluabit eiam ci a morte + opit multi
tudine peccoz Jacobi b.

Jacobz apts

Būdctus

Mons callini.

Et iohes

Jurta montē callinū ydolū fuit qp a pplo cristiano paganoz erroze colebat.
vbi gmozate mltitudine pdicaoc gtinua ad fidē bñdc votebat. ggozii lib dya·

ggozii p.

Apostolus destinatur: Benedictus ad callinum.
Qui populum exhortatur: Et dat ad cultū diuinū.
Ly vzay apostle dieu sains benoit. Fut envoyes a calline.
Ypluseurs gens la destournoit. Des errour al foid cristine.
Sint bñdctus godes bode. tot calliney waert ghelant
Daer hi sterkēde was te gode. Alle di hi guet willich vant.

N 7850 .K7813 2008
Krèuger, Kristina.
Monasteries and monastic orders